KU-730-489

01 057 575X

9

Writer / Letterer
Hideyuki Furuhashi

Penciller / Colorist
Betten Court

Original Concept
Kohei Horikoshi

【persona】

noun | per • so • na

: a public personality; a mask; in psychology, a social
facade that reflects one's role in life

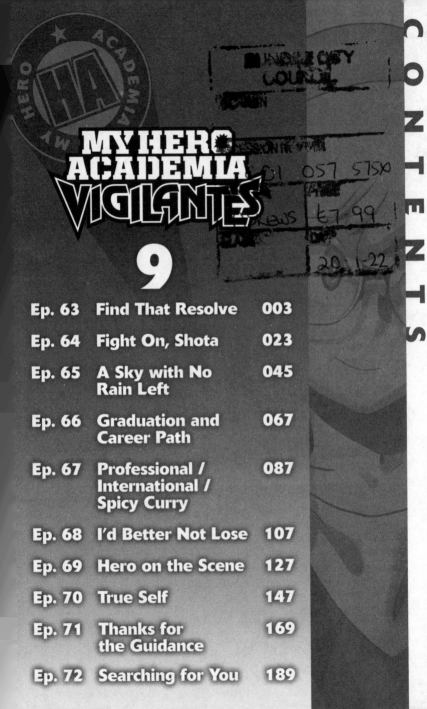

MY HERO ACADEMIA VIGILANTES

9

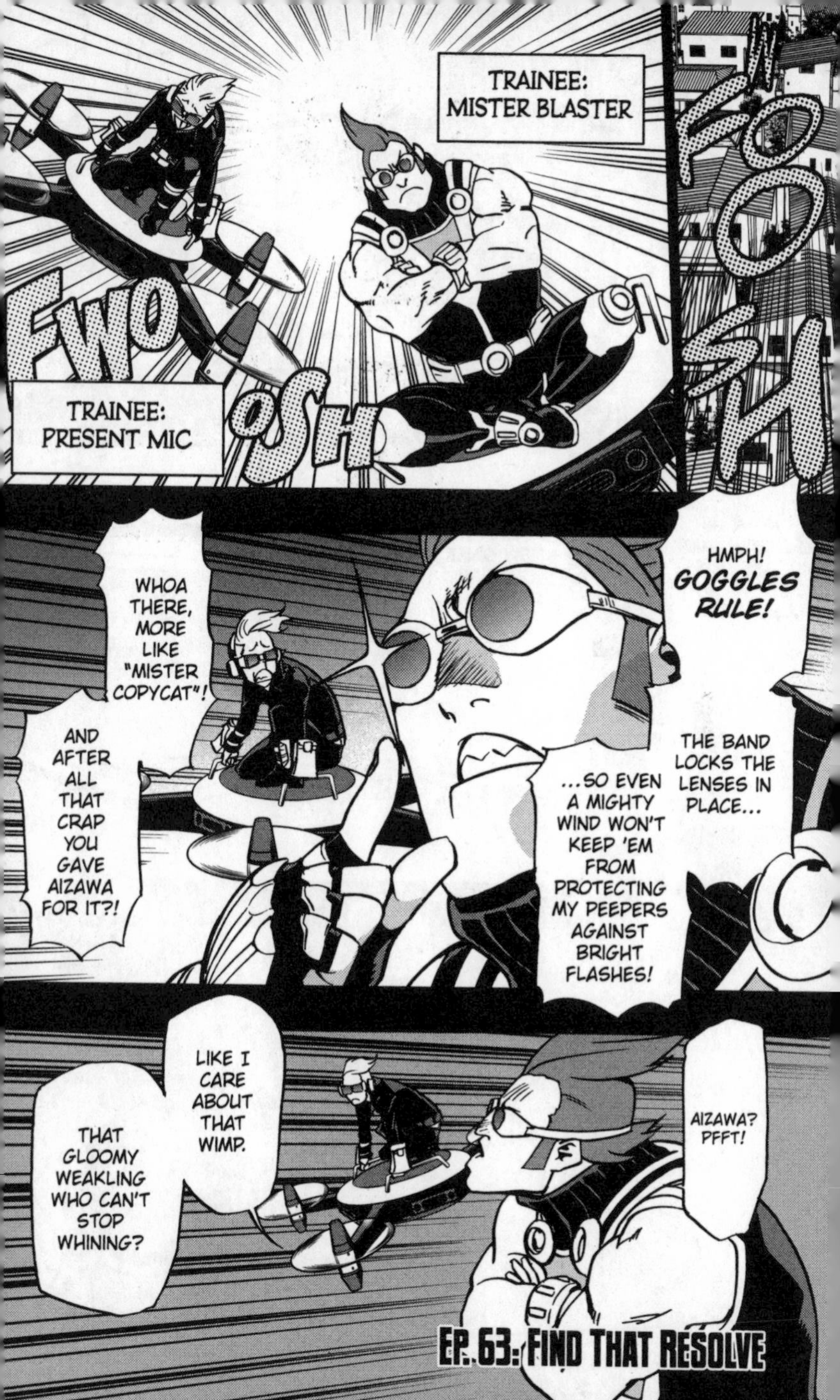
FWOOSH
TRAINEE: MISTER BLASTER
FWOOSH
TRAINEE: PRESENT MIC
HMPH! GOGGLES RULE!
THE BAND LOCKS THE LENSES IN PLACE...
...SO EVEN A MIGHTY WIND WON'T KEEP 'EM FROM PROTECTING MY PEEPERS AGAINST BRIGHT FLASHES!
WHOA THERE, MORE LIKE "MISTER COPYCAT"!
AND AFTER ALL THAT CRAP YOU GAVE AIZAWA FOR IT?!
AIZAWA? PFFT!
LIKE I CARE ABOUT THAT WIMP.
THAT GLOOMY WEAKLING WHO CAN'T STOP WHINING?
EP. 63: FIND THAT RESOLVE

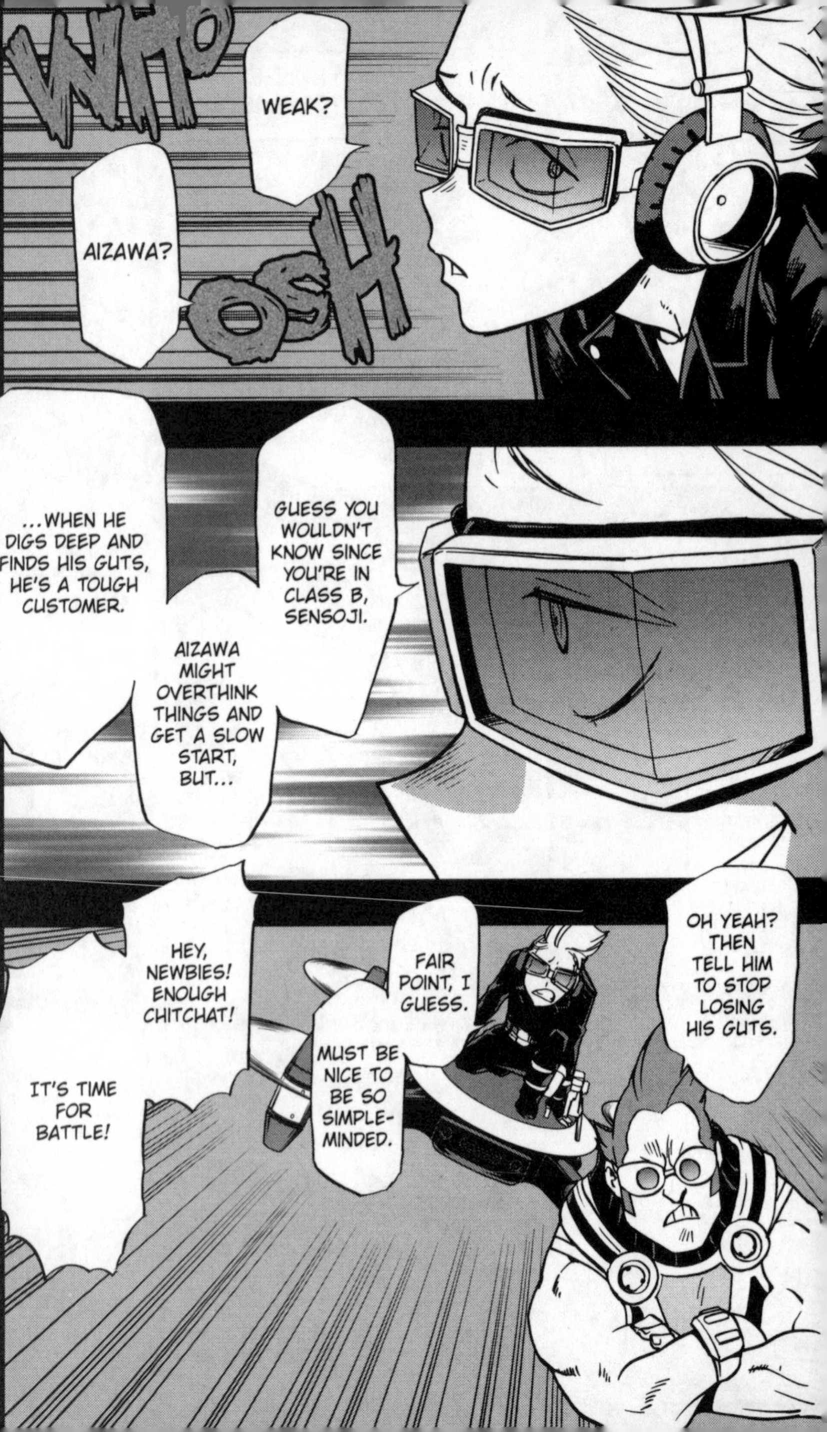
WHOOSH
WEAK?
AIZAWA?
GUESS YOU WOULDN'T KNOW SINCE YOU'RE IN CLASS B, SENSOJI.
AIZAWA MIGHT OVERTHINK THINGS AND GET A SLOW START, BUT...
...WHEN HE DIGS DEEP AND FINDS HIS GUTS, HE'S A TOUGH CUSTOMER.
OH YEAH? THEN TELL HIM TO STOP LOSING HIS GUTS.
FAIR POINT, I GUESS.
MUST BE NICE TO BE SO SIMPLE-MINDED.
HEY, NEWBIES! ENOUGH CHITCHAT!
IT'S TIME FOR BATTLE!

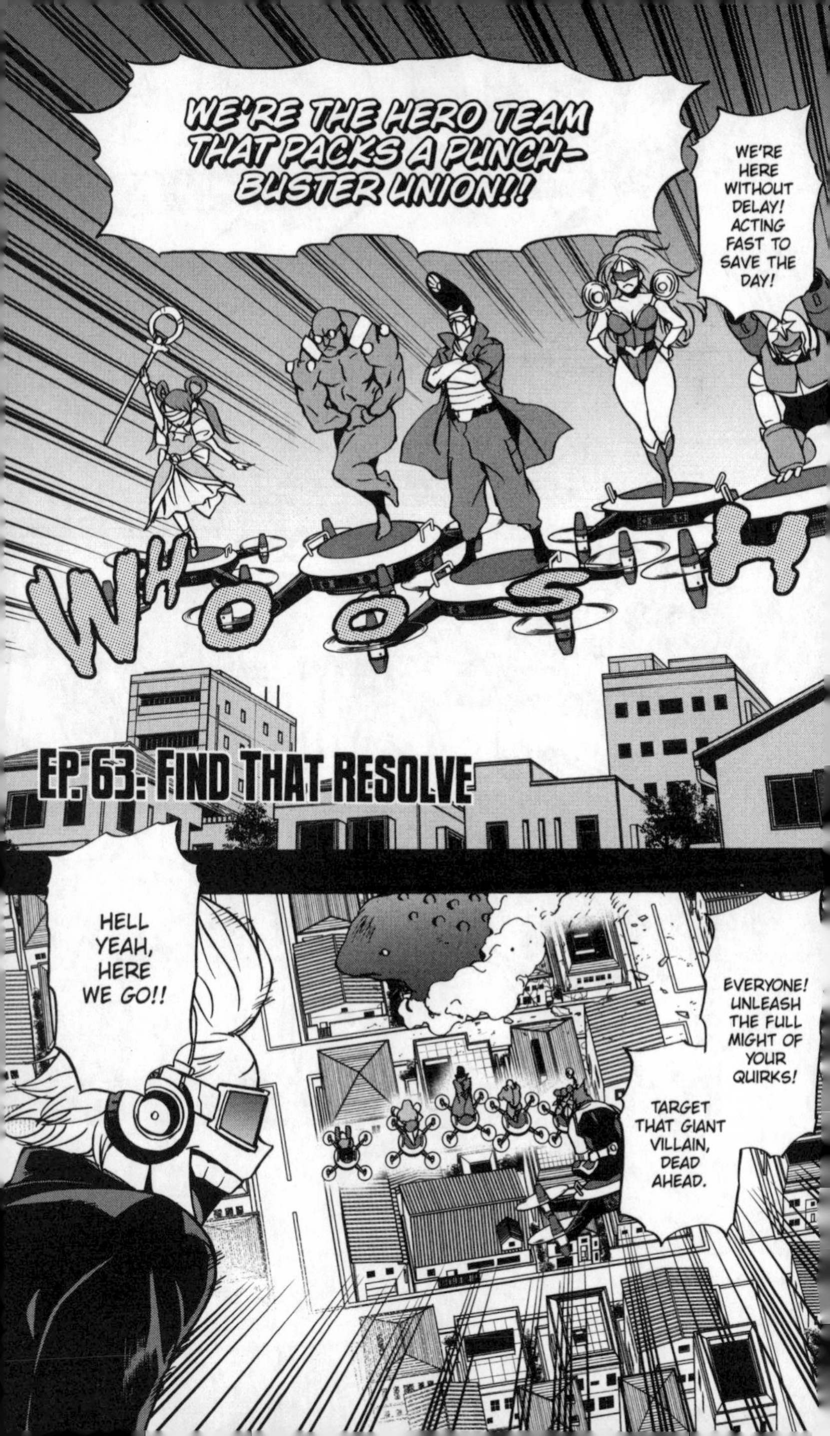
WE'RE HERE WITHOUT DELAY! ACTING FAST TO SAVE THE DAY!
WE'RE THE HERO TEAM THAT PACKS A PUNCH— BUSTER UNION!!
WHOOSH
EP. 63: FIND THAT RESOLVE
EVERYONE! UNLEASH THE FULL MIGHT OF YOUR QUIRKS!
TARGET THAT GIANT VILLAIN, DEAD AHEAD.
HELL YEAH, HERE WE GO!!

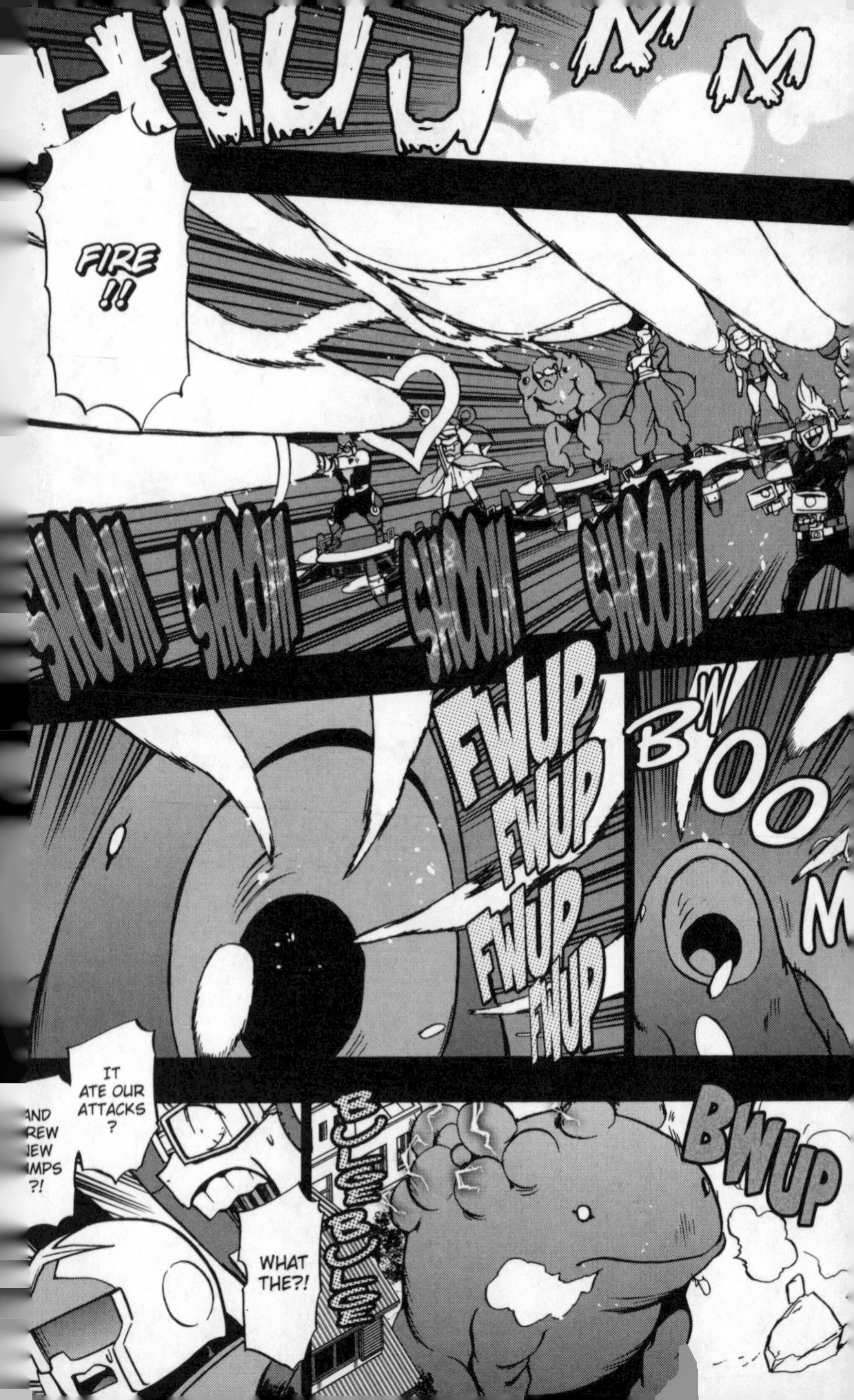

HUUUMM
FIRE!!
SHOOM SHOOM SHOOM SHOOM
BWOOM
FWUP FWUP FWUP FWUP
BWUP
BULGE BULGE
WHAT THE?!
IT ATE OUR ATTACKS?
AND REW EW MPS ?!

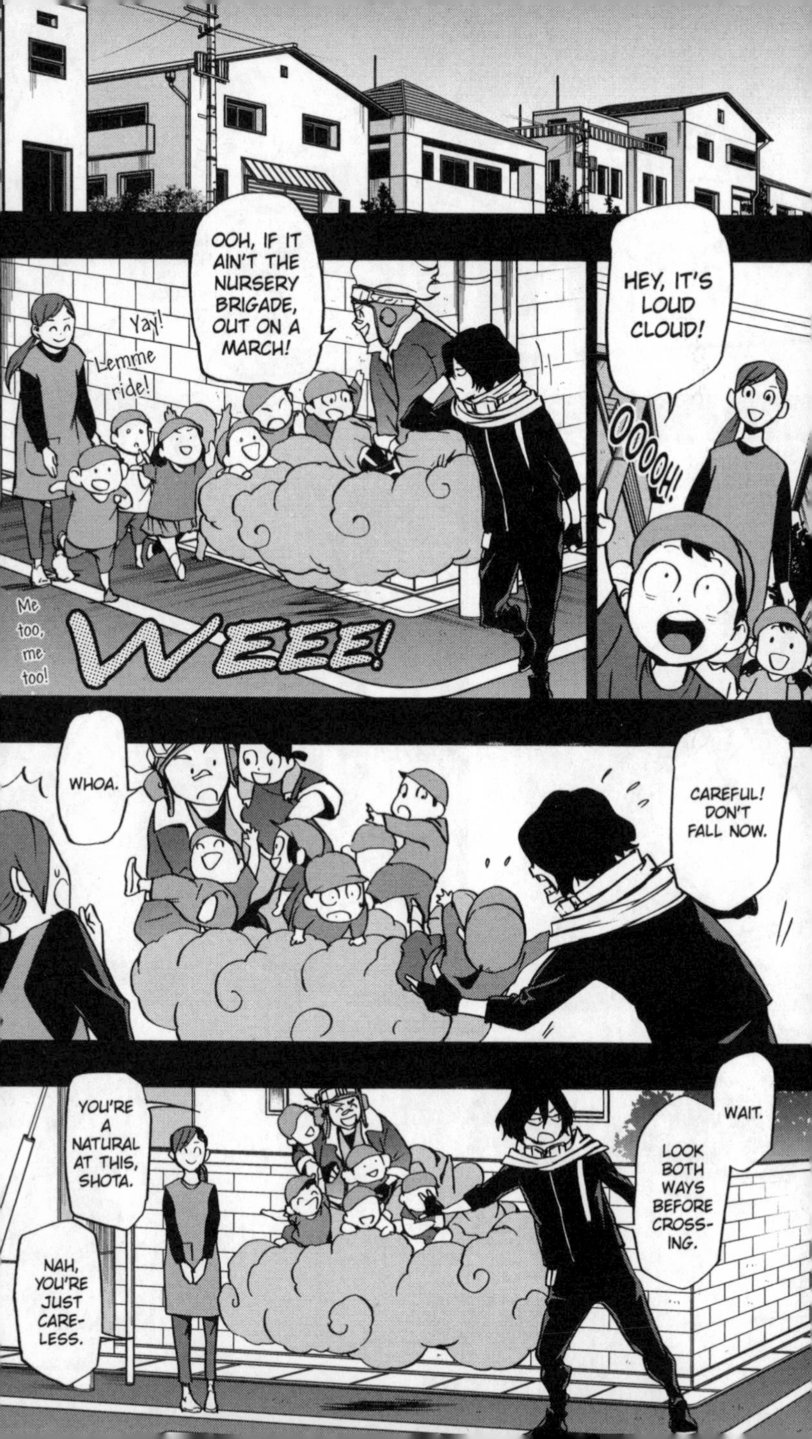
HEY, IT'S LOUD CLOUD!
OOOOOH!
OOH, IF IT AIN'T THE NURSERY BRIGADE, OUT ON A MARCH!
Yay!
Lemme ride!
WEEE!
Me too, me too!
CAREFUL! DON'T FALL NOW.
WHOA.
WAIT.
LOOK BOTH WAYS BEFORE CROSS-ING.
YOU'RE A NATURAL AT THIS, SHOTA.
NAH, YOU'RE JUST CARE-LESS.

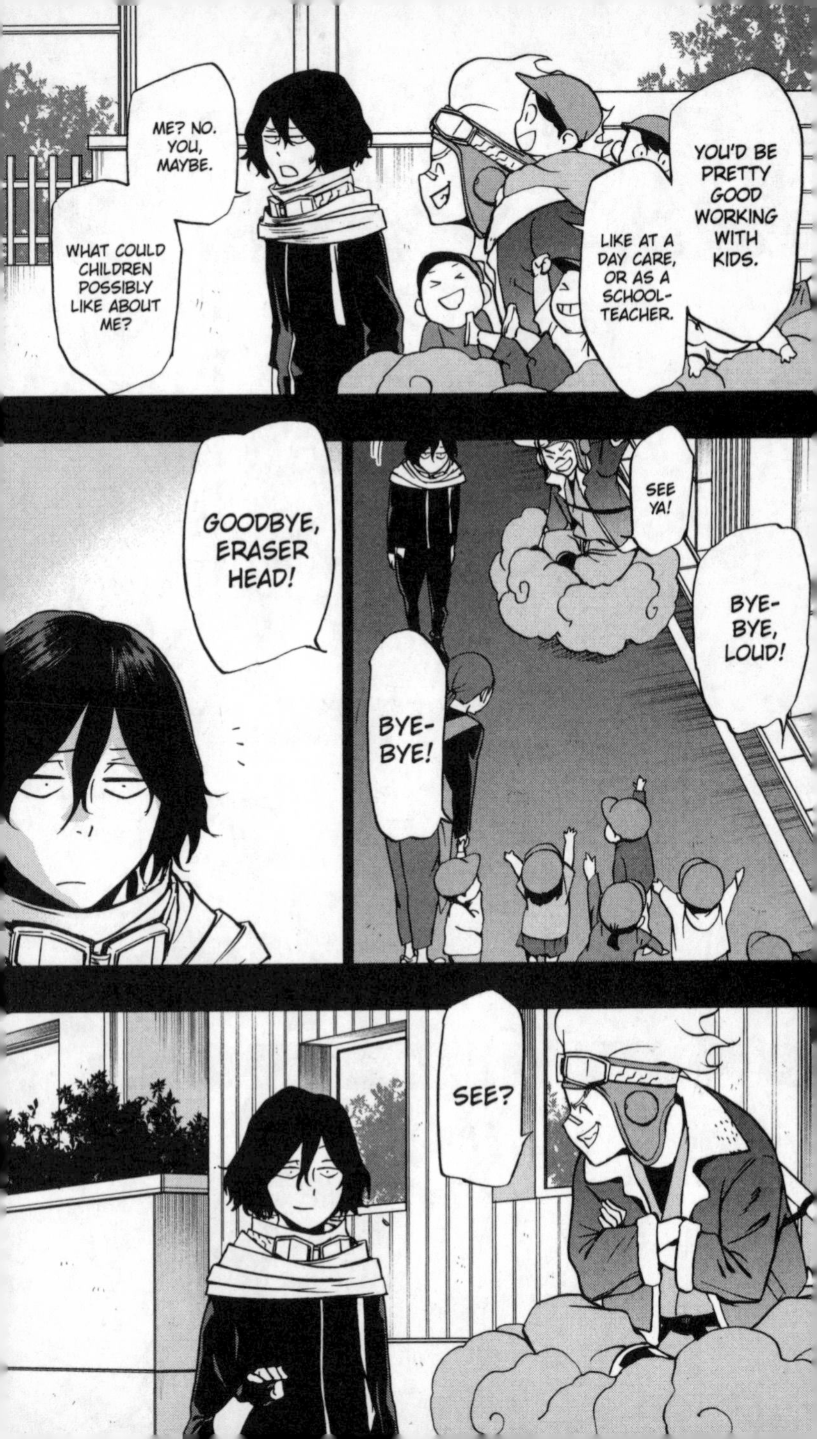
YOU'D BE PRETTY GOOD WORKING WITH KIDS.
LIKE AT A DAY CARE, OR AS A SCHOOL-TEACHER.
ME? NO. YOU, MAYBE.
WHAT COULD CHILDREN POSSIBLY LIKE ABOUT ME?
SEE YA!
BYE-BYE, LOUD!
BYE-BYE!
GOODBYE, ERASER HEAD!
SEE?

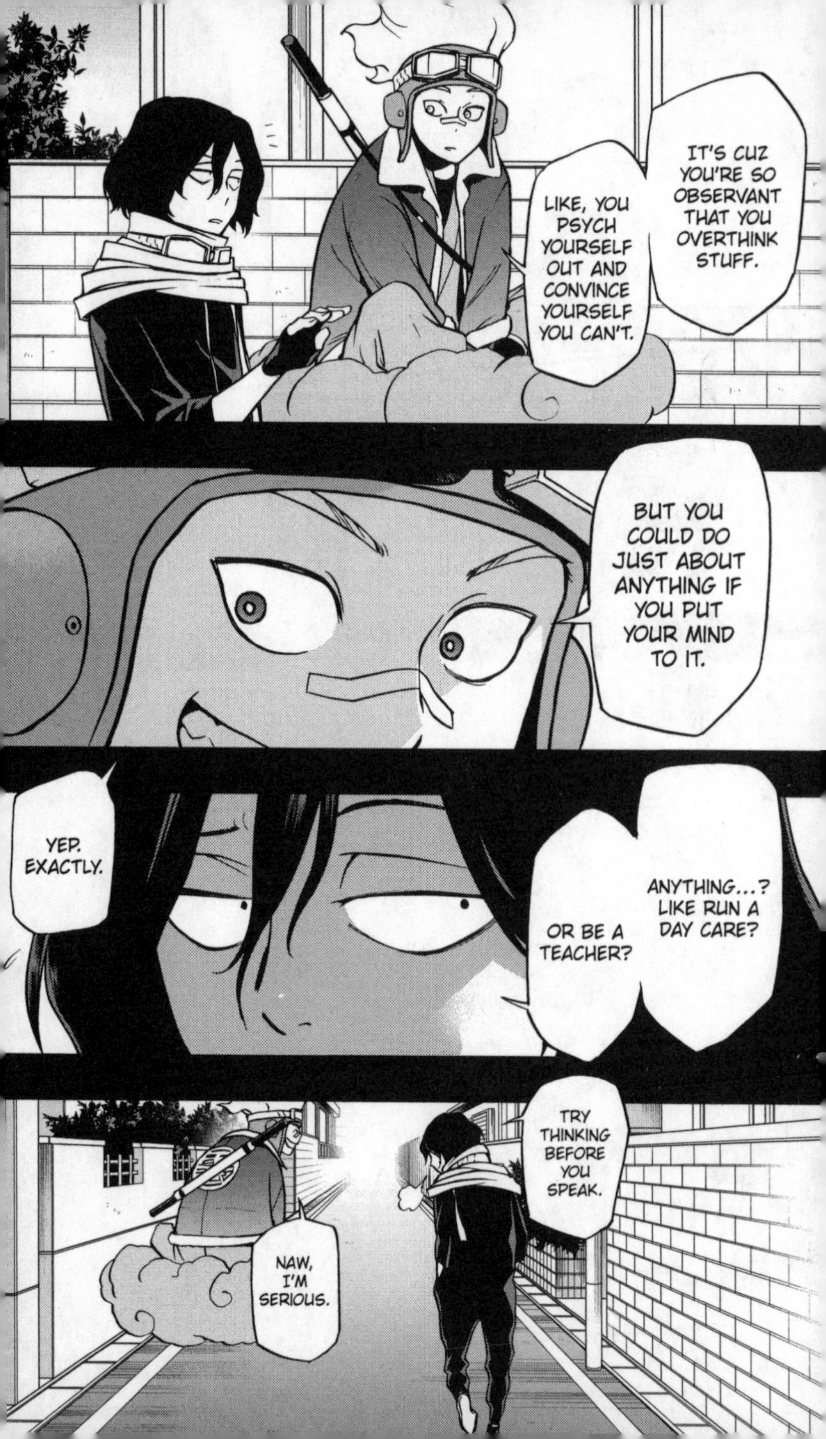
IT'S CUZ YOU'RE SO OBSERVANT THAT YOU OVERTHINK STUFF.
LIKE, YOU PSYCH YOURSELF OUT AND CONVINCE YOURSELF YOU CAN'T.
BUT YOU COULD DO JUST ABOUT ANYTHING IF YOU PUT YOUR MIND TO IT.
ANYTHING...? LIKE RUN A DAY CARE?
OR BE A TEACHER?
YEP. EXACTLY.
TRY THINKING BEFORE YOU SPEAK.
NAW, I'M SERIOUS.

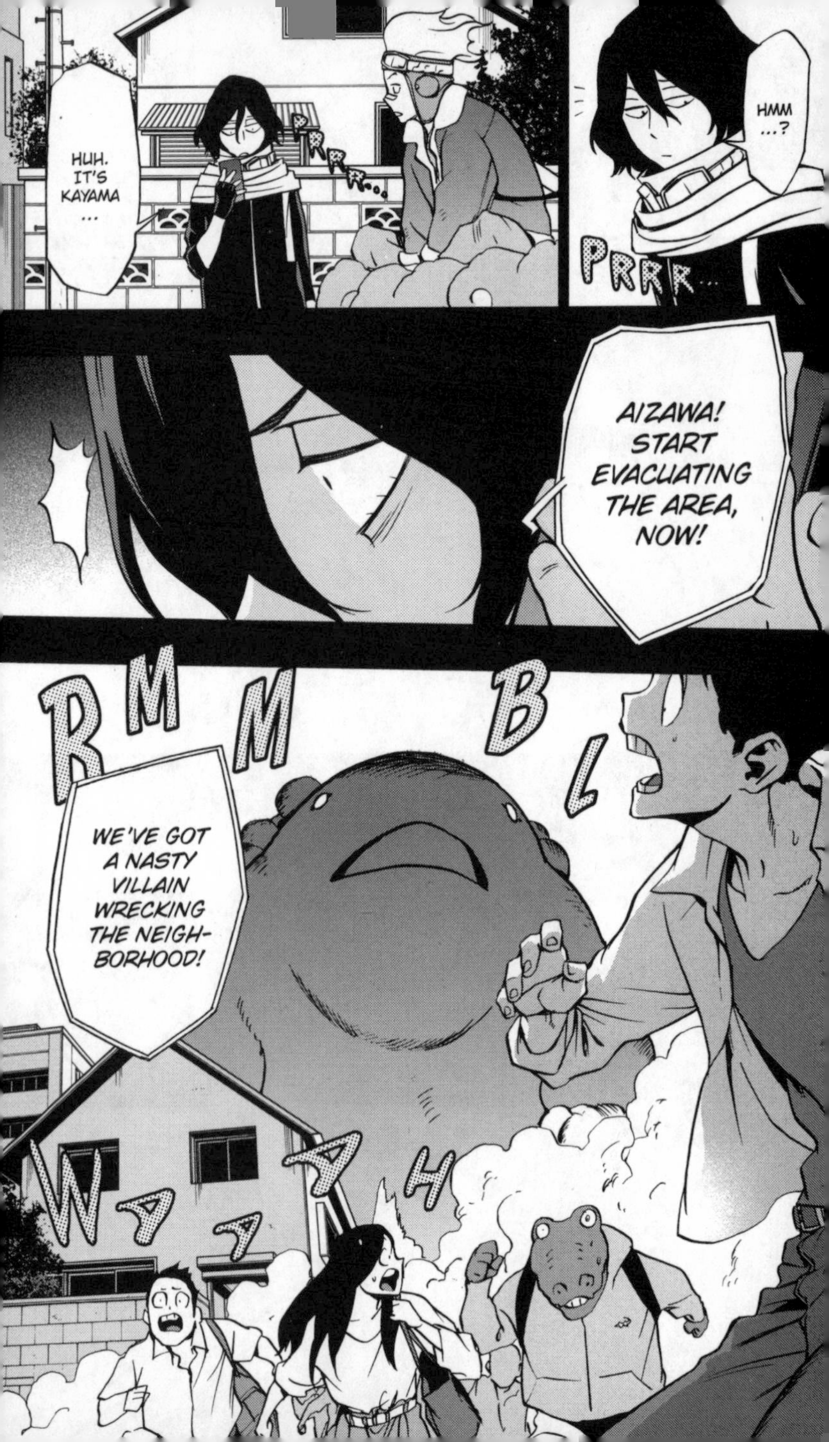
HMM ...?
PRRR...
HUH. IT'S KAYAMA ...
PRRR...
AIZAWA! START EVACUATING THE AREA, NOW!
RMMBL
WE'VE GOT A NASTY VILLAIN WRECKING THE NEIGH-BORHOOD!
WAAAH

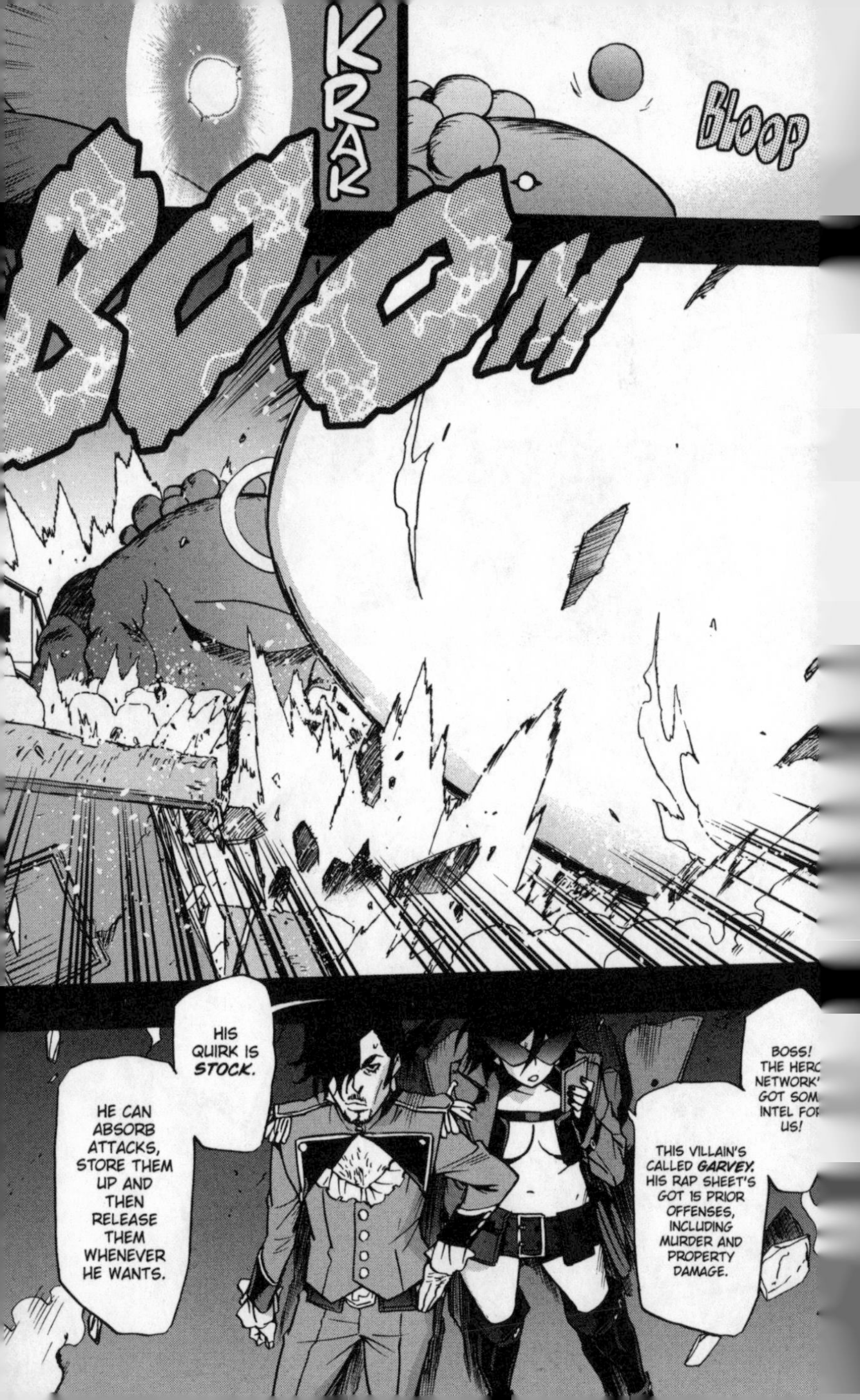
BLOOP
KRAK
BOOM
BOSS! THE HERO NETWORK' GOT SOM INTEL FOR US!
THIS VILLAIN'S CALLED **GARVEY.** HIS RAP SHEET'S GOT 15 PRIOR OFFENSES, INCLUDING MURDER AND PROPERTY DAMAGE.
HIS QUIRK IS **STOCK.**
HE CAN ABSORB ATTACKS, STORE THEM UP AND THEN RELEASE THEM WHENEVER HE WANTS.

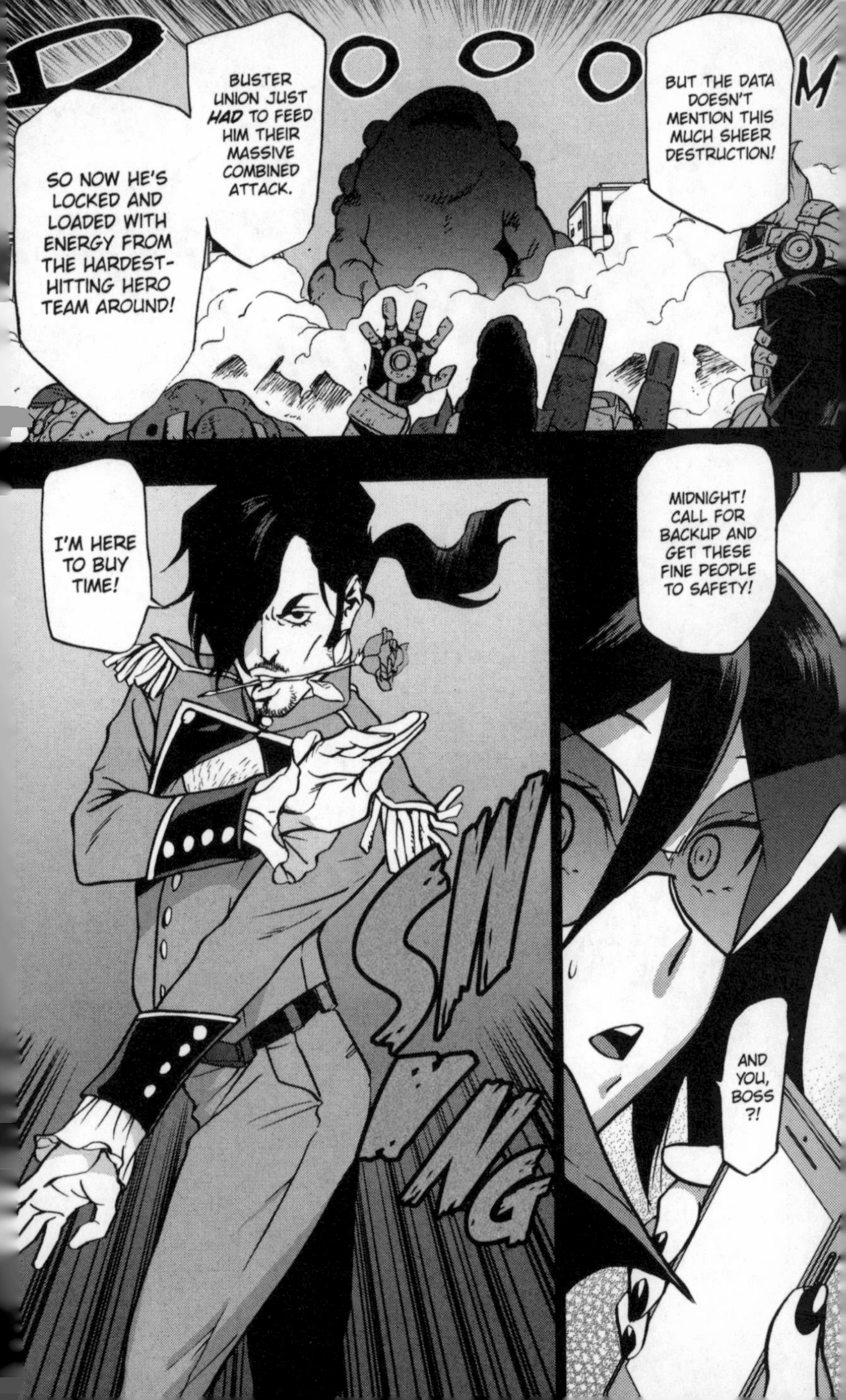

DOOOOM
BUT THE DATA DOESN'T MENTION THIS MUCH SHEER DESTRUCTION!
BUSTER UNION JUST *HAD* TO FEED HIM THEIR MASSIVE COMBINED ATTACK.
SO NOW HE'S LOCKED AND LOADED WITH ENERGY FROM THE HARDEST-HITTING HERO TEAM AROUND!
MIDNIGHT! CALL FOR BACKUP AND GET THESE FINE PEOPLE TO SAFETY!
AND YOU, BOSS ?!
I'M HERE TO BUY TIME!
SHING

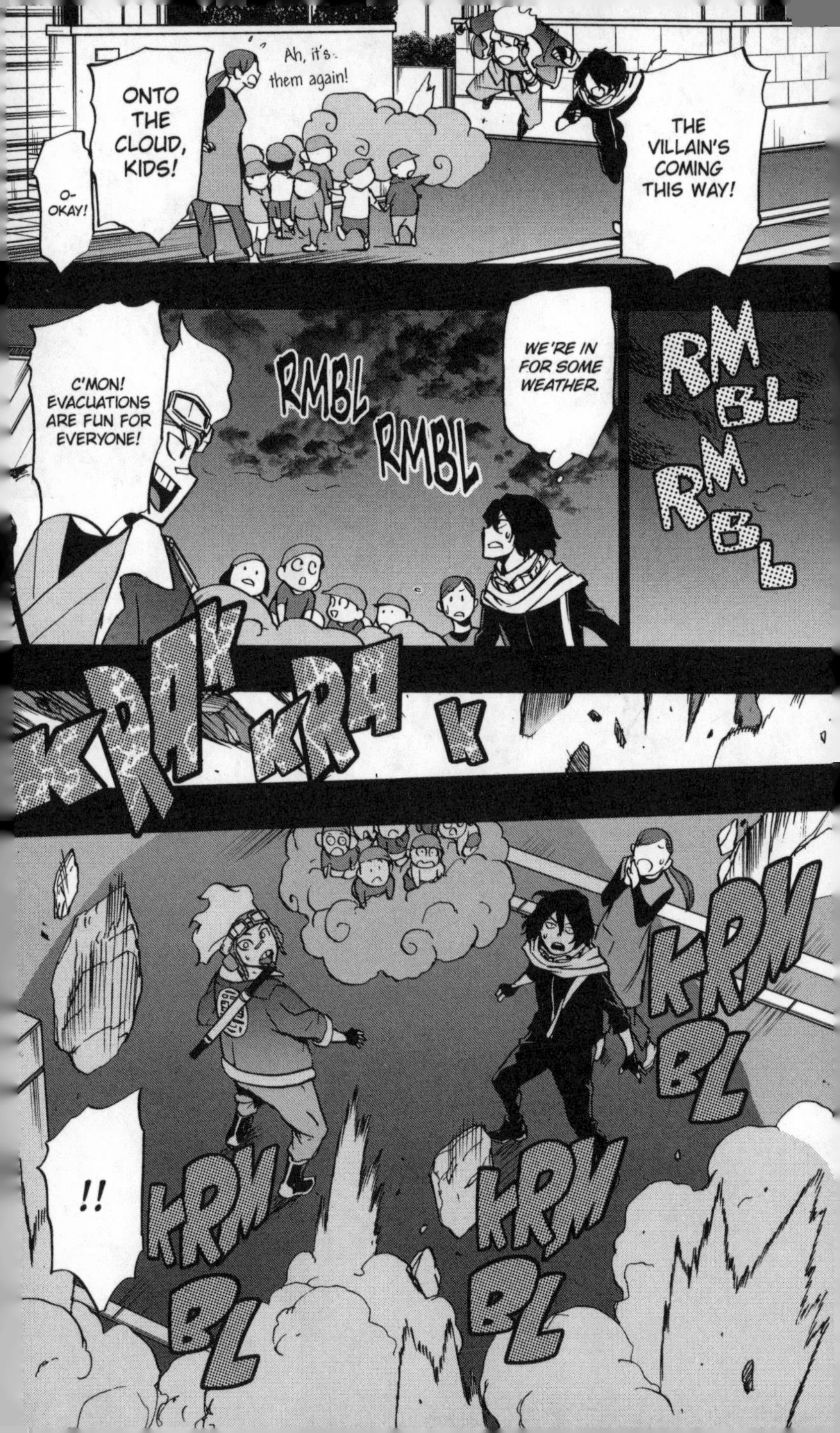
THE VILLAIN'S COMING THIS WAY!
Ah, it's them again!
ONTO THE CLOUD, KIDS!
O-OKAY!
RMBL RMBL
WE'RE IN FOR SOME WEATHER.
RMBL RMBL
C'MON! EVACUATIONS ARE FUN FOR EVERYONE!
KRAK KRAK
KRMBL
KRMBL
KRMBL
!!

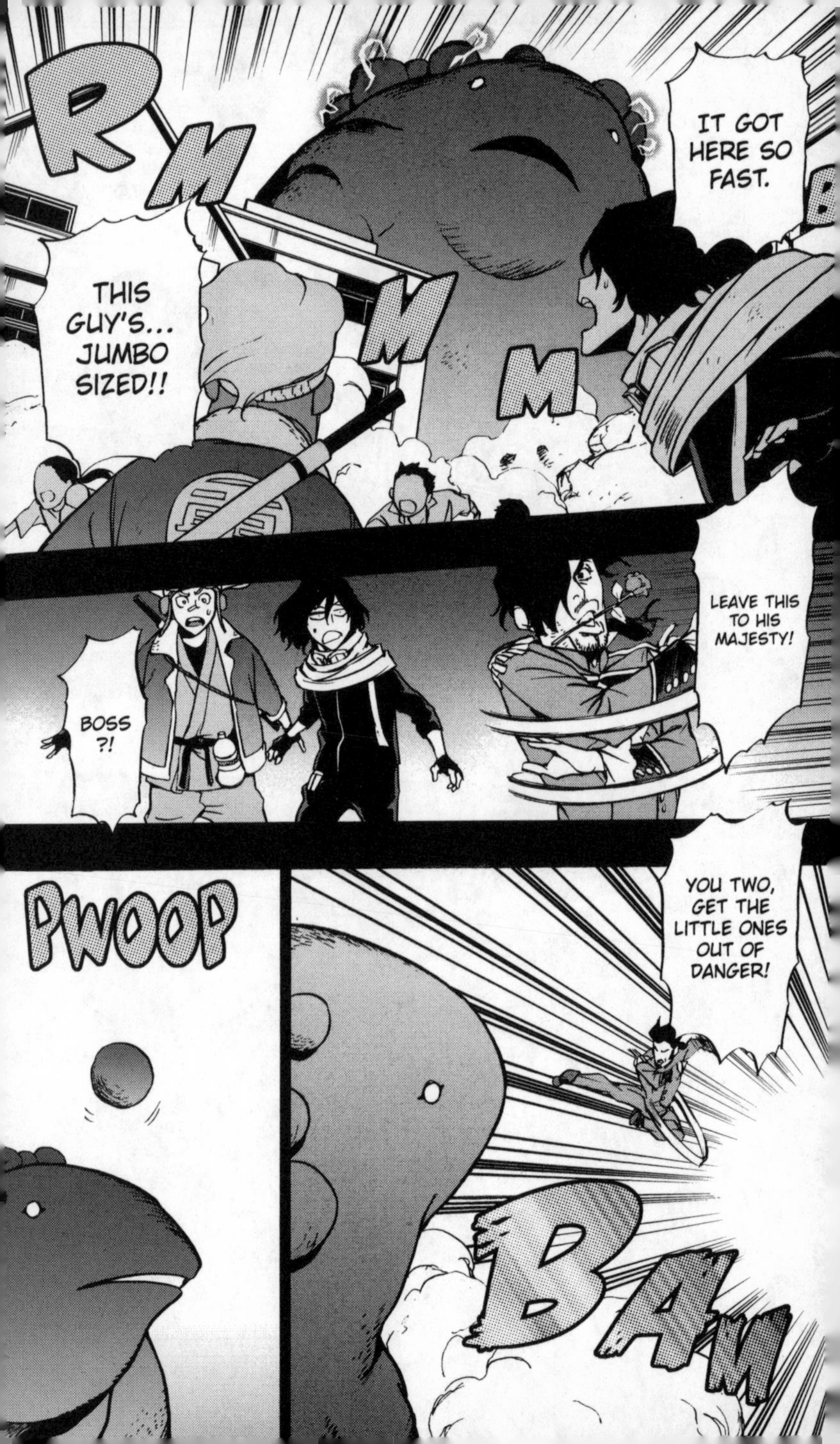
IT GOT HERE SO FAST.
RMMM
THIS GUY'S... JUMBO SIZED!!
LEAVE THIS TO HIS MAJESTY!
BOSS?!
YOU TWO, GET THE LITTLE ONES OUT OF DANGER!
BAM
PWOOP

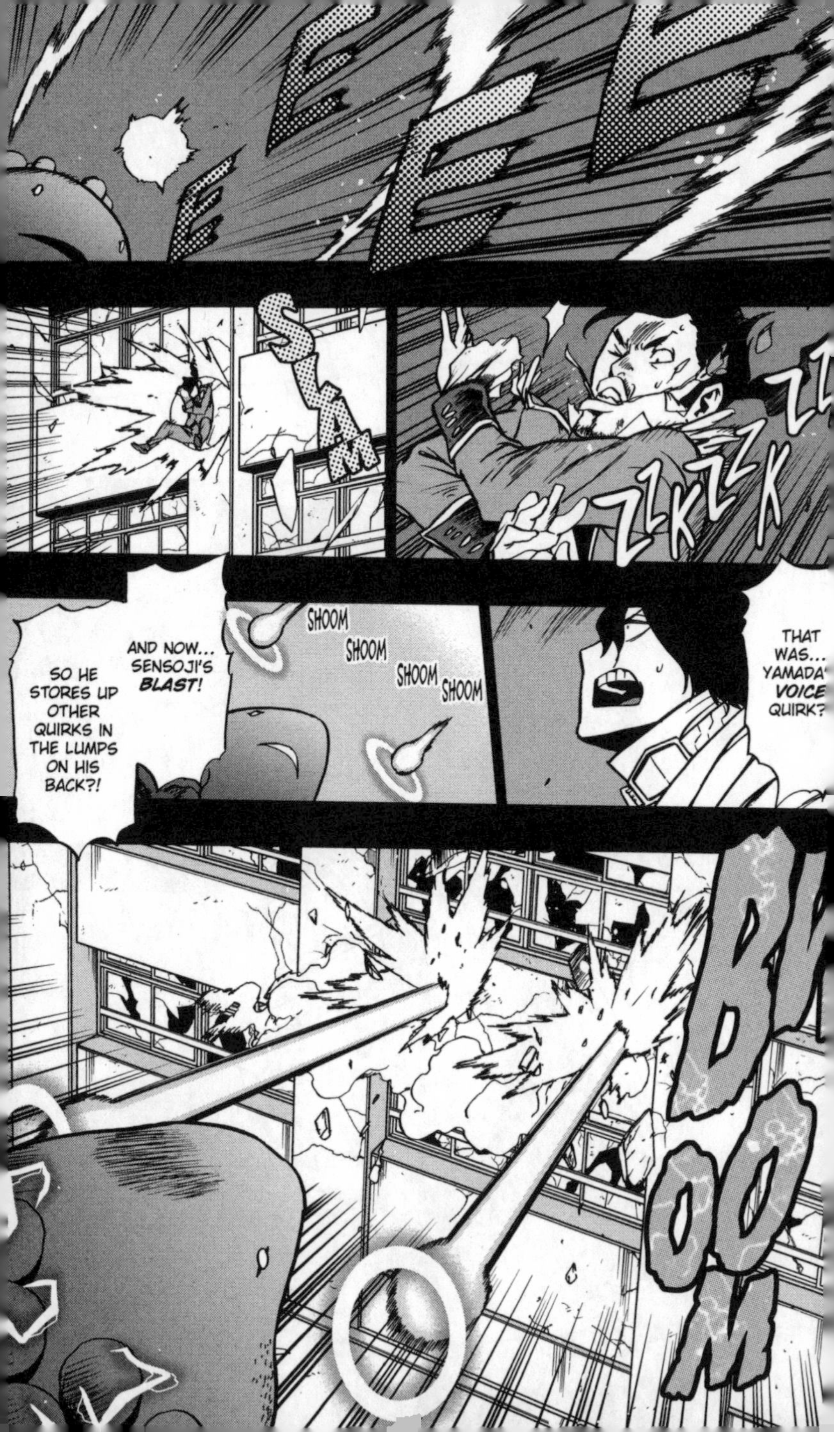
THAT WAS... YAMADA'S VOICE QUIRK?
SHOOM
SHOOM
SHOOM
SHOOM
AND NOW... SENSOJI'S BLAST!
SO HE STORES UP OTHER QUIRKS IN THE LUMPS ON HIS BACK?!

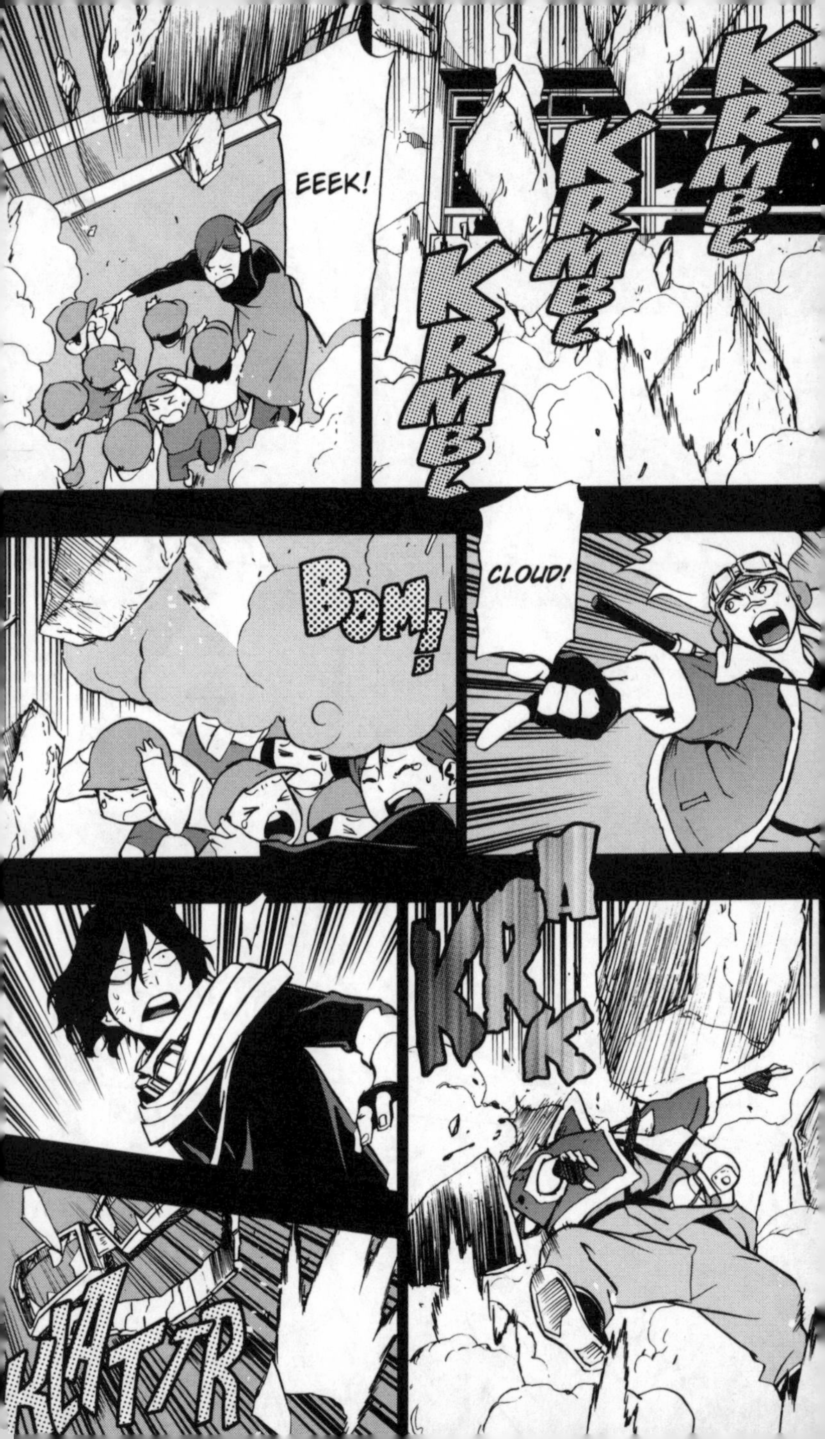
KRMBL
KRMBL
KRMBL
EEEK!
CLOUD!
BOM!
KRAK
KLATTR

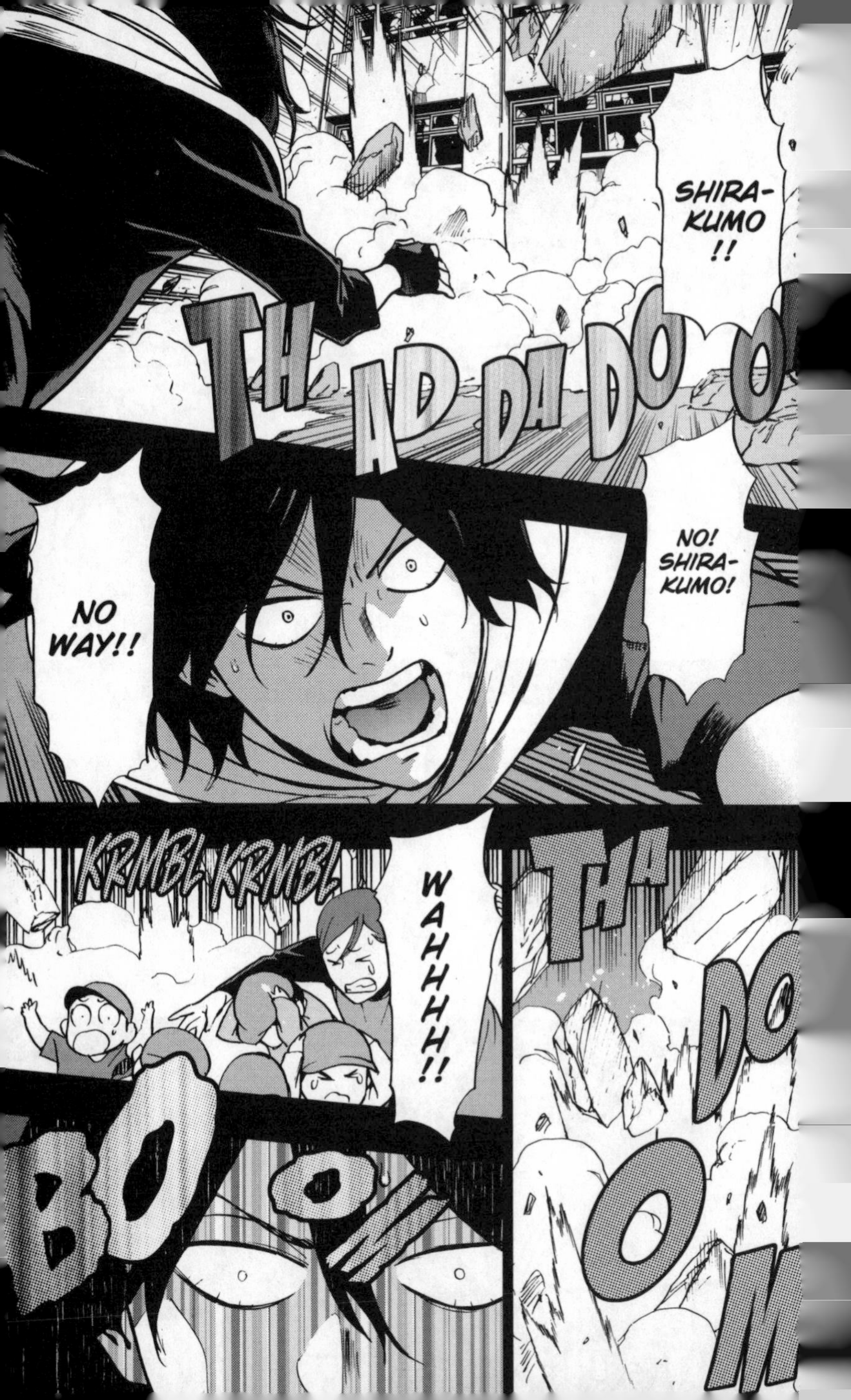
SHIRA-KUMO !!
TH AD DA DO O
NO! SHIRA-KUMO!
NO WAY!!
THA DO O
WAHHHHH!!
KRMBL KRMBL
BO O

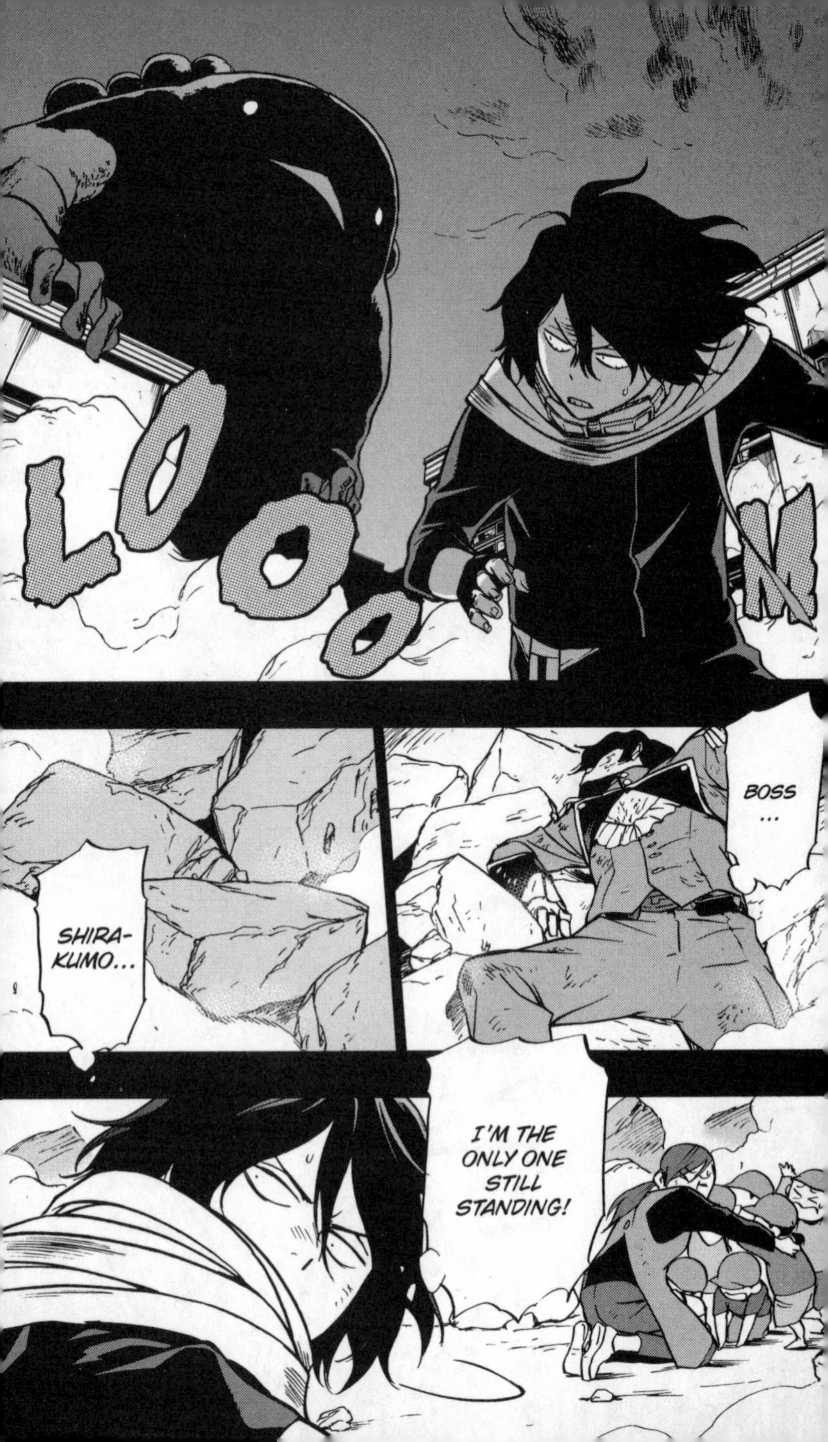
LOOOM
BOSS ...
SHIRA-KUMO...
I'M THE ONLY ONE STILL STANDING!

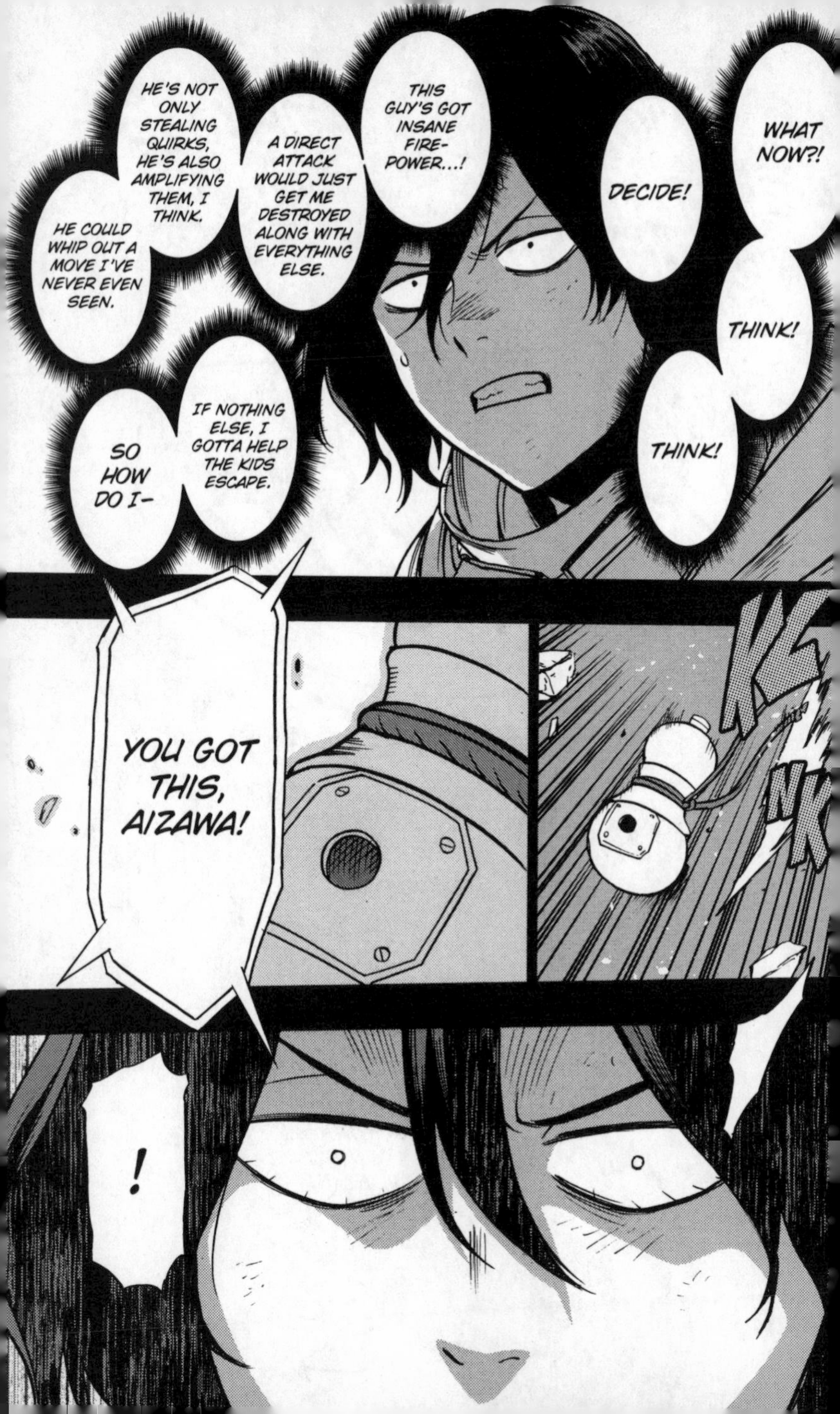
WHAT NOW?!
DECIDE!
THINK!
THINK!
THIS GUY'S GOT INSANE FIRE-POWER...!
A DIRECT ATTACK WOULD JUST GET ME DESTROYED ALONG WITH EVERYTHING ELSE.
HE'S NOT ONLY STEALING QUIRKS, HE'S ALSO AMPLIFYING THEM, I THINK.
HE COULD WHIP OUT A MOVE I'VE NEVER EVEN SEEN.
IF NOTHING ELSE, I GOTTA HELP THE KIDS ESCAPE.
SO HOW DO I-
YOU GOT THIS, AIZAWA!
!

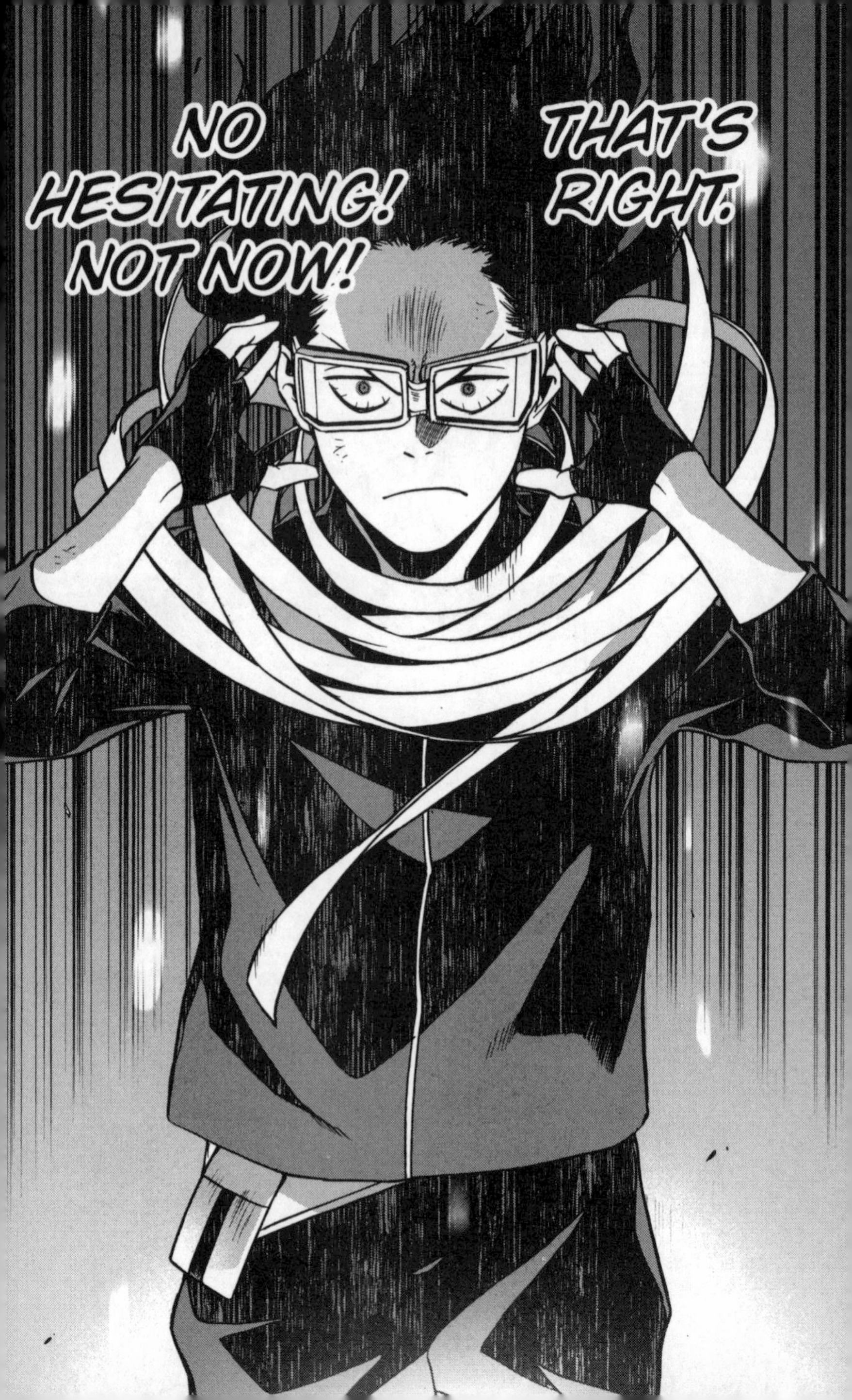
THAT'S RIGHT.
NO HESITATING! NOT NOW!

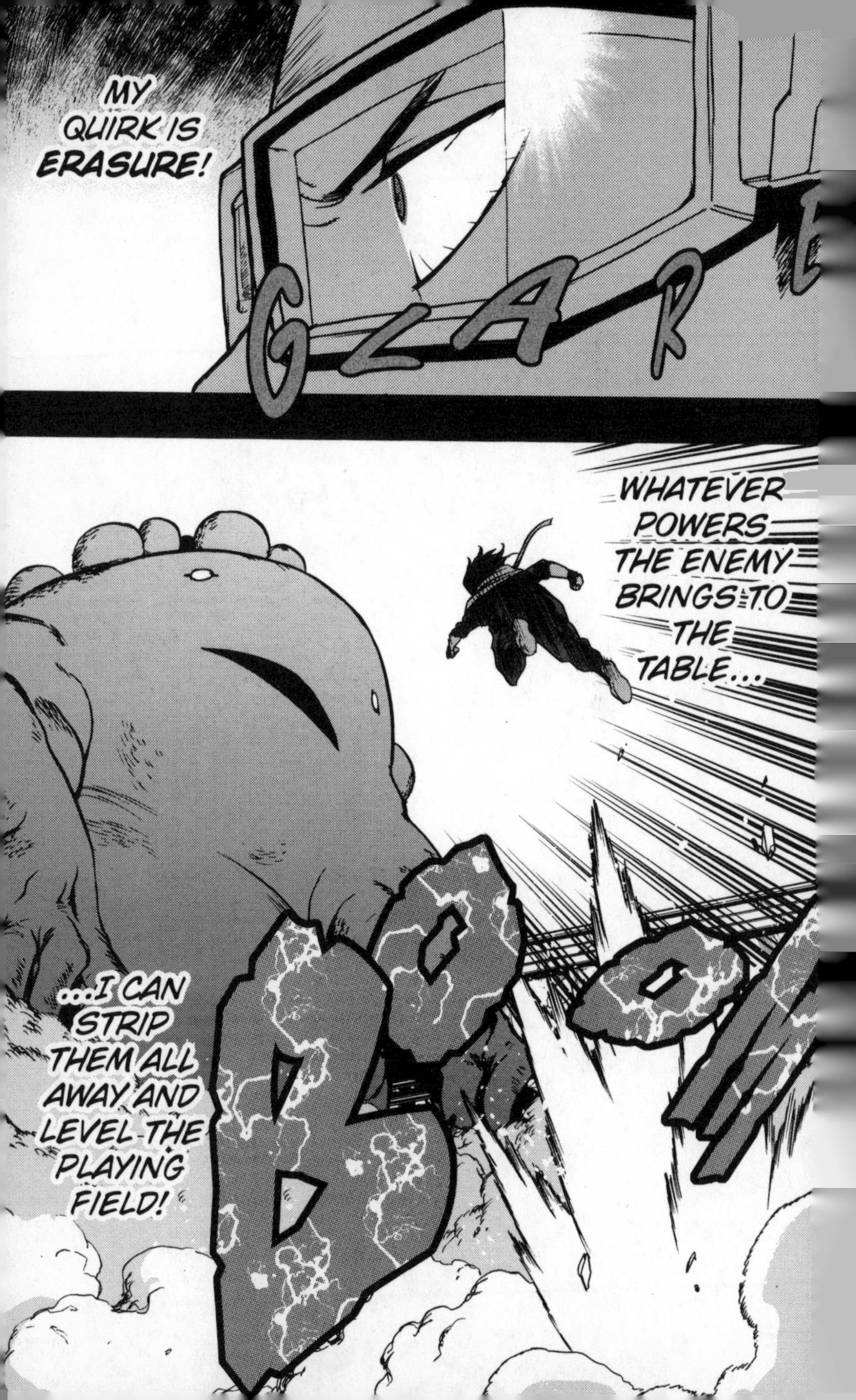
MY QUIRK IS ERASURE!
GLAR
WHATEVER POWERS THE ENEMY BRINGS TO THE TABLE...
...I CAN STRIP THEM ALL AWAY AND LEVEL THE PLAYING FIELD!

BUSTER UNION

THE ROUGH DESIGN

Buster Union

Bukkomi

Boobs

Cangunnon

Mellorine

Tech Magic

BEHIND THE SCENES

The requirements here were "They fly in, line up and fire off attacks all at once" plus "A team with enough variety that Mic and Sensoji don't feel out of place." So I did some reverse engineering and came up with these guys. Betten-san and I are from the same generation, so we both had some chuckles about the little touches here, like Cangunnon being inspired by *Gundam*'s Guncannon, or the guy who seems to be inspired by the *Cho Aniki* video games but is actually referencing Taro Yamamoto's Mellorine Q shtick.

—Furuhashi

I was short on time, so these are some pretty desperate attempts at characters. But shhh—that's a secret.

—Betten

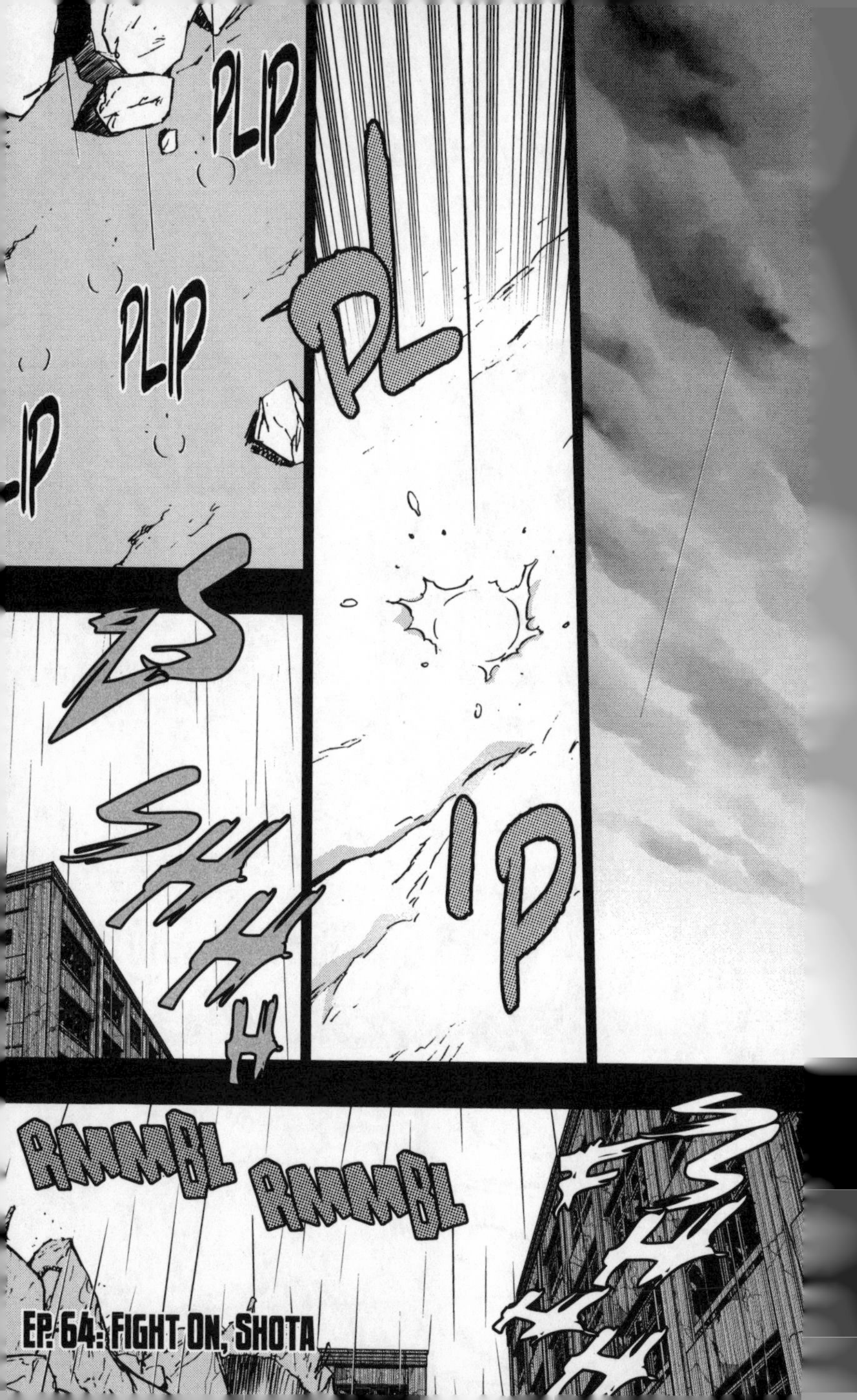
PLIP
PLIP
PLIP
SHHH
FSHHH
RMMMBL RMMMBL
EP. 64: FIGHT ON, SHOTA

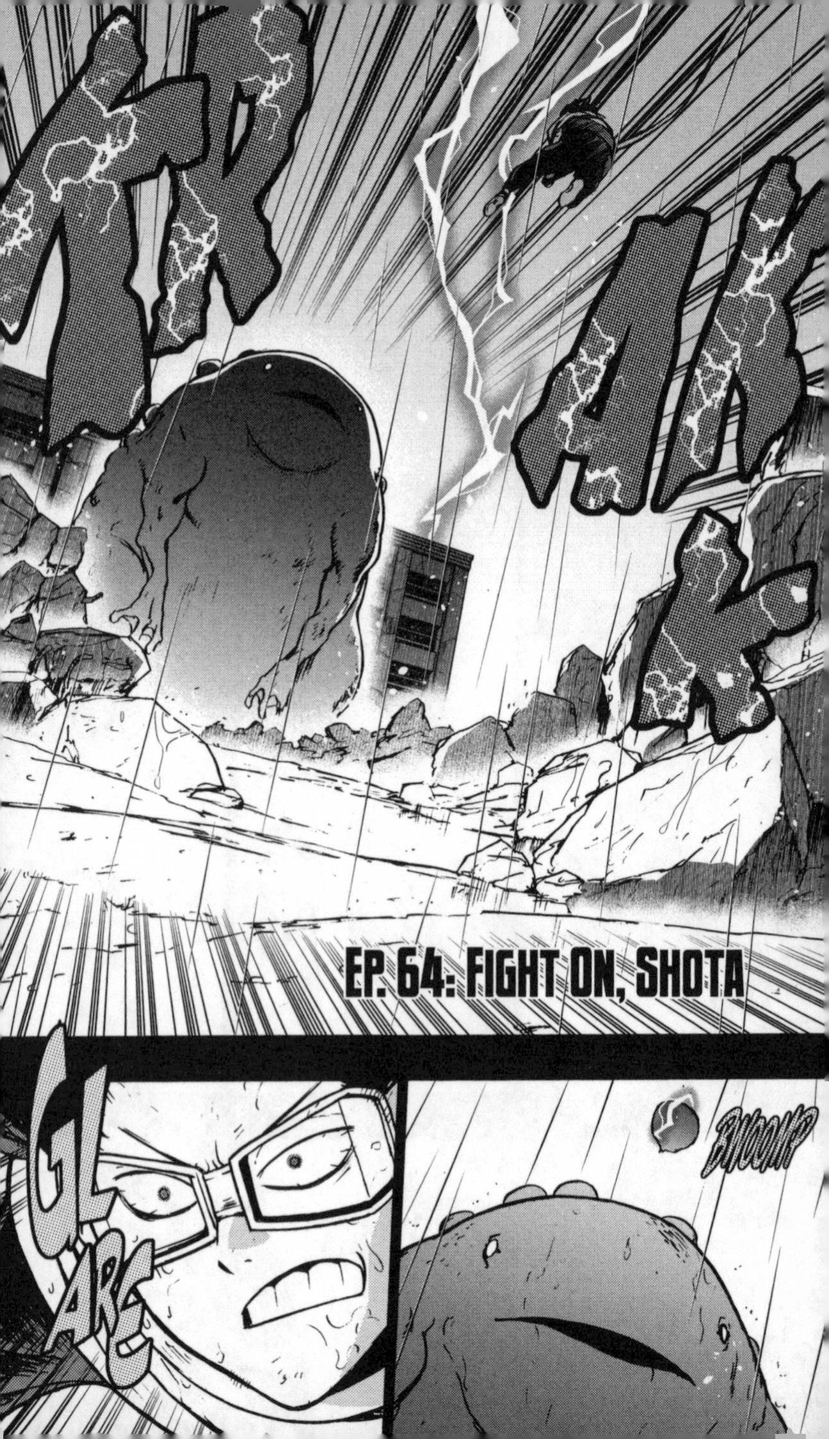
EP. 64: FIGHT ON, SHOTA
BWOOMP
GLARE

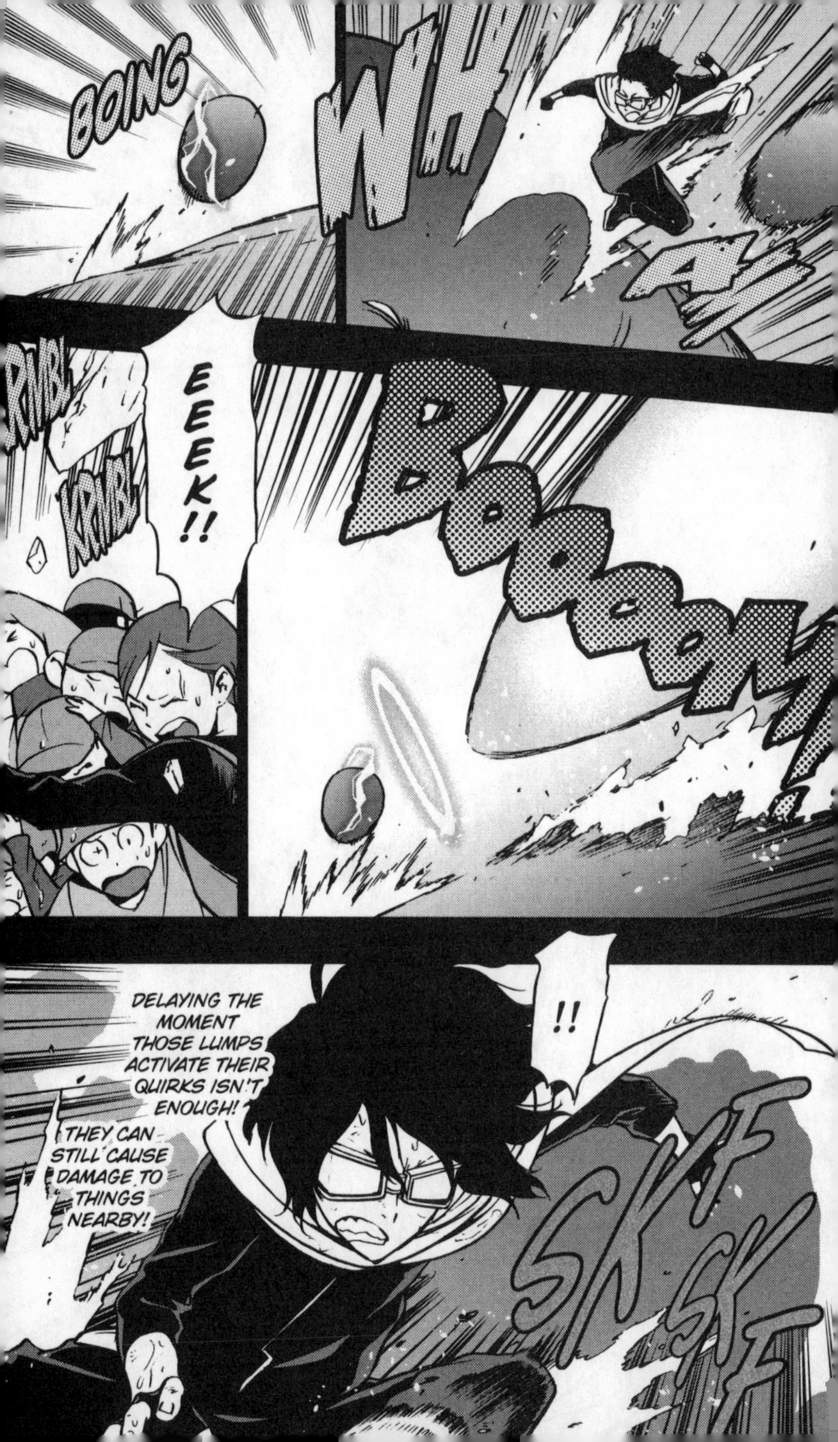
WHAM
BOING
BOOOOM
KRMBL
KRMBL
EEEEK!!
!!
DELAYING THE MOMENT THOSE LUMPS ACTIVATE THEIR QUIRKS ISN'T ENOUGH!
THEY CAN STILL CAUSE DAMAGE TO THINGS NEARBY!

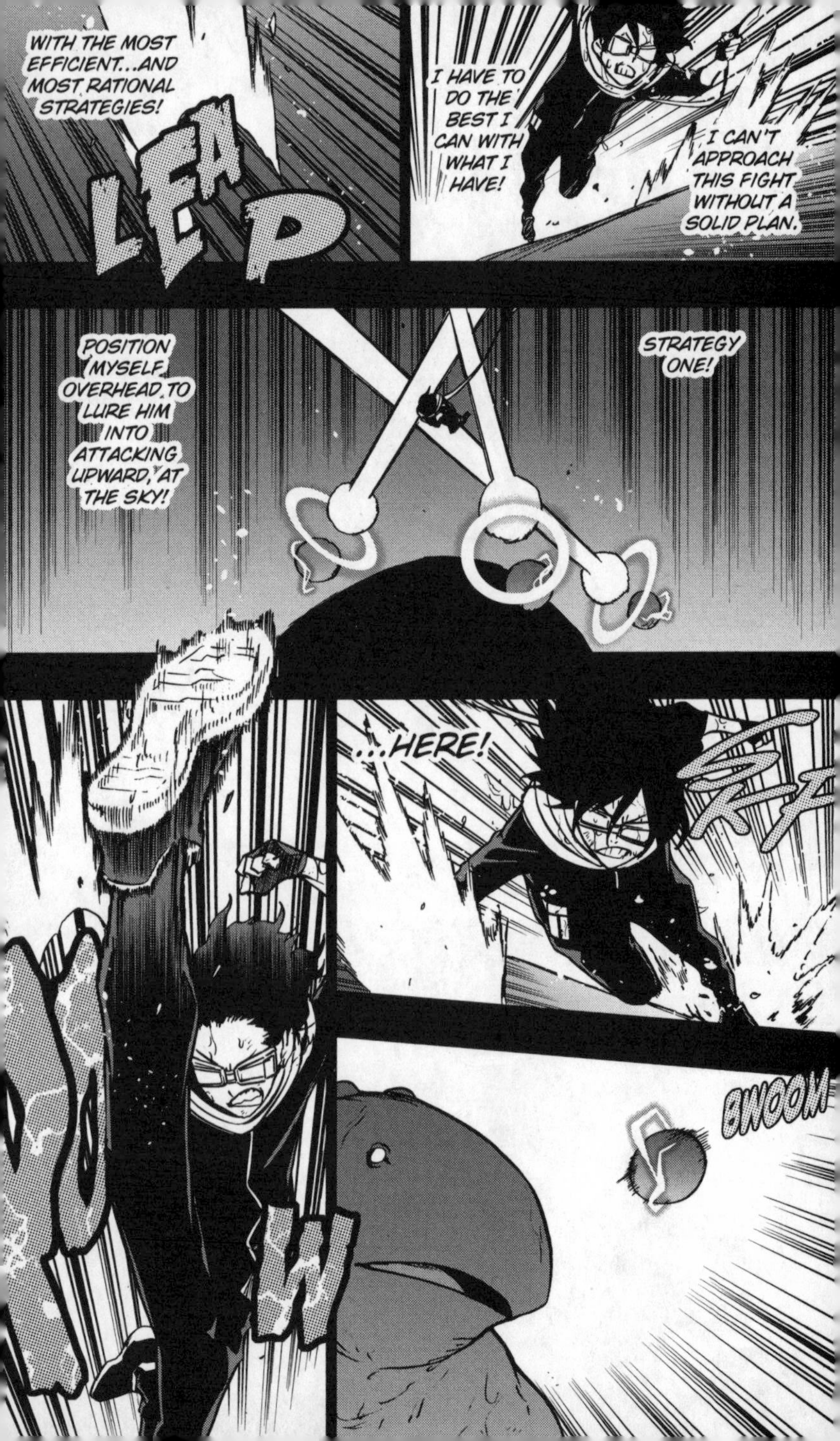
I HAVE TO DO THE BEST I CAN WITH WHAT I HAVE!
I CAN'T APPROACH THIS FIGHT WITHOUT A SOLID PLAN.
WITH THE MOST EFFICIENT...AND MOST RATIONAL STRATEGIES!
LEAP
STRATEGY ONE!
POSITION MYSELF OVERHEAD TO LURE HIM INTO ATTACKING UPWARD, AT THE SKY!
...HERE!
BWOOM

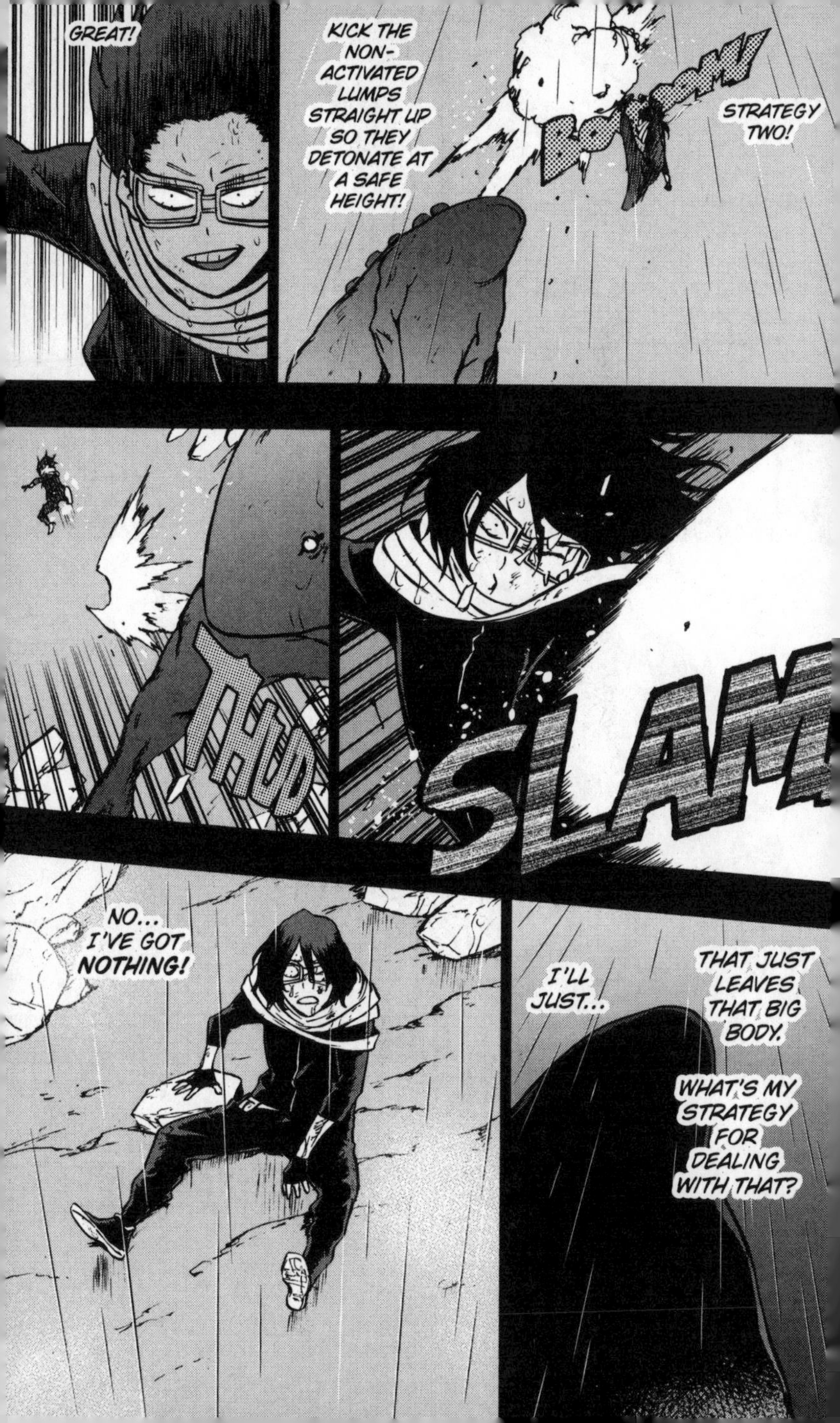
STRATEGY TWO!
KICK THE NON-ACTIVATED LUMPS STRAIGHT UP SO THEY DETONATE AT A SAFE HEIGHT!
GREAT!
SLAM
THUD
THAT JUST LEAVES THAT BIG BODY.
WHAT'S MY STRATEGY FOR DEALING WITH THAT?
I'LL JUST...
NO... I'VE GOT NOTHING!

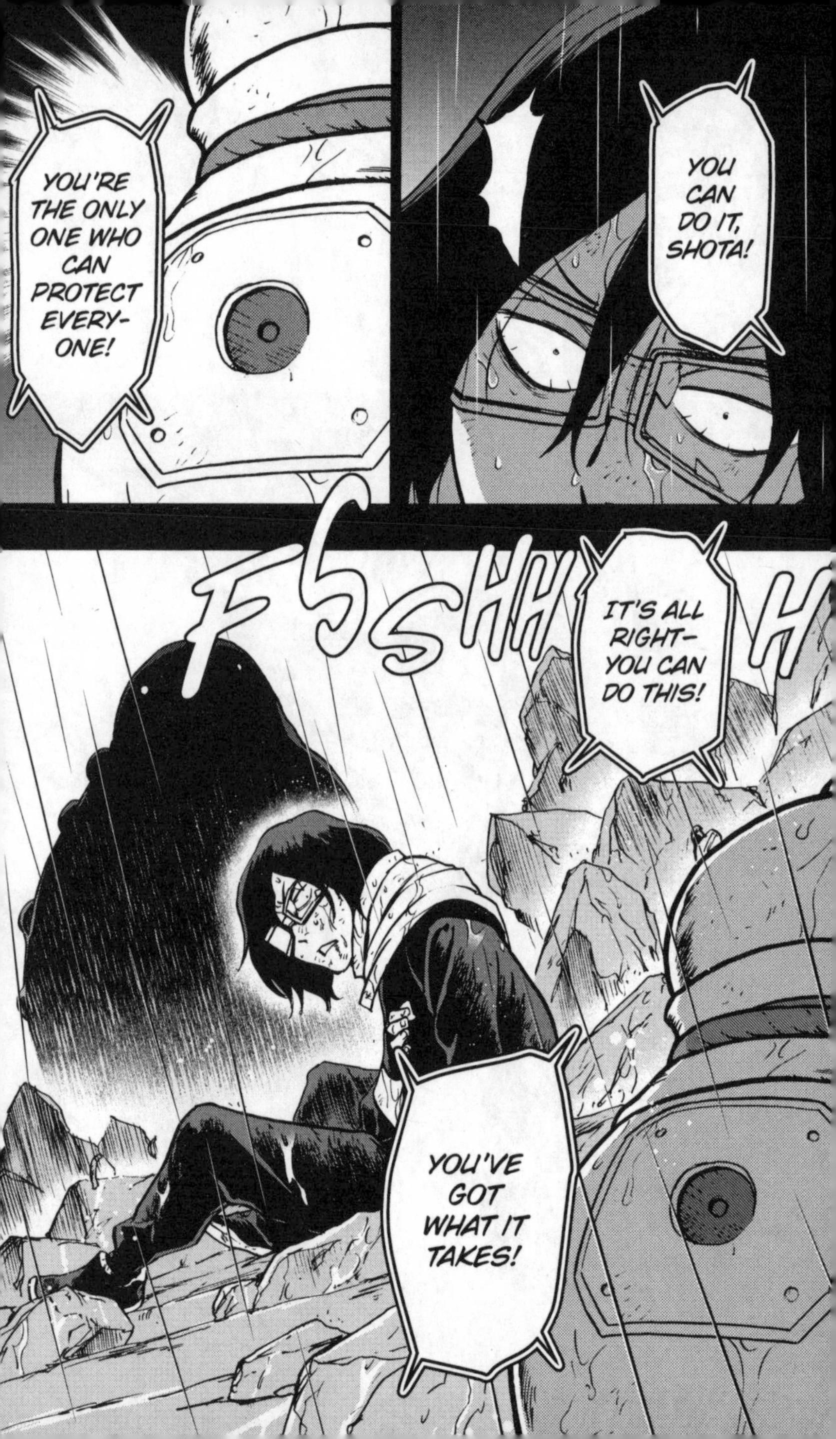
YOU CAN DO IT, SHOTA!
YOU'RE THE ONLY ONE WHO CAN PROTECT EVERY-ONE!
IT'S ALL RIGHT—YOU CAN DO THIS!
FSSHHHH
YOU'VE GOT WHAT IT TAKES!

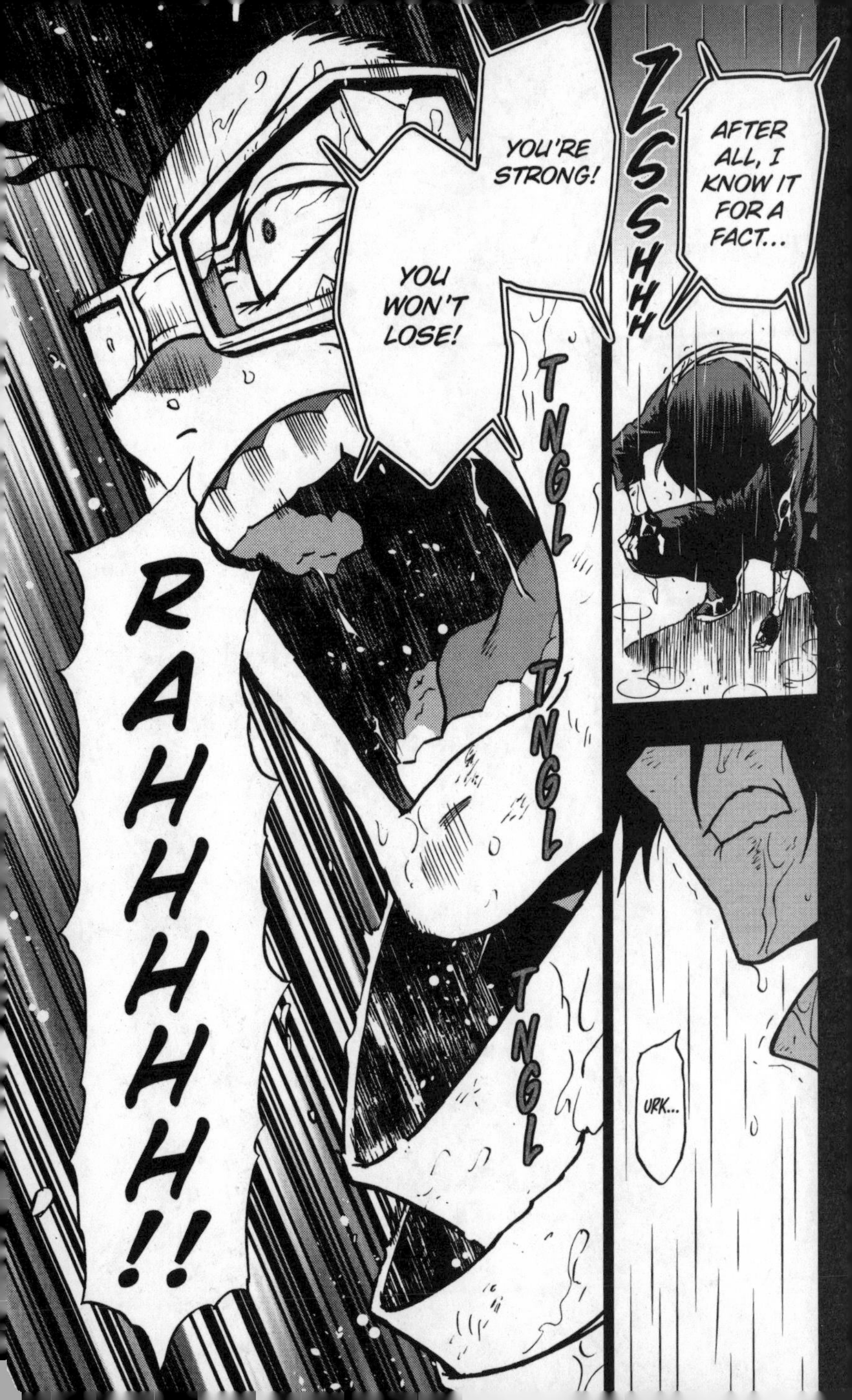
AFTER ALL, I KNOW IT FOR A FACT...
ZSSHHH
URK...
YOU'RE STRONG!
YOU WON'T LOSE!
TNGL
TNGL
TNGL
RAHHHHH!!

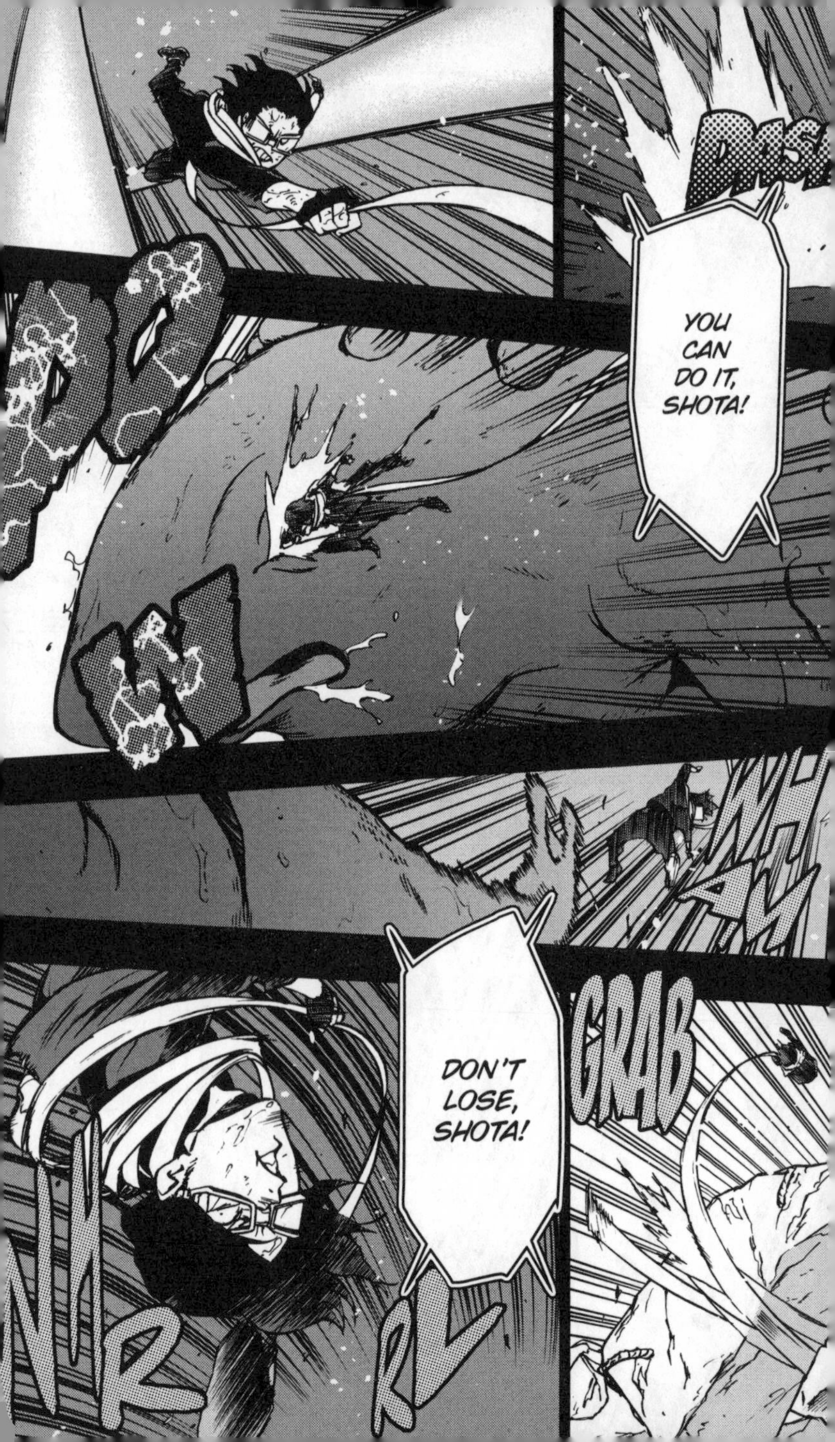
YOU CAN DO IT, SHOTA!
WHAM
GRAB
DON'T LOSE, SHOTA!

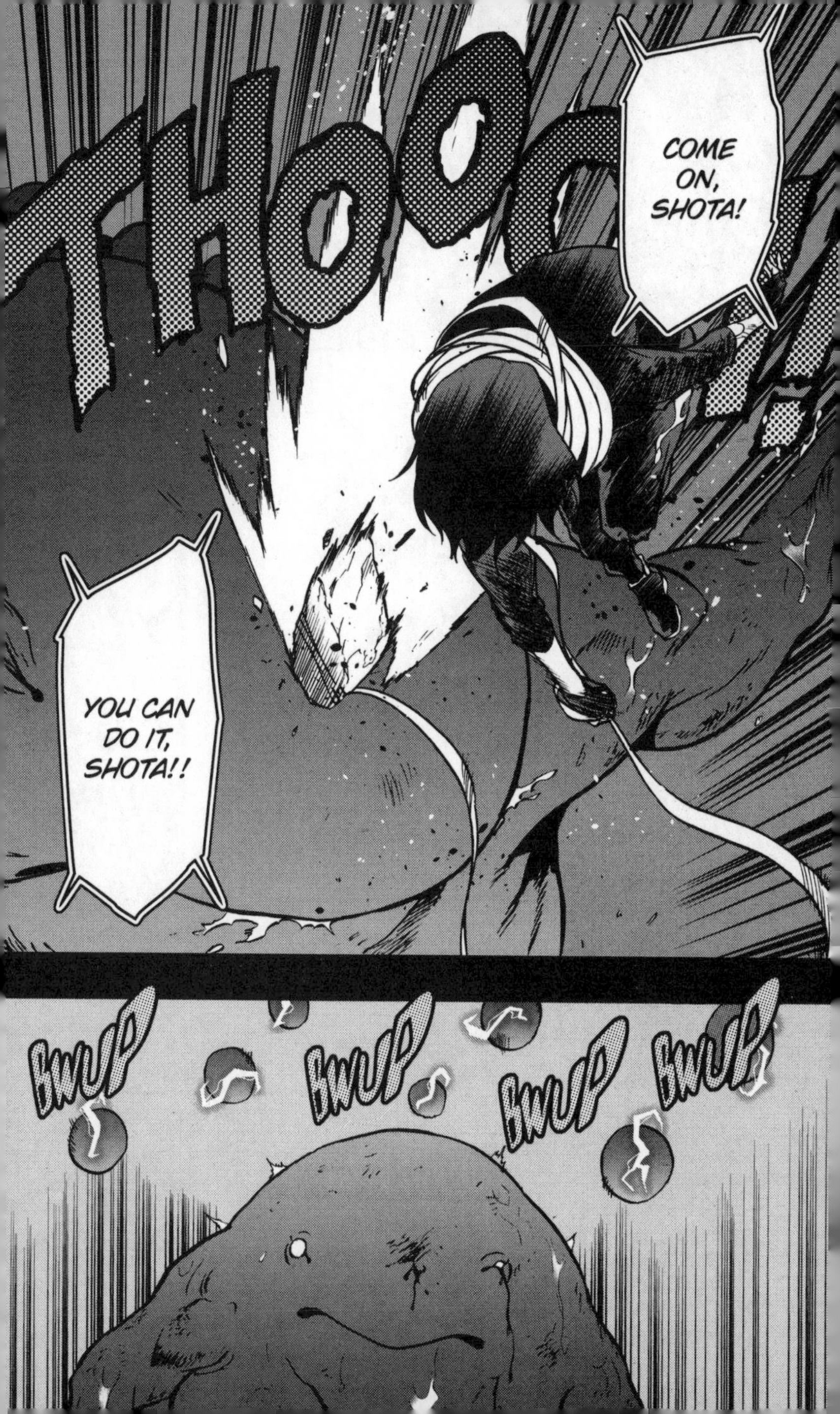
COME ON, SHOTA!
THOOO
YOU CAN DO IT, SHOTA!!
BWUP
BWUP
BWUP
BWUP

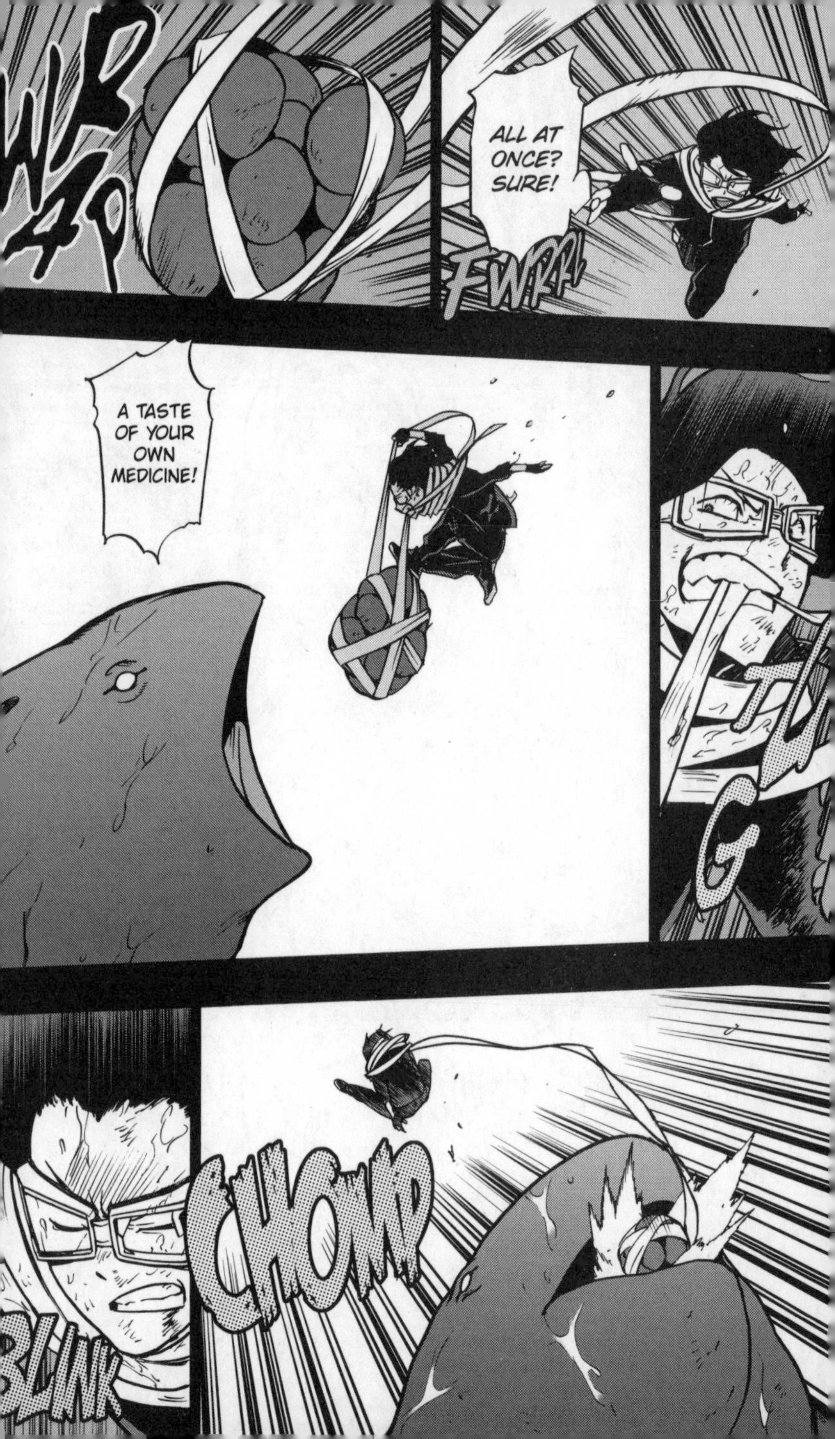
ALL AT ONCE? SURE!
FWAA
WHAP
TUG
A TASTE OF YOUR OWN MEDICINE!
CHOMP
BLINK

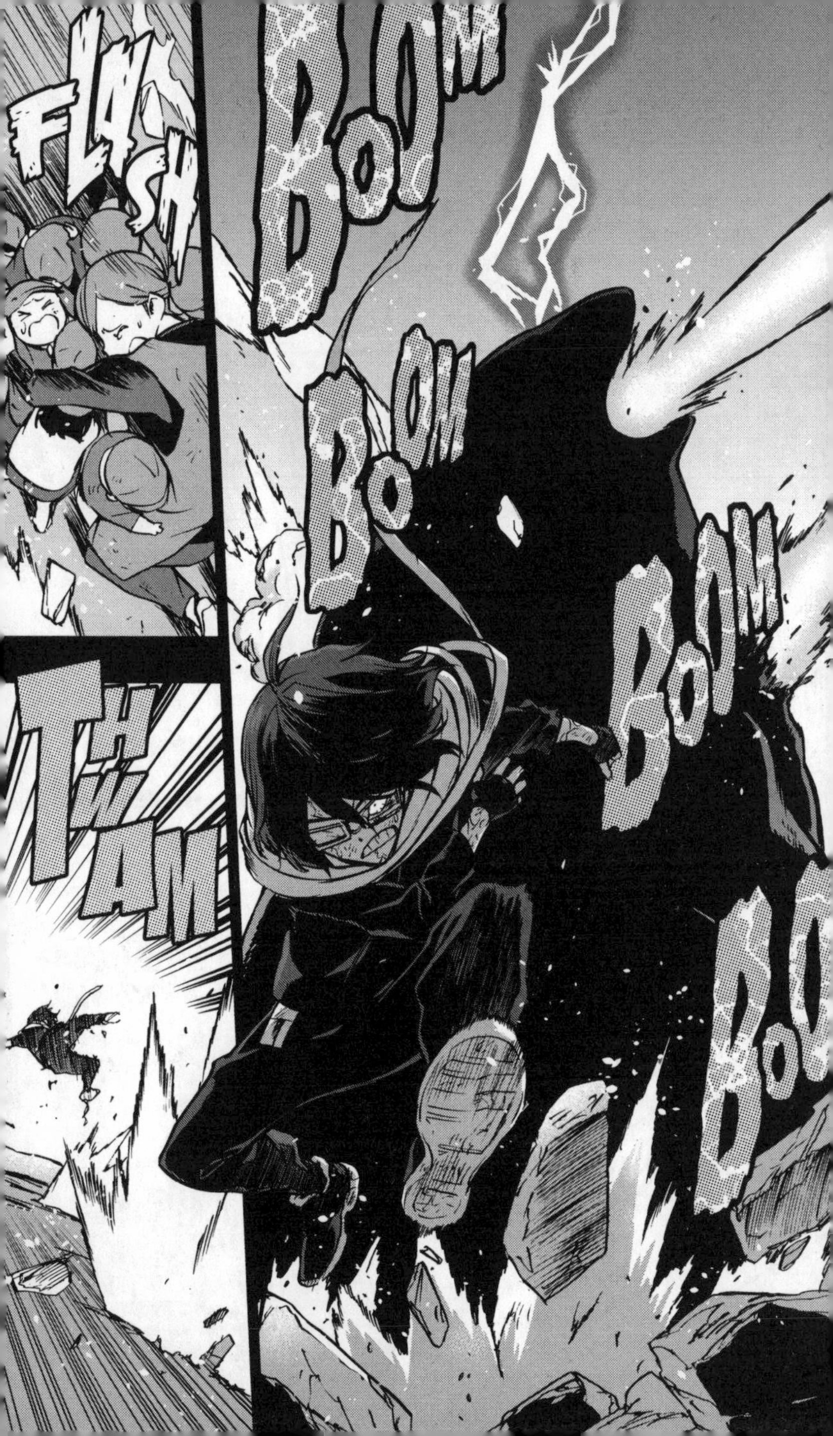
BOOM
BOOM
BOOM
BOO
FLASH
THWAM

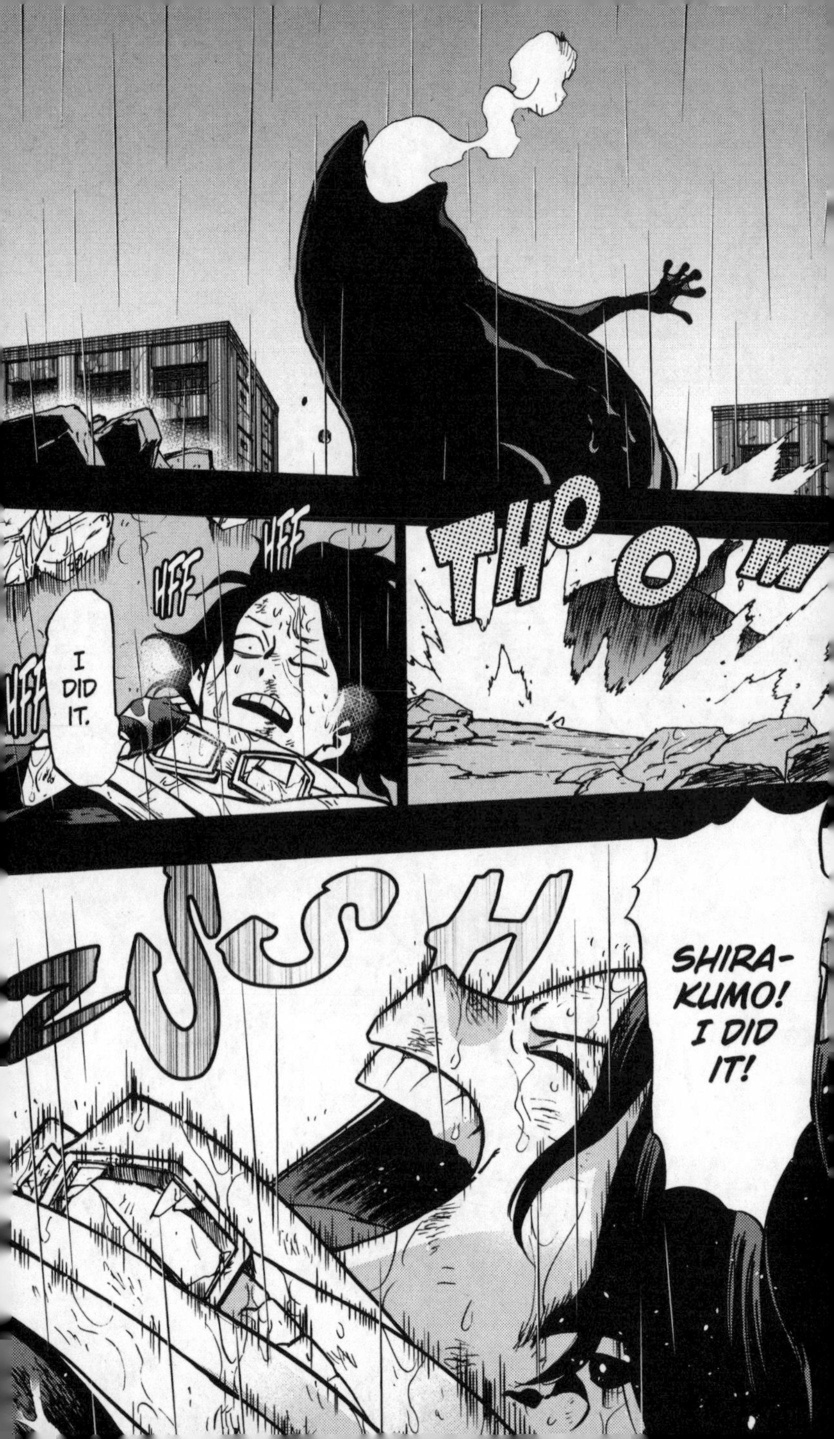
THOOM
HFF
HFF
HFF
I DID IT.
SHIRA-KUMO! I DID IT!
ZUSH

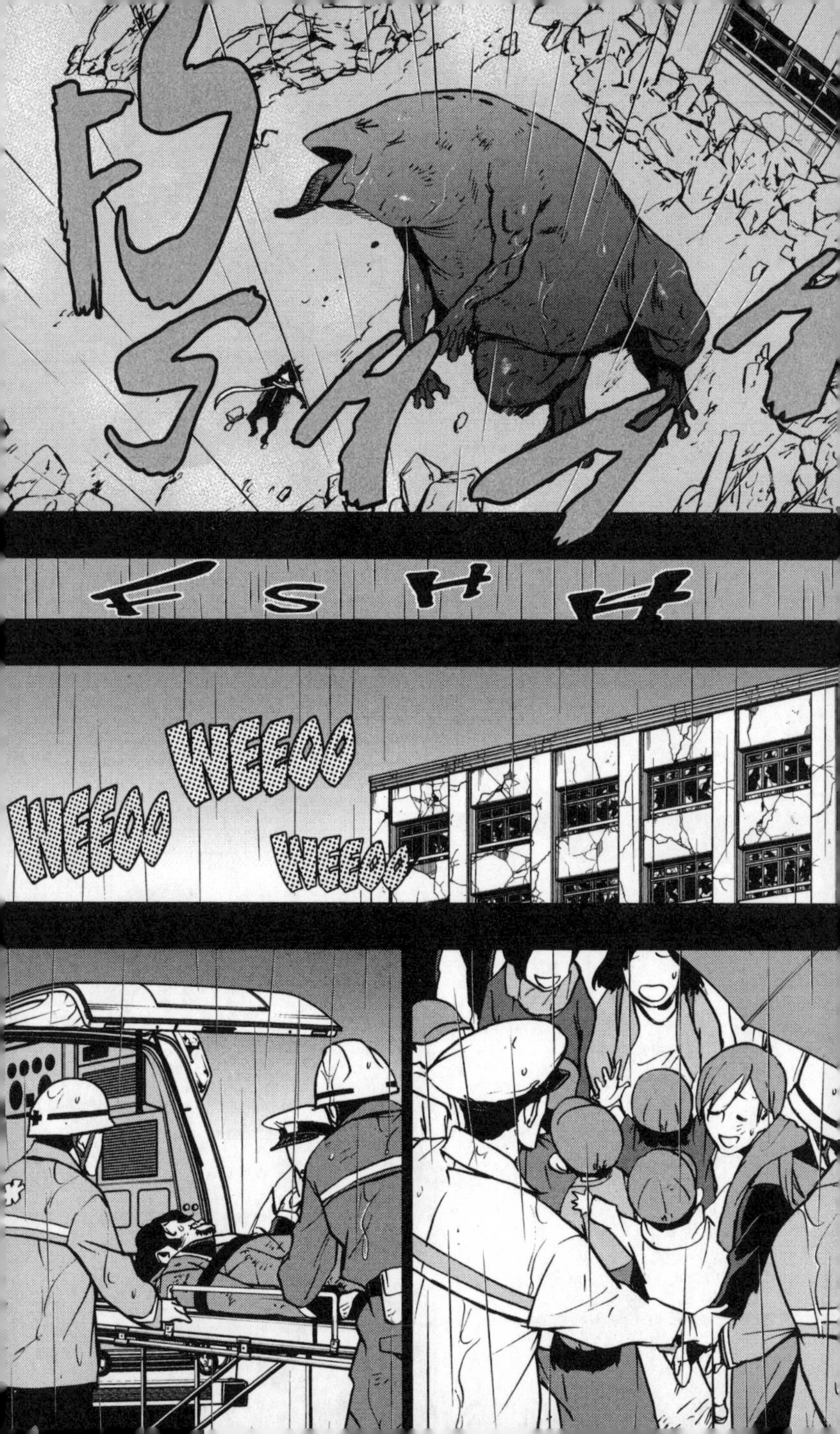
FSHH
WEEOO
WEEOO
WEEOO

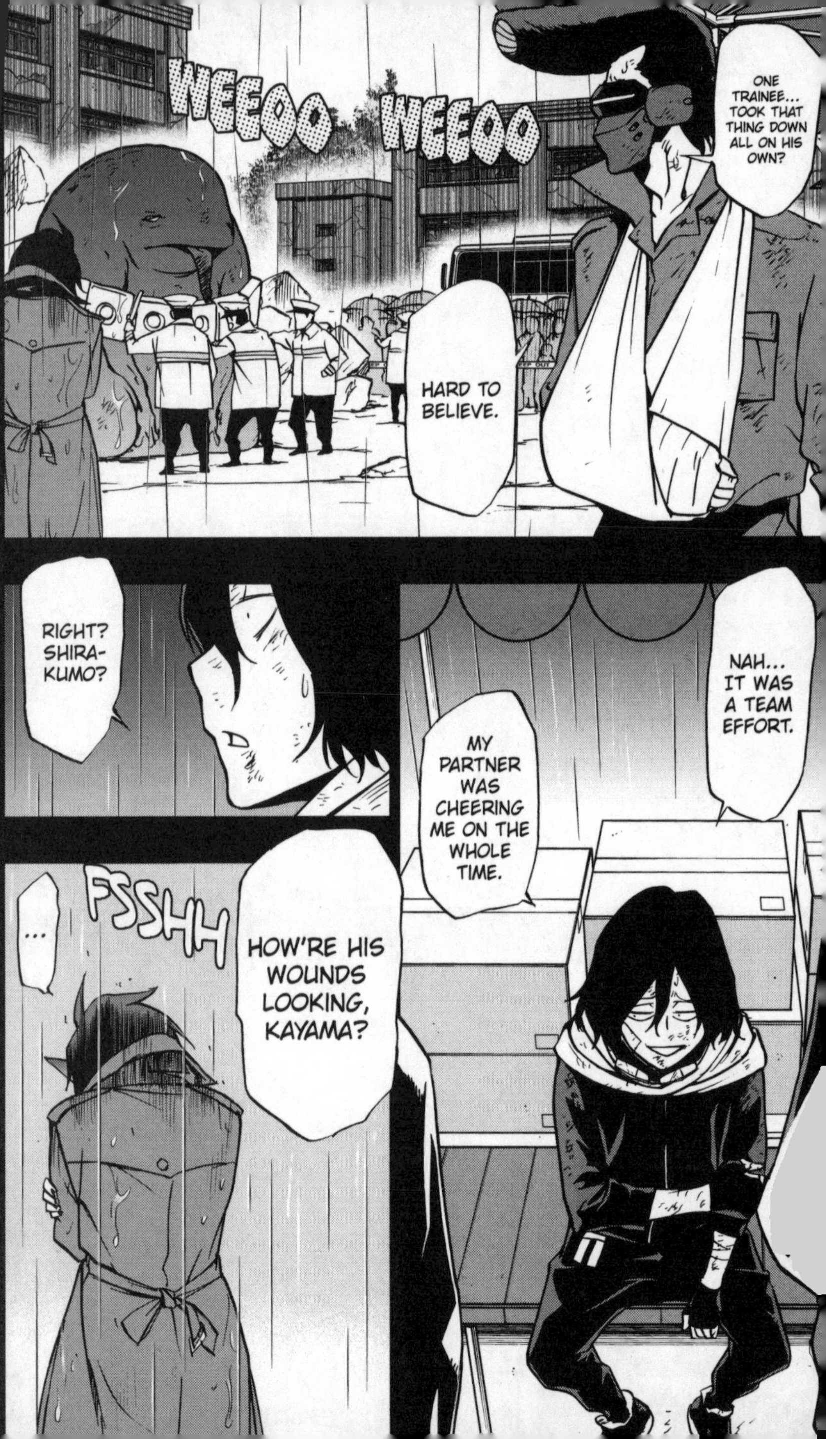
ONE TRAINEE... TOOK THAT THING DOWN ALL ON HIS OWN?
WEEOO WEEOO
HARD TO BELIEVE.
NAH... IT WAS A TEAM EFFORT.
MY PARTNER WAS CHEERING ME ON THE WHOLE TIME.
RIGHT? SHIRA-KUMO?
HOW'RE HIS WOUNDS LOOKING, KAYAMA?
FSSHH
...

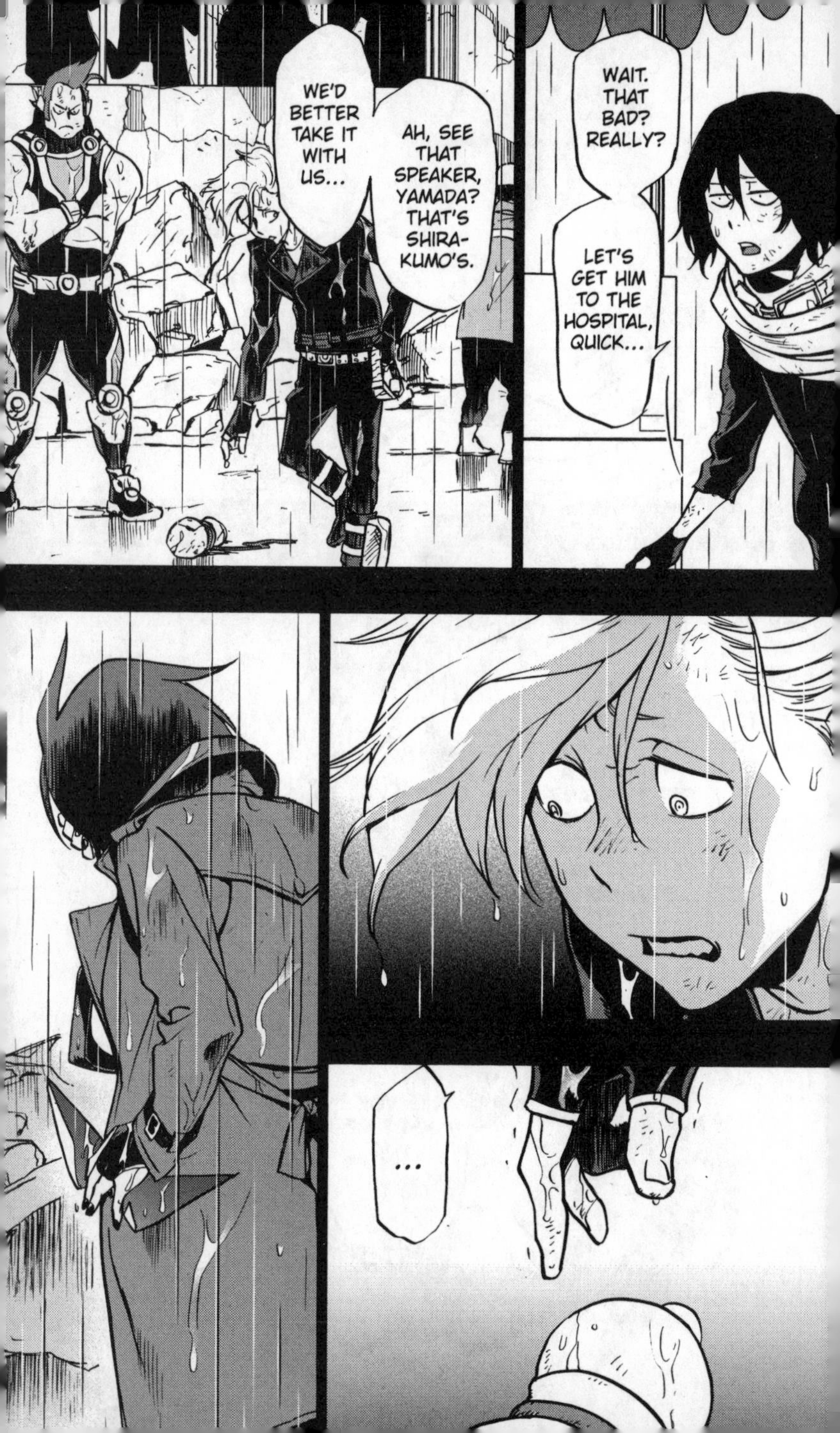
WAIT. THAT BAD? REALLY?
LET'S GET HIM TO THE HOSPITAL, QUICK...
AH, SEE THAT SPEAKER, YAMADA? THAT'S SHIRA-KUMO'S.
WE'D BETTER TAKE IT WITH US...
...

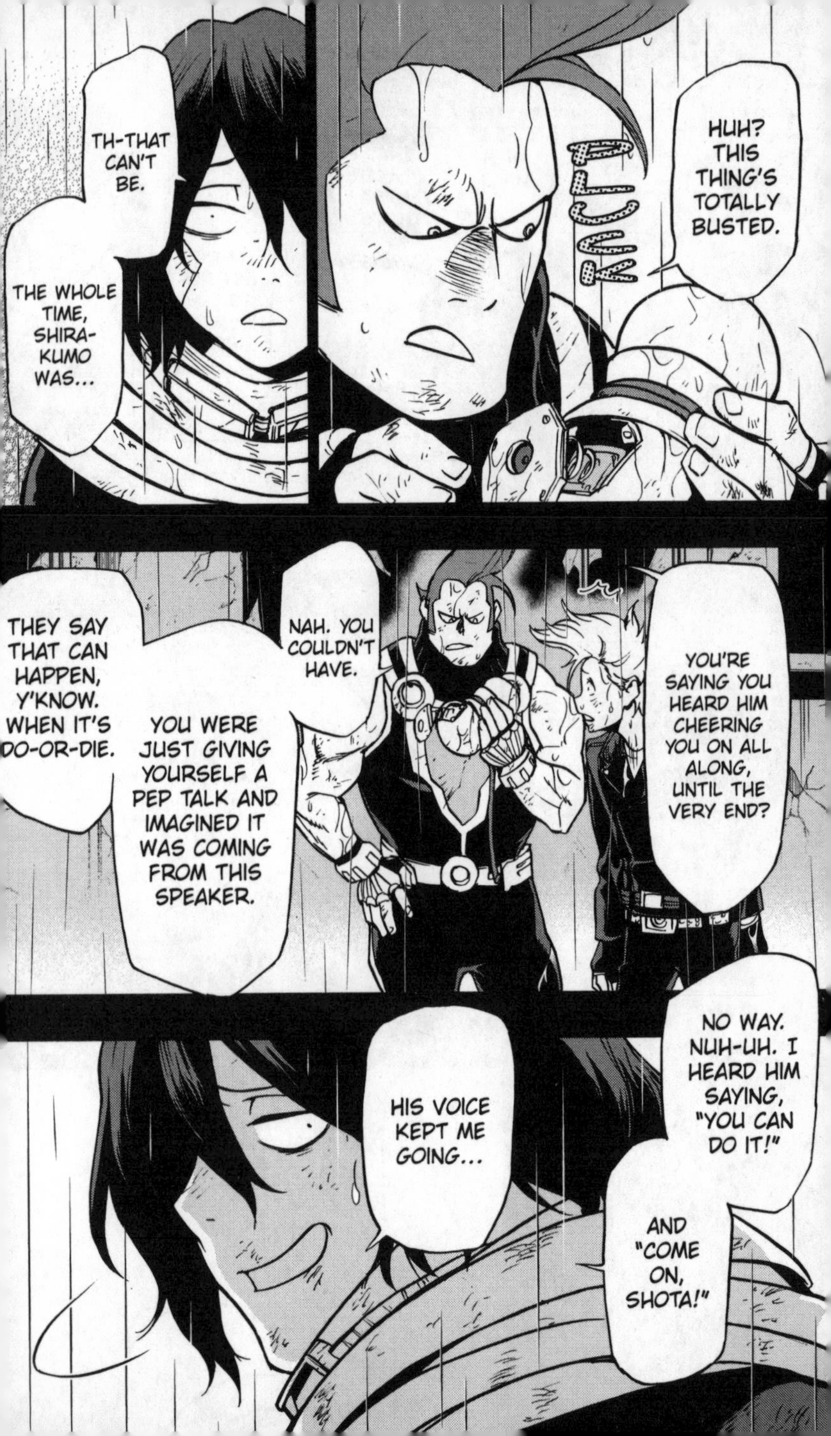
HUH? THIS THING'S TOTALLY BUSTED.
TH-THAT CAN'T BE.
THE WHOLE TIME, SHIRA-KUMO WAS...
YOU'RE SAYING YOU HEARD HIM CHEERING YOU ON ALL ALONG, UNTIL THE VERY END?
NAH. YOU COULDN'T HAVE.
YOU WERE JUST GIVING YOURSELF A PEP TALK AND IMAGINED IT WAS COMING FROM THIS SPEAKER.
THEY SAY THAT CAN HAPPEN, Y'KNOW. WHEN IT'S DO-OR-DIE.
NO WAY. NUH-UH. I HEARD HIM SAYING, "YOU CAN DO IT!"
AND "COME ON, SHOTA!"
HIS VOICE KEPT ME GOING...

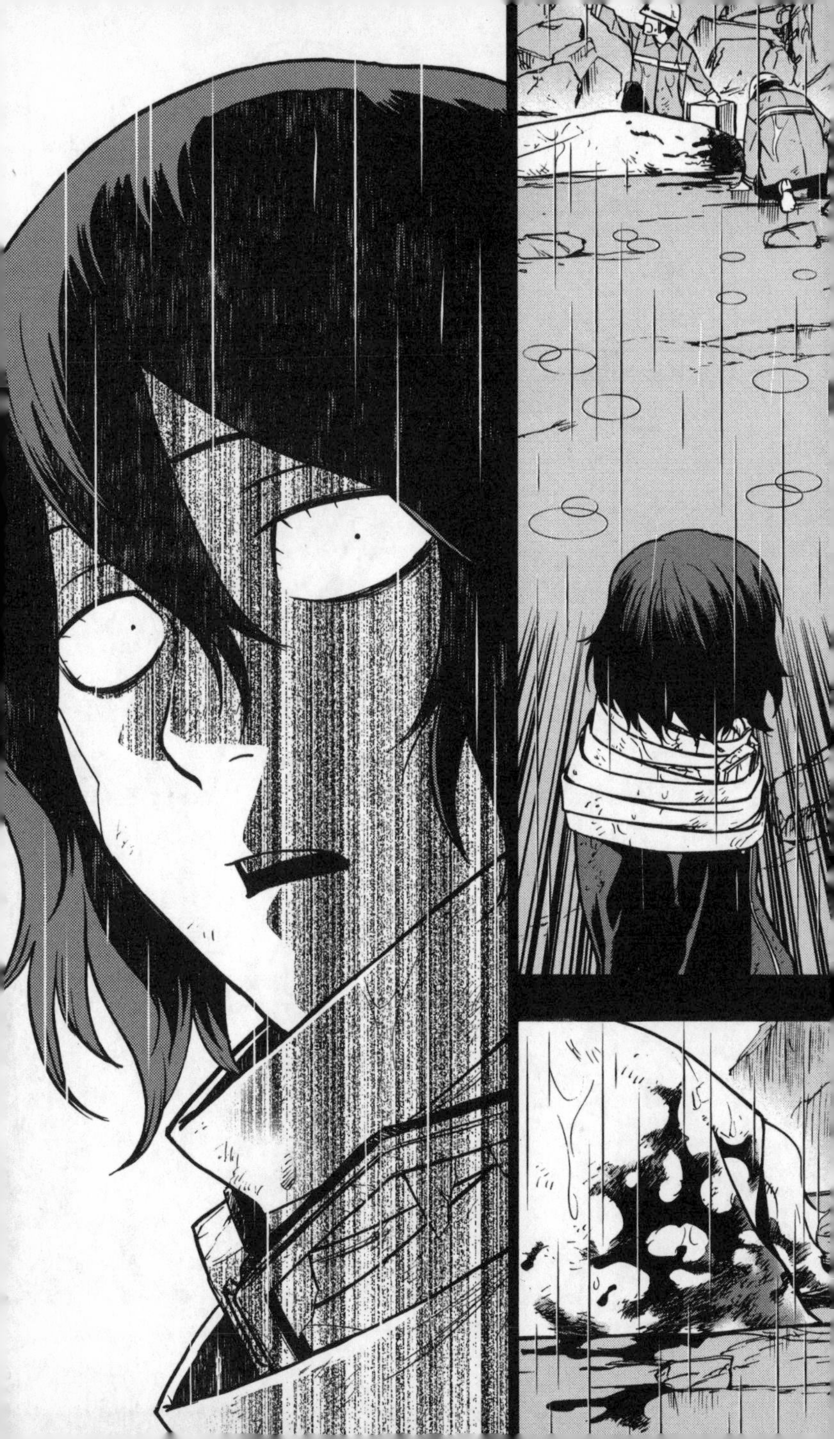

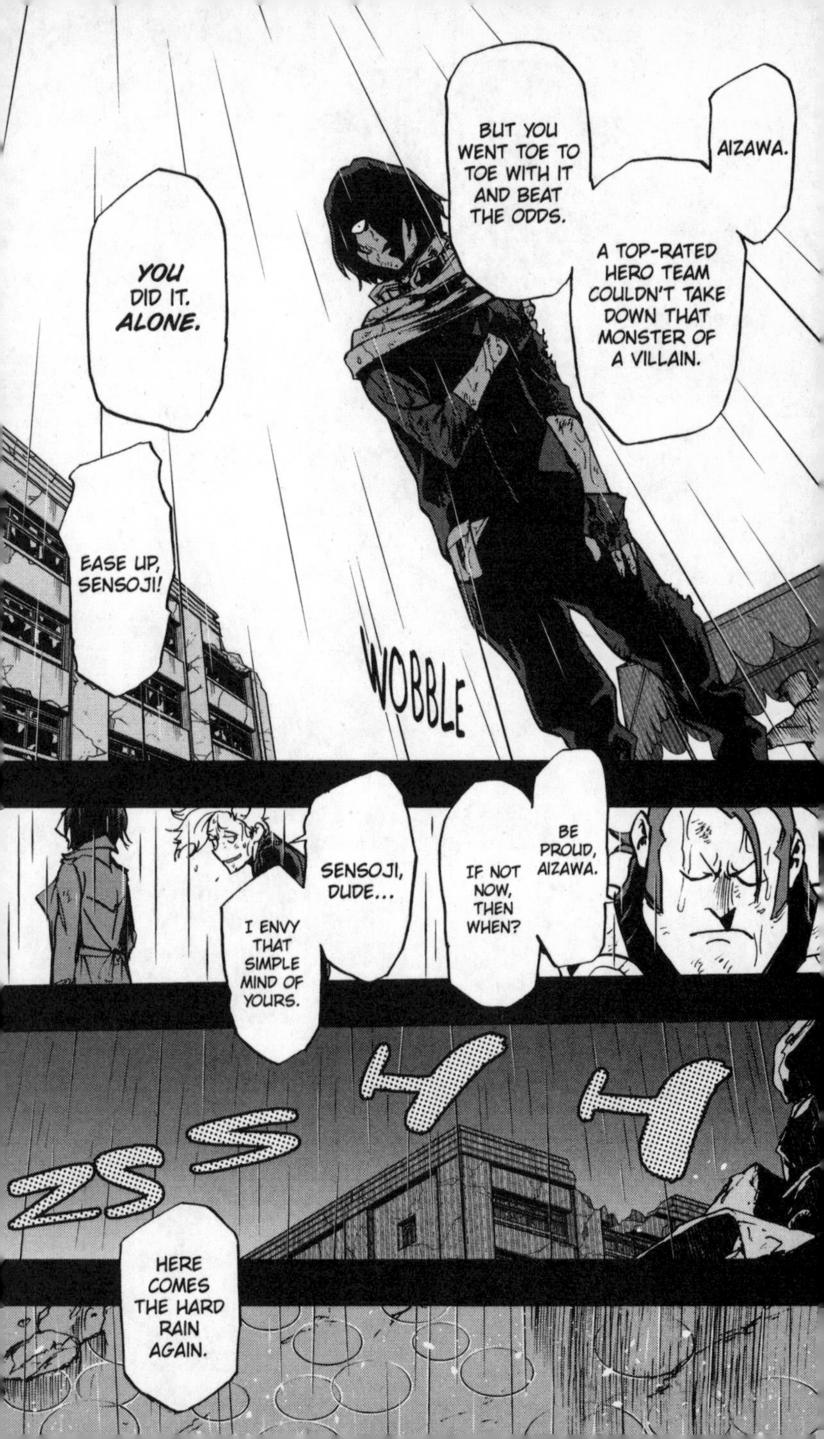
AIZAWA.
A TOP-RATED HERO TEAM COULDN'T TAKE DOWN THAT MONSTER OF A VILLAIN.
BUT YOU WENT TOE TO TOE WITH IT AND BEAT THE ODDS.
YOU DID IT. ALONE.
WOBBLE
EASE UP, SENSOJI!
BE PROUD, AIZAWA.
IF NOT NOW, THEN WHEN?
SENSOJI, DUDE...
I ENVY THAT SIMPLE MIND OF YOURS.
ZSSHH
HERE COMES THE HARD RAIN AGAIN.

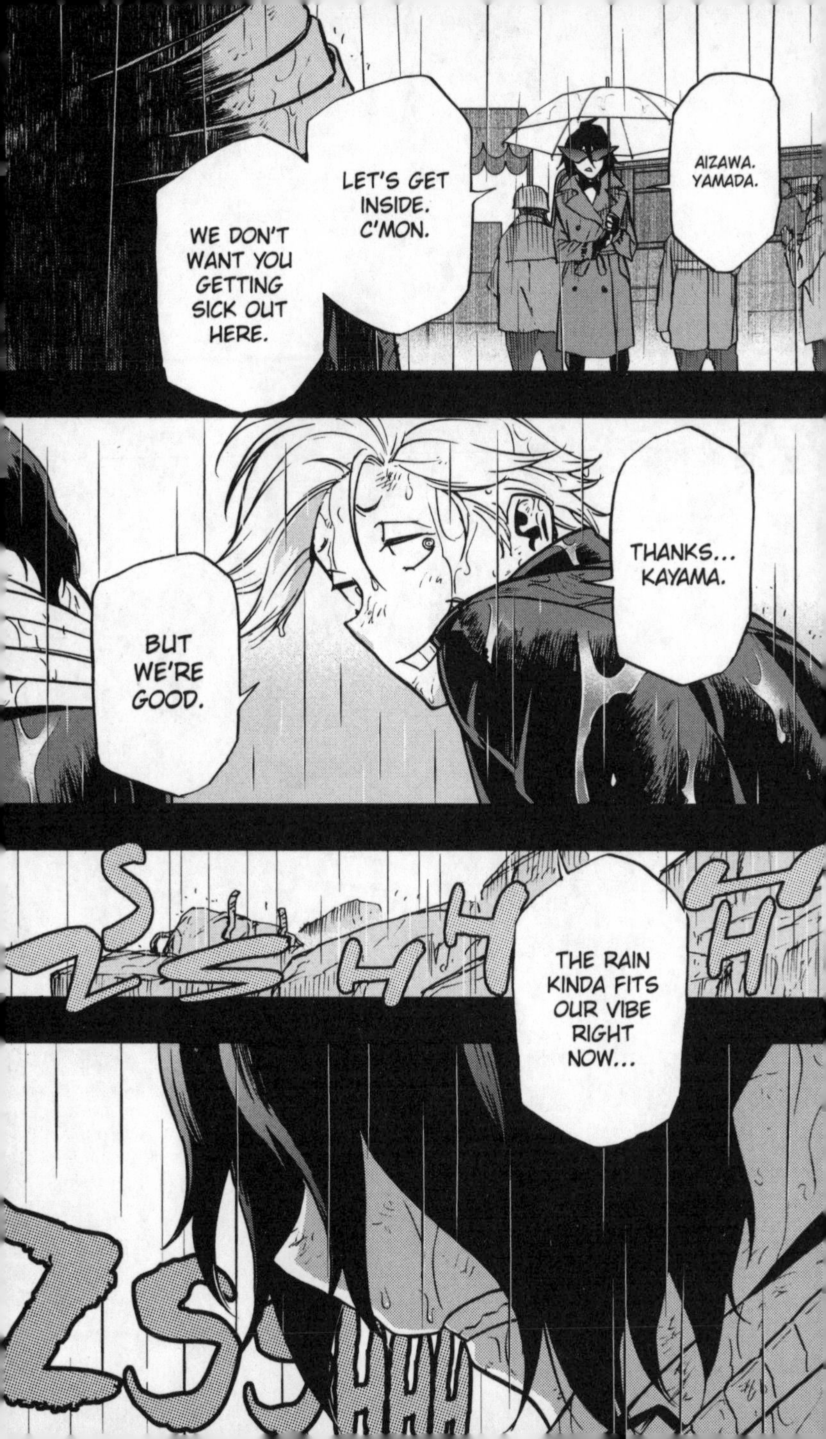

AIZAWA. YAMADA.
LET'S GET INSIDE. C'MON.
WE DON'T WANT YOU GETTING SICK OUT HERE.
THANKS... KAYAMA.
BUT WE'RE GOOD.
ZSSHHHH
THE RAIN KINDA FITS OUR VIBE RIGHT NOW...
ZSSHHH

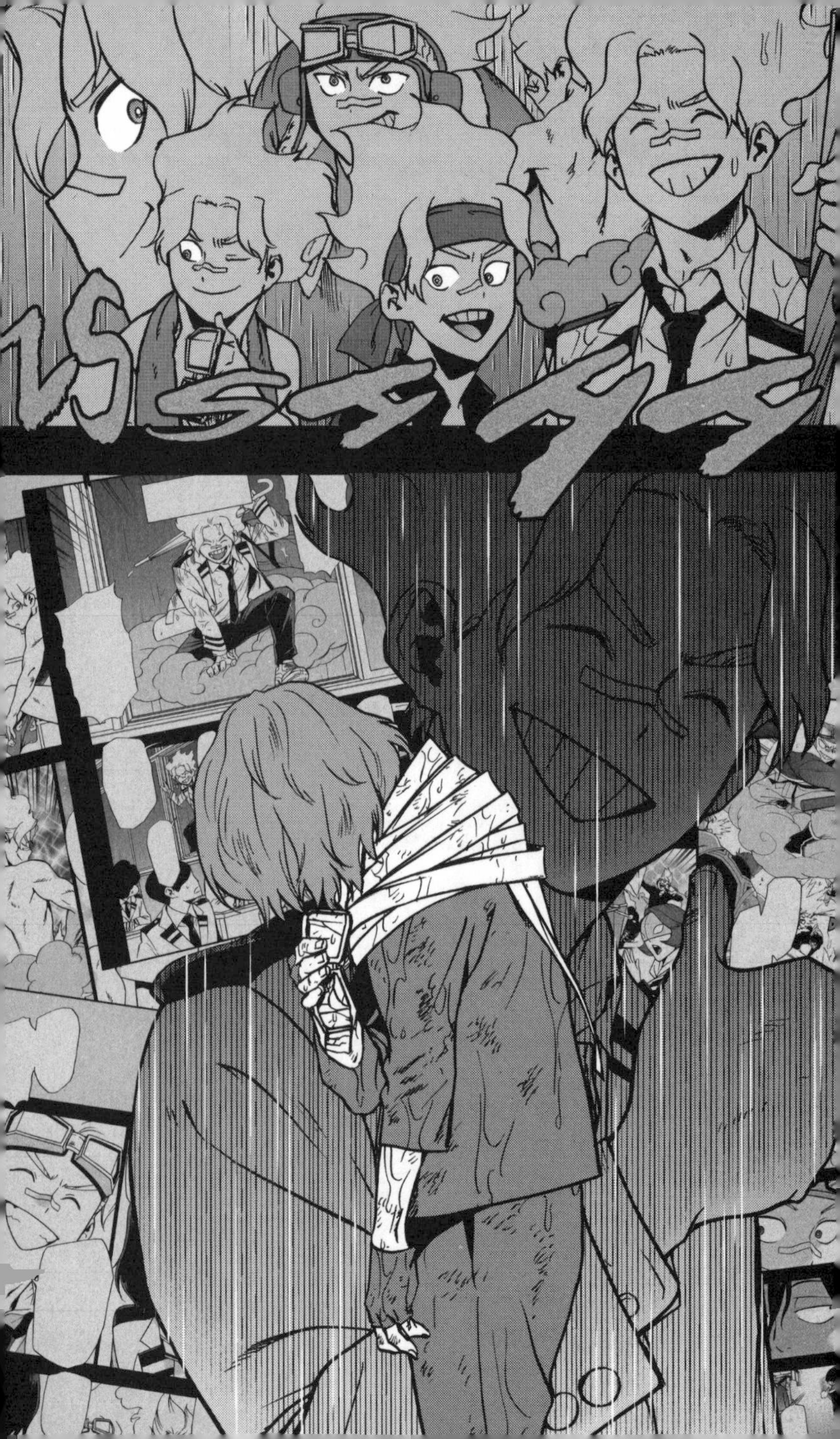

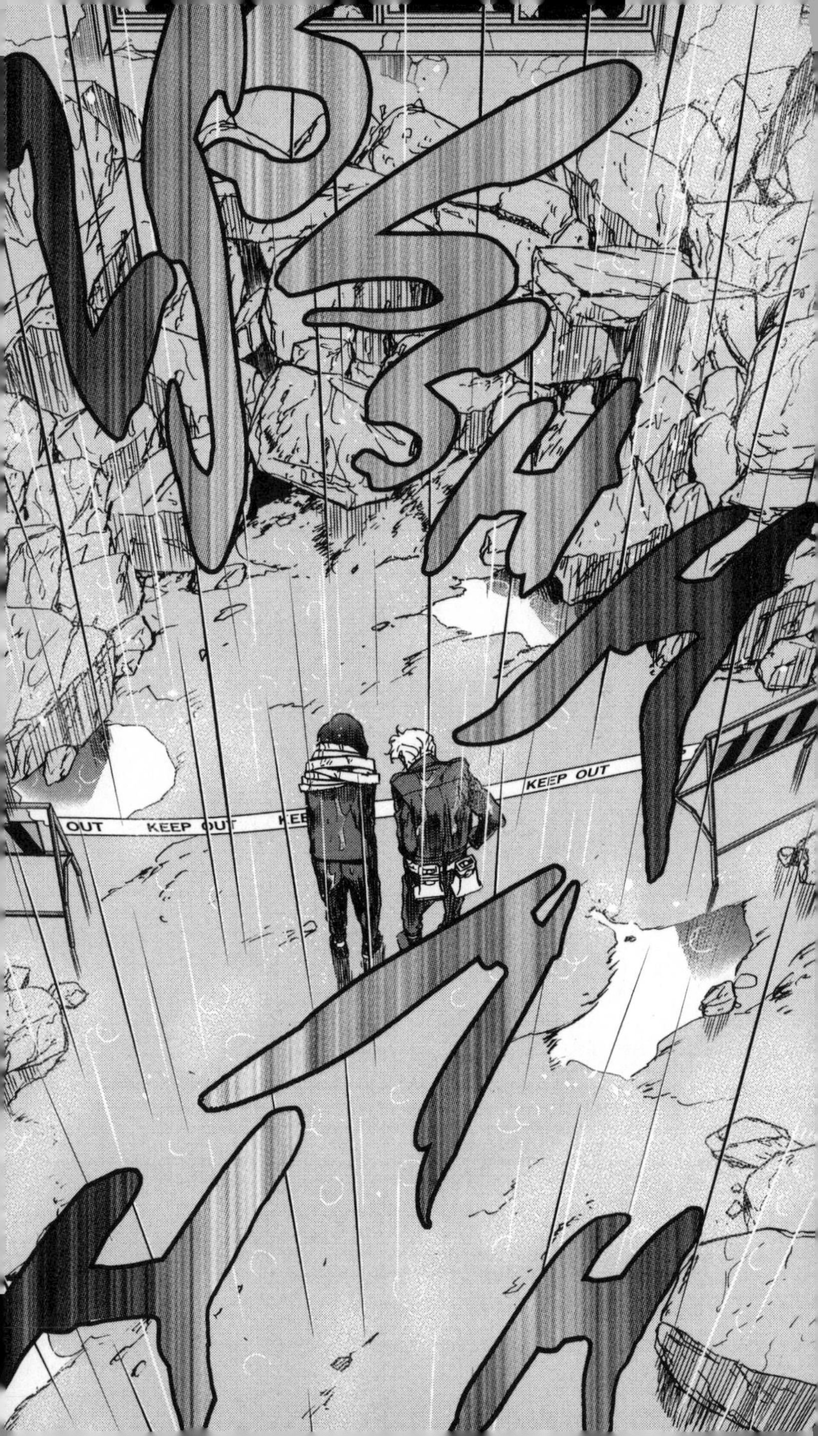
KEEP OUT
OUT KEEP OUT

LUMP VILLAIN / SENSOJI

THE ROUGH DESIGN

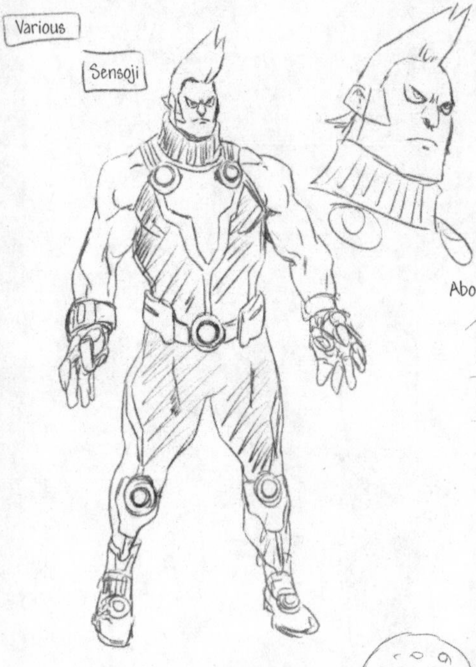
Various
Sensoji

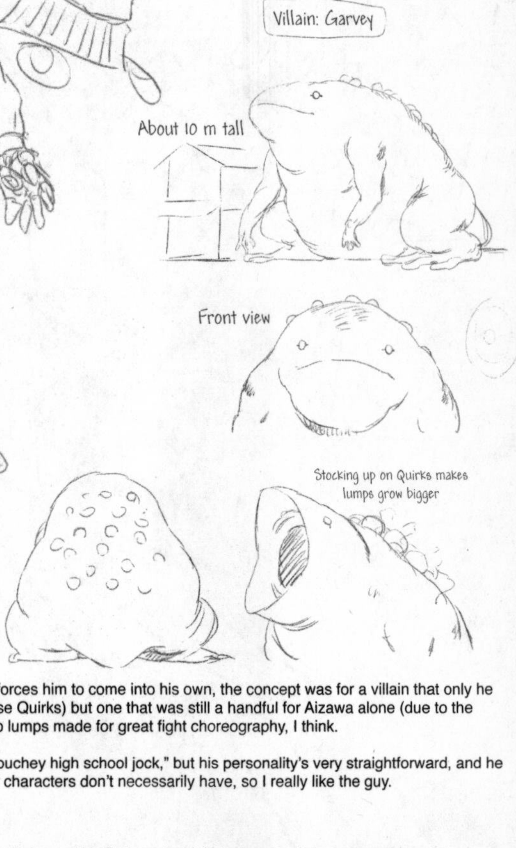
Villain: Garvey
About 10 m tall
Front view
Stocking up on Quirks makes lumps grow bigger

BEHIND THE SCENES

For Aizawa's first life-and-death battle that forces him to come into his own, the concept was for a villain that only he could deal with (since it uses multiple diverse Quirks) but one that was still a handful for Aizawa alone (due to the difference in physical size). The stocking-up lumps made for great fight choreography, I think.

Sensoji comes off as your basic, clichéd "douchey high school jock," but his personality's very straightforward, and he tells it like it is from a perspective that other characters don't necessarily have, so I really like the guy.

—Furuhashi

One of the original inspirations for the lump villain was the Surinam toad, but when I watched some videos for research, the toad turned out to be way grosser than I imagined, so I moved away from that as an inspiration. (LOL)

Sensoji's costume is the same as Aoyama's, from the main *MHA* series.

Sensoji's energy emits from somewhere on his body, but the costume channels it through those lines so he can shoot it from his hands and legs.

—Betten

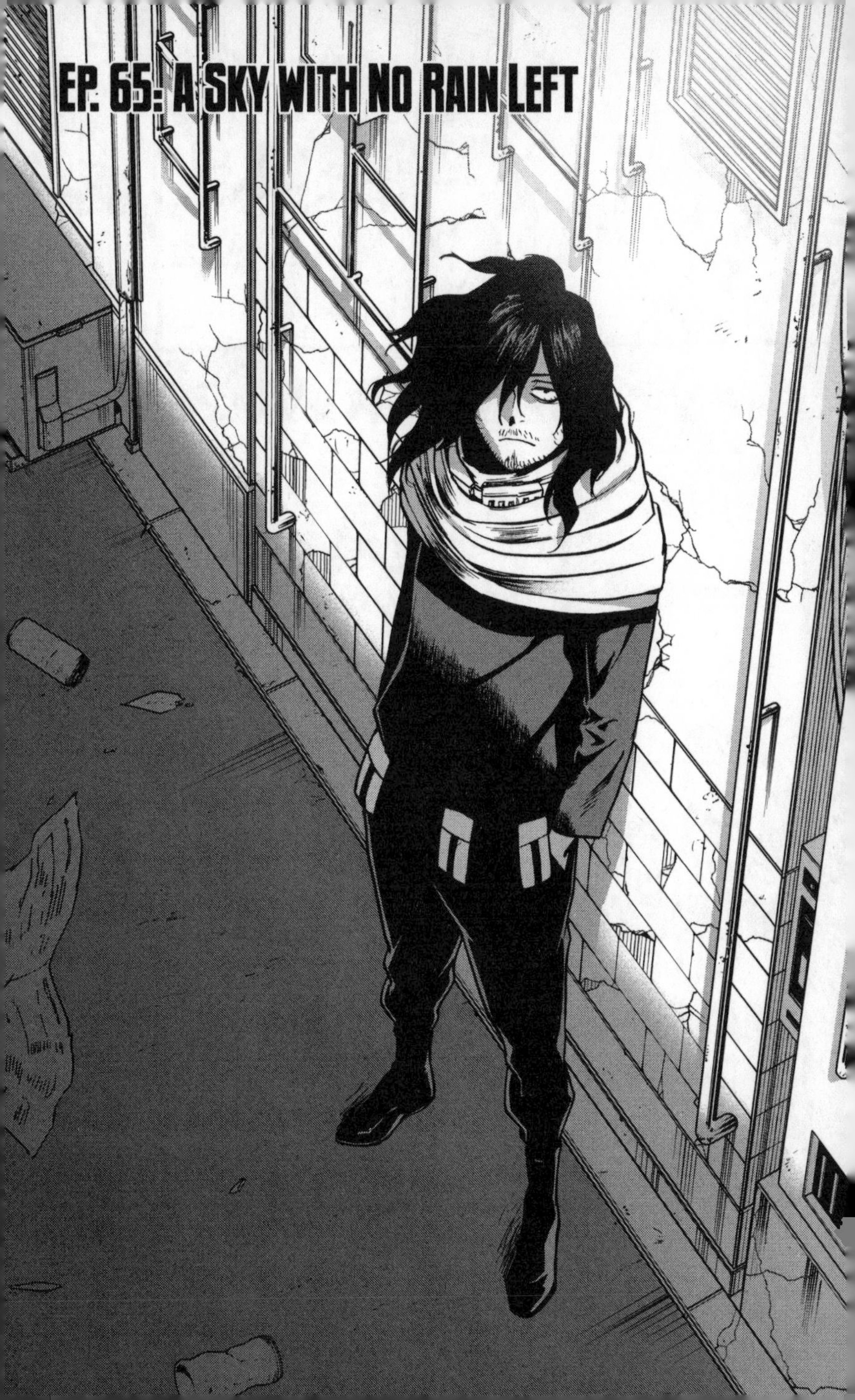
EP. 65: A SKY WITH NO RAIN LEFT

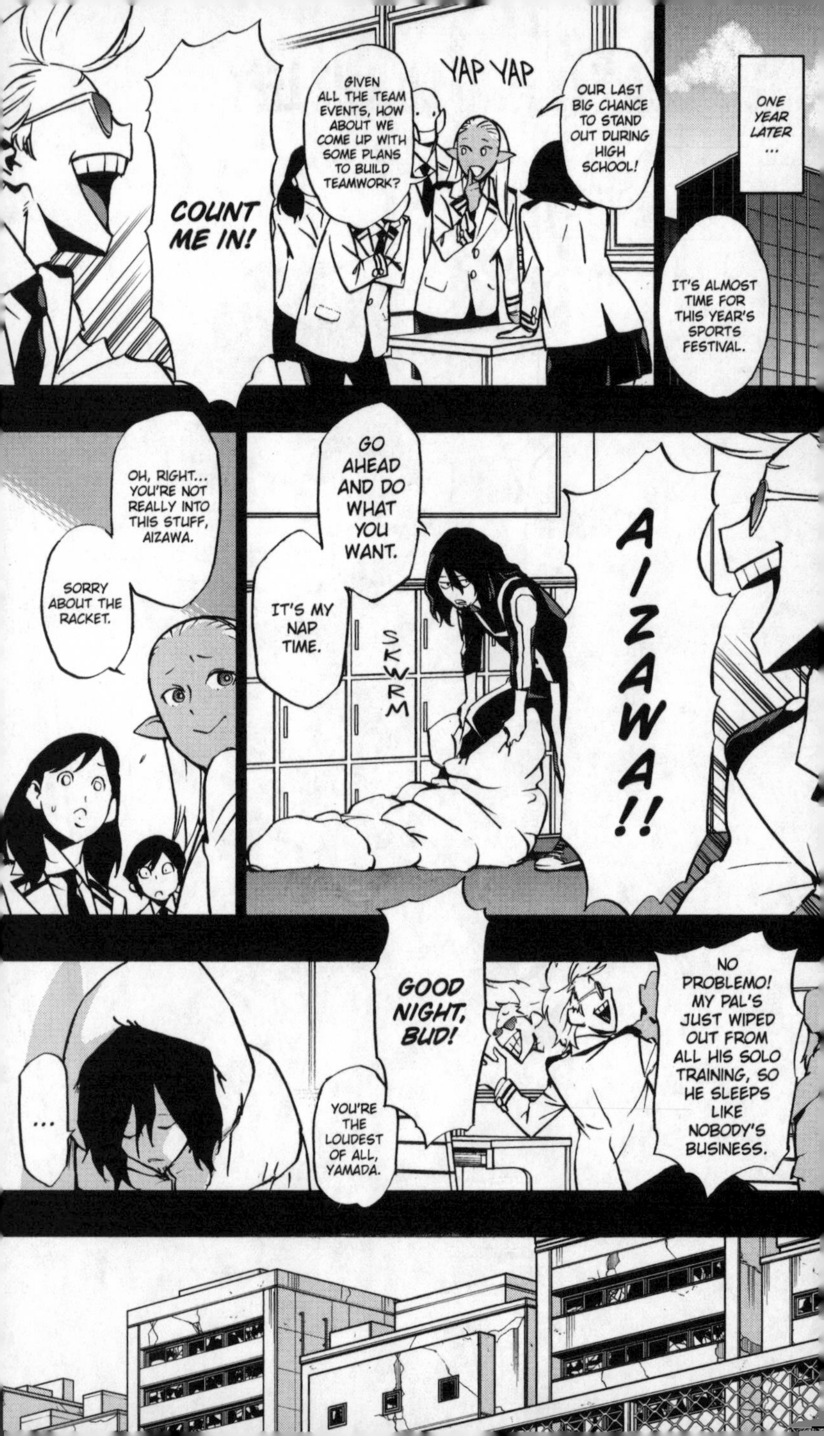
ONE YEAR LATER...
IT'S ALMOST TIME FOR THIS YEAR'S SPORTS FESTIVAL.
OUR LAST BIG CHANCE TO STAND OUT DURING HIGH SCHOOL!
YAP YAP
GIVEN ALL THE TEAM EVENTS, HOW ABOUT WE COME UP WITH SOME PLANS TO BUILD TEAMWORK?
COUNT ME IN!
AIZAWA!!
GO AHEAD AND DO WHAT YOU WANT.
IT'S MY NAP TIME.
SKWRM
OH, RIGHT... YOU'RE NOT REALLY INTO THIS STUFF, AIZAWA.
SORRY ABOUT THE RACKET.
NO PROBLEMO! MY PAL'S JUST WIPED OUT FROM ALL HIS SOLO TRAINING, SO HE SLEEPS LIKE NOBODY'S BUSINESS.
GOOD NIGHT, BUD!
YOU'RE THE LOUDEST OF ALL, YAMADA.
...

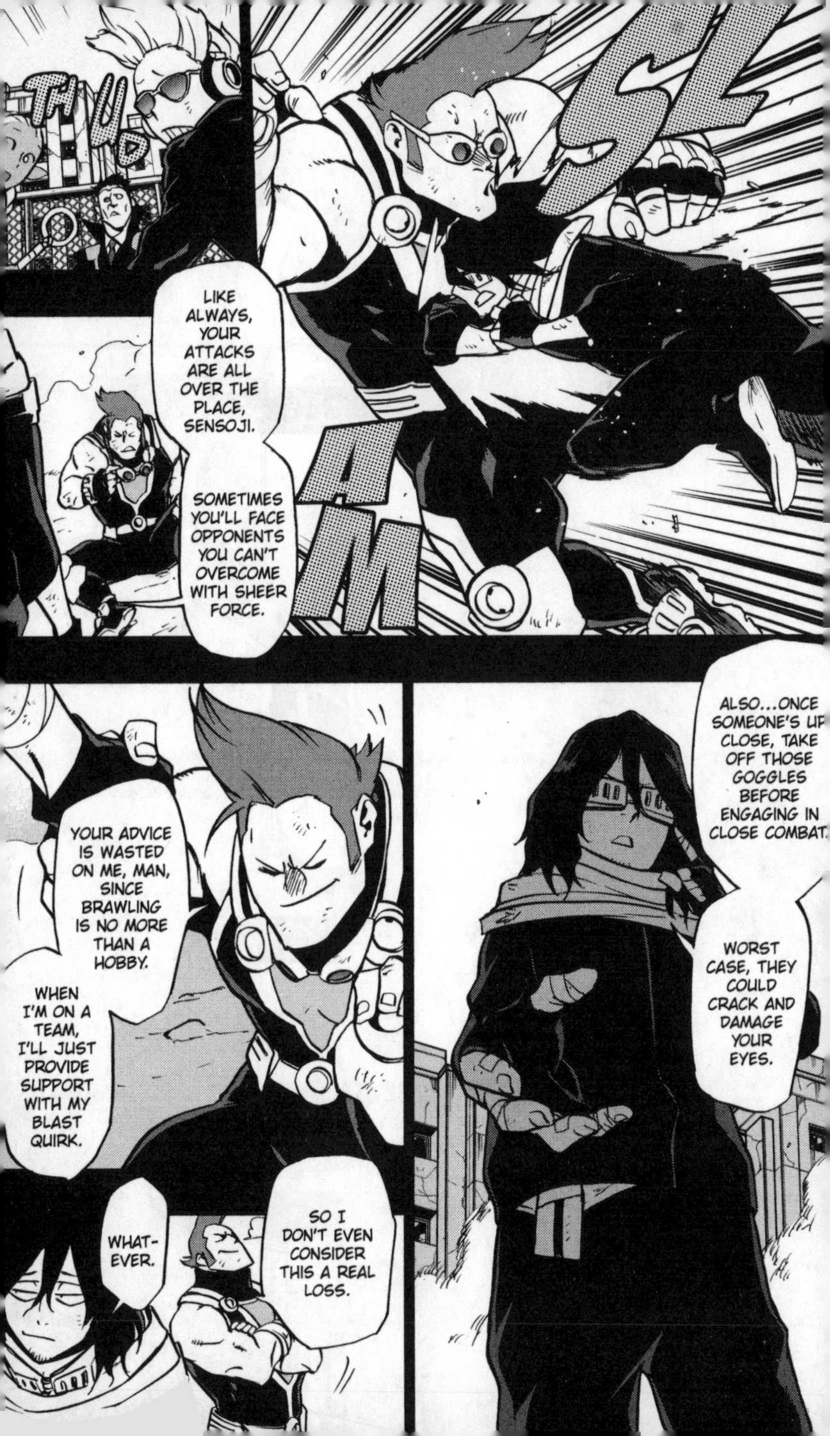
SL
AM
THUD
LIKE ALWAYS, YOUR ATTACKS ARE ALL OVER THE PLACE, SENSOJI.
SOMETIMES YOU'LL FACE OPPONENTS YOU CAN'T OVERCOME WITH SHEER FORCE.
ALSO...ONCE SOMEONE'S UP CLOSE, TAKE OFF THOSE GOGGLES BEFORE ENGAGING IN CLOSE COMBAT.
WORST CASE, THEY COULD CRACK AND DAMAGE YOUR EYES.
YOUR ADVICE IS WASTED ON ME, MAN, SINCE BRAWLING IS NO MORE THAN A HOBBY.
WHEN I'M ON A TEAM, I'LL JUST PROVIDE SUPPORT WITH MY BLAST QUIRK.
SO I DON'T EVEN CONSIDER THIS A REAL LOSS.
WHAT-EVER.

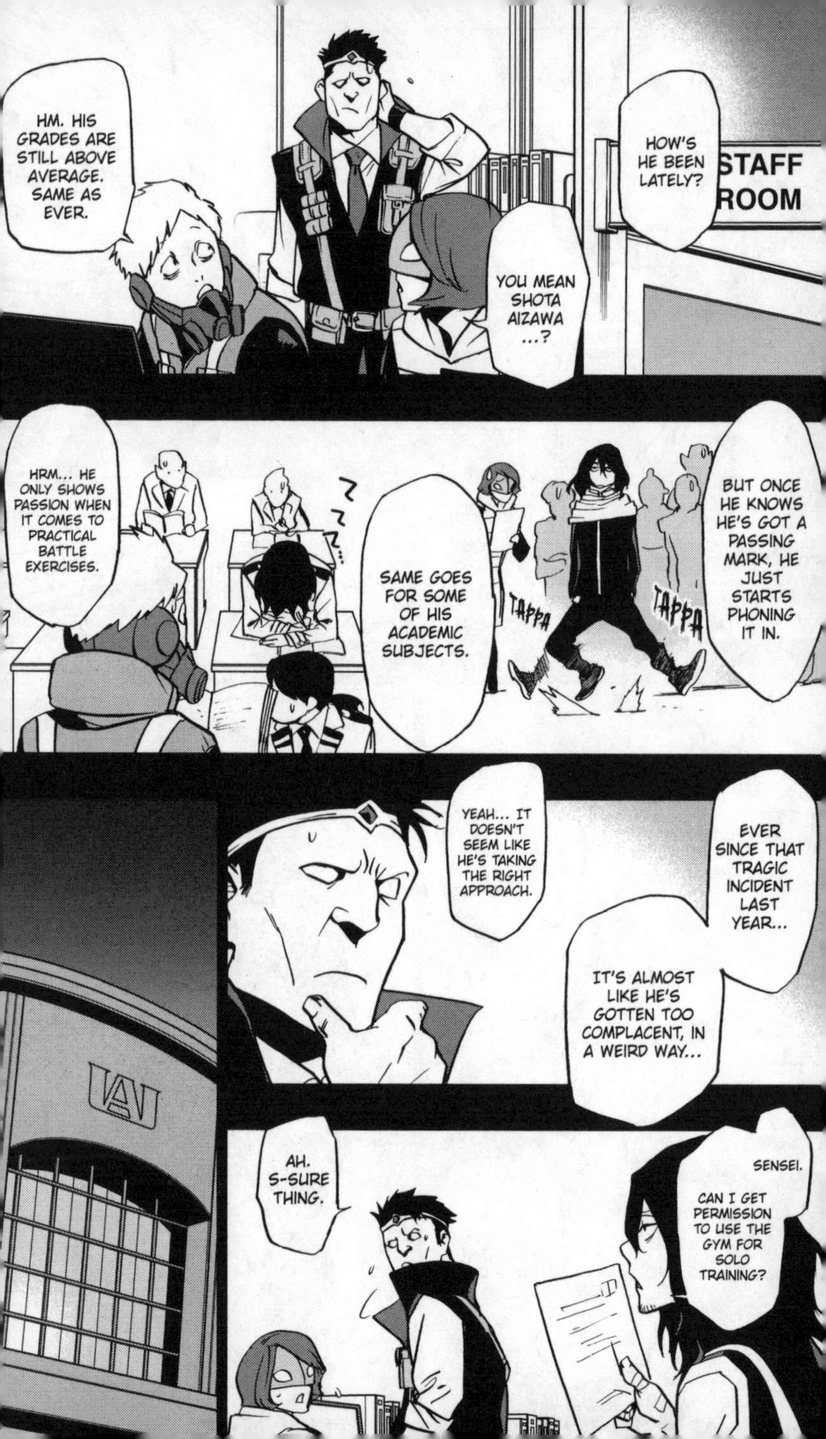
HOW'S HE BEEN LATELY?
STAFF ROOM
YOU MEAN SHOTA AIZAWA ...?
HM. HIS GRADES ARE STILL ABOVE AVERAGE. SAME AS EVER.
BUT ONCE HE KNOWS HE'S GOT A PASSING MARK, HE JUST STARTS PHONING IT IN.
TAPPA
TAPPA
SAME GOES FOR SOME OF HIS ACADEMIC SUBJECTS.
Z Z Z...
HRM... HE ONLY SHOWS PASSION WHEN IT COMES TO PRACTICAL BATTLE EXERCISES.
EVER SINCE THAT TRAGIC INCIDENT LAST YEAR...
YEAH... IT DOESN'T SEEM LIKE HE'S TAKING THE RIGHT APPROACH.
IT'S ALMOST LIKE HE'S GOTTEN TOO COMPLACENT, IN A WEIRD WAY...
SENSEI.
CAN I GET PERMISSION TO USE THE GYM FOR SOLO TRAINING?
AH. S-SURE THING.
UA

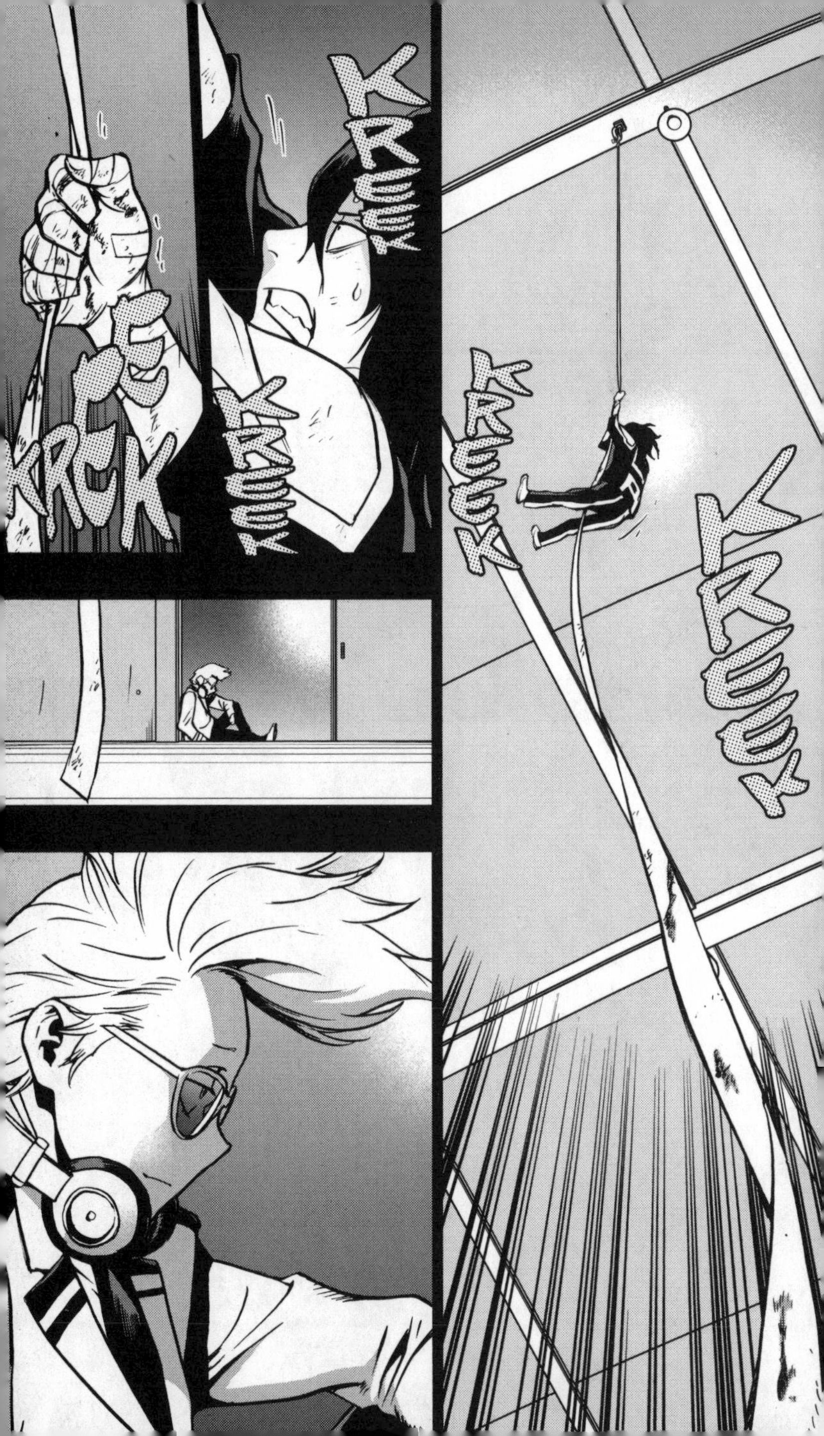
KREEEK
KREEK
KREEK
KREEEK
KRECK

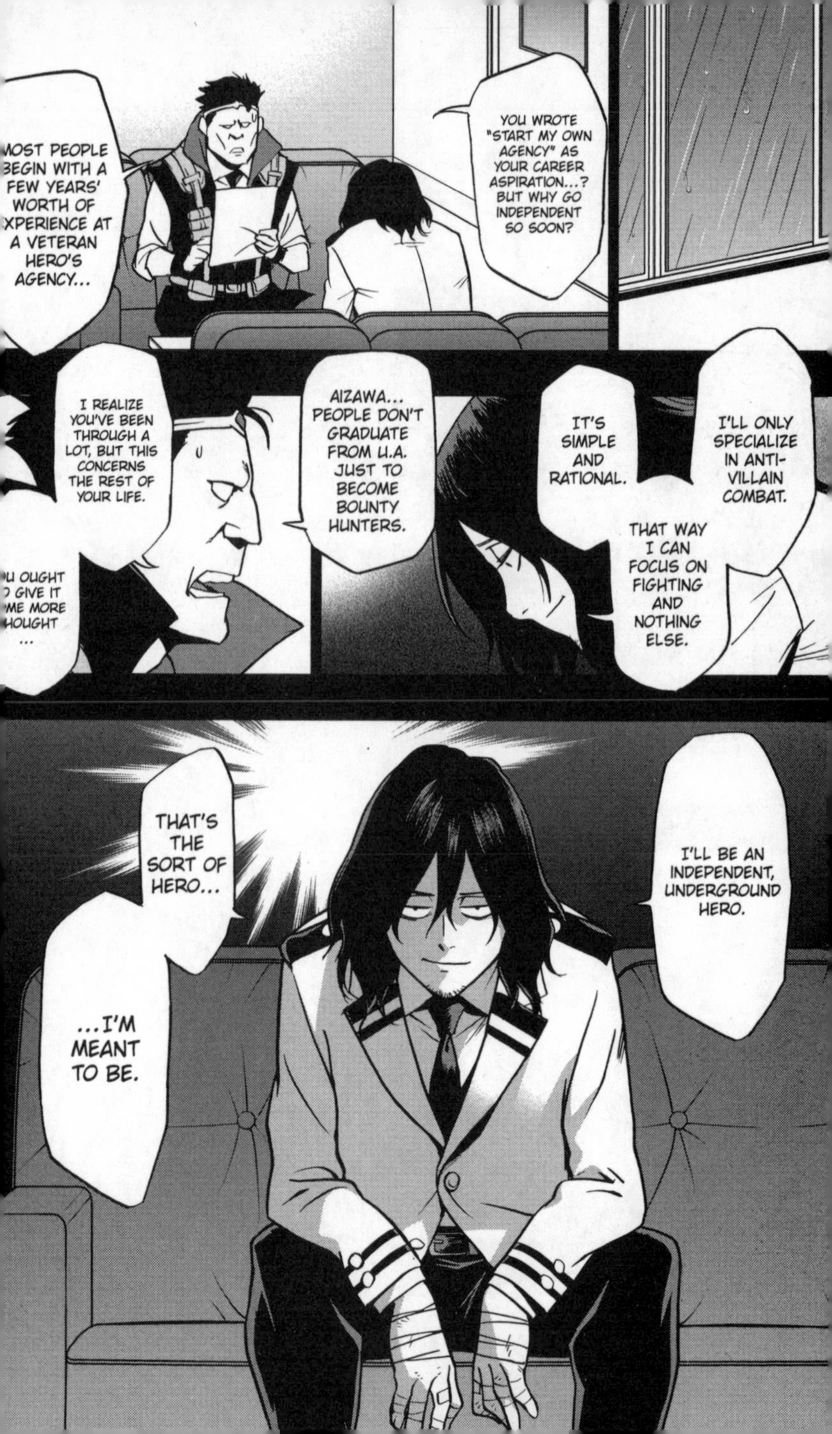
YOU WROTE "START MY OWN AGENCY" AS YOUR CAREER ASPIRATION...? BUT WHY GO INDEPENDENT SO SOON?
MOST PEOPLE BEGIN WITH A FEW YEARS' WORTH OF EXPERIENCE AT A VETERAN HERO'S AGENCY...
I'LL ONLY SPECIALIZE IN ANTI-VILLAIN COMBAT.
IT'S SIMPLE AND RATIONAL.
THAT WAY I CAN FOCUS ON FIGHTING AND NOTHING ELSE.
AIZAWA... PEOPLE DON'T GRADUATE FROM U.A. JUST TO BECOME BOUNTY HUNTERS.
I REALIZE YOU'VE BEEN THROUGH A LOT, BUT THIS CONCERNS THE REST OF YOUR LIFE.
U OUGHT GIVE IT ME MORE HOUGHT ...
I'LL BE AN INDEPENDENT, UNDERGROUND HERO.
THAT'S THE SORT OF HERO...
...I'M MEANT TO BE.

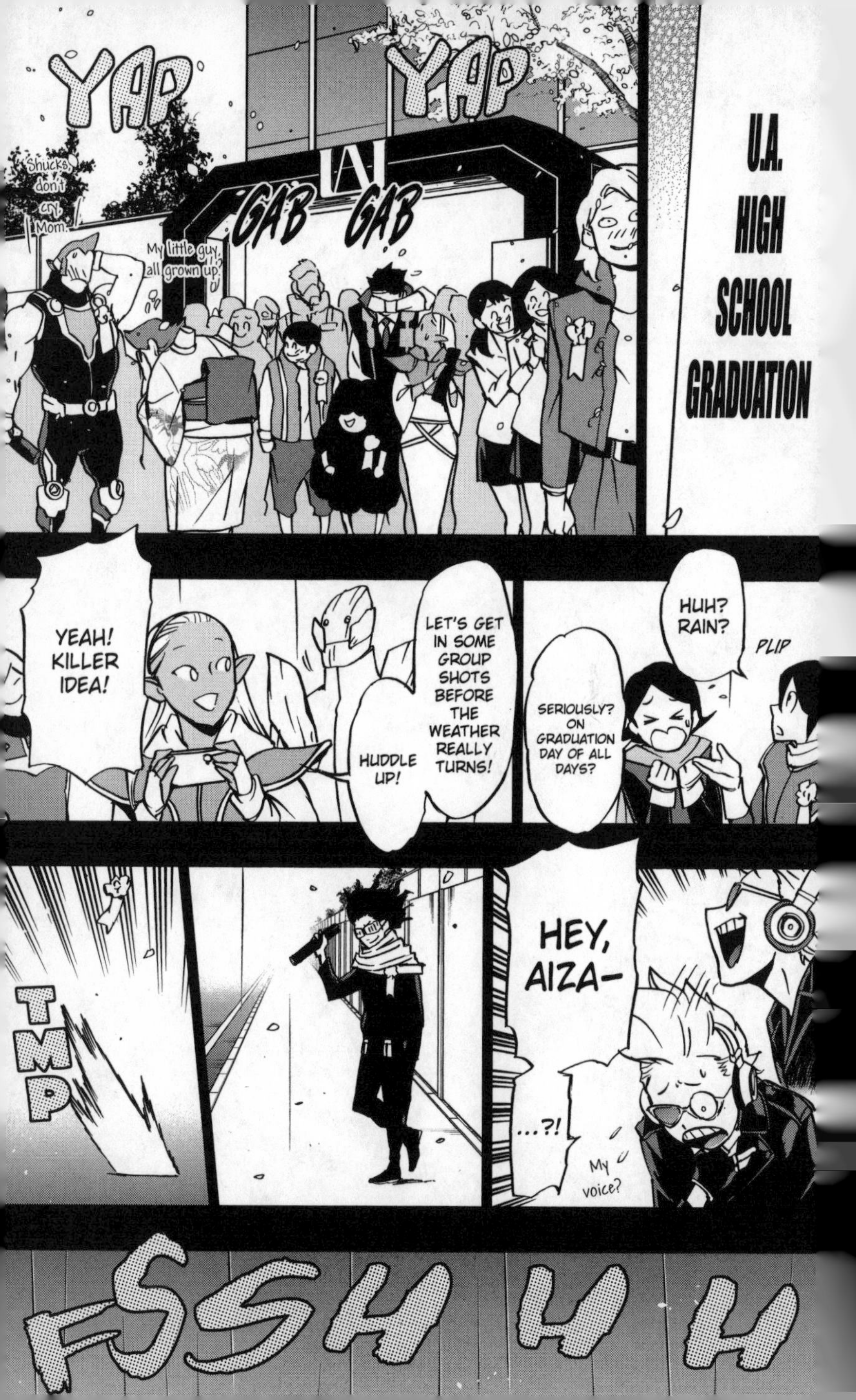
U.A. HIGH SCHOOL GRADUATION
YAP
YAP
GAB GAB
My little guy, all grown up?
Shucks, don't cry, Mom.
HUH? RAIN?
PLIP
SERIOUSLY? ON GRADUATION DAY OF ALL DAYS?
LET'S GET IN SOME GROUP SHOTS BEFORE THE WEATHER REALLY TURNS!
HUDDLE UP!
YEAH! KILLER IDEA!
HEY, AIZA-
...?!
My voice?
TMP
FSSHHH

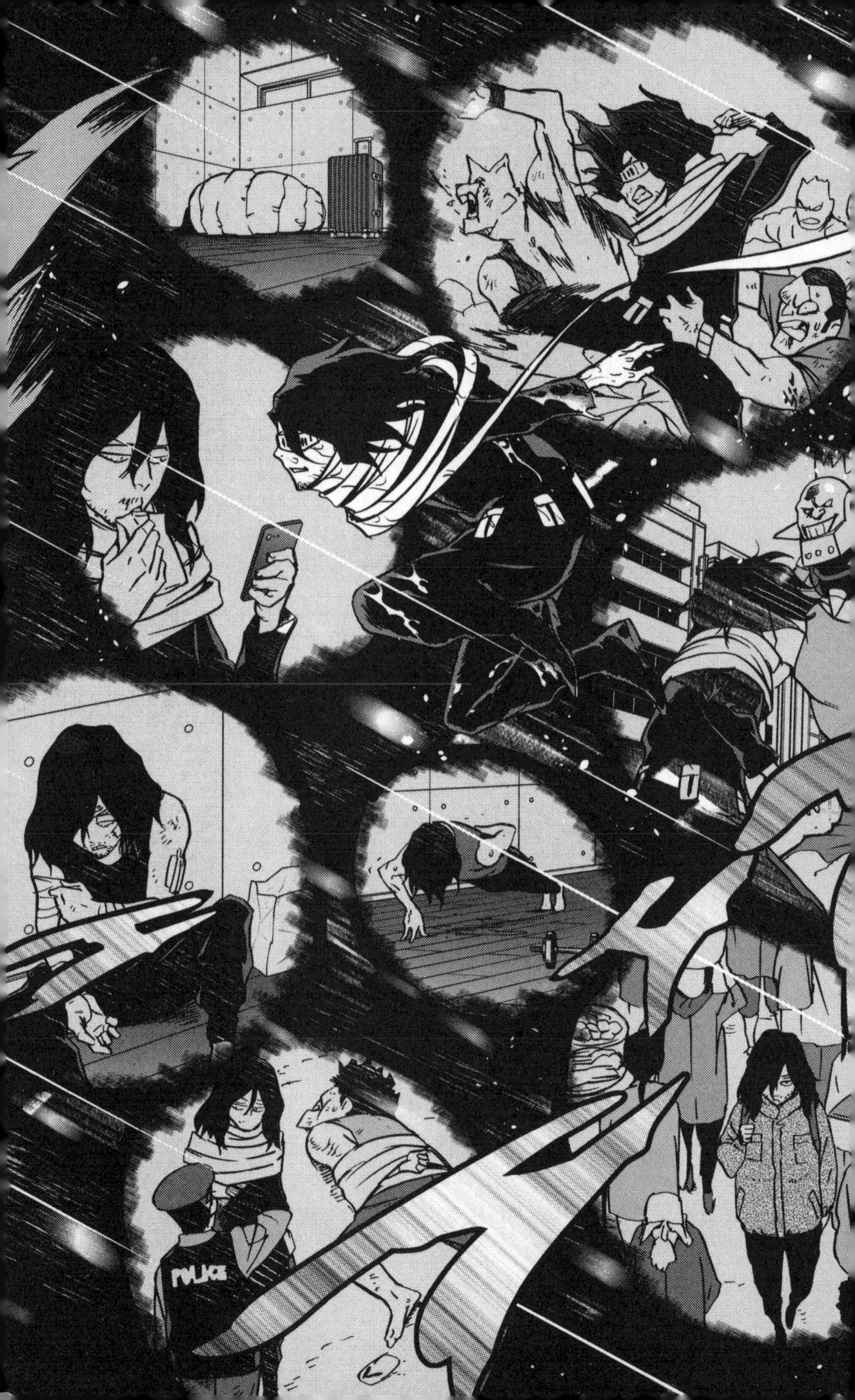

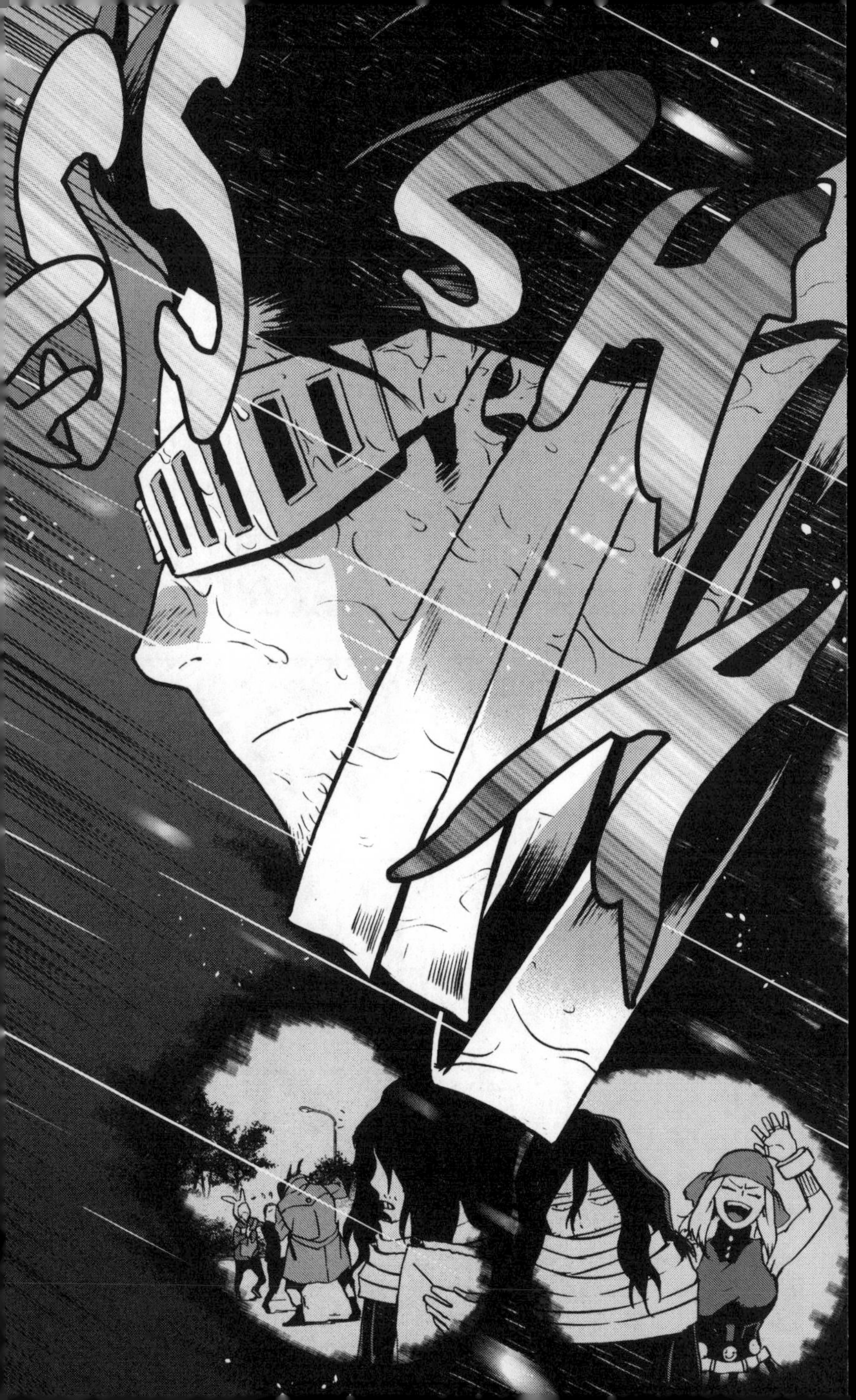

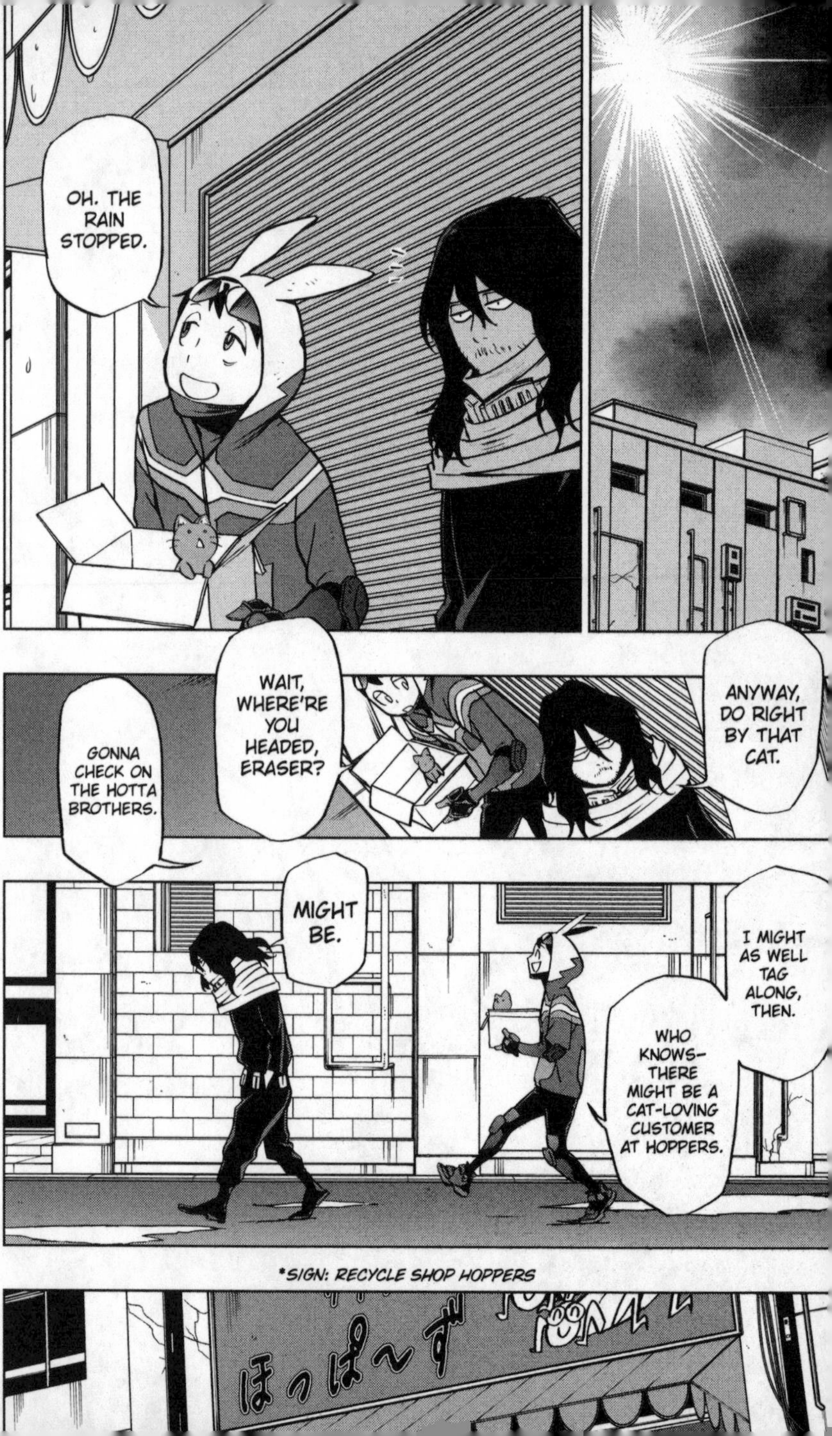
OH. THE RAIN STOPPED.
ANYWAY, DO RIGHT BY THAT CAT.
WAIT, WHERE'RE YOU HEADED, ERASER?
GONNA CHECK ON THE HOTTA BROTHERS.
I MIGHT AS WELL TAG ALONG, THEN.
WHO KNOWS— THERE MIGHT BE A CAT-LOVING CUSTOMER AT HOPPERS.
MIGHT BE.
*SIGN: RECYCLE SHOP HOPPERS
ほっぱ〜ず

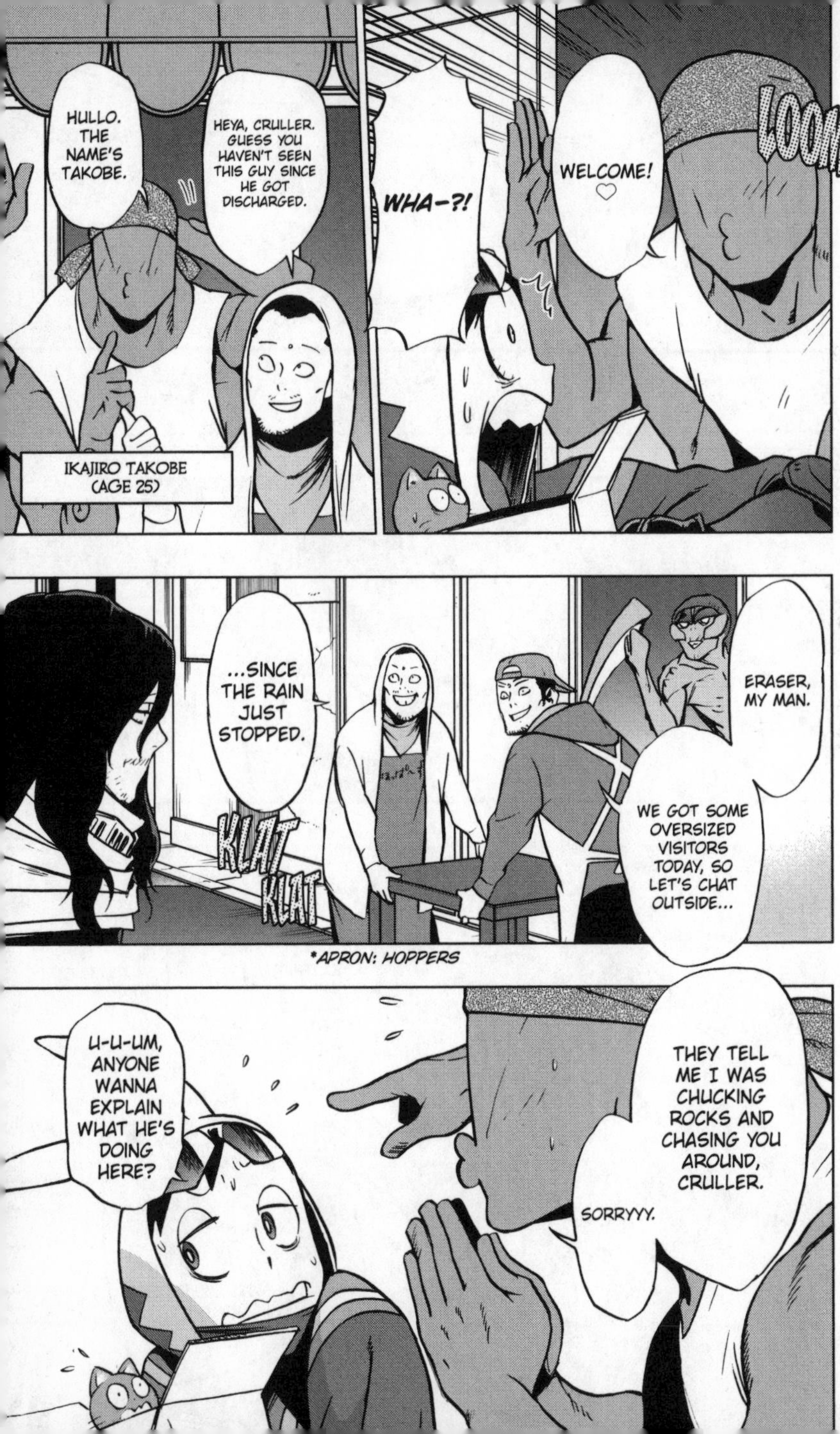
LOOM
WELCOME! ♡
WHA-?!
HEYA, CRULLER. GUESS YOU HAVEN'T SEEN THIS GUY SINCE HE GOT DISCHARGED.
HULLO. THE NAME'S TAKOBE.
IKAJIRO TAKOBE (AGE 25)
ERASER, MY MAN.
WE GOT SOME OVERSIZED VISITORS TODAY, SO LET'S CHAT OUTSIDE...
...SINCE THE RAIN JUST STOPPED.
KLAT KLAT
*APRON: HOPPERS
THEY TELL ME I WAS CHUCKING ROCKS AND CHASING YOU AROUND, CRULLER.
SORRYYY.
U-U-UM, ANYONE WANNA EXPLAIN WHAT HE'S DOING HERE?

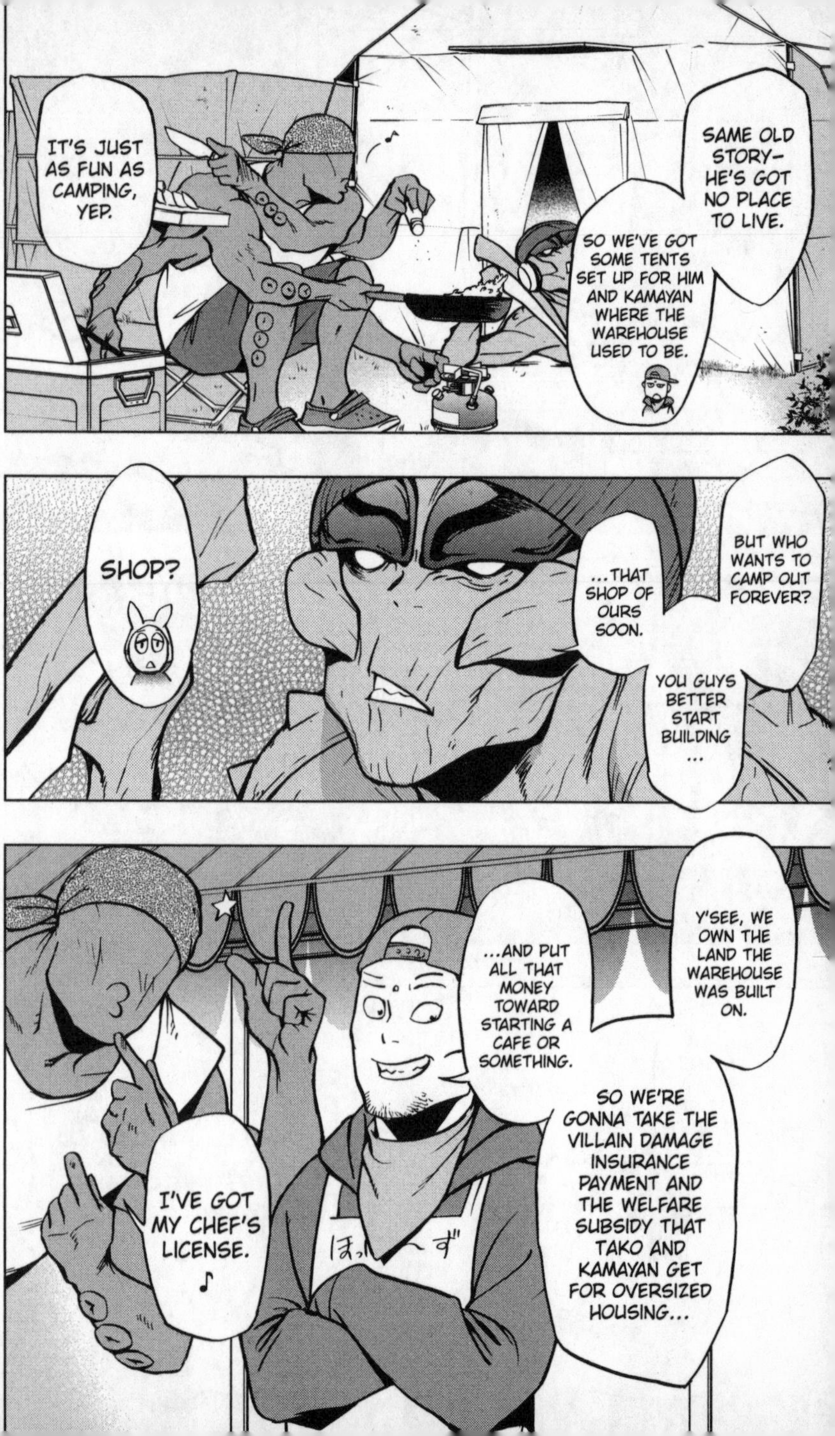

SAME OLD STORY— HE'S GOT NO PLACE TO LIVE.
SO WE'VE GOT SOME TENTS SET UP FOR HIM AND KAMAYAN WHERE THE WAREHOUSE USED TO BE.
IT'S JUST AS FUN AS CAMPING, YEP.
BUT WHO WANTS TO CAMP OUT FOREVER?
YOU GUYS BETTER START BUILDING...
...THAT SHOP OF OURS SOON.
SHOP?
Y'SEE, WE OWN THE LAND THE WAREHOUSE WAS BUILT ON.
SO WE'RE GONNA TAKE THE VILLAIN DAMAGE INSURANCE PAYMENT AND THE WELFARE SUBSIDY THAT TAKO AND KAMAYAN GET FOR OVERSIZED HOUSING...
...AND PUT ALL THAT MONEY TOWARD STARTING A CAFE OR SOMETHING.
I'VE GOT MY CHEF'S LICENSE. ♪

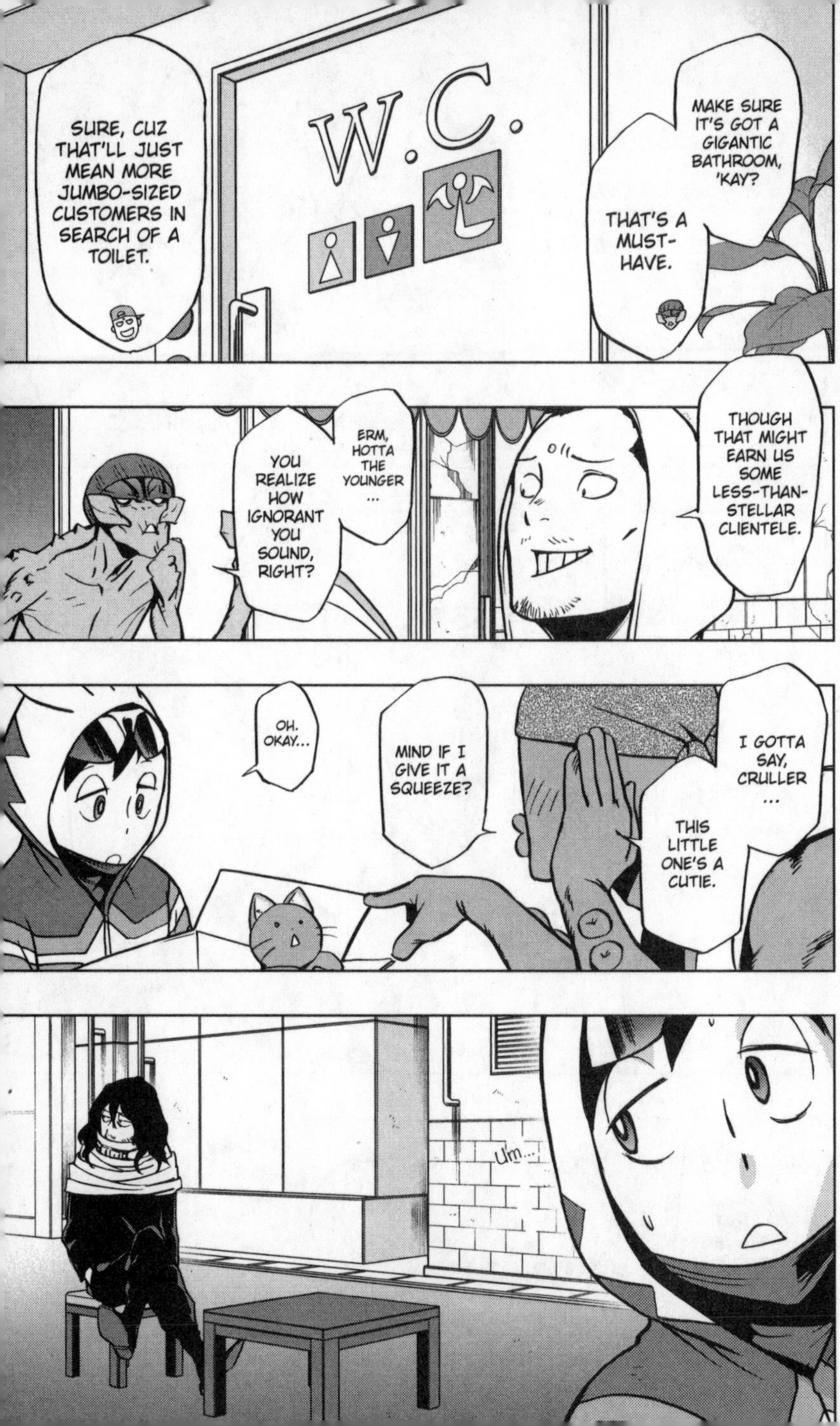
MAKE SURE IT'S GOT A GIGANTIC BATHROOM, 'KAY?
THAT'S A MUST-HAVE.
W.C.
SURE, CUZ THAT'LL JUST MEAN MORE JUMBO-SIZED CUSTOMERS IN SEARCH OF A TOILET.
THOUGH THAT MIGHT EARN US SOME LESS-THAN-STELLAR CLIENTELE.
ERM, HOTTA THE YOUNGER...
YOU REALIZE HOW IGNORANT YOU SOUND, RIGHT?
I GOTTA SAY, CRULLER...
THIS LITTLE ONE'S A CUTIE.
MIND IF I GIVE IT A SQUEEZE?
OH. OKAY...
Um...

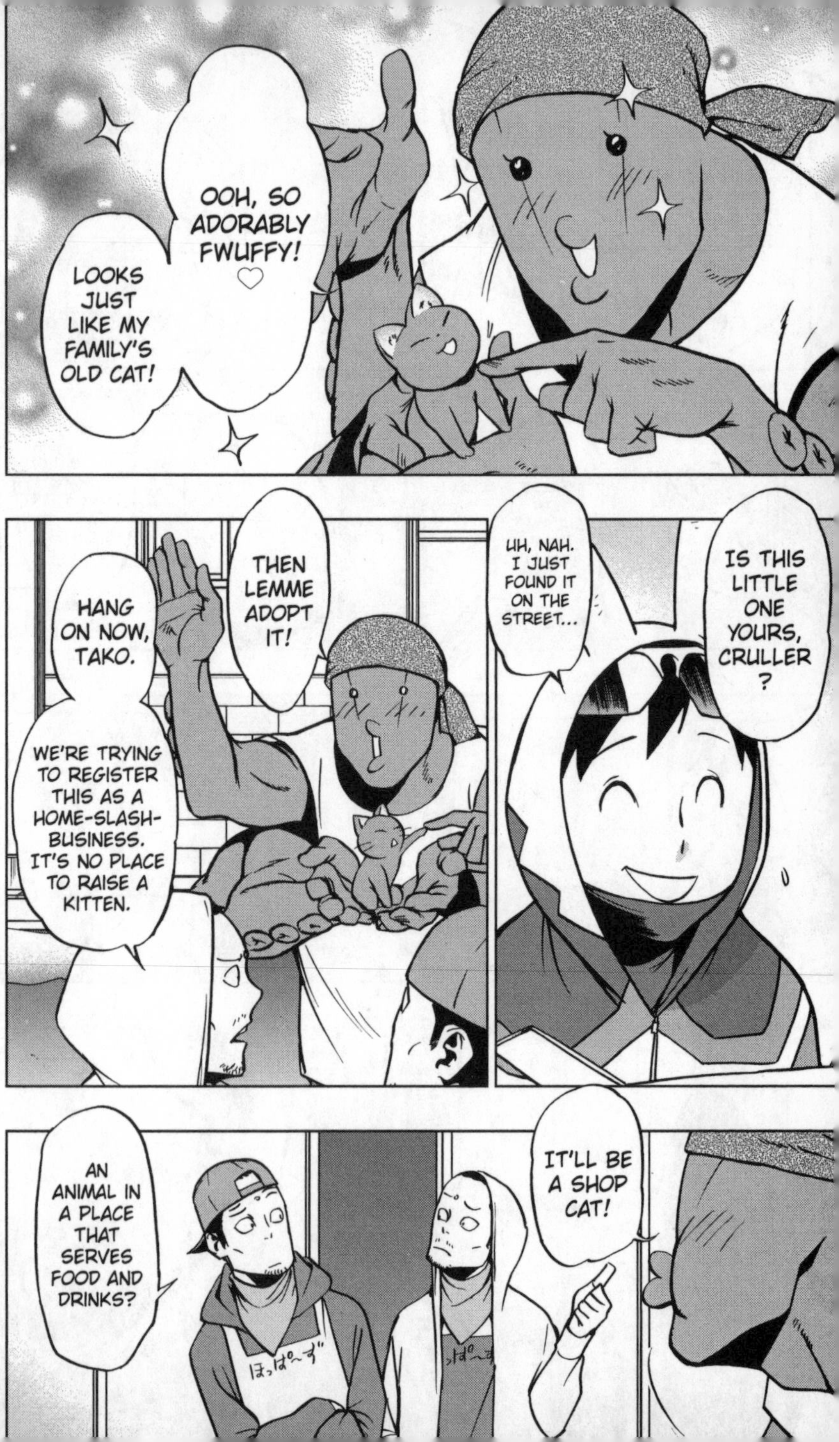
OOH, SO ADORABLY FWUFFY! ♡
LOOKS JUST LIKE MY FAMILY'S OLD CAT!
IS THIS LITTLE ONE YOURS, CRULLER?
UH, NAH. I JUST FOUND IT ON THE STREET...
THEN LEMME ADOPT IT!
HANG ON NOW, TAKO.
WE'RE TRYING TO REGISTER THIS AS A HOME-SLASH-BUSINESS. IT'S NO PLACE TO RAISE A KITTEN.
IT'LL BE A SHOP CAT!
AN ANIMAL IN A PLACE THAT SERVES FOOD AND DRINKS?
ほっぱ〜ず

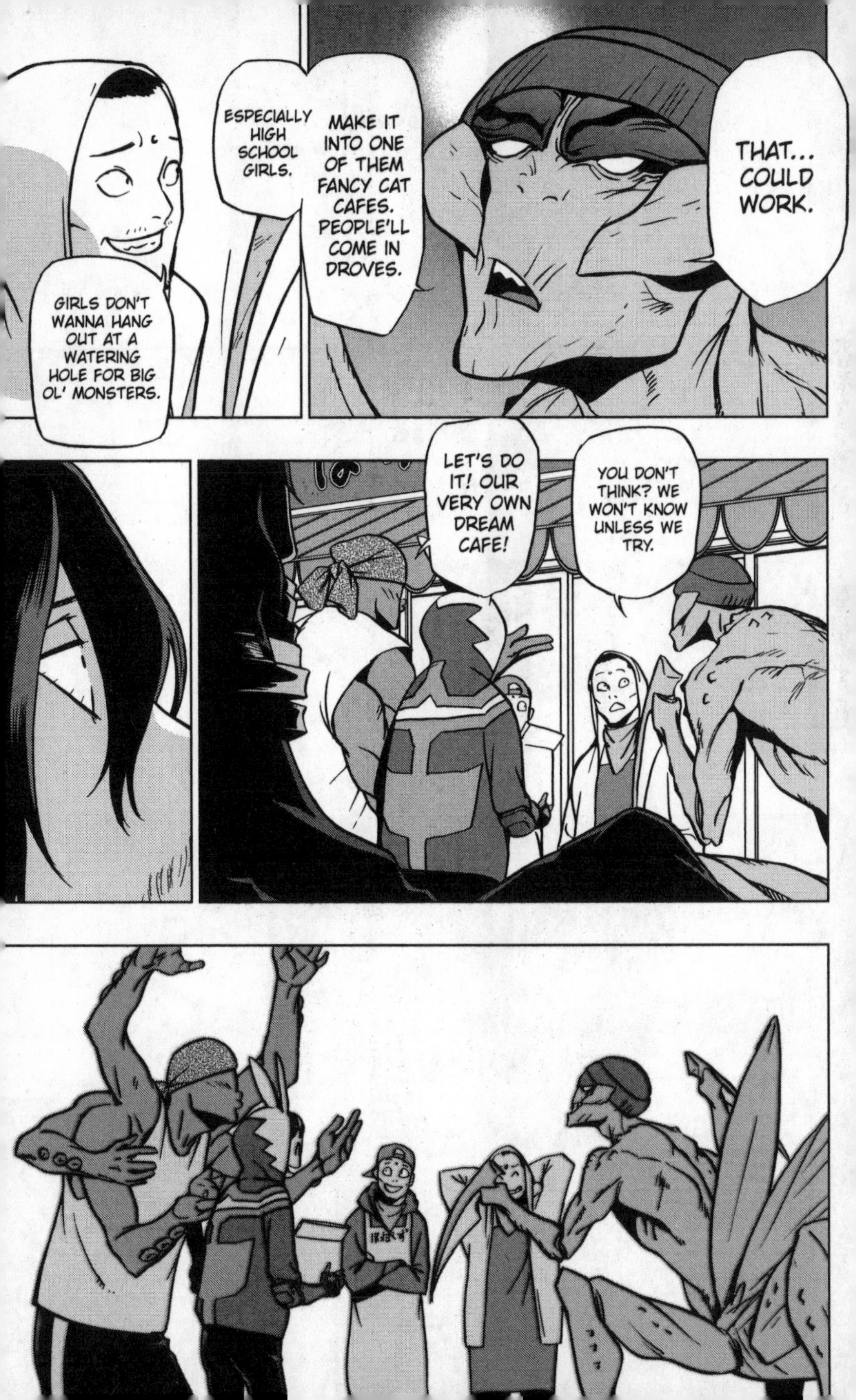
THAT... COULD WORK.
MAKE IT INTO ONE OF THEM FANCY CAT CAFES. PEOPLE'LL COME IN DROVES.
ESPECIALLY HIGH SCHOOL GIRLS.
GIRLS DON'T WANNA HANG OUT AT A WATERING HOLE FOR BIG OL' MONSTERS.
YOU DON'T THINK? WE WON'T KNOW UNLESS WE TRY.
LET'S DO IT! OUR VERY OWN DREAM CAFE!

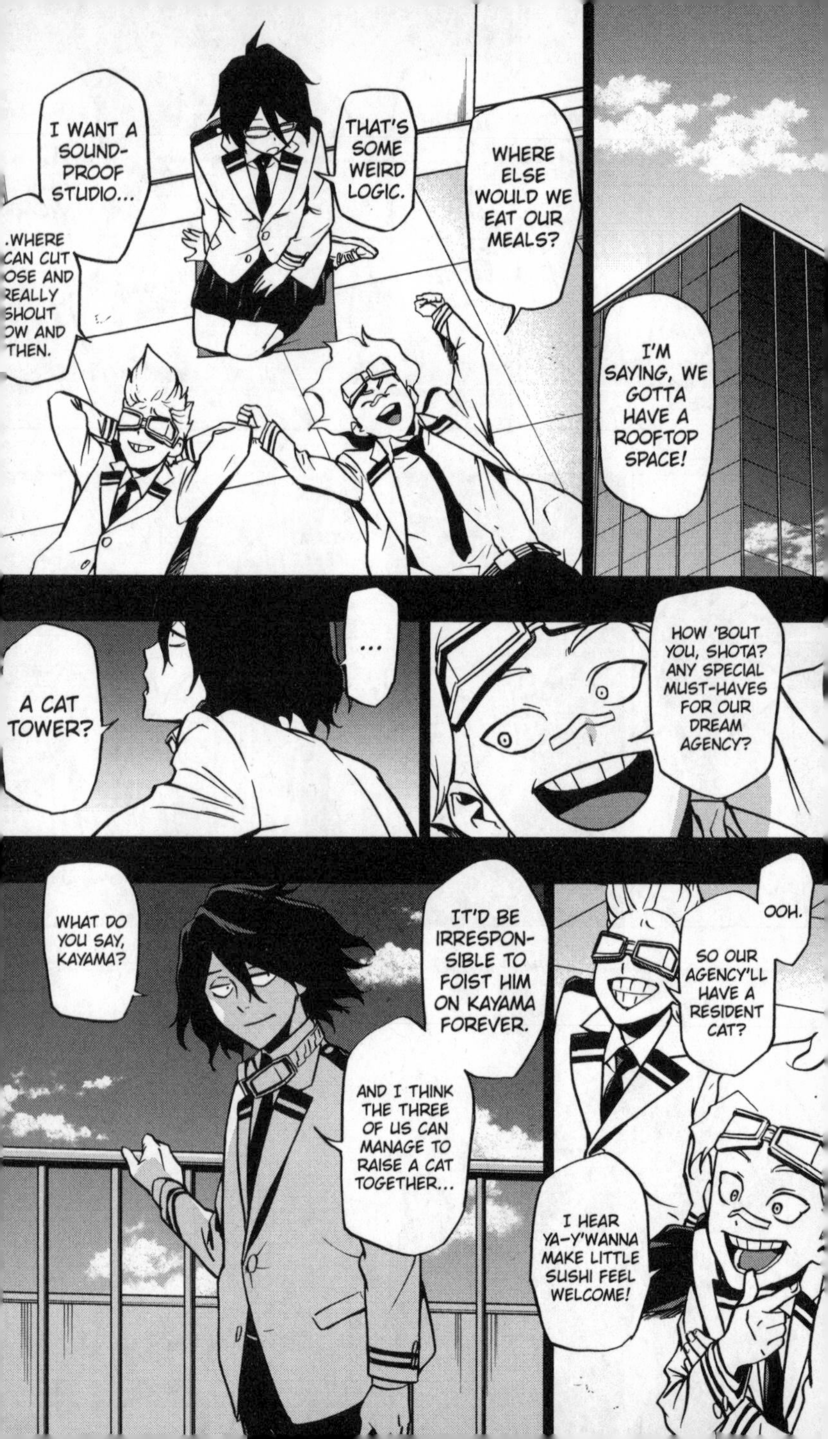
I'M SAYING, WE GOTTA HAVE A ROOFTOP SPACE!
WHERE ELSE WOULD WE EAT OUR MEALS?
THAT'S SOME WEIRD LOGIC.
I WANT A SOUND-PROOF STUDIO...
.WHERE CAN CUT OSE AND REALLY SHOUT OW AND THEN.
HOW 'BOUT YOU, SHOTA? ANY SPECIAL MUST-HAVES FOR OUR DREAM AGENCY?
...
A CAT TOWER?
OOH.
SO OUR AGENCY'LL HAVE A RESIDENT CAT?
I HEAR YA-Y'WANNA MAKE LITTLE SUSHI FEEL WELCOME!
IT'D BE IRRESPON-SIBLE TO FOIST HIM ON KAYAMA FOREVER.
WHAT DO YOU SAY, KAYAMA?
AND I THINK THE THREE OF US CAN MANAGE TO RAISE A CAT TOGETHER...

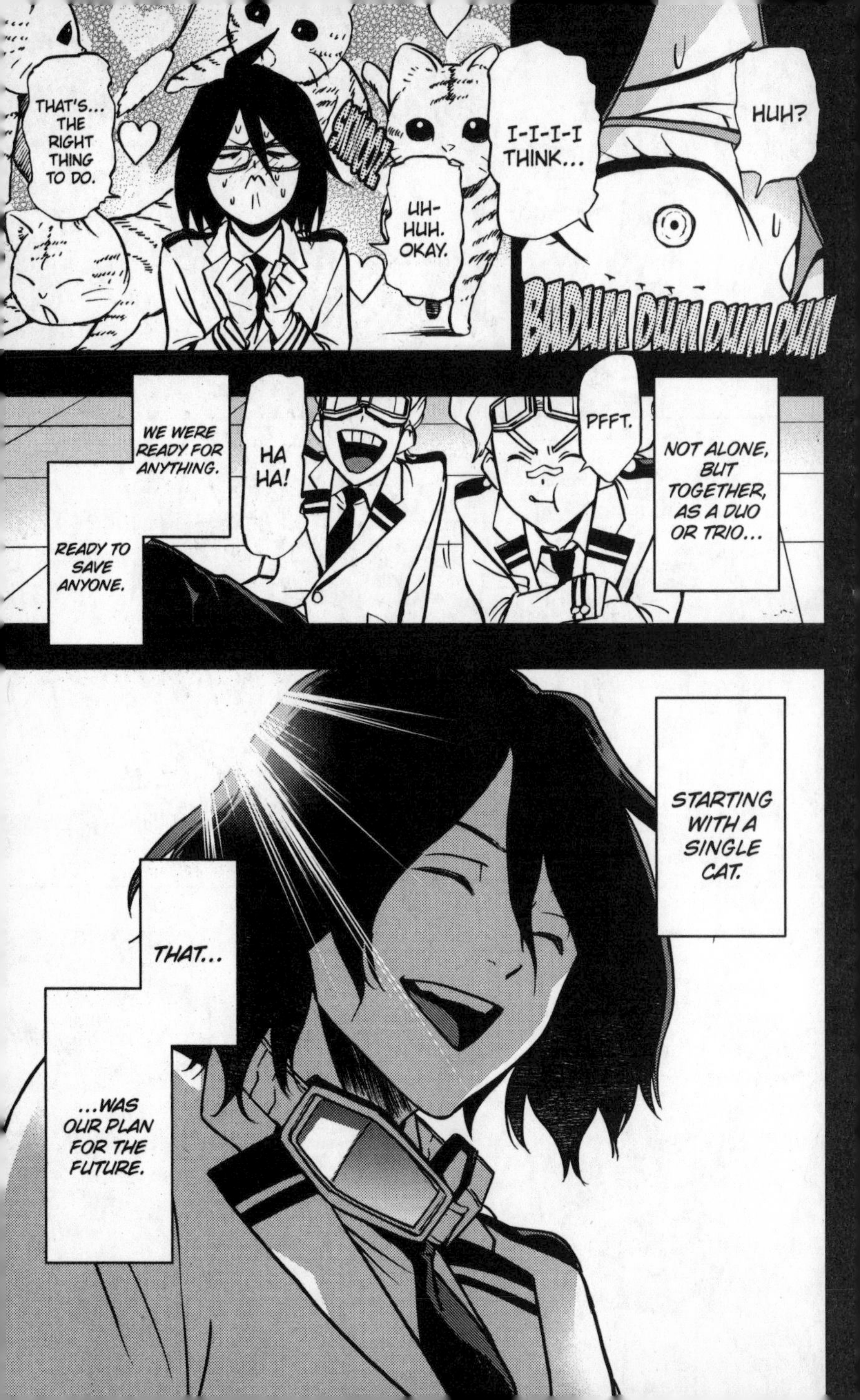
HUH?
BADUM DUM DUM DUM
I-I-I-I THINK...
UH-HUH. OKAY.
THAT'S... THE RIGHT THING TO DO.
NOT ALONE, BUT TOGETHER, AS A DUO OR TRIO...
PFFT.
HA HA!
WE WERE READY FOR ANYTHING.
READY TO SAVE ANYONE.
STARTING WITH A SINGLE CAT.
THAT...
...WAS OUR PLAN FOR THE FUTURE.

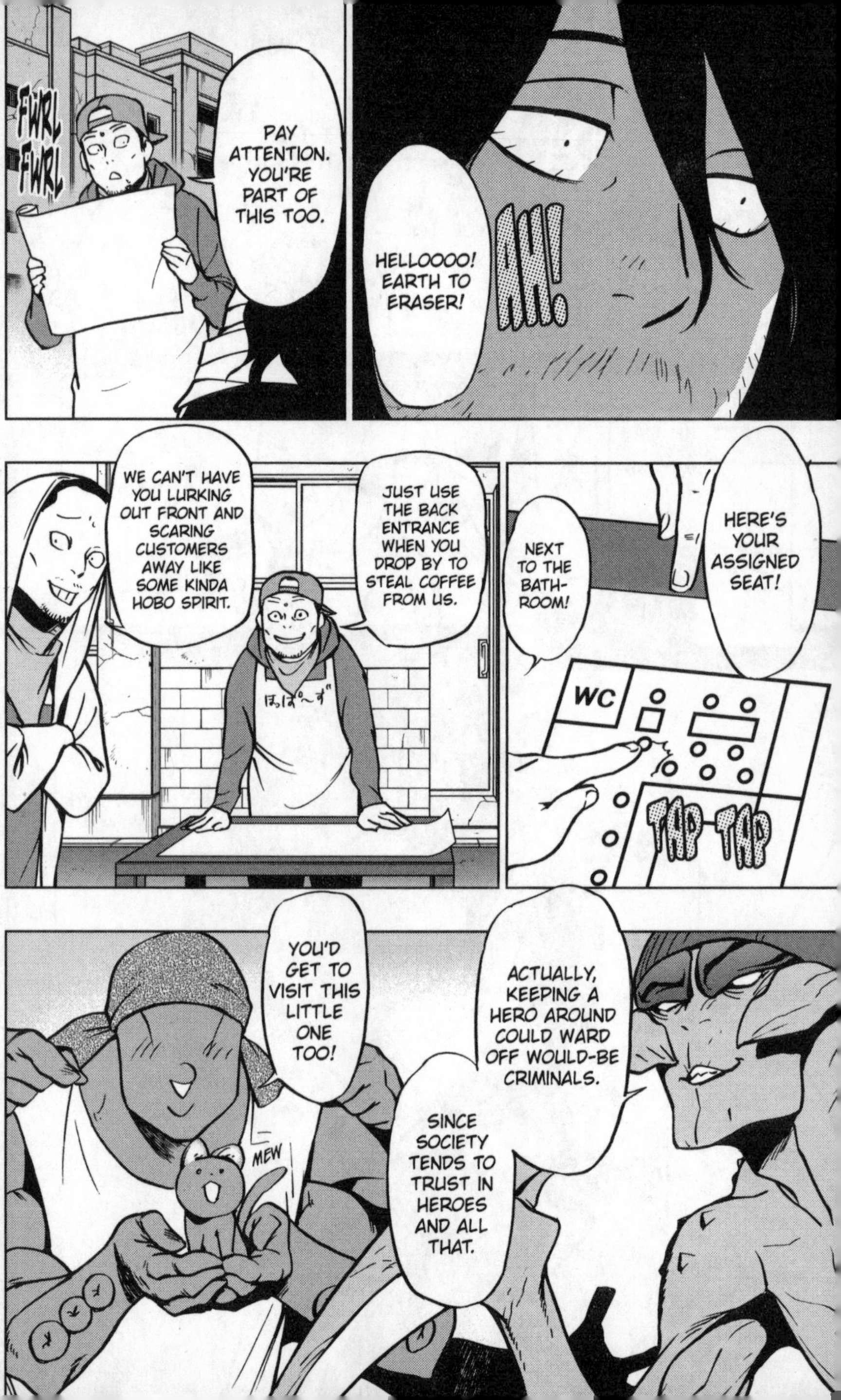
HELLOOOO! EARTH TO ERASER!
AH!
PAY ATTENTION. YOU'RE PART OF THIS TOO.
FWRL FWRL
HERE'S YOUR ASSIGNED SEAT!
NEXT TO THE BATH-ROOM!
WC
TAP TAP
JUST USE THE BACK ENTRANCE WHEN YOU DROP BY TO STEAL COFFEE FROM US.
WE CAN'T HAVE YOU LURKING OUT FRONT AND SCARING CUSTOMERS AWAY LIKE SOME KINDA HOBO SPIRIT.
ほっぱ〜ず
ACTUALLY, KEEPING A HERO AROUND COULD WARD OFF WOULD-BE CRIMINALS.
SINCE SOCIETY TENDS TO TRUST IN HEROES AND ALL THAT.
YOU'D GET TO VISIT THIS LITTLE ONE TOO!
MEW

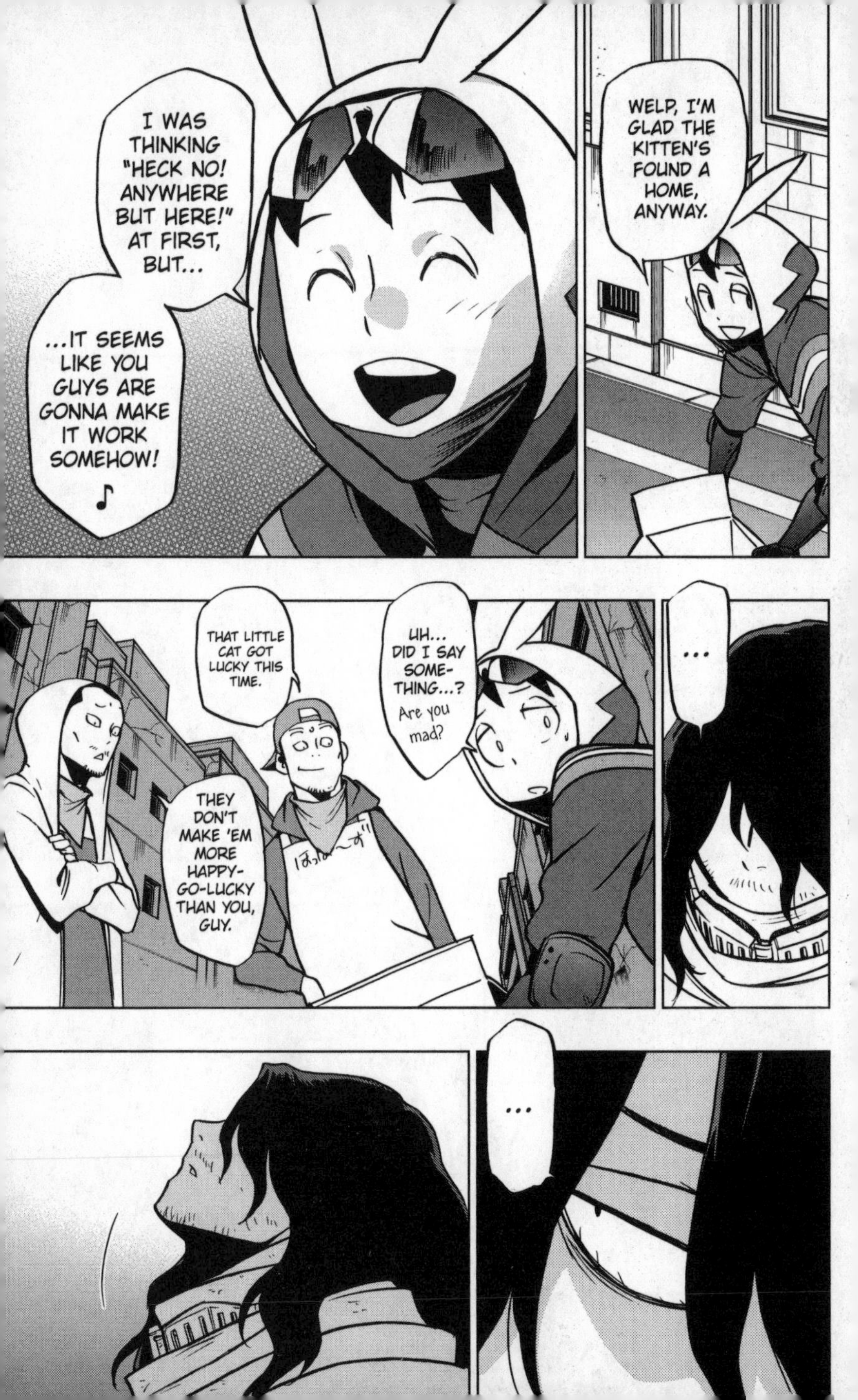
WELP, I'M GLAD THE KITTEN'S FOUND A HOME, ANYWAY.
I WAS THINKING "HECK NO! ANYWHERE BUT HERE!" AT FIRST, BUT...
...IT SEEMS LIKE YOU GUYS ARE GONNA MAKE IT WORK SOMEHOW! ♪
...
UH... DID I SAY SOME-THING...? Are you mad?
THAT LITTLE CAT GOT LUCKY THIS TIME.
THEY DON'T MAKE 'EM MORE HAPPY-GO-LUCKY THAN YOU, GUY.
...

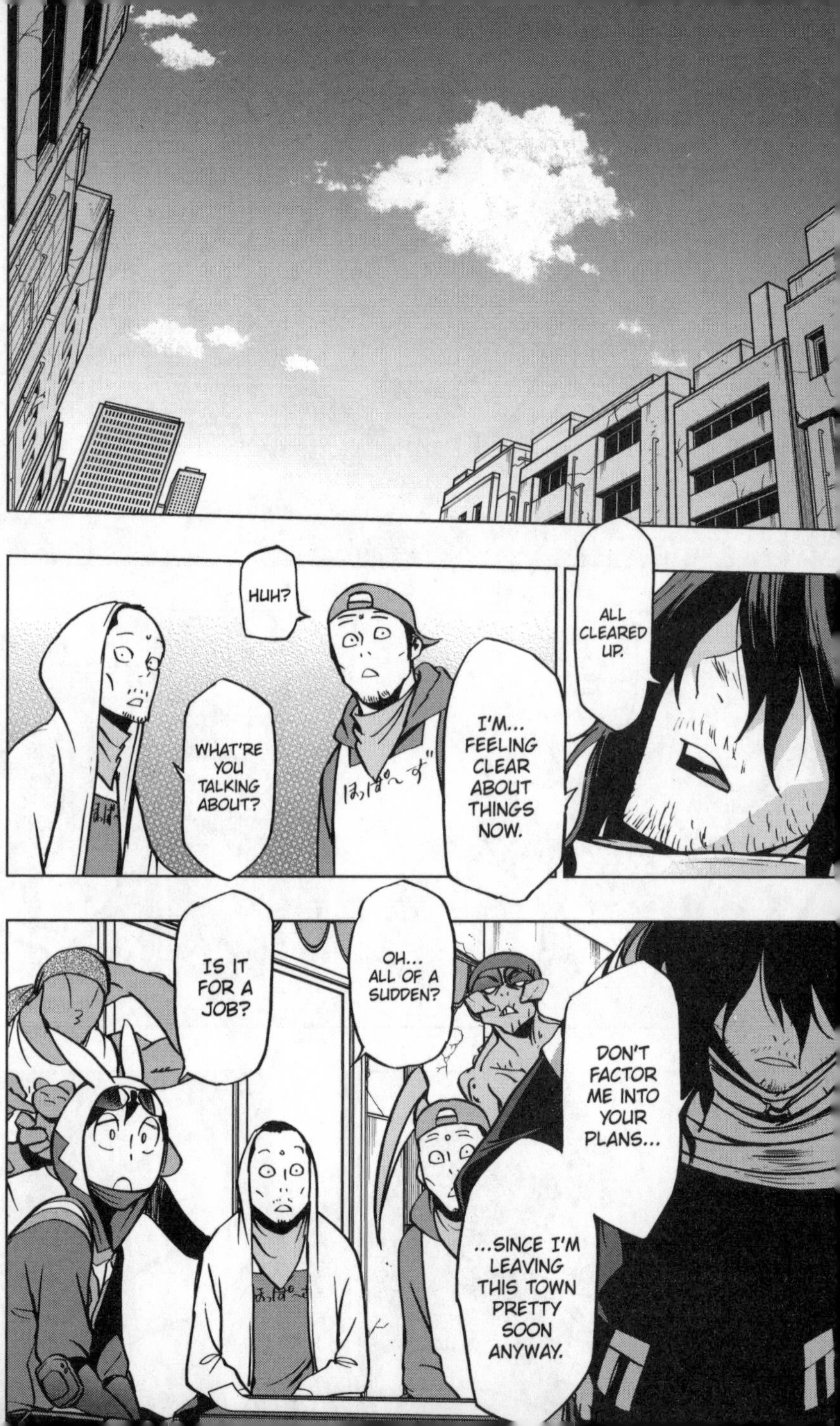
ALL CLEARED UP.
I'M... FEELING CLEAR ABOUT THINGS NOW.
HUH?
WHAT'RE YOU TALKING ABOUT?
はっぱ〜ず
DON'T FACTOR ME INTO YOUR PLANS...
...SINCE I'M LEAVING THIS TOWN PRETTY SOON ANYWAY.
OH... ALL OF A SUDDEN?
IS IT FOR A JOB?

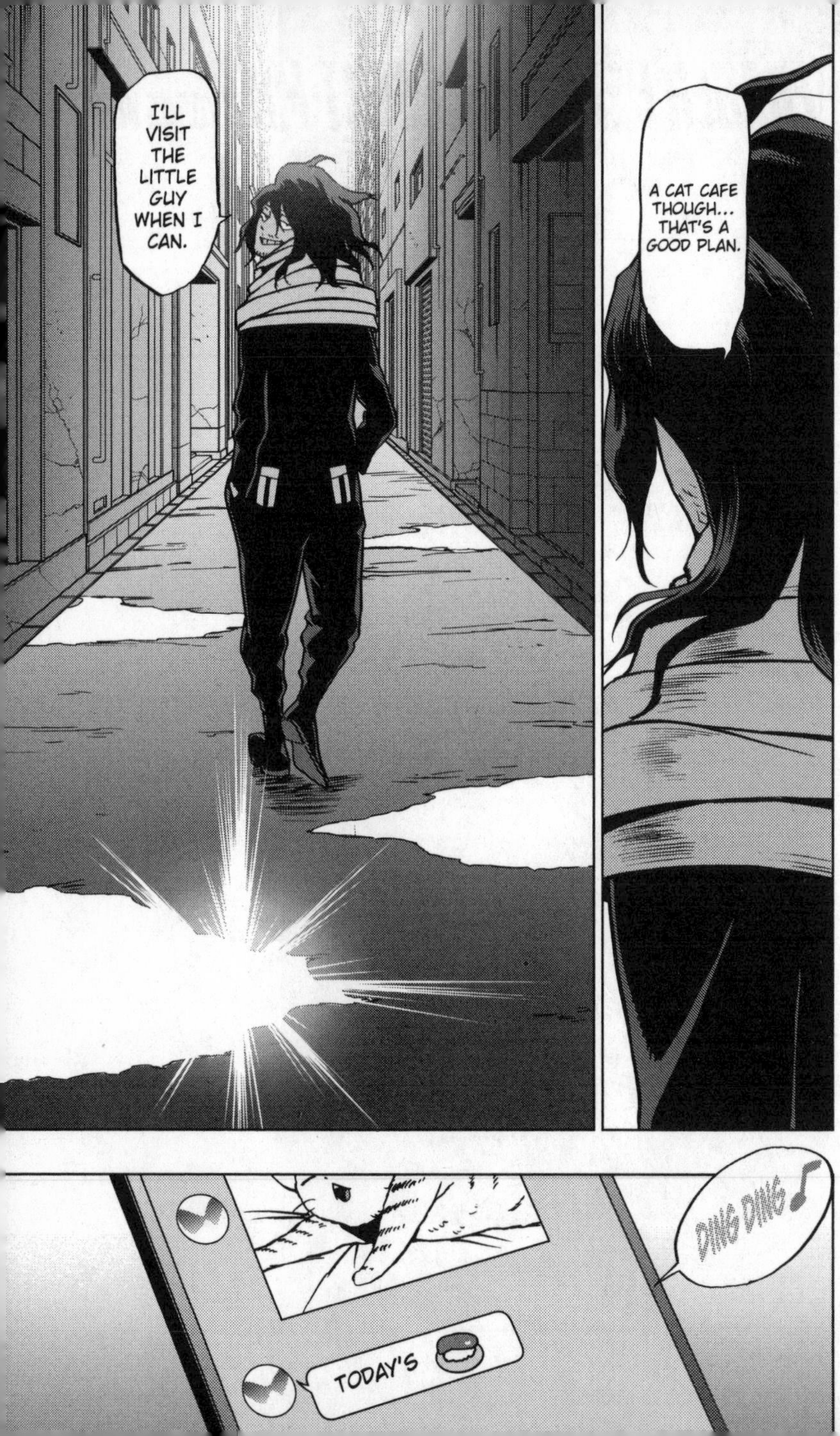
A CAT CAFE THOUGH... THAT'S A GOOD PLAN.
I'LL VISIT THE LITTLE GUY WHEN I CAN.
DING DING
TODAY'S

ERASER HEAD & PRESENT MIC (YOUNG VER.)

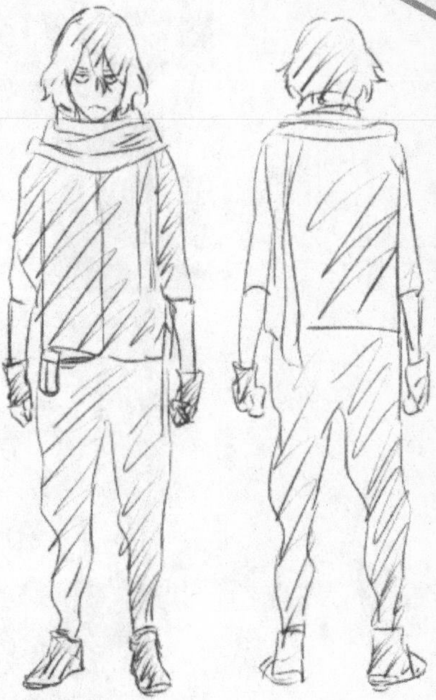
Student Hero Costumes
Aizawa
Simple

BEHIND THE SCENES

For both of these guys, my requests were “lighter equipment than present day,” “transitional period” and “shonen-ish.” Once you add those goggles, young Eraser Head is complete, so to speak.

—Furuhashi

Since these two are in their powered-up forms in the main *MHA* story, I wanted to imagine these versions as an earlier stage of that. As if they would improve on these designs over time to achieve their eventual styles… Kind of like that.

—Betten

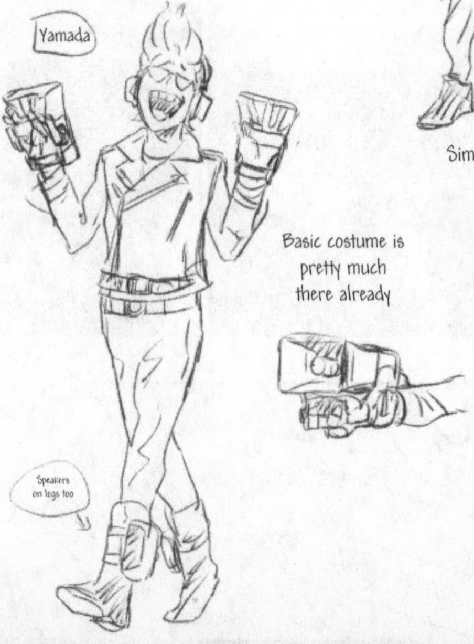
Yamada
Basic costume is pretty much there already
Speakers on legs too

THE ROUGH DESIGN

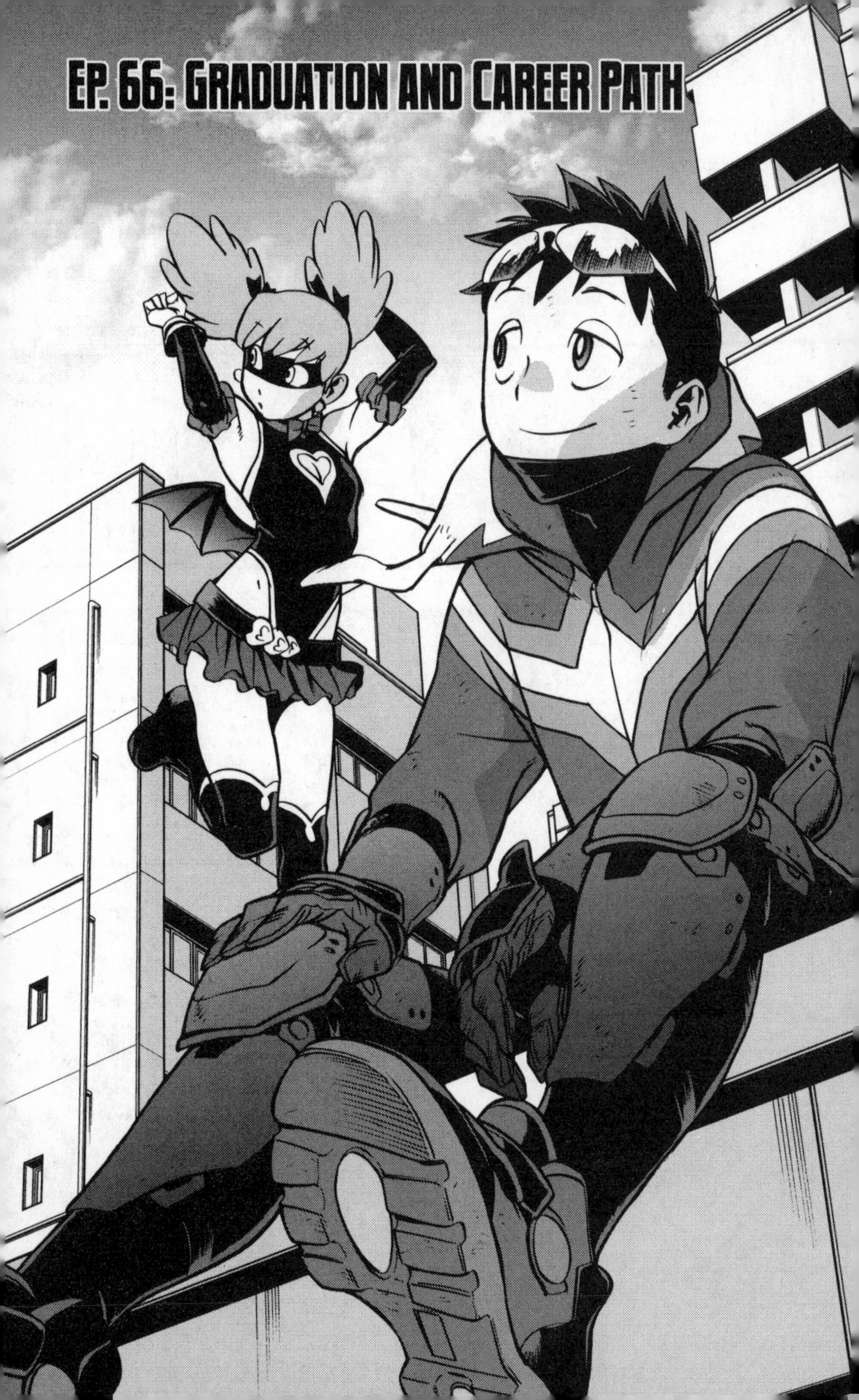
Ep. 66: Graduation and Career Path

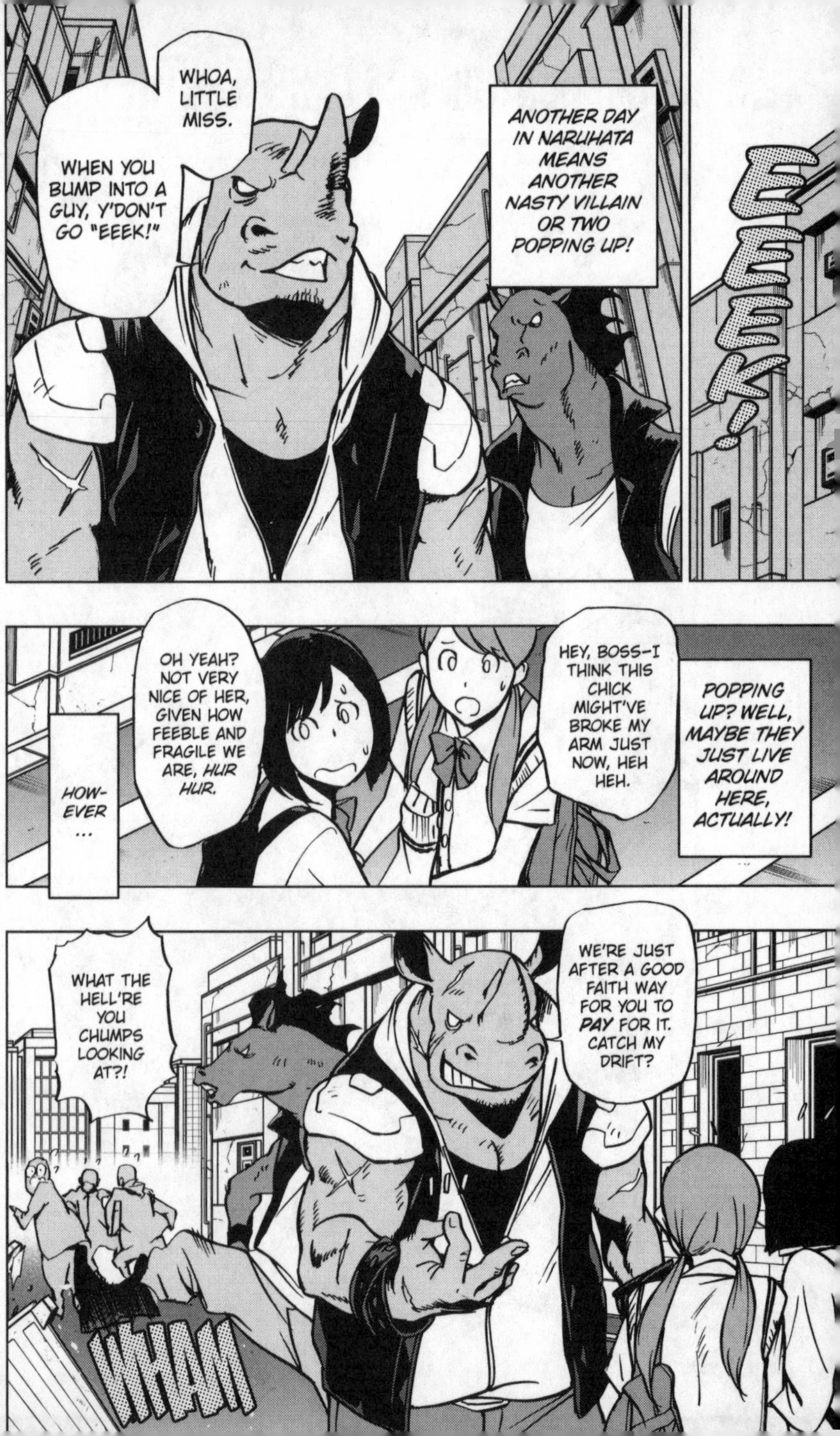
EEEEK!!
ANOTHER DAY IN NARUHATA MEANS ANOTHER NASTY VILLAIN OR TWO POPPING UP!
WHOA, LITTLE MISS.
WHEN YOU BUMP INTO A GUY, Y'DON'T GO "EEEK!"
POPPING UP? WELL, MAYBE THEY JUST LIVE AROUND HERE, ACTUALLY!
HEY, BOSS—I THINK THIS CHICK MIGHT'VE BROKE MY ARM JUST NOW, HEH HEH.
OH YEAH? NOT VERY NICE OF HER, GIVEN HOW FEEBLE AND FRAGILE WE ARE, *HUR HUR.*
HOW-EVER ...
WE'RE JUST AFTER A GOOD FAITH WAY FOR YOU TO *PAY* FOR IT. CATCH MY DRIFT?
WHAT THE HELL'RE YOU CHUMPS LOOKING AT?!
WHAM

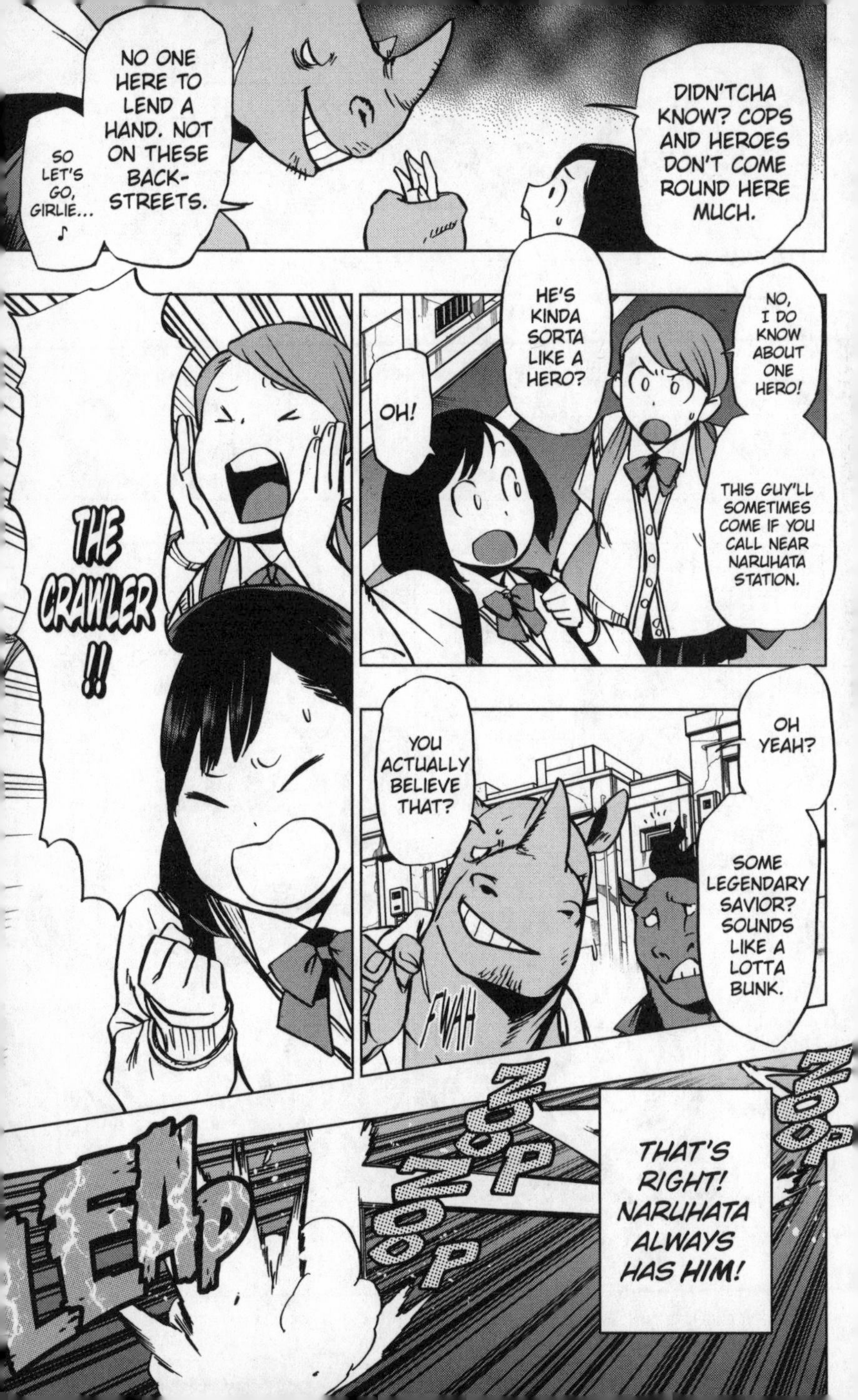
DIDN'TCHA KNOW? COPS AND HEROES DON'T COME ROUND HERE MUCH.
NO ONE HERE TO LEND A HAND. NOT ON THESE BACK-STREETS.
SO LET'S GO, GIRLIE... ♪
NO, I DO KNOW ABOUT ONE HERO!
THIS GUY'LL SOMETIMES COME IF YOU CALL NEAR NARUHATA STATION.
HE'S KINDA SORTA LIKE A HERO?
OH!
OH YEAH?
SOME LEGENDARY SAVIOR? SOUNDS LIKE A LOTTA BUNK.
YOU ACTUALLY BELIEVE THAT?
FWAH
THE CRAWLER!!
THAT'S RIGHT! NARUHATA ALWAYS HAS HIM!
ZOOP
ZOOP ZOOP

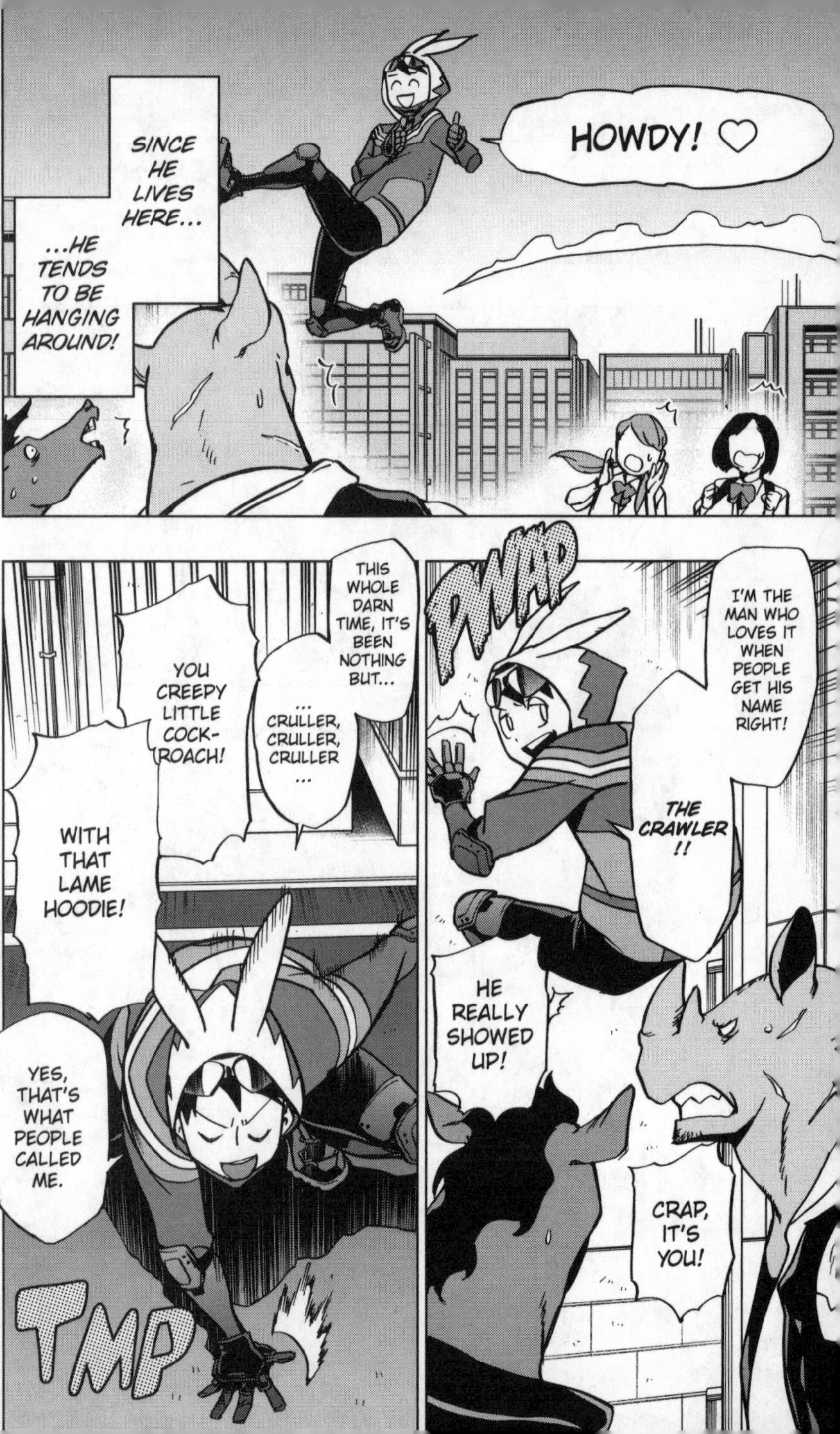
HOWDY! ♡
SINCE HE LIVES HERE...
...HE TENDS TO BE HANGING AROUND!
DWAP
I'M THE MAN WHO LOVES IT WHEN PEOPLE GET HIS NAME RIGHT!
THE CRAWLER!!
HE REALLY SHOWED UP!
CRAP, IT'S YOU!
THIS WHOLE DARN TIME, IT'S BEEN NOTHING BUT...
...CRULLER, CRULLER, CRULLER...
YOU CREEPY LITTLE COCK-ROACH!
WITH THAT LAME HOODIE!
YES, THAT'S WHAT PEOPLE CALLED ME.
TMP

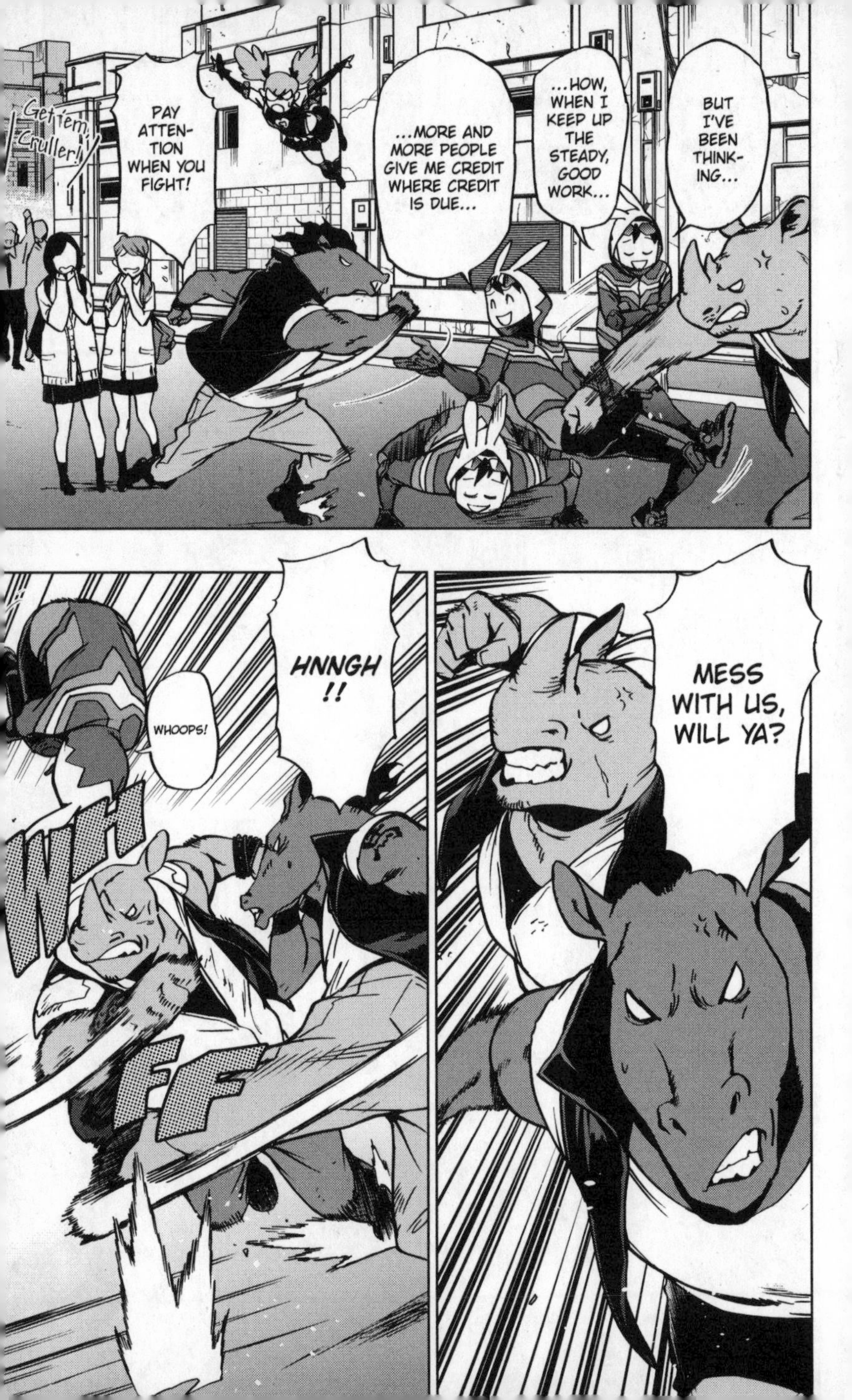
BUT I'VE BEEN THINKING...
...HOW, WHEN I KEEP UP THE STEADY, GOOD WORK...
...MORE AND MORE PEOPLE GIVE ME CREDIT WHERE CREDIT IS DUE...
PAY ATTENTION WHEN YOU FIGHT!
Get 'em, Cruller!!
MESS WITH US, WILL YA?
HNNGH!!
WHOOPS!

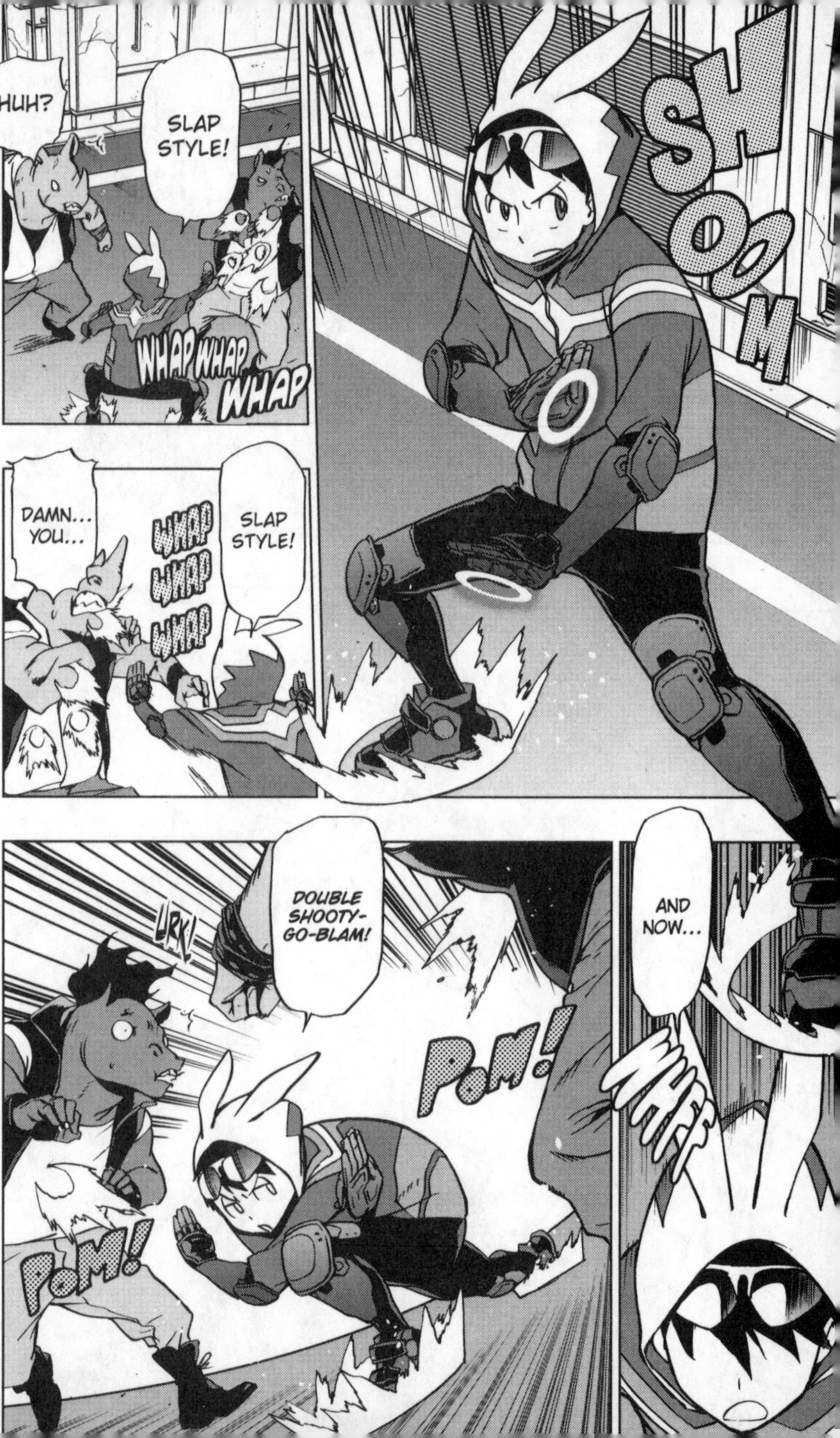
SHOOOM
SLAP STYLE!
HUH?
WHAP WHAP WHAP
SLAP STYLE!
WHAP WHAP WHAP
DAMN... YOU...
AND NOW...
DOUBLE SHOOTY-GO-BLAM!
URK!
POM!
POM!

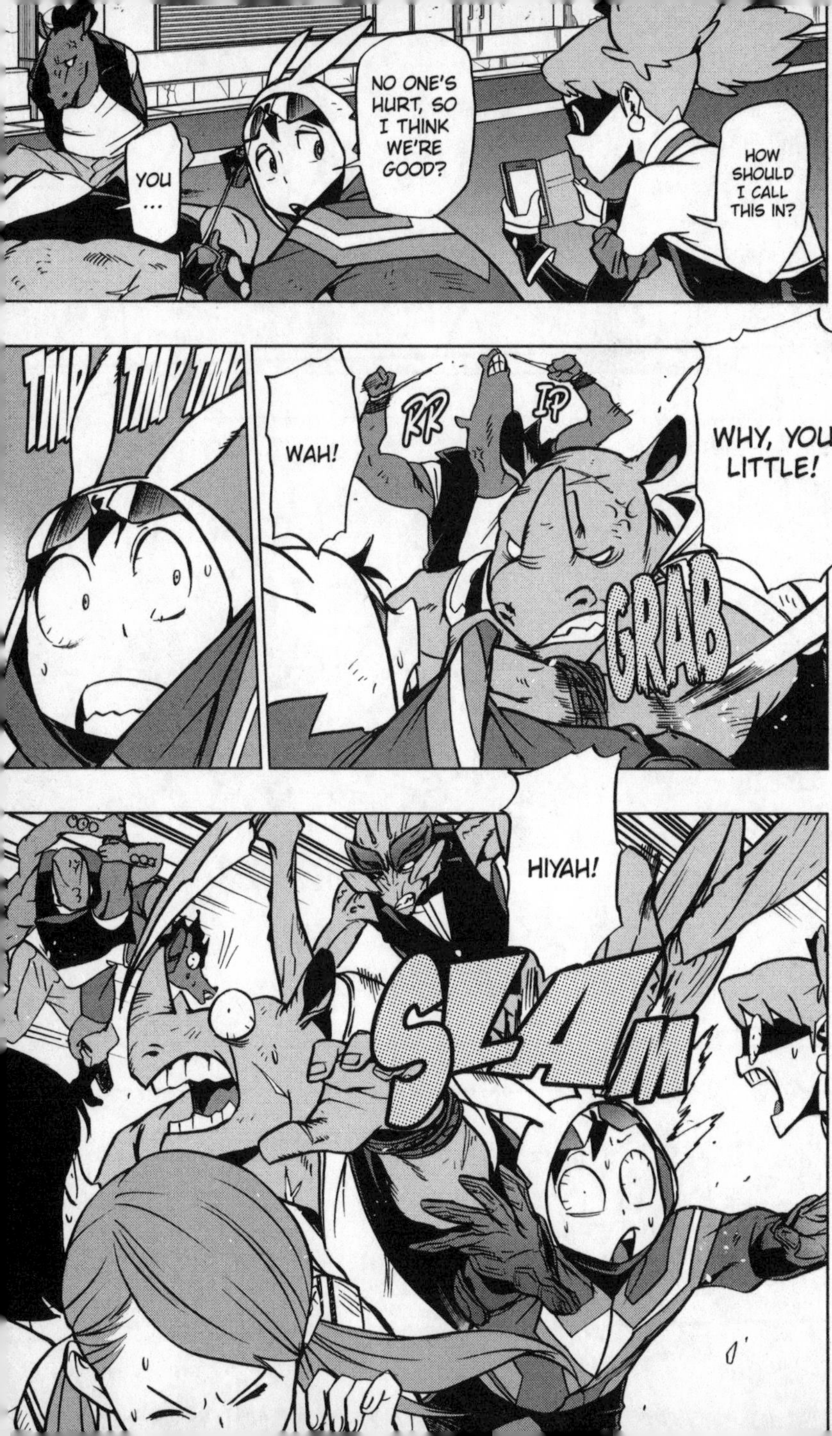
HOW SHOULD I CALL THIS IN?
NO ONE'S HURT, SO I THINK WE'RE GOOD?
YOU ...
WHY, YOU LITTLE!
RRIP
WAH!
GRAB
TMP TMP TMP
HIYAH!
SLAM

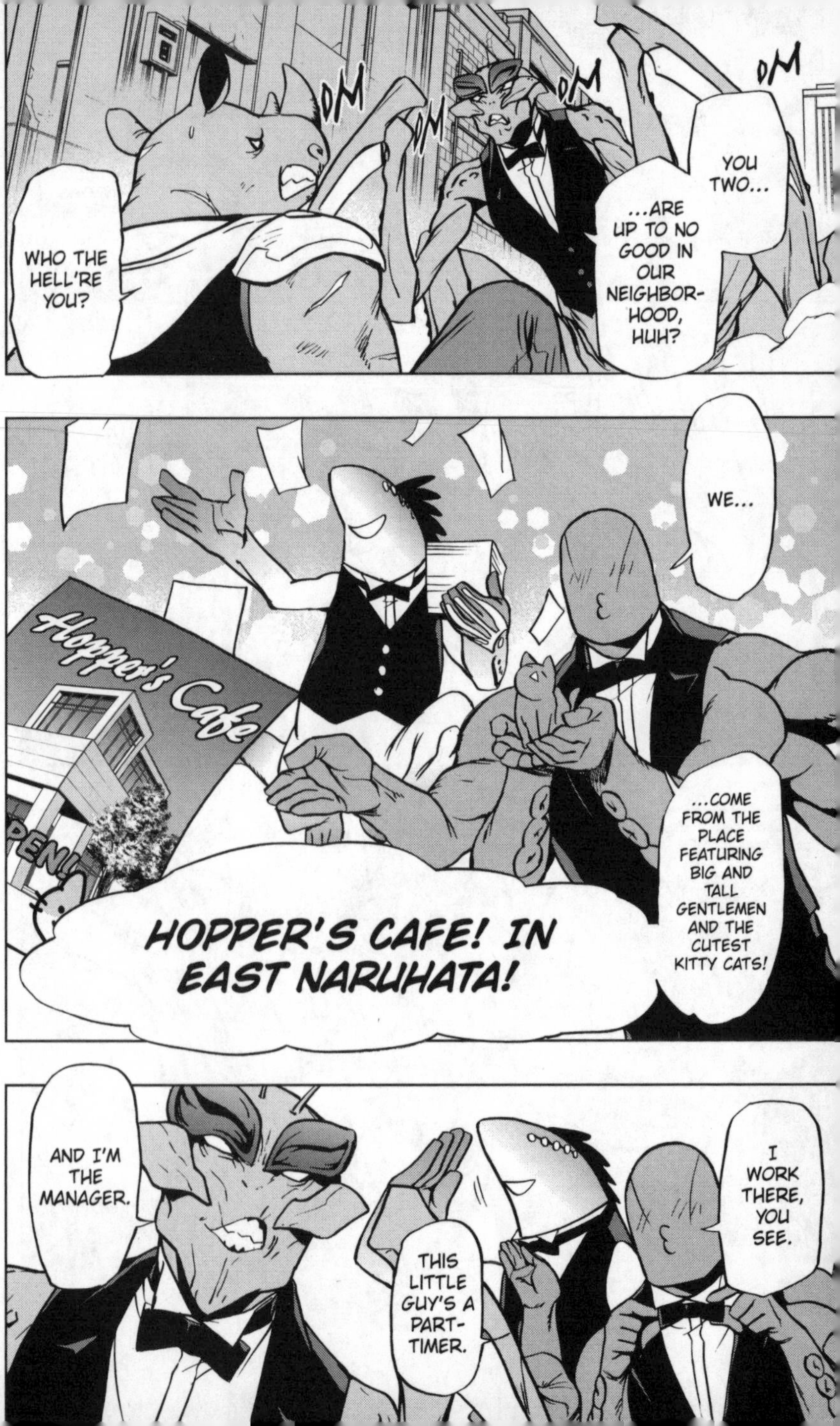
YOU TWO...
...ARE UP TO NO GOOD IN OUR NEIGHBOR-HOOD, HUH?
WHO THE HELL'RE YOU?
WE...
...COME FROM THE PLACE FEATURING BIG AND TALL GENTLEMEN AND THE CUTEST KITTY CATS!
Hopper's Cafe
HOPPER'S CAFE! IN EAST NARUHATA!
I WORK THERE, YOU SEE.
THIS LITTLE GUY'S A PART-TIMER.
AND I'M THE MANAGER.

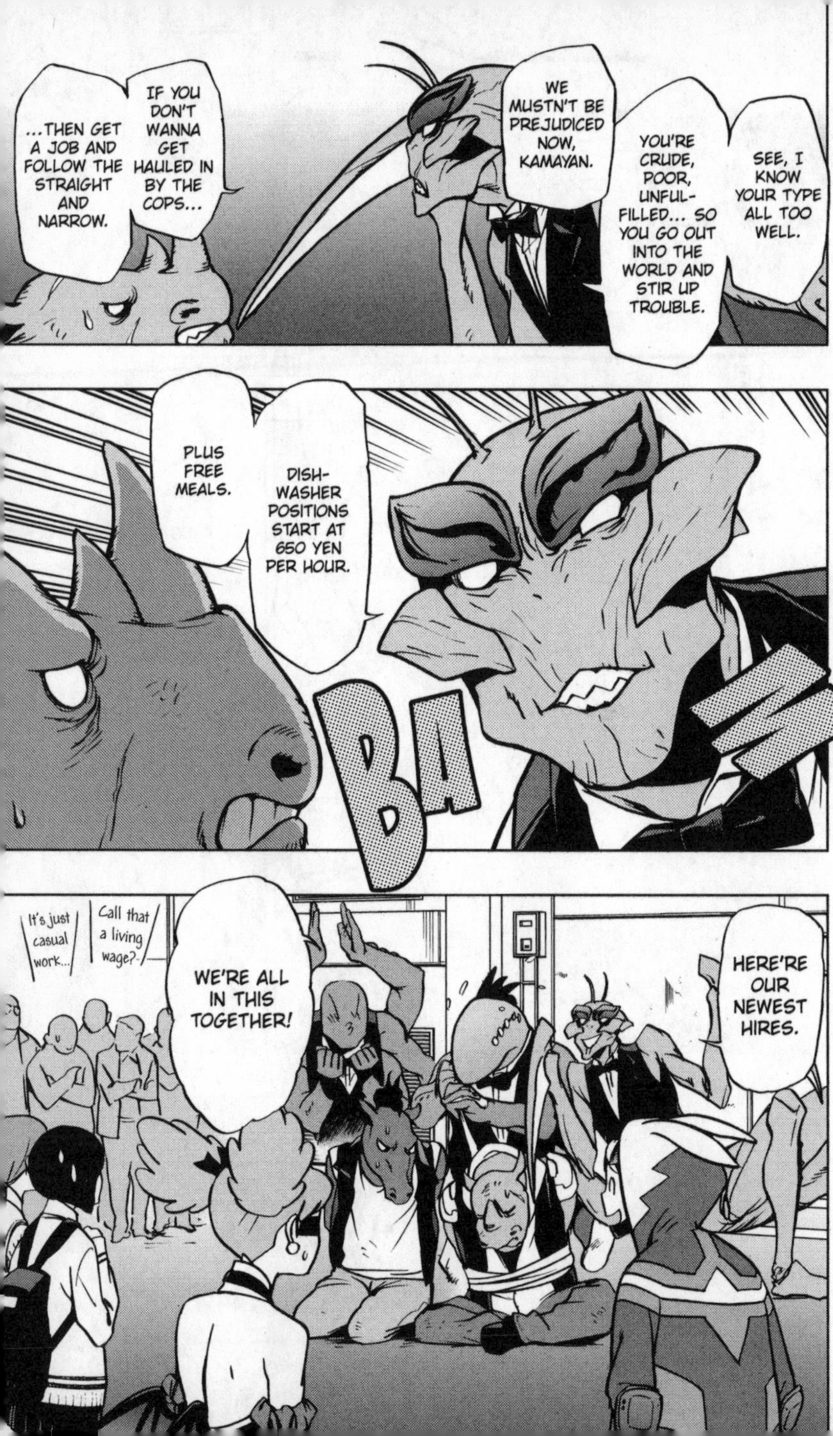
SEE, I KNOW YOUR TYPE ALL TOO WELL.
YOU'RE CRUDE, POOR, UNFUL-FILLED... SO YOU GO OUT INTO THE WORLD AND STIR UP TROUBLE.
WE MUSTN'T BE PREJUDICED NOW, KAMAYAN.
IF YOU DON'T WANNA GET HAULED IN BY THE COPS...
...THEN GET A JOB AND FOLLOW THE STRAIGHT AND NARROW.
DISH-WASHER POSITIONS START AT 650 YEN PER HOUR.
PLUS FREE MEALS.
BAM
HERE'RE OUR NEWEST HIRES.
WE'RE ALL IN THIS TOGETHER!
Call that a living wage?
It's just casual work...

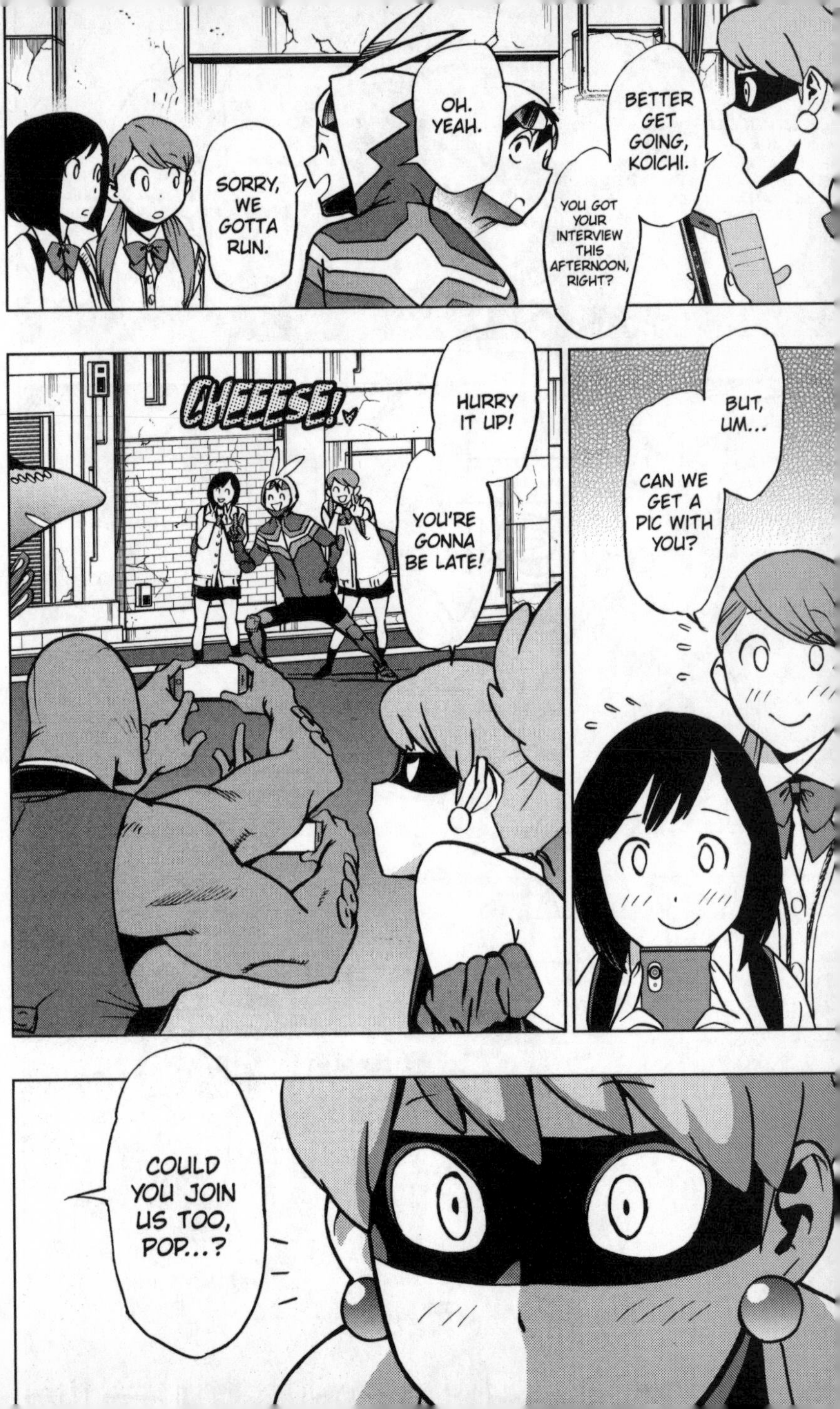
BETTER GET GOING, KOICHI.
YOU GOT YOUR INTERVIEW THIS AFTERNOON, RIGHT?
OH. YEAH.
SORRY, WE GOTTA RUN.
BUT, UM...
CAN WE GET A PIC WITH YOU?
HURRY IT UP!
YOU'RE GONNA BE LATE!
CHEEESE!
COULD YOU JOIN US TOO, POP...?

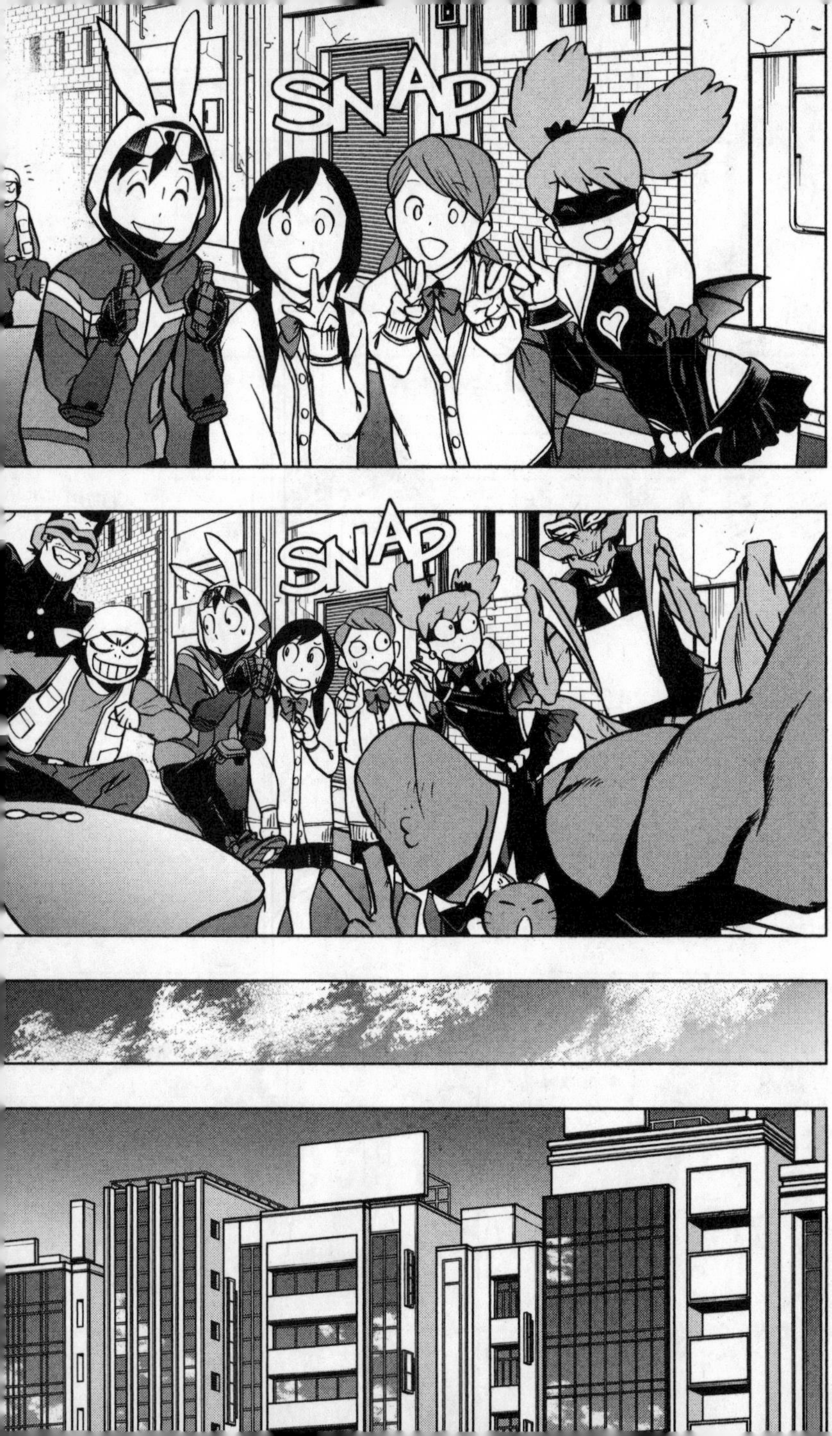
SNAP
SNAP

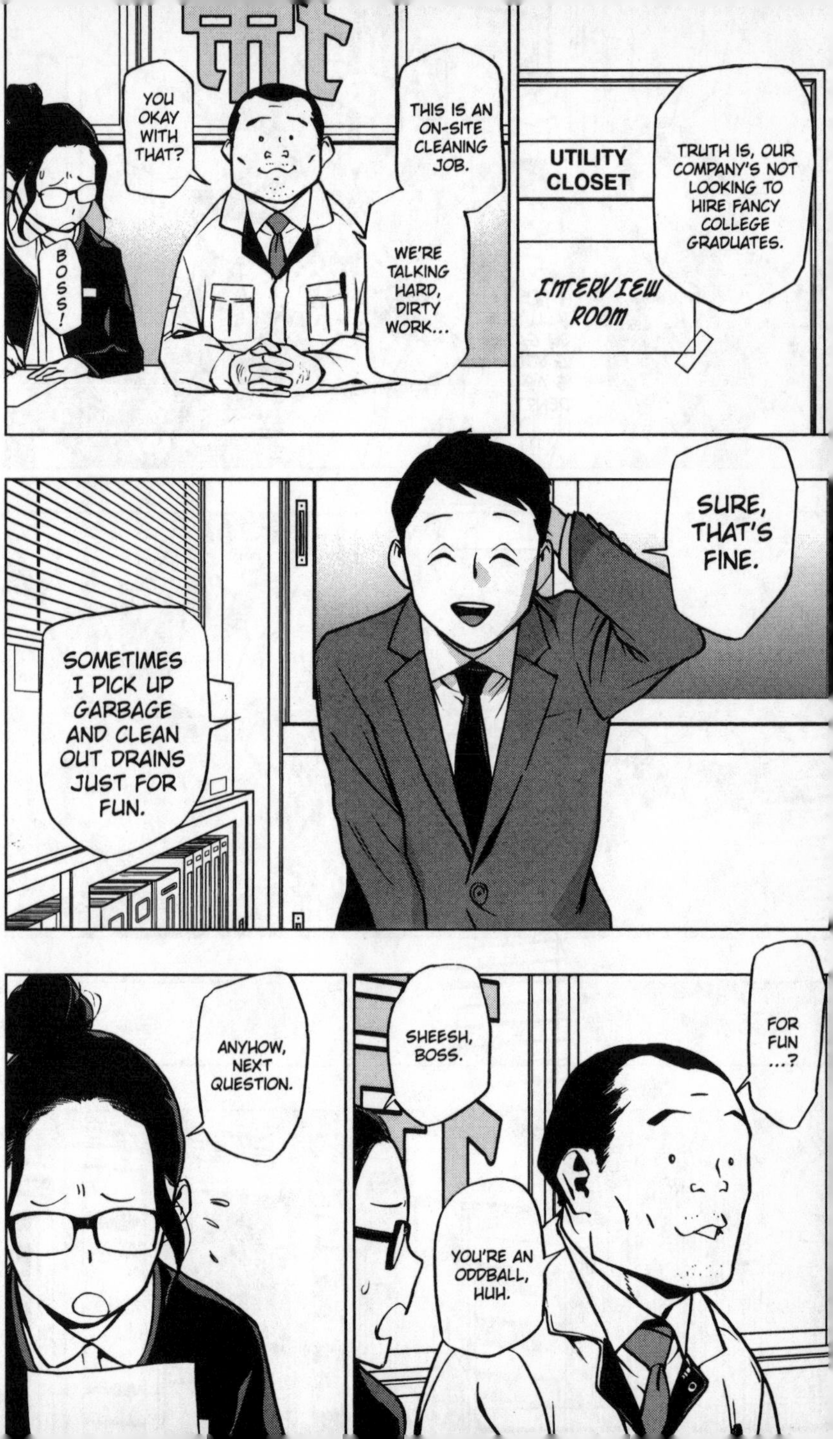
TRUTH IS, OUR COMPANY'S NOT LOOKING TO HIRE FANCY COLLEGE GRADUATES.
UTILITY CLOSET
INTERVIEW ROOM
THIS IS AN ON-SITE CLEANING JOB.
WE'RE TALKING HARD, DIRTY WORK...
YOU OKAY WITH THAT?
BOSS!
SURE, THAT'S FINE.
SOMETIMES I PICK UP GARBAGE AND CLEAN OUT DRAINS JUST FOR FUN.
FOR FUN ...?
SHEESH, BOSS.
YOU'RE AN ODDBALL, HUH.
ANYHOW, NEXT QUESTION.

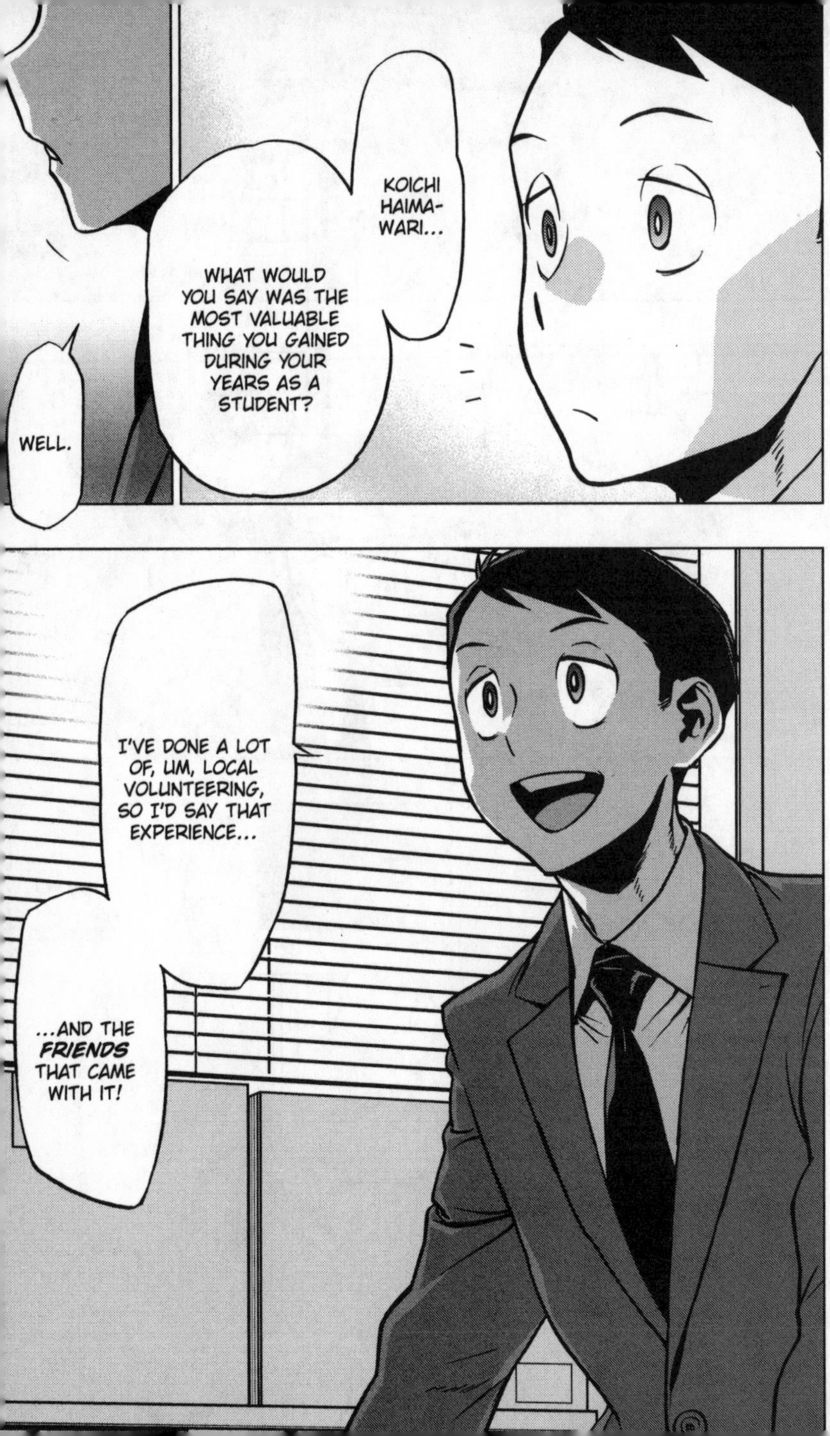
KOICHI HAIMA-WARI...
WHAT WOULD YOU SAY WAS THE MOST VALUABLE THING YOU GAINED DURING YOUR YEARS AS A STUDENT?
WELL.
I'VE DONE A LOT OF, UM, LOCAL VOLUNTEERING, SO I'D SAY THAT EXPERIENCE...
...AND THE *FRIENDS* THAT CAME WITH IT!

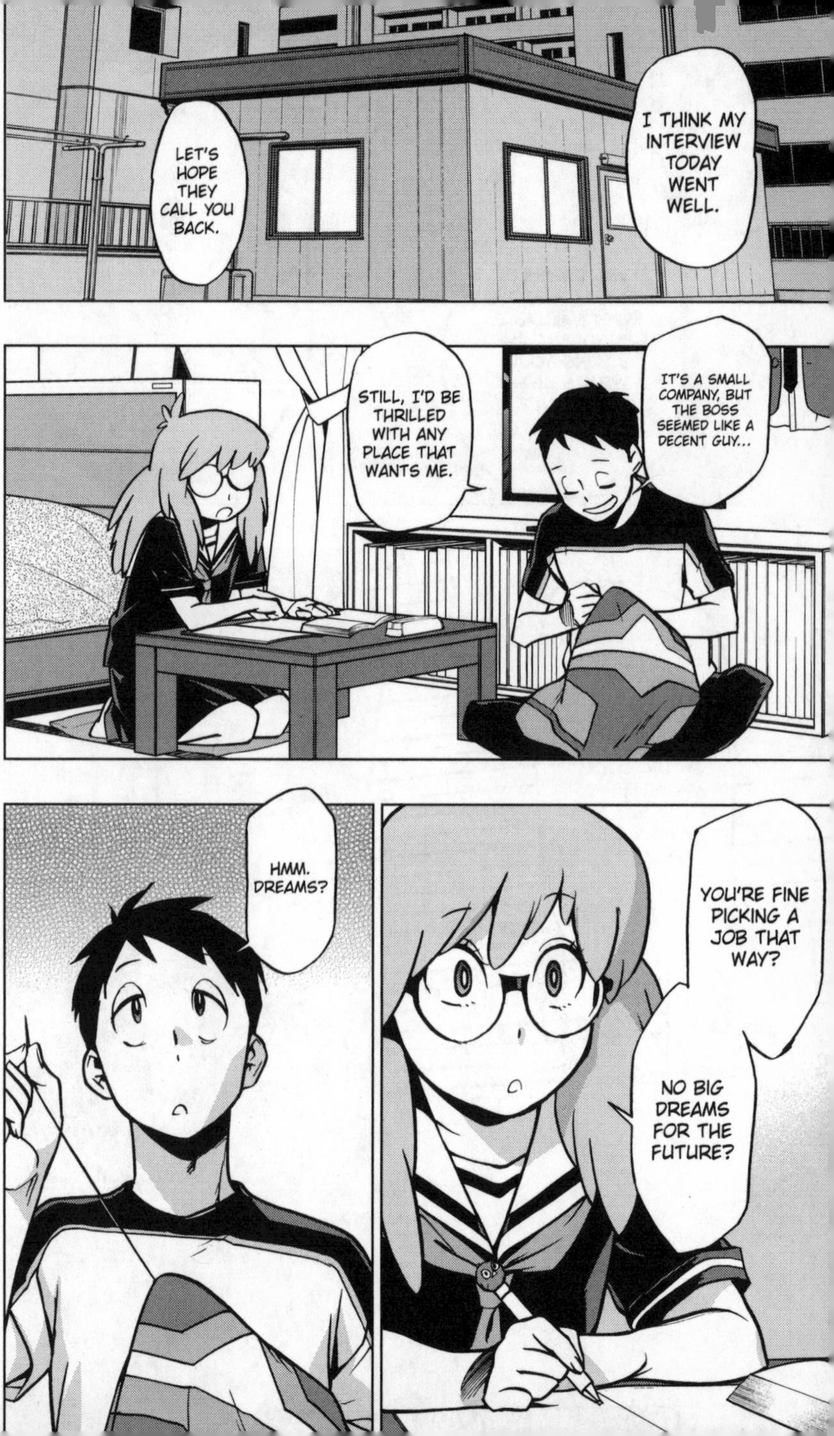
I THINK MY INTERVIEW TODAY WENT WELL.
LET'S HOPE THEY CALL YOU BACK.
IT'S A SMALL COMPANY, BUT THE BOSS SEEMED LIKE A DECENT GUY...
STILL, I'D BE THRILLED WITH ANY PLACE THAT WANTS ME.
YOU'RE FINE PICKING A JOB THAT WAY?
NO BIG DREAMS FOR THE FUTURE?
HMM. DREAMS?

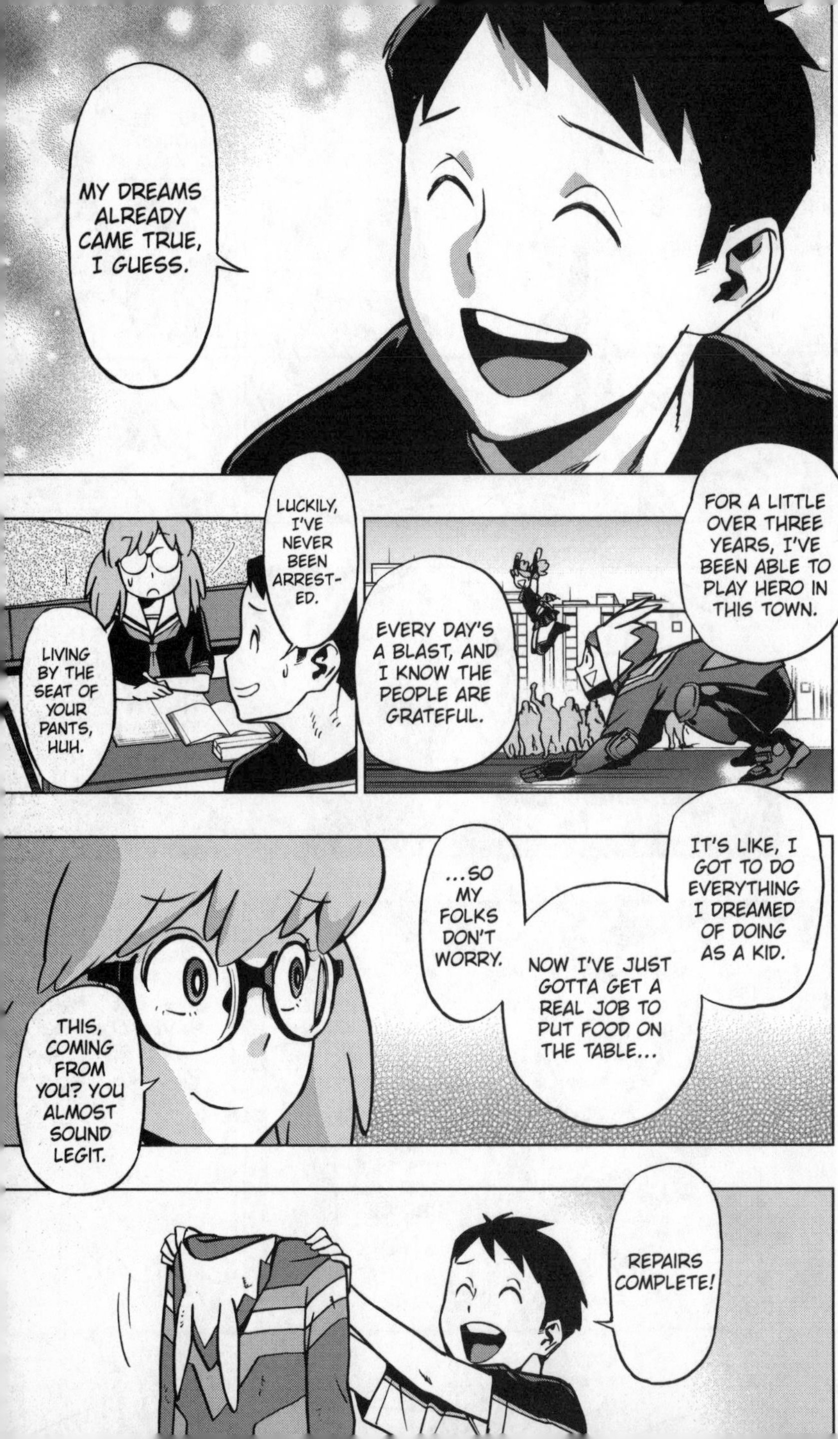
MY DREAMS ALREADY CAME TRUE, I GUESS.
FOR A LITTLE OVER THREE YEARS, I'VE BEEN ABLE TO PLAY HERO IN THIS TOWN.
EVERY DAY'S A BLAST, AND I KNOW THE PEOPLE ARE GRATEFUL.
LUCKILY, I'VE NEVER BEEN ARREST-ED.
LIVING BY THE SEAT OF YOUR PANTS, HUH.
IT'S LIKE, I GOT TO DO EVERYTHING I DREAMED OF DOING AS A KID.
NOW I'VE JUST GOTTA GET A REAL JOB TO PUT FOOD ON THE TABLE...
...SO MY FOLKS DON'T WORRY.
THIS, COMING FROM YOU? YOU ALMOST SOUND LEGIT.
REPAIRS COMPLETE!

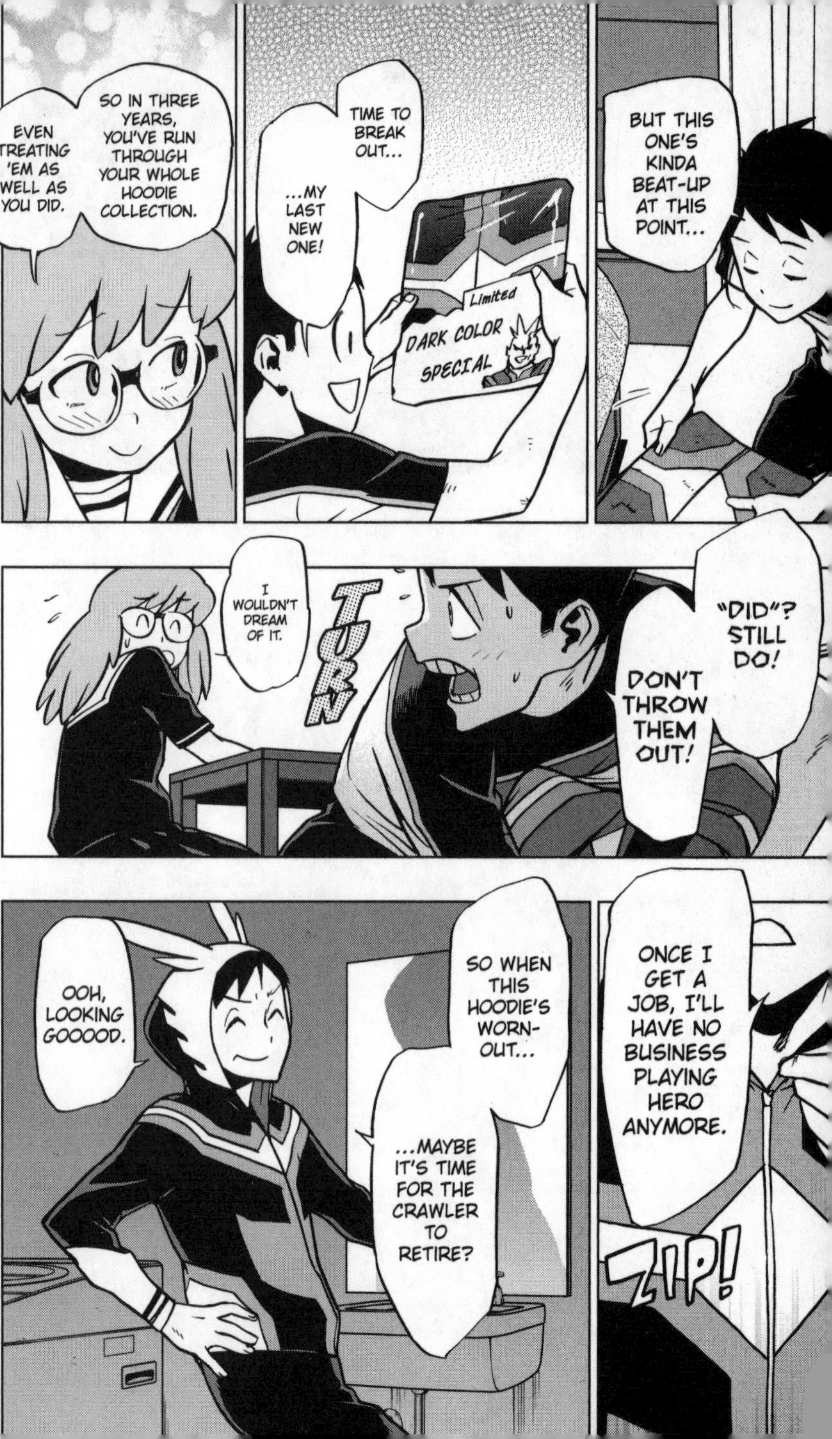
BUT THIS ONE'S KINDA BEAT-UP AT THIS POINT...
TIME TO BREAK OUT...
...MY LAST NEW ONE!
Limited DARK COLOR SPECIAL
SO IN THREE YEARS, YOU'VE RUN THROUGH YOUR WHOLE HOODIE COLLECTION.
EVEN TREATING 'EM AS WELL AS YOU DID.
"DID"? STILL DO!
DON'T THROW THEM OUT!
TURN
I WOULDN'T DREAM OF IT.
ONCE I GET A JOB, I'LL HAVE NO BUSINESS PLAYING HERO ANYMORE.
ZIP!
SO WHEN THIS HOODIE'S WORN-OUT...
...MAYBE IT'S TIME FOR THE CRAWLER TO RETIRE?
OOH, LOOKING GOOOOD.

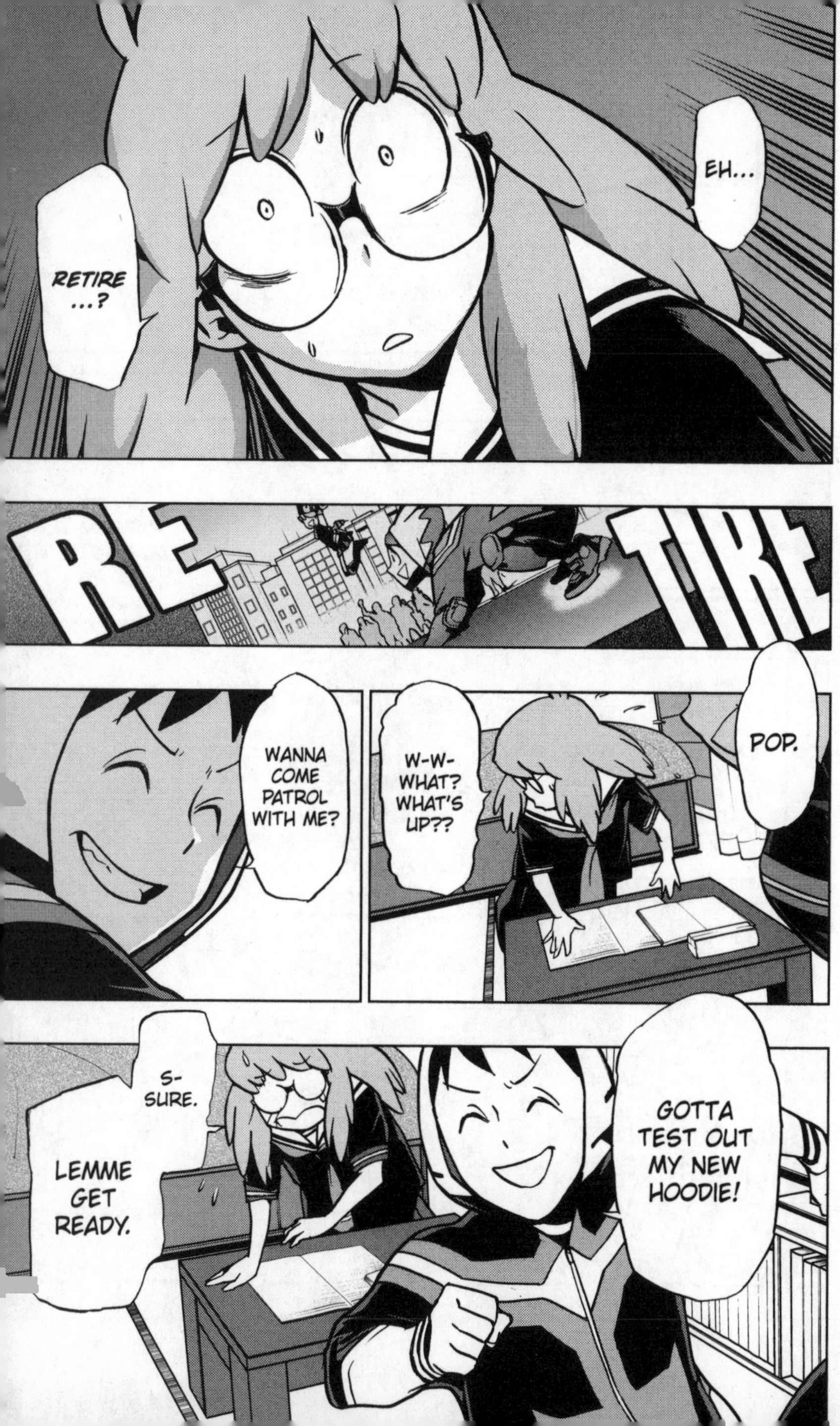
EH...
RETIRE ...?
RE TIRE
POP.
W-W-WHAT? WHAT'S UP??
WANNA COME PATROL WITH ME?
GOTTA TEST OUT MY NEW HOODIE!
S-SURE.
LEMME GET READY.

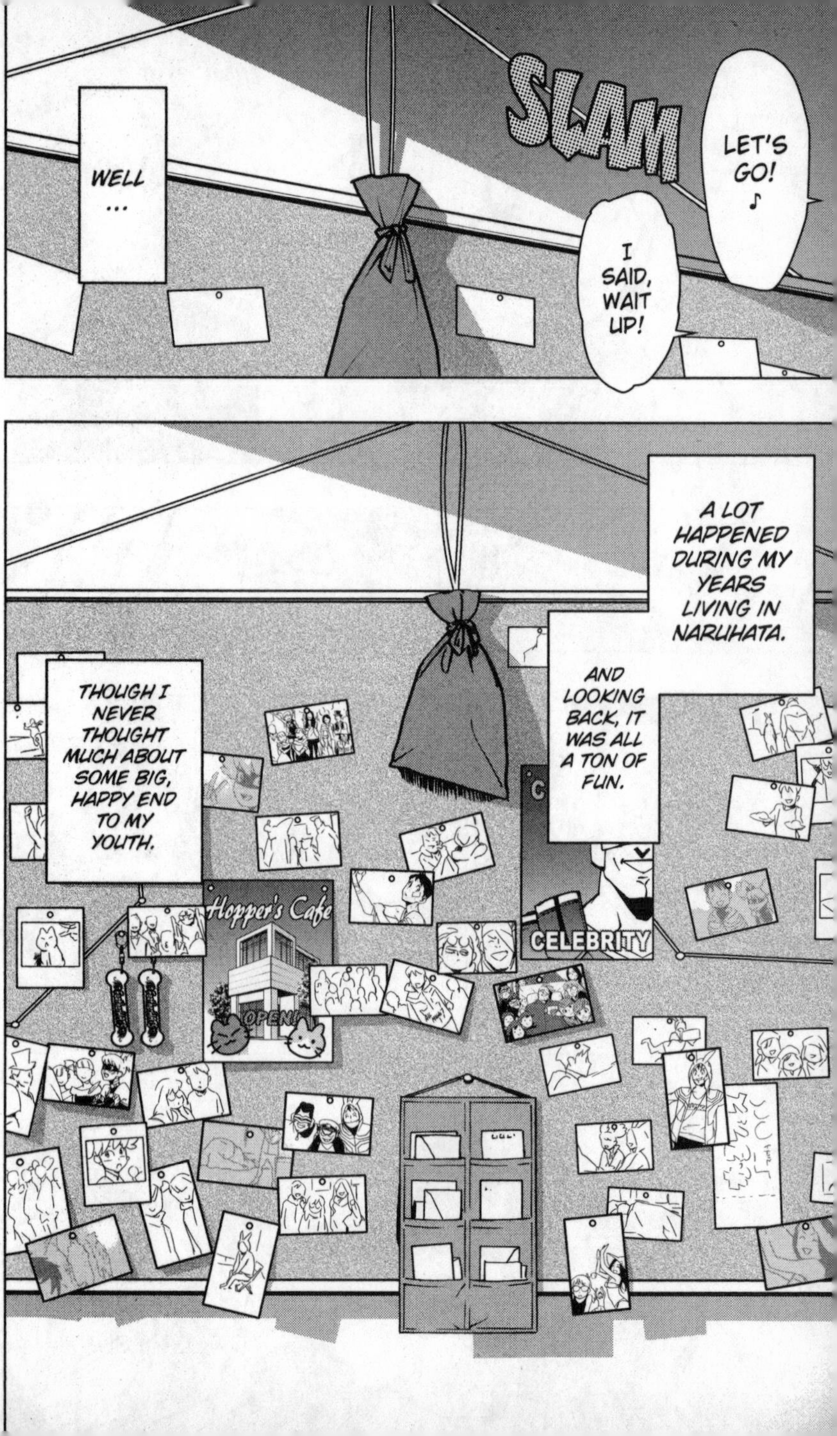
LET'S GO! ♪
SLAM
I SAID, WAIT UP!
WELL...
A LOT HAPPENED DURING MY YEARS LIVING IN NARUHATA.
AND LOOKING BACK, IT WAS ALL A TON OF FUN.
CELEBRITY
THOUGH I NEVER THOUGHT MUCH ABOUT SOME BIG, HAPPY END TO MY YOUTH.
Hopper's Cafe
OPEN!

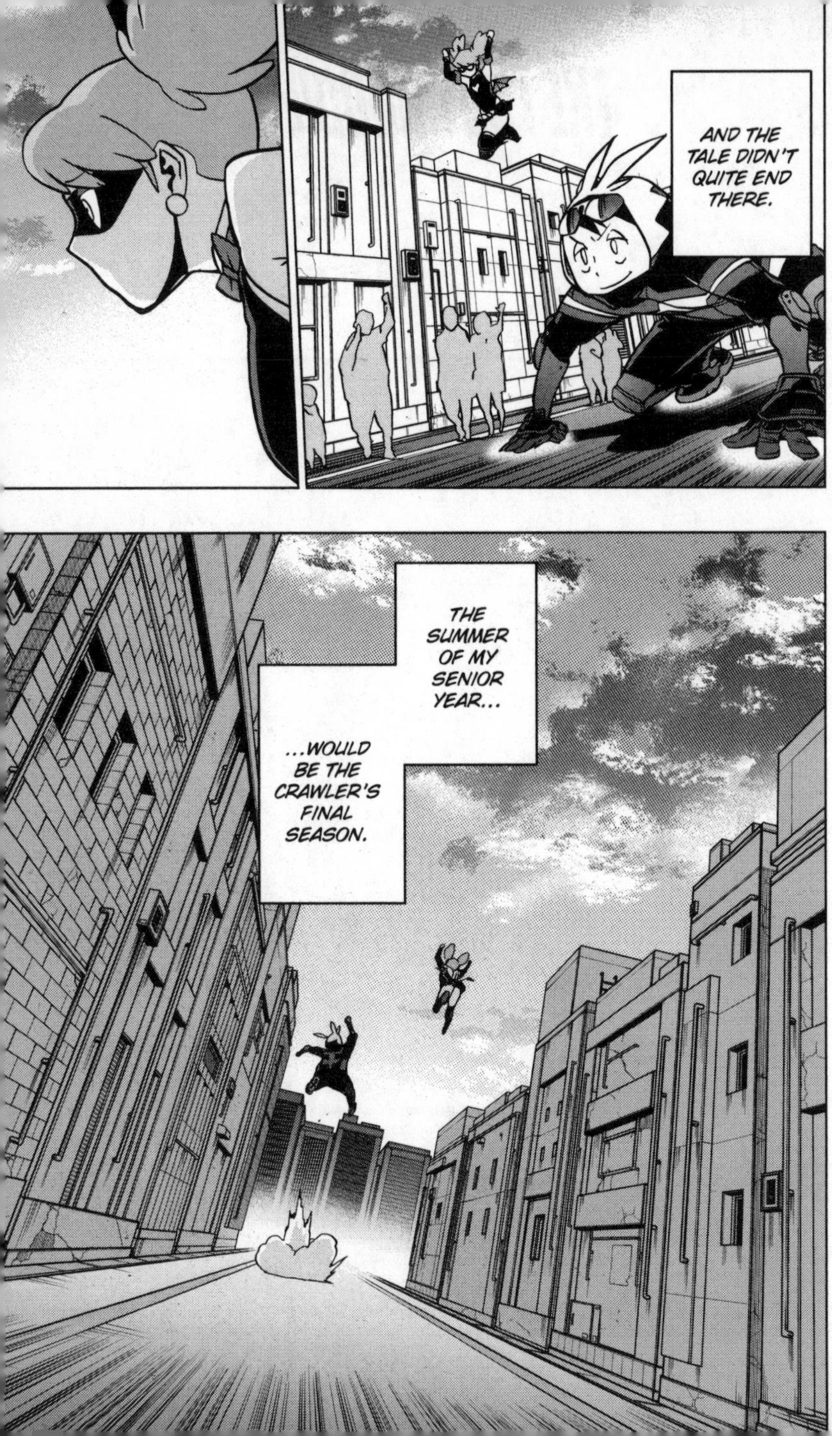
AND THE TALE DIDN'T QUITE END THERE.
THE SUMMER OF MY SENIOR YEAR...
...WOULD BE THE CRAWLER'S FINAL SEASON.

THE LAST HOODIE

THE ROUGH DESIGN

Koichi
Dark-colored
hoodie

BEHIND THE SCENES

It's a new version of the old hoodie, to give off that fresh and shiny feeling of a new season. I wanted it darker to make him look a little stronger and to hint at the serious story developments to come. But also, from a narrative standpoint, I wanted to make the distinction between the hoodies up to now (with the All Might color scheme) versus this final dark one. That said, it's not like he's literally been wearing just a single hoodie all along, so I wanted the final hoodie to look mostly like the standard ones.

All these minute differences also play into the "only a fanatic could even tell" aspect, as if Koichi might declare, "They're totally different!" That's also kind of fun.

—Furuhashi

Since it's been three whole years since the start of the story, I designed this hoping it would give Koichi a slight air of reliability—but only a little bit. Fine-tuning is tricky.

—Betten

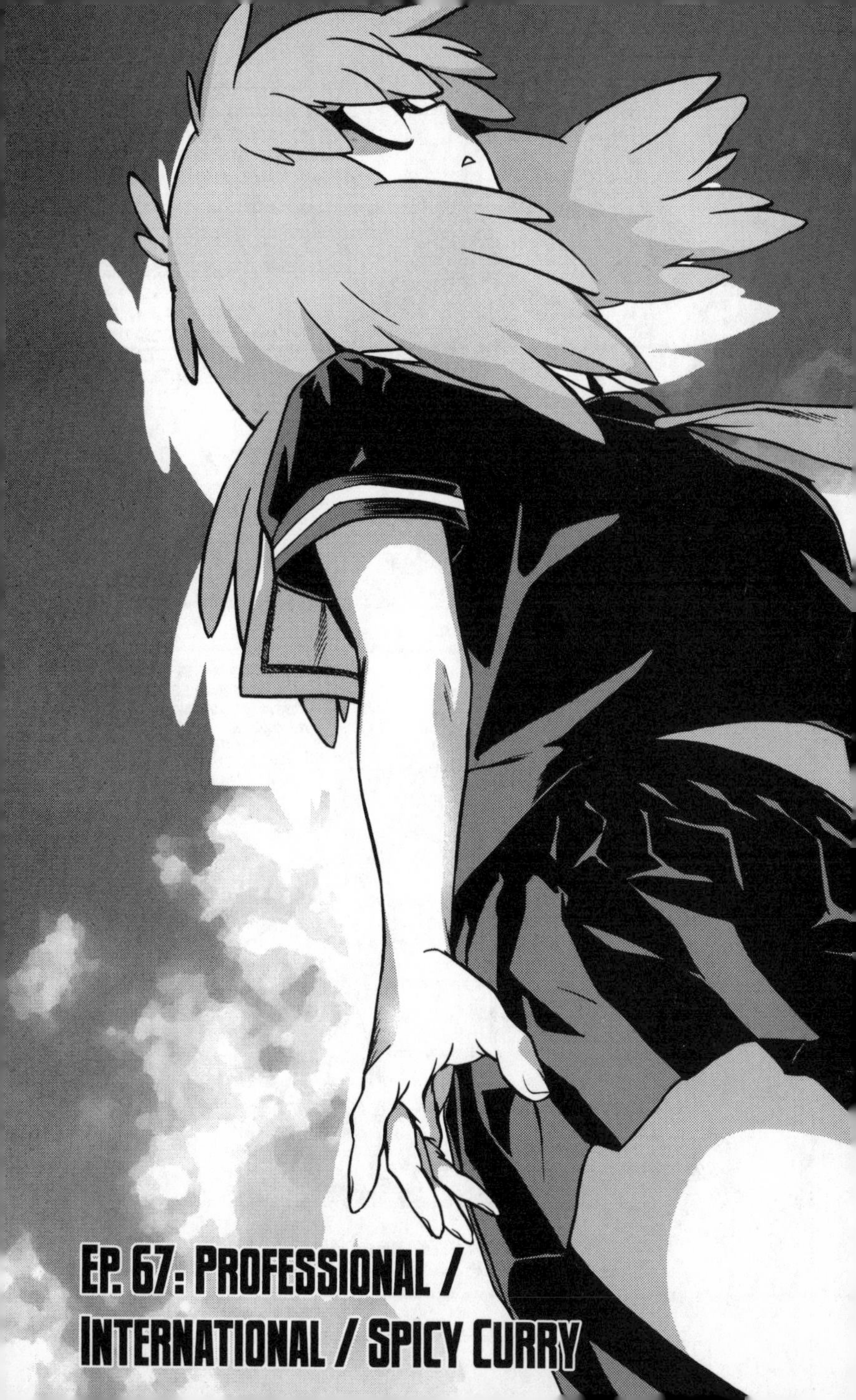
Ep. 67: Professional /
International / Spicy Curry

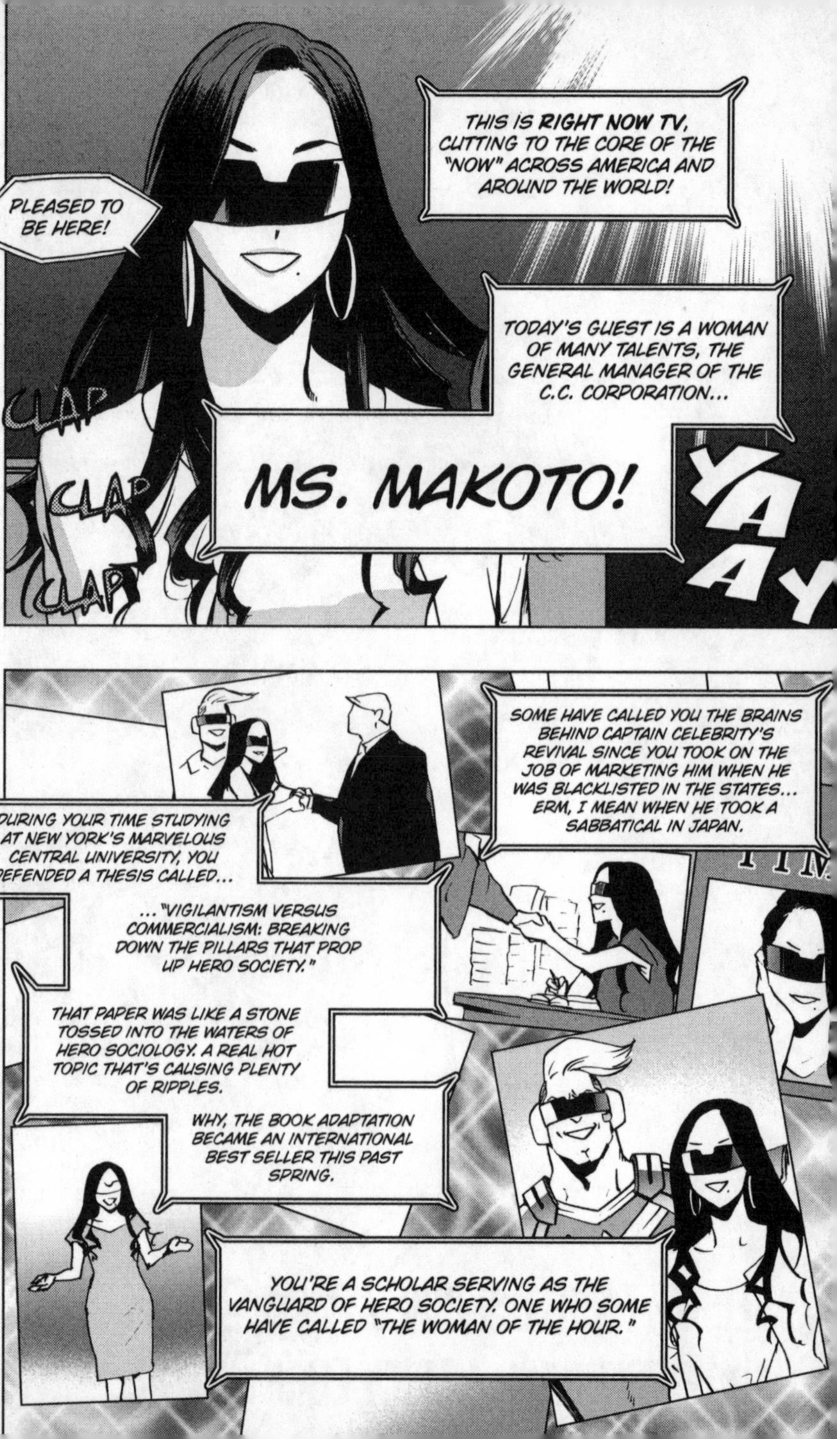
THIS IS **RIGHT NOW TV**, CUTTING TO THE CORE OF THE "NOW" ACROSS AMERICA AND AROUND THE WORLD!
PLEASED TO BE HERE!
TODAY'S GUEST IS A WOMAN OF MANY TALENTS, THE GENERAL MANAGER OF THE C.C. CORPORATION...
MS. MAKOTO!
YAAAY
CLAP
CLAP
CLAP
SOME HAVE CALLED YOU THE BRAINS BEHIND CAPTAIN CELEBRITY'S REVIVAL SINCE YOU TOOK ON THE JOB OF MARKETING HIM WHEN HE WAS BLACKLISTED IN THE STATES... ERM, I MEAN WHEN HE TOOK A SABBATICAL IN JAPAN.
DURING YOUR TIME STUDYING AT NEW YORK'S MARVELOUS CENTRAL UNIVERSITY, YOU DEFENDED A THESIS CALLED...
..."VIGILANTISM VERSUS COMMERCIALISM: BREAKING DOWN THE PILLARS THAT PROP UP HERO SOCIETY."
THAT PAPER WAS LIKE A STONE TOSSED INTO THE WATERS OF HERO SOCIOLOGY. A REAL HOT TOPIC THAT'S CAUSING PLENTY OF RIPPLES.
WHY, THE BOOK ADAPTATION BECAME AN INTERNATIONAL BEST SELLER THIS PAST SPRING.
YOU'RE A SCHOLAR SERVING AS THE VANGUARD OF HERO SOCIETY. ONE WHO SOME HAVE CALLED "THE WOMAN OF THE HOUR."

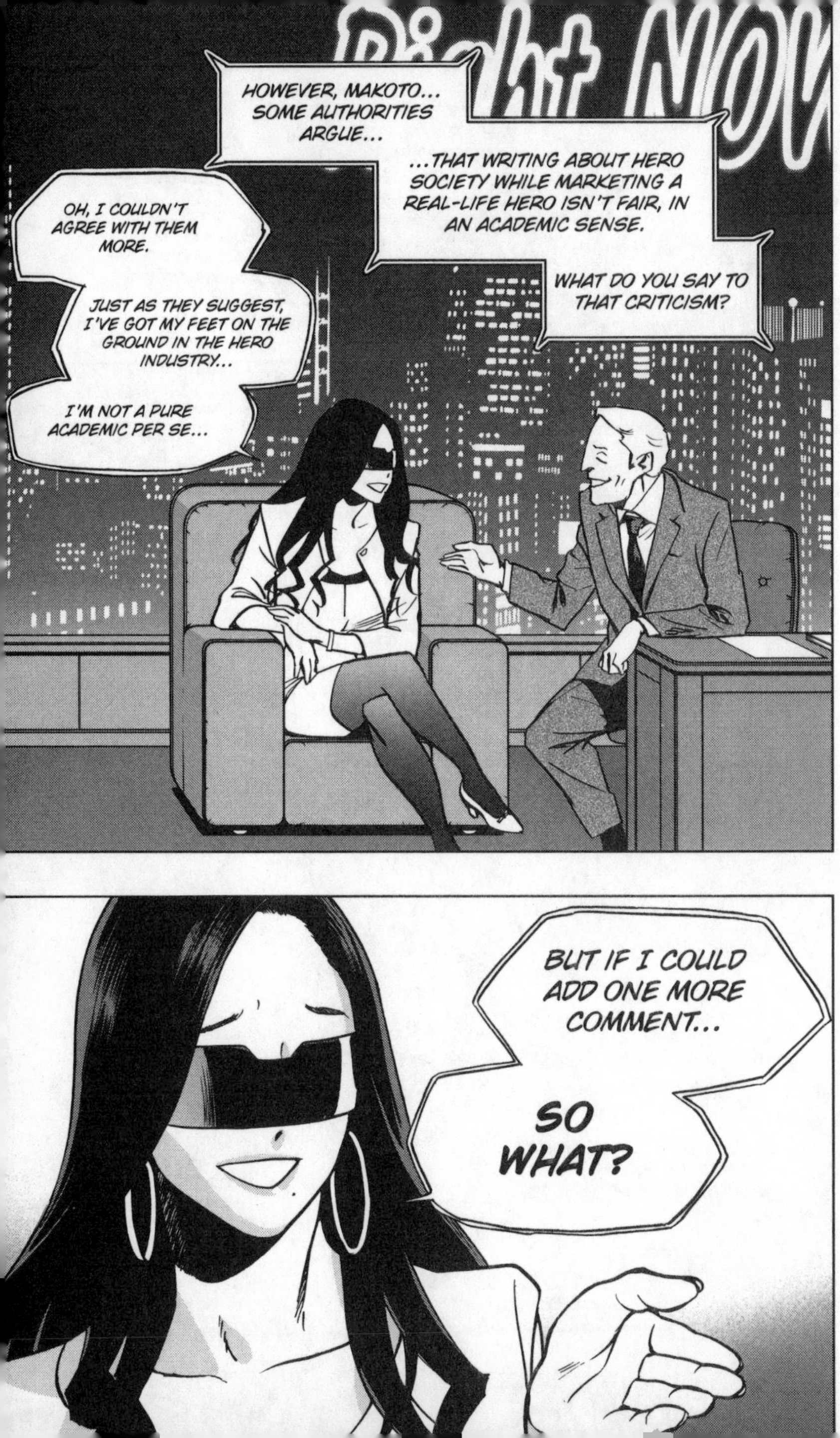
HOWEVER, MAKOTO... SOME AUTHORITIES ARGUE...
...THAT WRITING ABOUT HERO SOCIETY WHILE MARKETING A REAL-LIFE HERO ISN'T FAIR, IN AN ACADEMIC SENSE.
WHAT DO YOU SAY TO THAT CRITICISM?
OH, I COULDN'T AGREE WITH THEM MORE.
JUST AS THEY SUGGEST, I'VE GOT MY FEET ON THE GROUND IN THE HERO INDUSTRY...
I'M NOT A PURE ACADEMIC PER SE...
BUT IF I COULD ADD ONE MORE COMMENT...
SO WHAT?

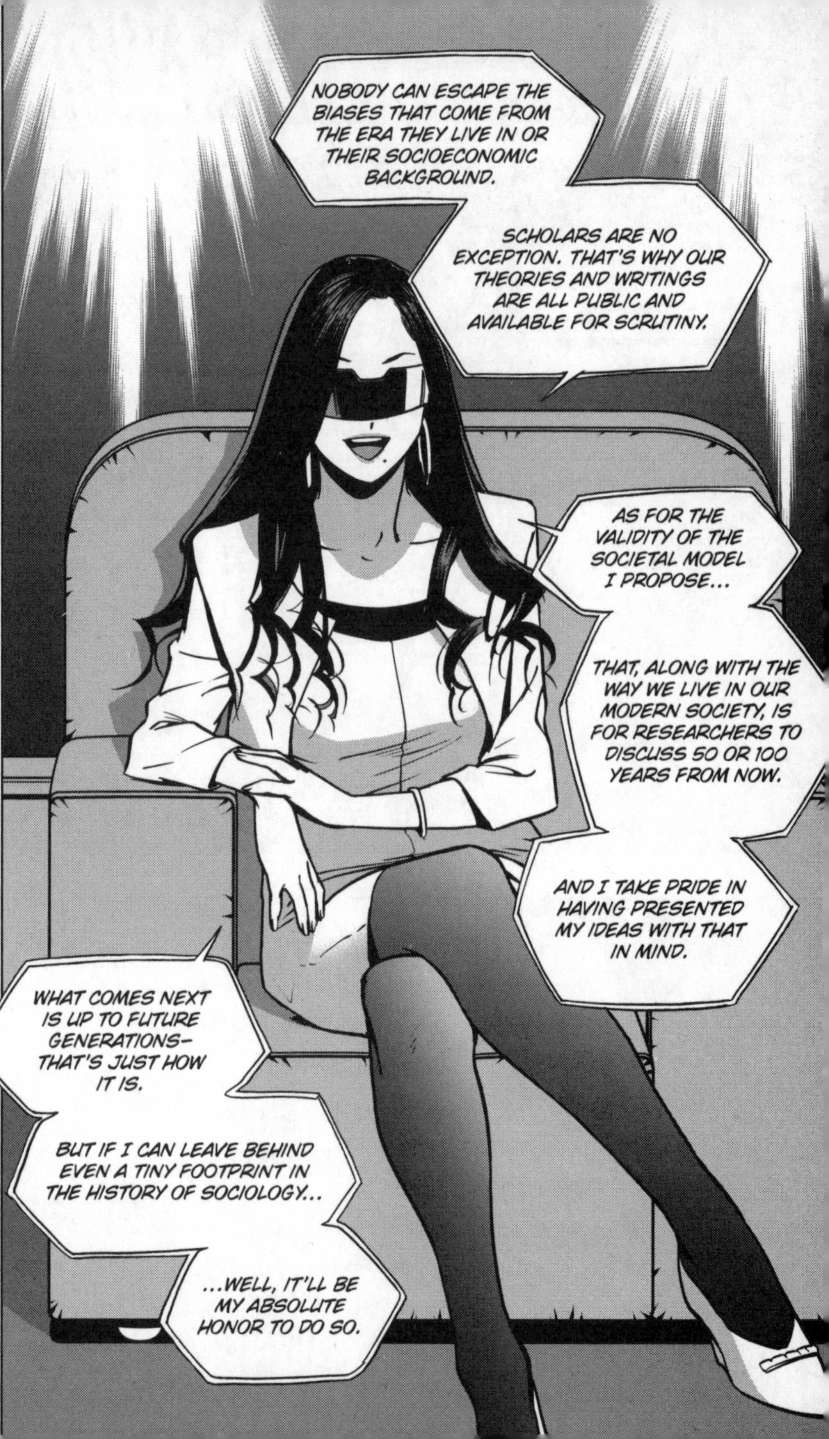
NOBODY CAN ESCAPE THE BIASES THAT COME FROM THE ERA THEY LIVE IN OR THEIR SOCIOECONOMIC BACKGROUND.
SCHOLARS ARE NO EXCEPTION. THAT'S WHY OUR THEORIES AND WRITINGS ARE ALL PUBLIC AND AVAILABLE FOR SCRUTINY.
AS FOR THE VALIDITY OF THE SOCIETAL MODEL I PROPOSE...
THAT, ALONG WITH THE WAY WE LIVE IN OUR MODERN SOCIETY, IS FOR RESEARCHERS TO DISCUSS 50 OR 100 YEARS FROM NOW.
AND I TAKE PRIDE IN HAVING PRESENTED MY IDEAS WITH THAT IN MIND.
WHAT COMES NEXT IS UP TO FUTURE GENERATIONS—THAT'S JUST HOW IT IS.
BUT IF I CAN LEAVE BEHIND EVEN A TINY FOOTPRINT IN THE HISTORY OF SOCIOLOGY...
...WELL, IT'LL BE MY ABSOLUTE HONOR TO DO SO.

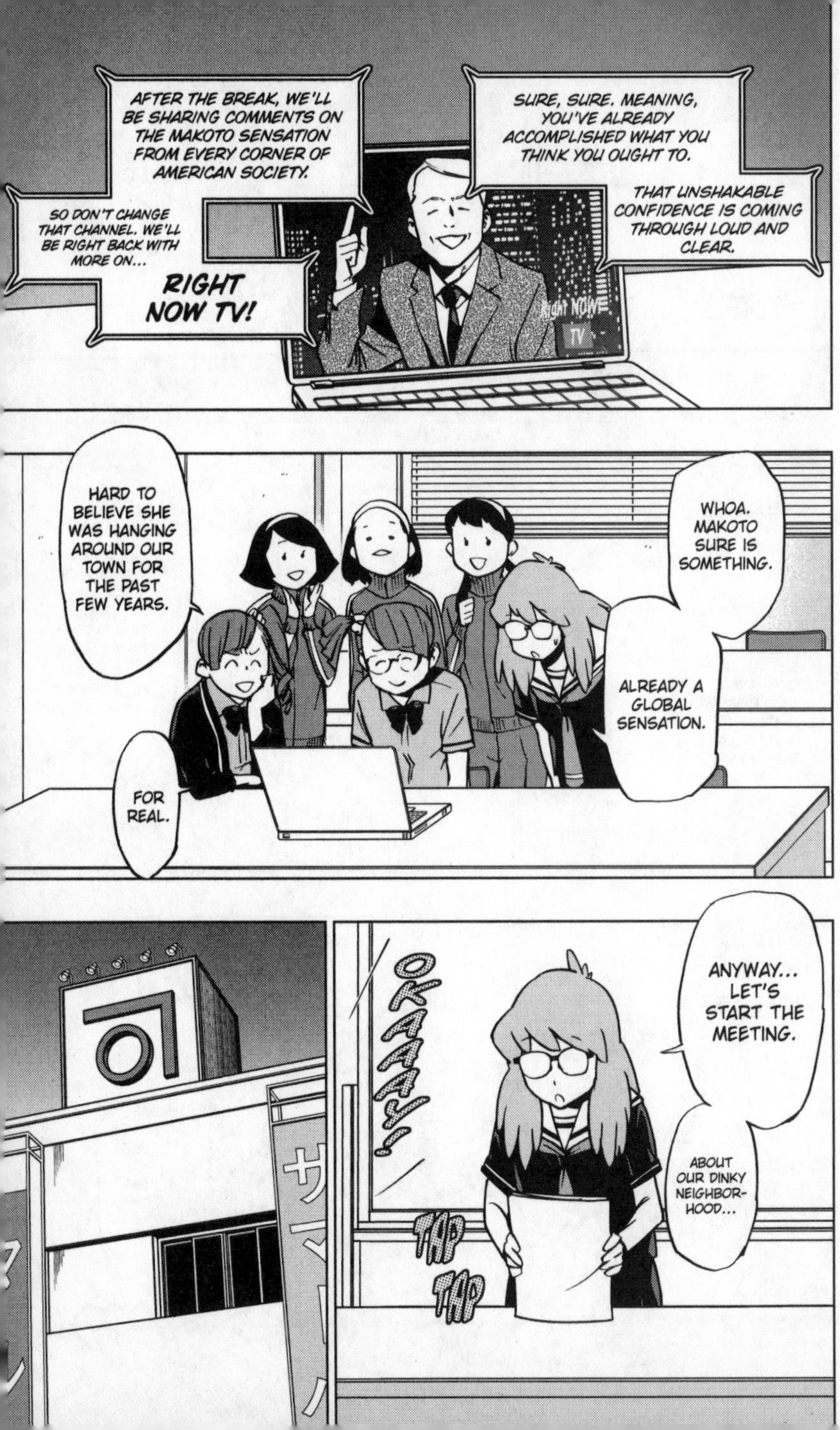
SURE, SURE. MEANING, YOU'VE ALREADY ACCOMPLISHED WHAT YOU THINK YOU OUGHT TO.
THAT UNSHAKABLE CONFIDENCE IS COMING THROUGH LOUD AND CLEAR.
AFTER THE BREAK, WE'LL BE SHARING COMMENTS ON THE MAKOTO SENSATION FROM EVERY CORNER OF AMERICAN SOCIETY.
SO DON'T CHANGE THAT CHANNEL. WE'LL BE RIGHT BACK WITH MORE ON...
RIGHT NOW TV!
Right NOW TV
WHOA. MAKOTO SURE IS SOMETHING.
ALREADY A GLOBAL SENSATION.
HARD TO BELIEVE SHE WAS HANGING AROUND OUR TOWN FOR THE PAST FEW YEARS.
FOR REAL.
ANYWAY... LET'S START THE MEETING.
ABOUT OUR DINKY NEIGHBOR-HOOD...
OKAAAY!
TAP
TAP

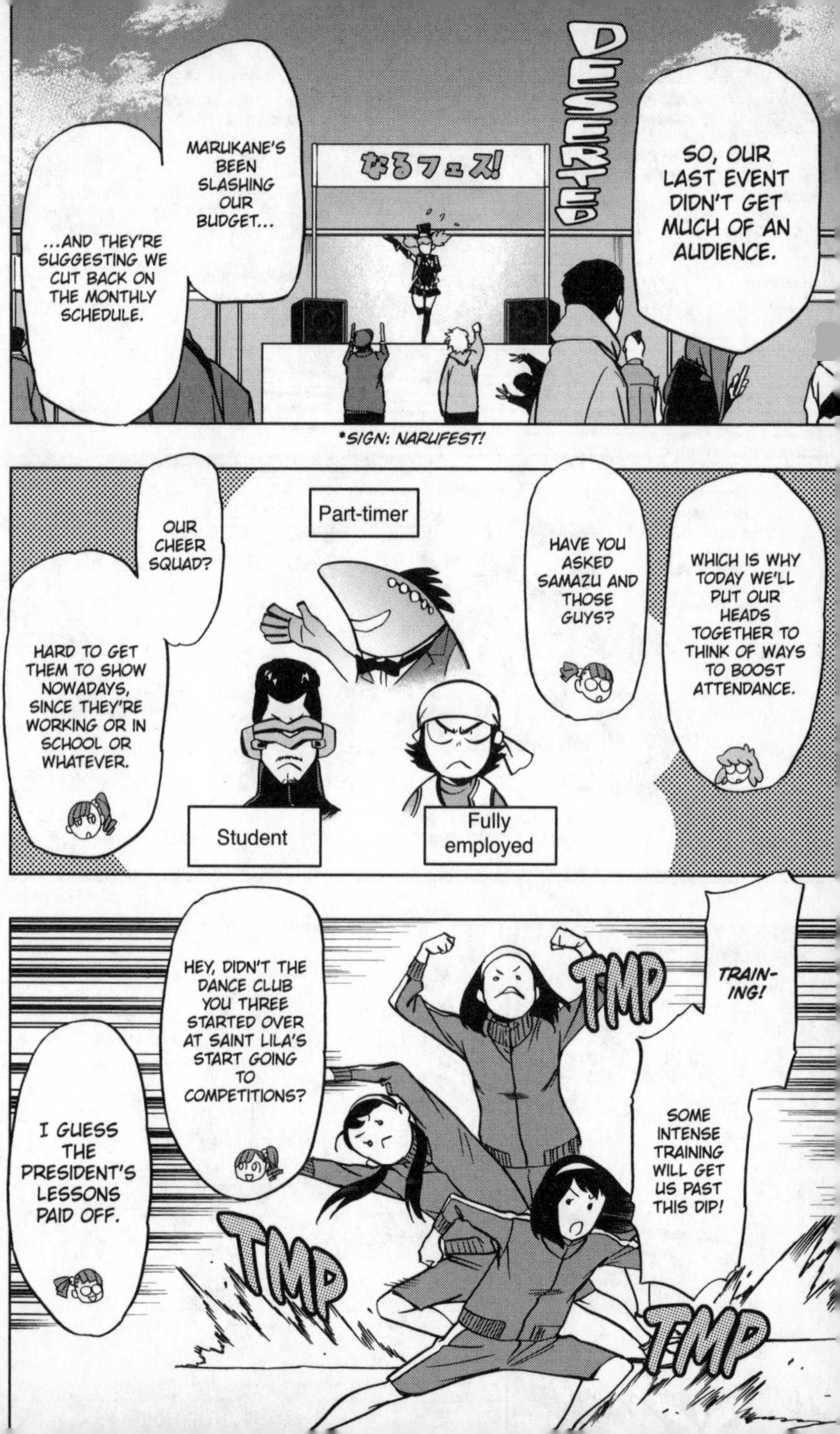
SO, OUR LAST EVENT DIDN'T GET MUCH OF AN AUDIENCE.
DESERTED
なるフェス!
MARUKANE'S BEEN SLASHING OUR BUDGET...
...AND THEY'RE SUGGESTING WE CUT BACK ON THE MONTHLY SCHEDULE.
*SIGN: NARUFEST!
WHICH IS WHY TODAY WE'LL PUT OUR HEADS TOGETHER TO THINK OF WAYS TO BOOST ATTENDANCE.
HAVE YOU ASKED SAMAZU AND THOSE GUYS?
Part-timer
OUR CHEER SQUAD?
Fully employed
Student
HARD TO GET THEM TO SHOW NOWADAYS, SINCE THEY'RE WORKING OR IN SCHOOL OR WHATEVER.
TRAIN-ING!
TMP
SOME INTENSE TRAINING WILL GET US PAST THIS DIP!
HEY, DIDN'T THE DANCE CLUB YOU THREE STARTED OVER AT SAINT LILA'S START GOING TO COMPETITIONS?
I GUESS THE PRESIDENT'S LESSONS PAID OFF.
TMP
TMP

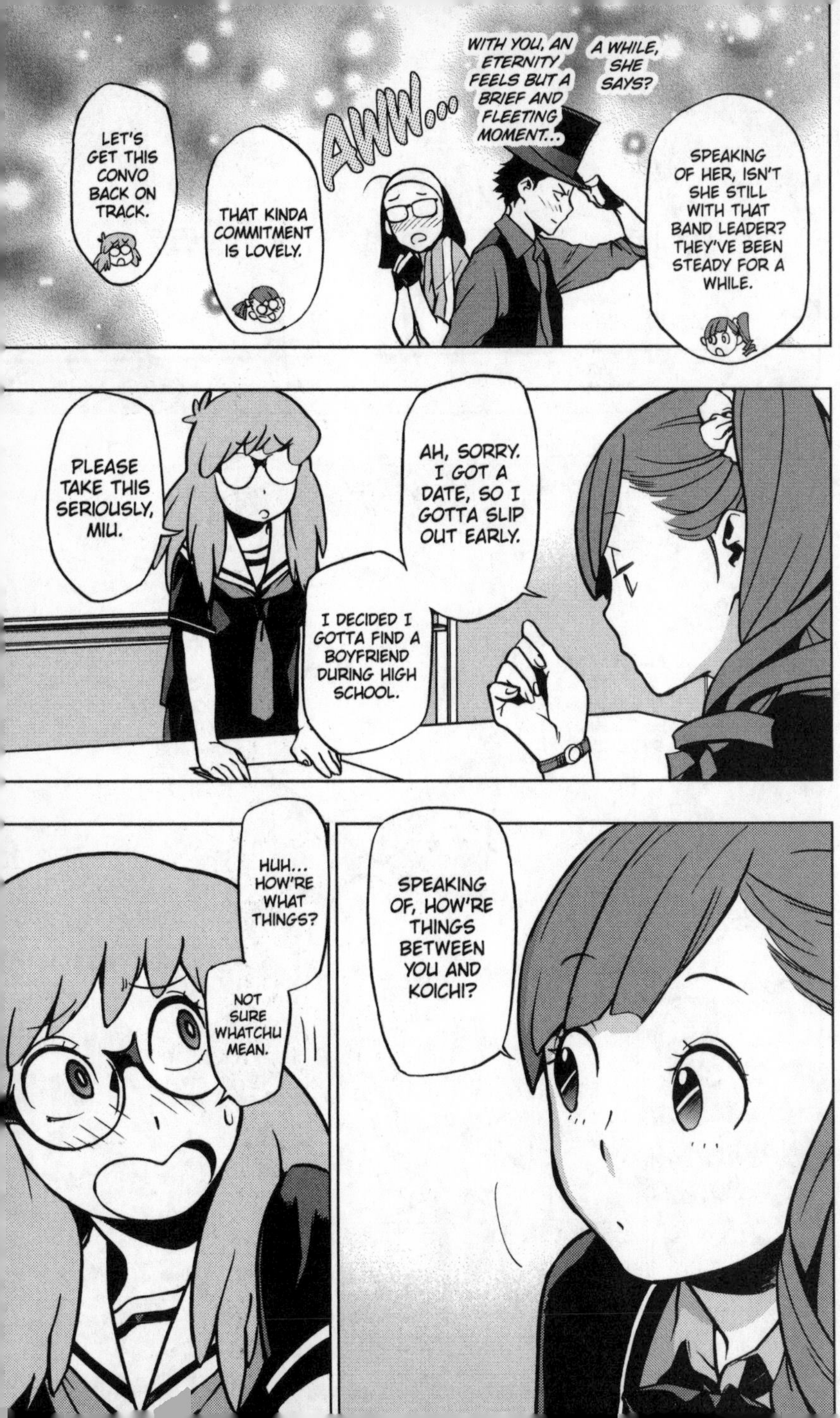
SPEAKING OF HER, ISN'T SHE STILL WITH THAT BAND LEADER? THEY'VE BEEN STEADY FOR A WHILE.
A WHILE, SHE SAYS?
WITH YOU, AN ETERNITY FEELS BUT A BRIEF AND FLEETING MOMENT...
AWW...
THAT KINDA COMMITMENT IS LOVELY.
LET'S GET THIS CONVO BACK ON TRACK.
AH, SORRY. I GOT A DATE, SO I GOTTA SLIP OUT EARLY.
I DECIDED I GOTTA FIND A BOYFRIEND DURING HIGH SCHOOL.
PLEASE TAKE THIS SERIOUSLY, MIU.
SPEAKING OF, HOW'RE THINGS BETWEEN YOU AND KOICHI?
HUH... HOW'RE WHAT THINGS?
NOT SURE WHATCHU MEAN.

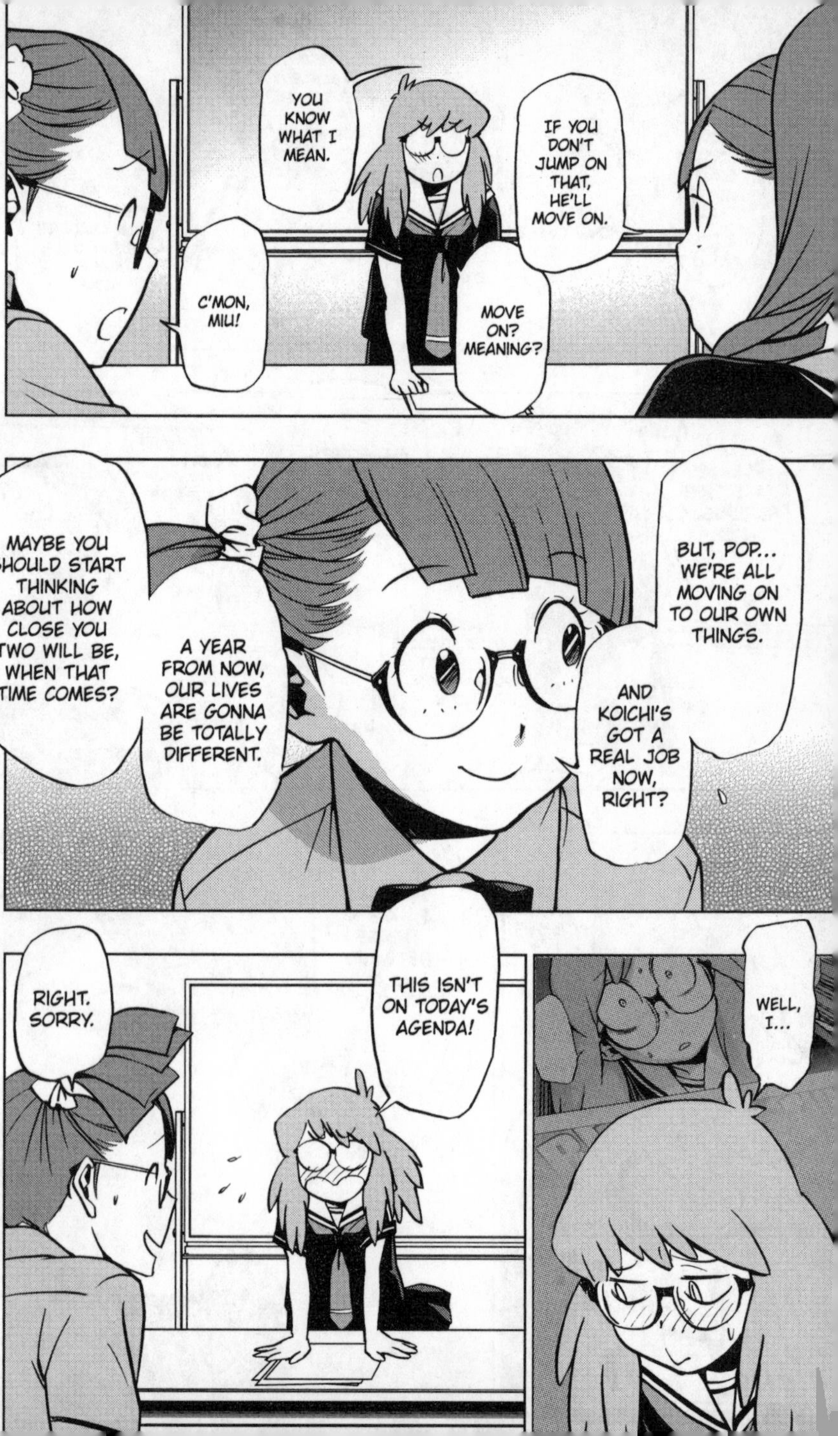
IF YOU DON'T JUMP ON THAT, HE'LL MOVE ON.
MOVE ON? MEANING?
YOU KNOW WHAT I MEAN.
C'MON, MIU!
BUT, POP... WE'RE ALL MOVING ON TO OUR OWN THINGS.
AND KOICHI'S GOT A REAL JOB NOW, RIGHT?
A YEAR FROM NOW, OUR LIVES ARE GONNA BE TOTALLY DIFFERENT.
MAYBE YOU SHOULD START THINKING ABOUT HOW CLOSE YOU TWO WILL BE, WHEN THAT TIME COMES?
WELL, I...
THIS ISN'T ON TODAY'S AGENDA!
RIGHT. SORRY.

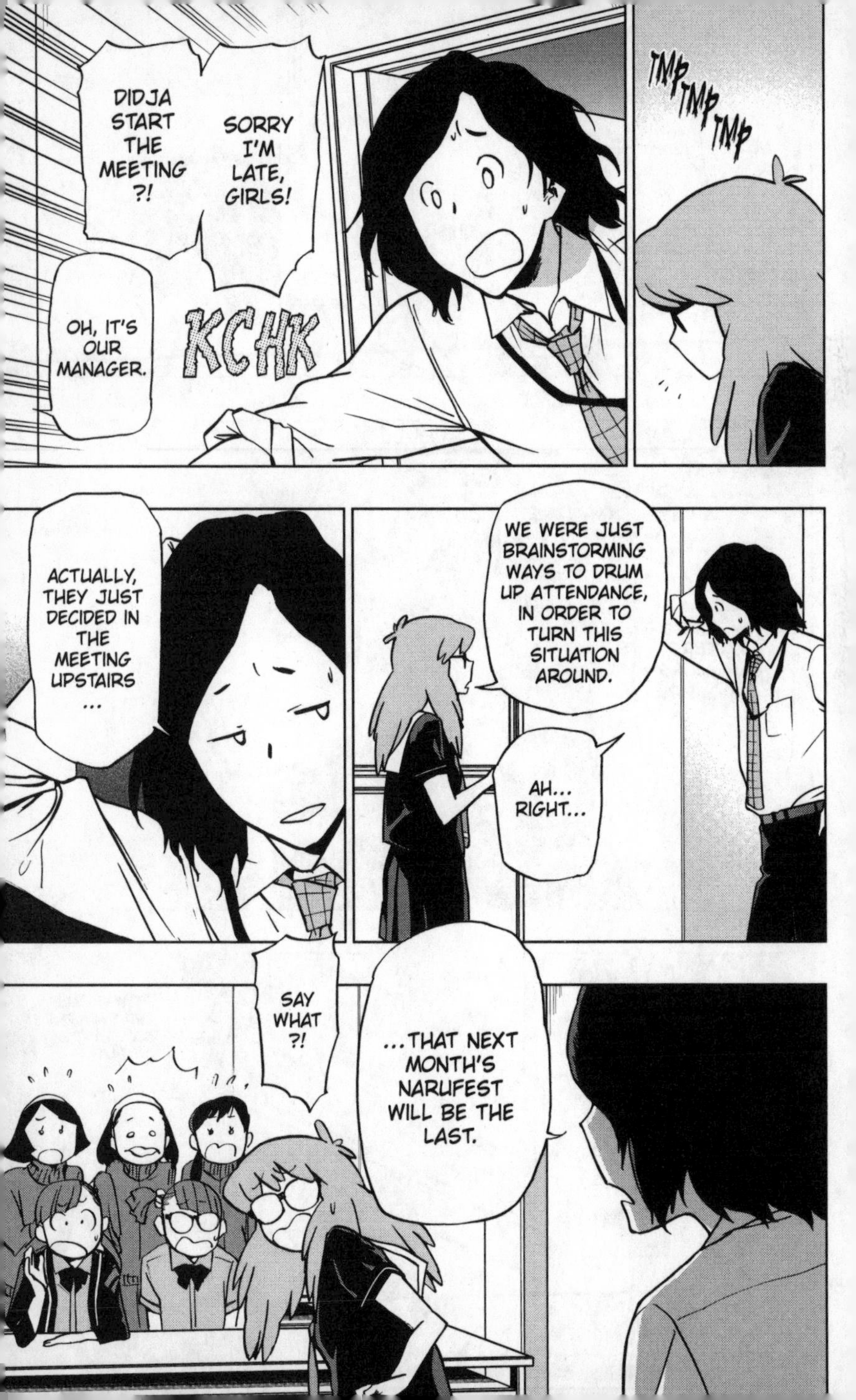
TMP TMP TMP
SORRY I'M LATE, GIRLS!
DIDJA START THE MEETING?!
KCHK
OH, IT'S OUR MANAGER.
WE WERE JUST BRAINSTORMING WAYS TO DRUM UP ATTENDANCE, IN ORDER TO TURN THIS SITUATION AROUND.
AH... RIGHT...
ACTUALLY, THEY JUST DECIDED IN THE MEETING UPSTAIRS...
...THAT NEXT MONTH'S NARUFEST WILL BE THE LAST.
SAY WHAT?!

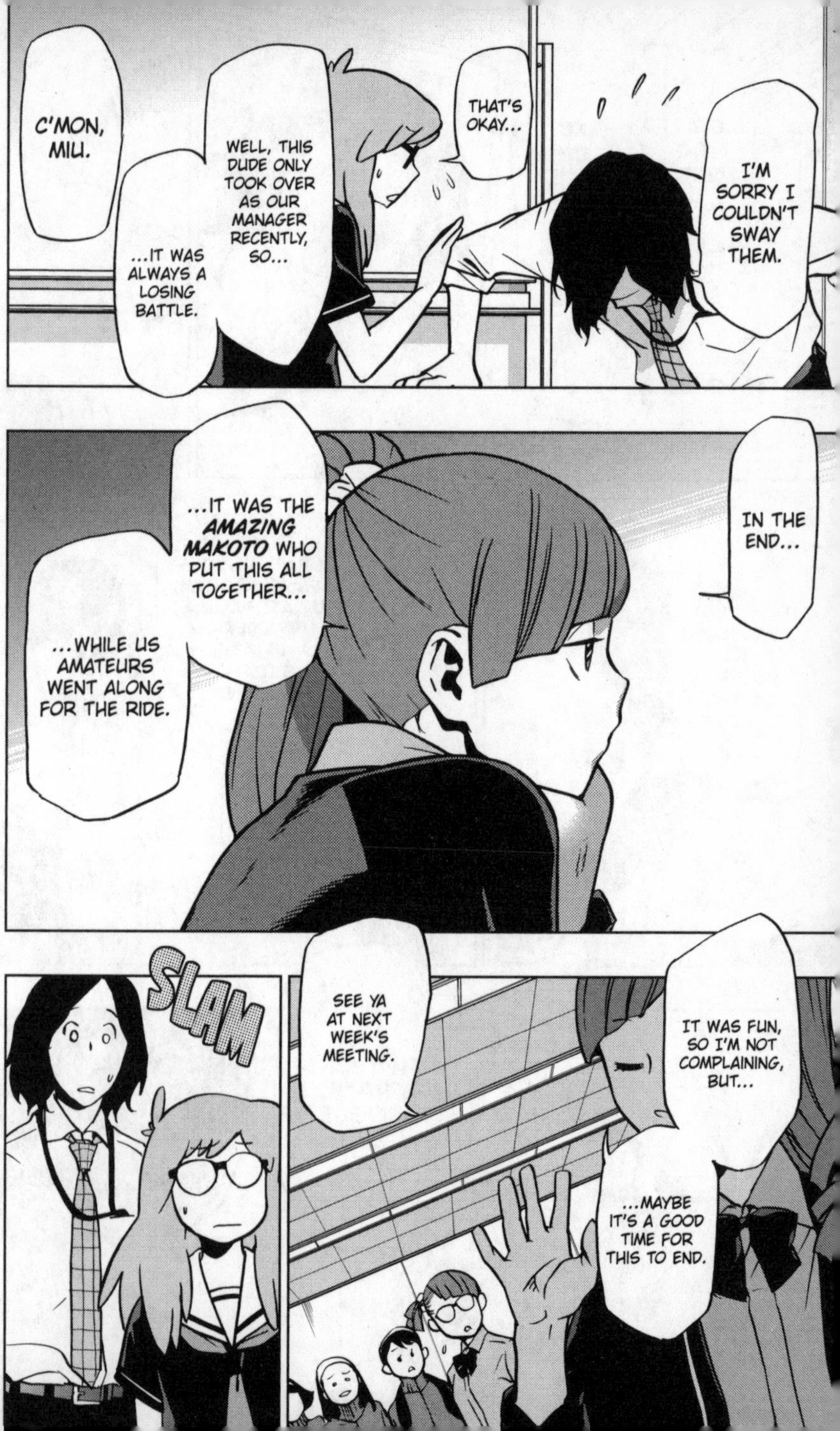
I'M SORRY I COULDN'T SWAY THEM.
THAT'S OKAY...
WELL, THIS DUDE ONLY TOOK OVER AS OUR MANAGER RECENTLY, SO...
...IT WAS ALWAYS A LOSING BATTLE.
C'MON, MIU.
IN THE END...
...IT WAS THE ***AMAZING MAKOTO*** WHO PUT THIS ALL TOGETHER...
...WHILE US AMATEURS WENT ALONG FOR THE RIDE.
IT WAS FUN, SO I'M NOT COMPLAINING, BUT...
...MAYBE IT'S A GOOD TIME FOR THIS TO END.
SEE YA AT NEXT WEEK'S MEETING.
SLAM

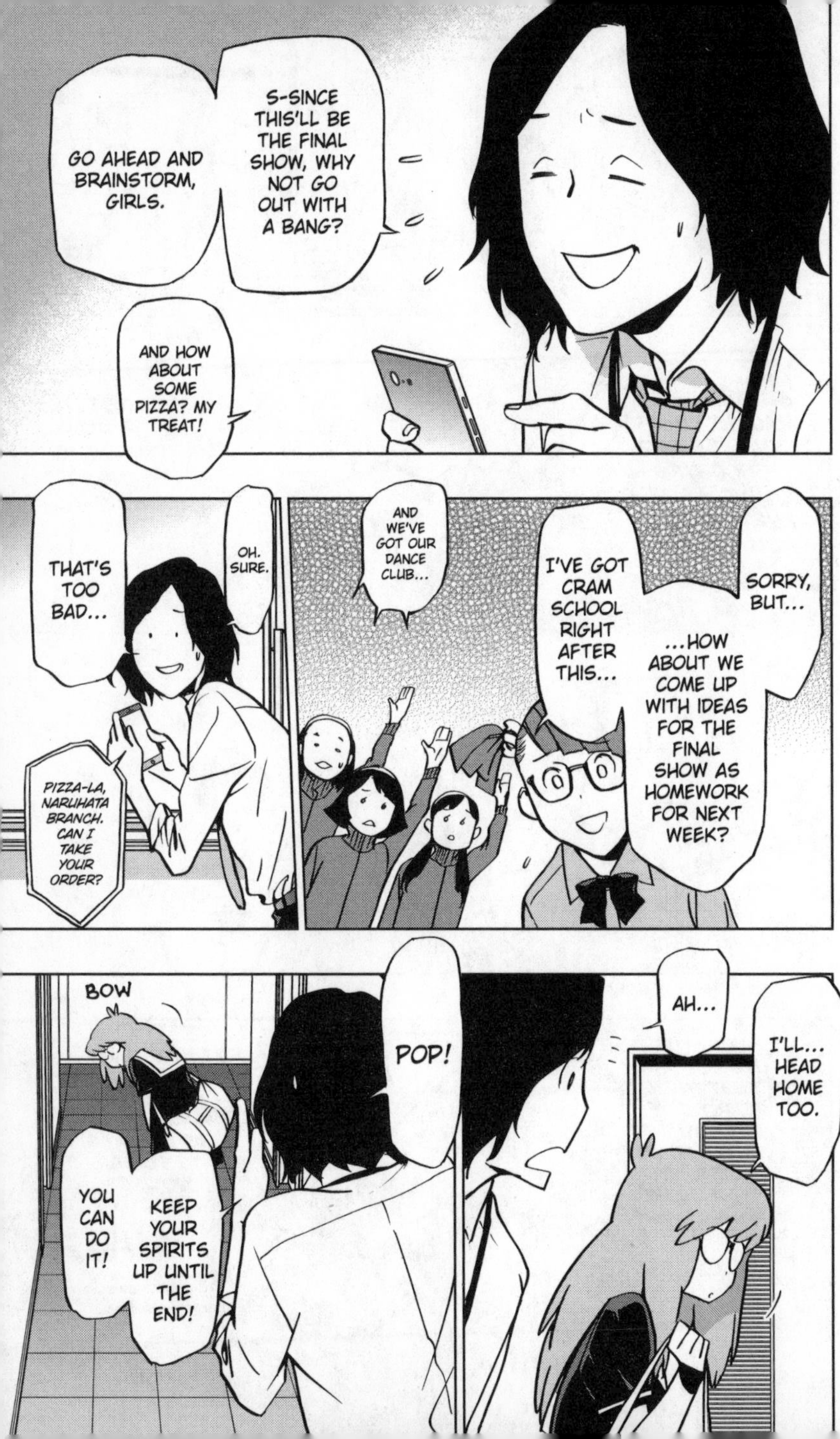
S-SINCE THIS'LL BE THE FINAL SHOW, WHY NOT GO OUT WITH A BANG?
GO AHEAD AND BRAINSTORM, GIRLS.
AND HOW ABOUT SOME PIZZA? MY TREAT!
SORRY, BUT...
...HOW ABOUT WE COME UP WITH IDEAS FOR THE FINAL SHOW AS HOMEWORK FOR NEXT WEEK?
I'VE GOT CRAM SCHOOL RIGHT AFTER THIS...
AND WE'VE GOT OUR DANCE CLUB...
OH. SURE.
THAT'S TOO BAD...
PIZZA-LA, NARUHATA BRANCH. CAN I TAKE YOUR ORDER?
AH...
I'LL... HEAD HOME TOO.
POP!
BOW
KEEP YOUR SPIRITS UP UNTIL THE END!
YOU CAN DO IT!

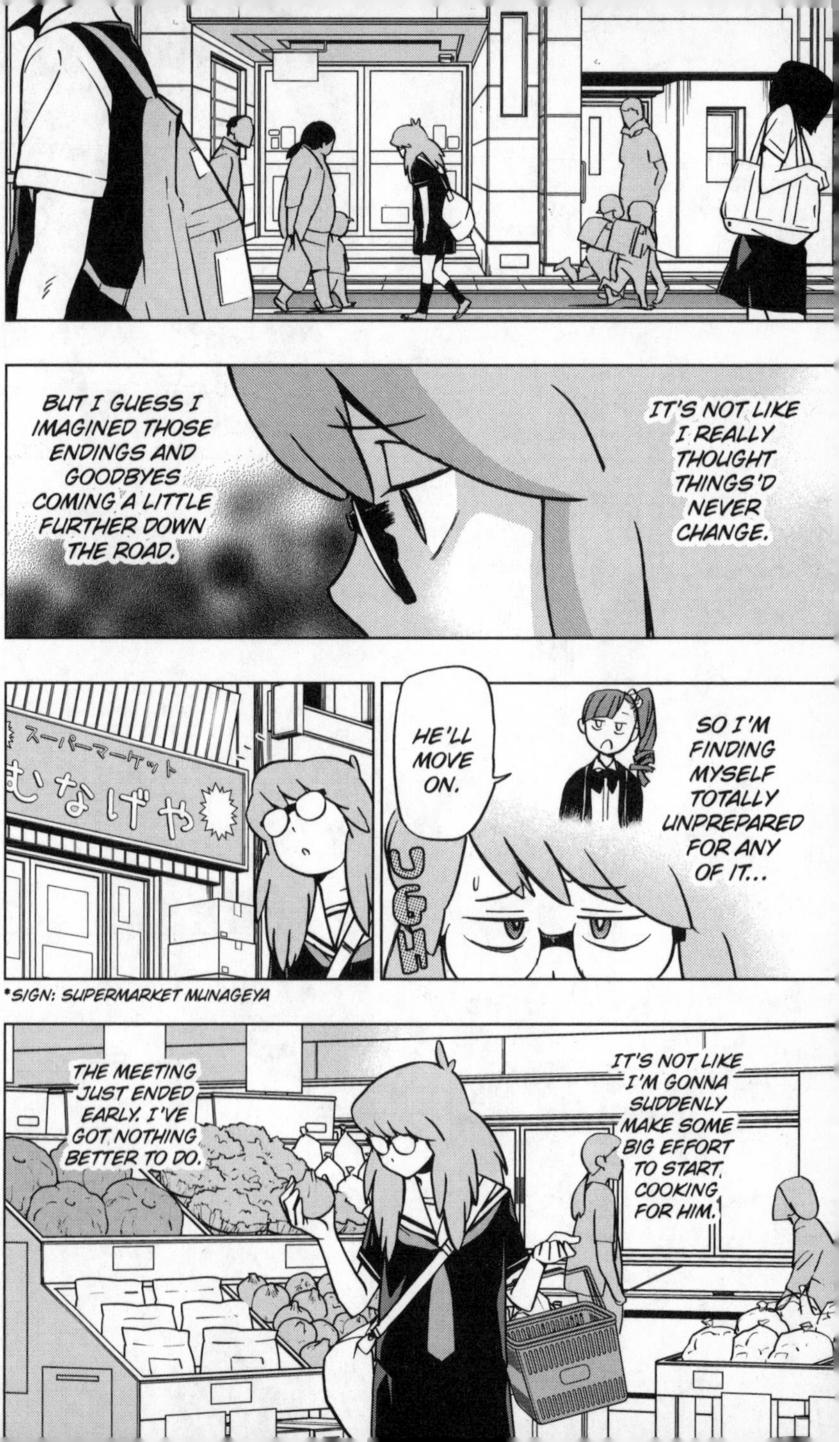
IT'S NOT LIKE I REALLY THOUGHT THINGS'D NEVER CHANGE.
BUT I GUESS I IMAGINED THOSE ENDINGS AND GOODBYES COMING A LITTLE FURTHER DOWN THE ROAD.
HE'LL MOVE ON.
SO I'M FINDING MYSELF TOTALLY UNPREPARED FOR ANY OF IT...
UGH
スーパーマーケット
むなげや
*SIGN: SUPERMARKET MUNAGEYA
IT'S NOT LIKE I'M GONNA SUDDENLY MAKE SOME BIG EFFORT TO START COOKING FOR HIM.
THE MEETING JUST ENDED EARLY. I'VE GOT NOTHING BETTER TO DO.

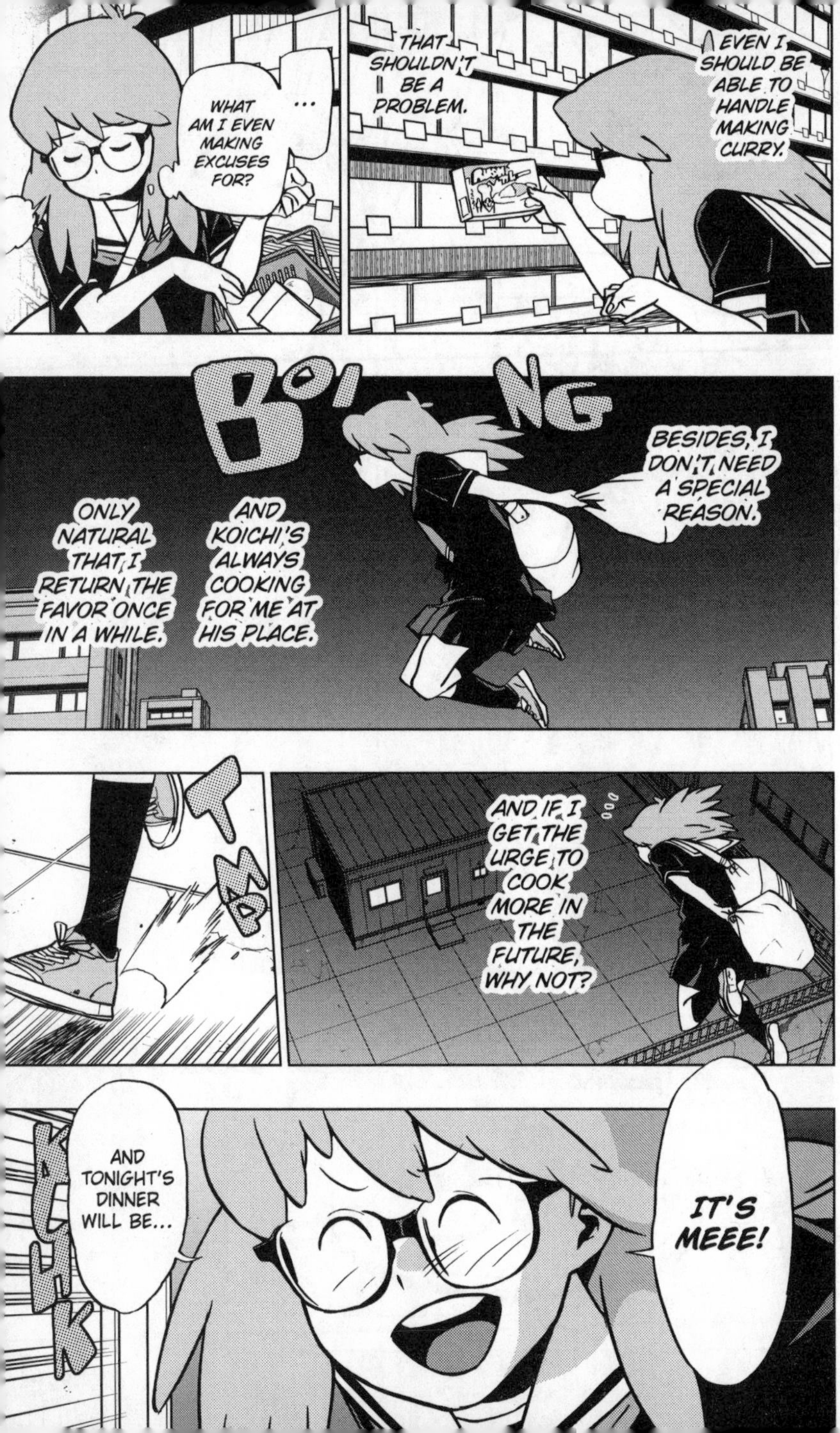
EVEN I SHOULD BE ABLE TO HANDLE MAKING CURRY.
THAT SHOULDN'T BE A PROBLEM.
...
WHAT AM I EVEN MAKING EXCUSES FOR?
BOING
BESIDES, I DON'T NEED A SPECIAL REASON.
AND KOICHI'S ALWAYS COOKING FOR ME AT HIS PLACE.
ONLY NATURAL THAT I RETURN THE FAVOR ONCE IN A WHILE.
AND IF I GET THE URGE TO COOK MORE IN THE FUTURE, WHY NOT?
TMP
AND TONIGHT'S DINNER WILL BE...
IT'S MEEE!
KSHK

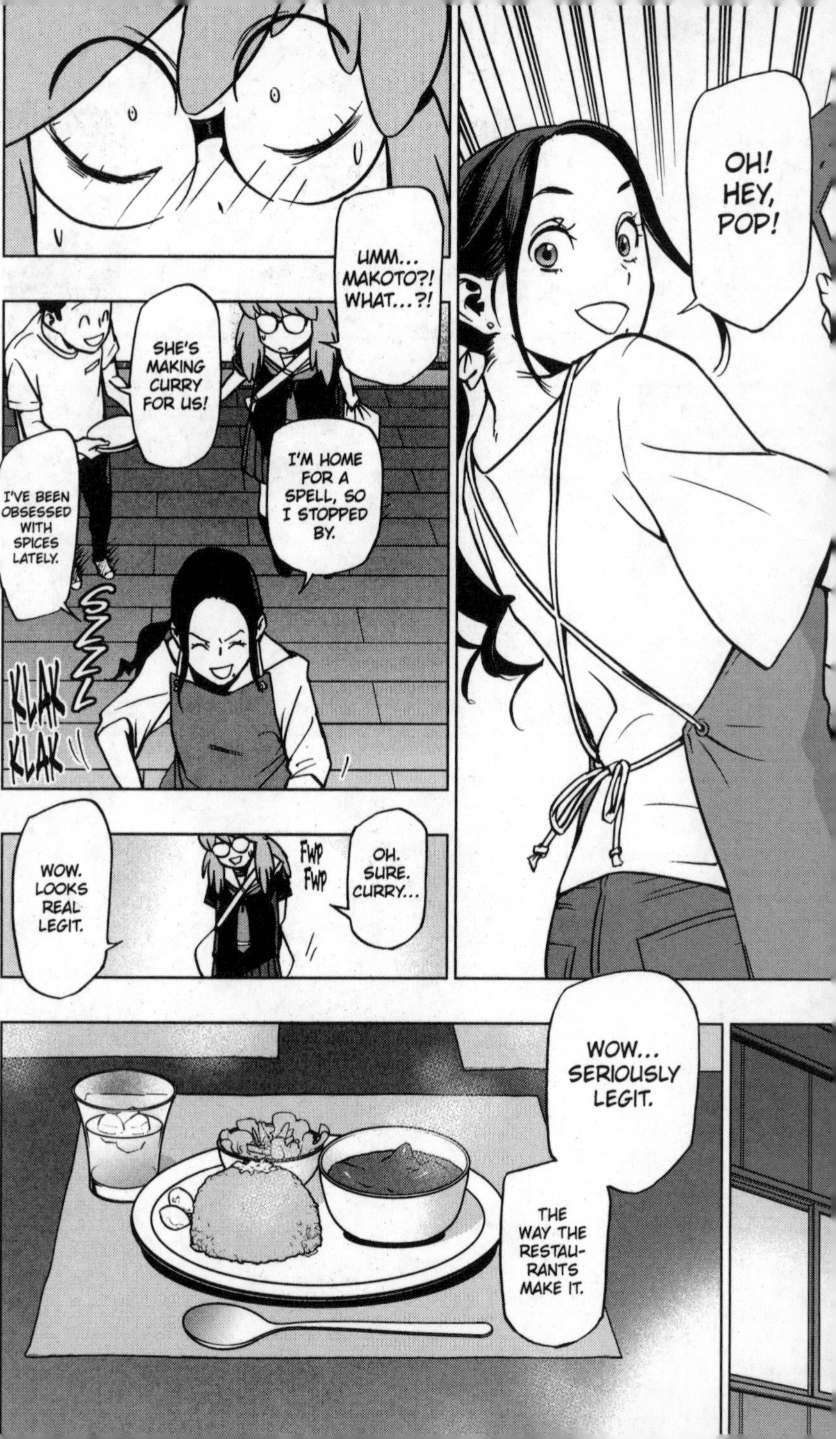
OH! HEY, POP!
UMM... MAKOTO?! WHAT...?!
SHE'S MAKING CURRY FOR US!
I'M HOME FOR A SPELL, SO I STOPPED BY.
I'VE BEEN OBSESSED WITH SPICES LATELY.
SZZZ
KLAK KLAK
FWP FWP
OH. SURE. CURRY...
WOW. LOOKS REAL LEGIT.
WOW... SERIOUSLY LEGIT.
THE WAY THE RESTAU-RANTS MAKE IT.

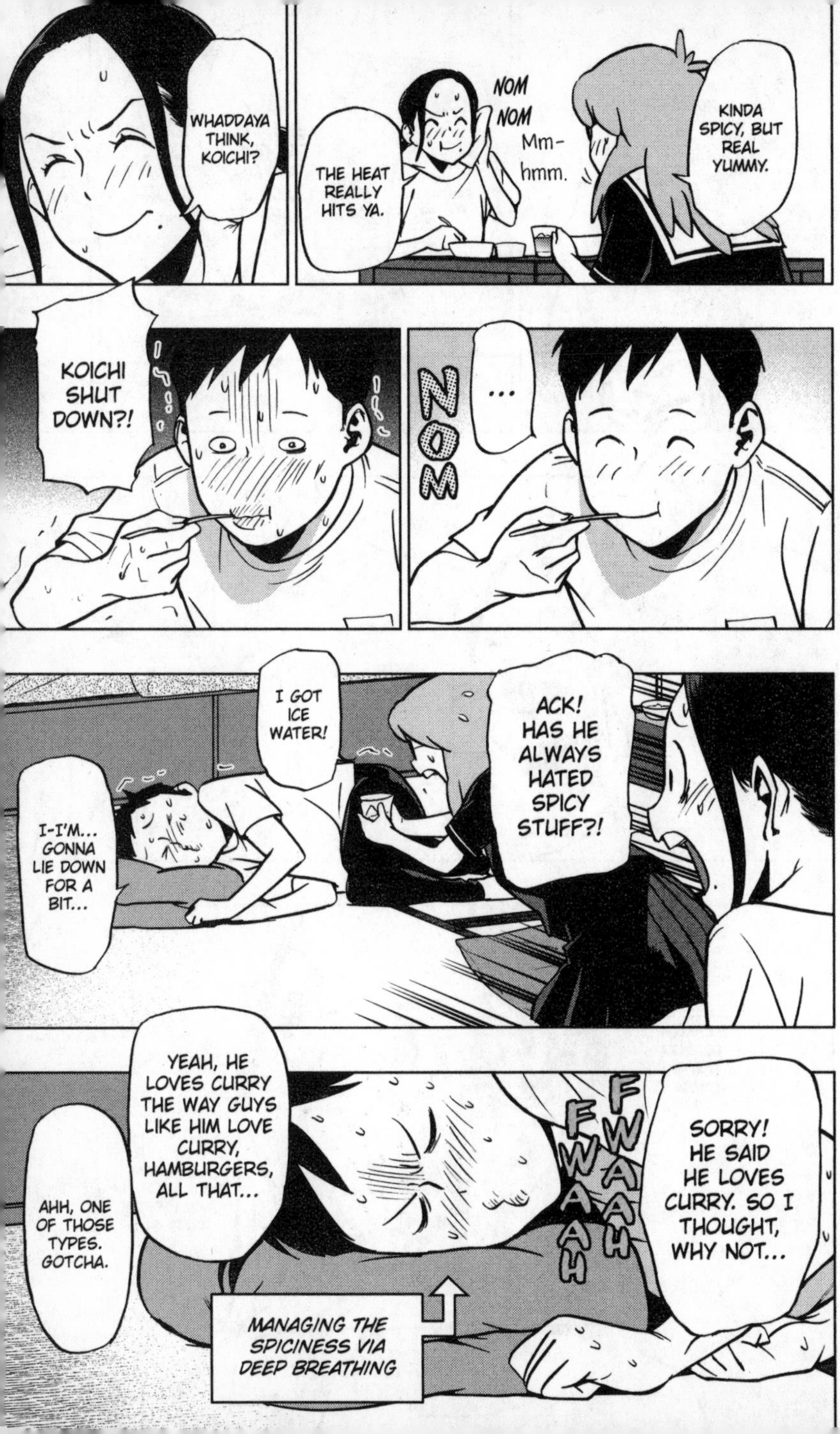
KINDA SPICY, BUT REAL YUMMY.
Mm-hmm.
NOM NOM
THE HEAT REALLY HITS YA.
WHADDAYA THINK, KOICHI?
...
NOM
KOICHI SHUT DOWN?!
ACK! HAS HE ALWAYS HATED SPICY STUFF?!
I GOT ICE WATER!
I-I'M... GONNA LIE DOWN FOR A BIT...
SORRY! HE SAID HE LOVES CURRY. SO I THOUGHT, WHY NOT...
FWAAH
FWAAH
YEAH, HE LOVES CURRY THE WAY GUYS LIKE HIM LOVE CURRY, HAMBURGERS, ALL THAT...
AHH, ONE OF THOSE TYPES. GOTCHA.
MANAGING THE SPICINESS VIA DEEP BREATHING

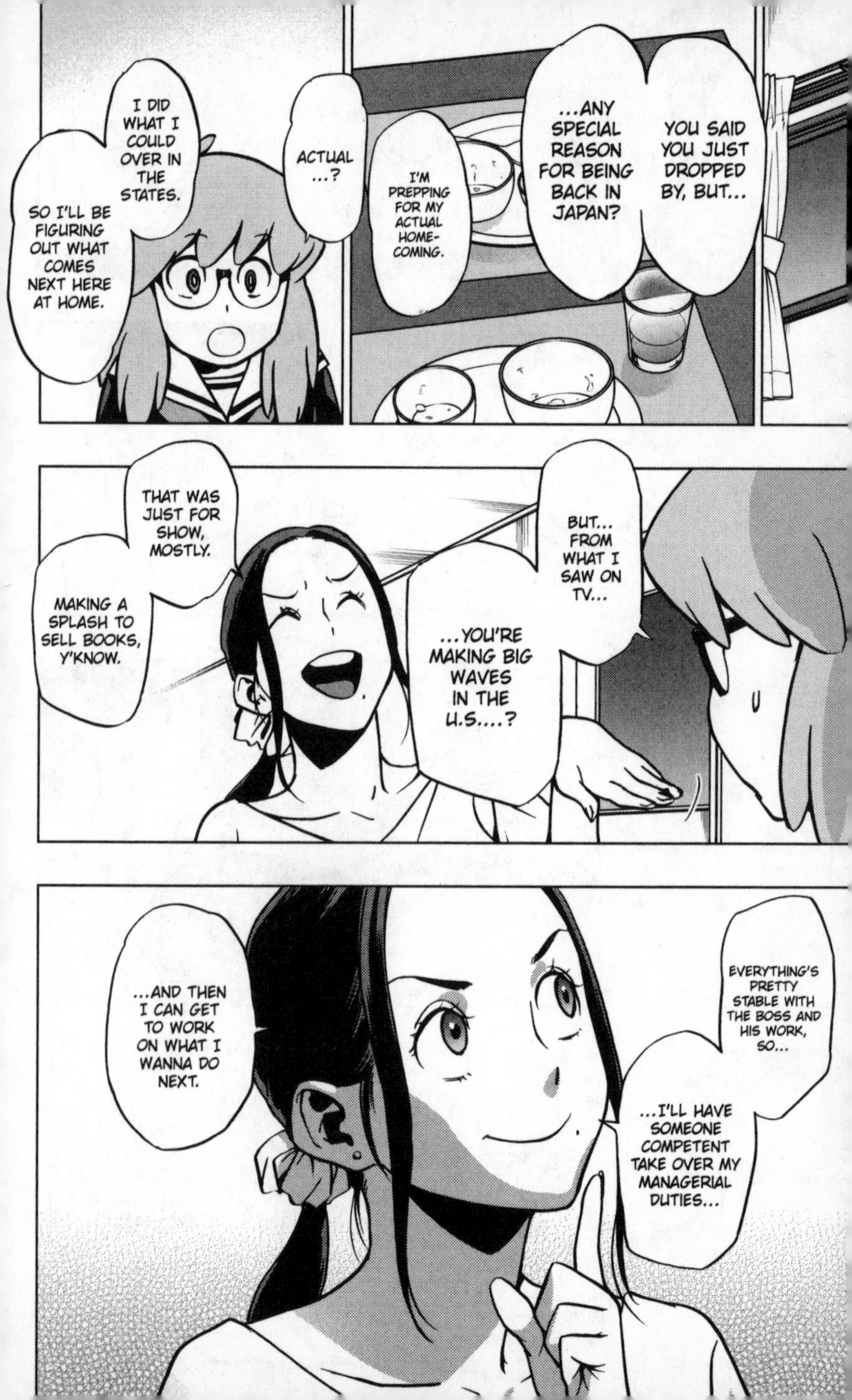
YOU SAID YOU JUST DROPPED BY, BUT...
...ANY SPECIAL REASON FOR BEING BACK IN JAPAN?
I'M PREPPING FOR MY ACTUAL HOME-COMING.
ACTUAL ...?
I DID WHAT I COULD OVER IN THE STATES.
SO I'LL BE FIGURING OUT WHAT COMES NEXT HERE AT HOME.
BUT... FROM WHAT I SAW ON TV...
...YOU'RE MAKING BIG WAVES IN THE U.S....?
THAT WAS JUST FOR SHOW, MOSTLY.
MAKING A SPLASH TO SELL BOOKS, Y'KNOW.
EVERYTHING'S PRETTY STABLE WITH THE BOSS AND HIS WORK, SO...
...I'LL HAVE SOMEONE COMPETENT TAKE OVER MY MANAGERIAL DUTIES...
...AND THEN I CAN GET TO WORK ON WHAT I WANNA DO NEXT.

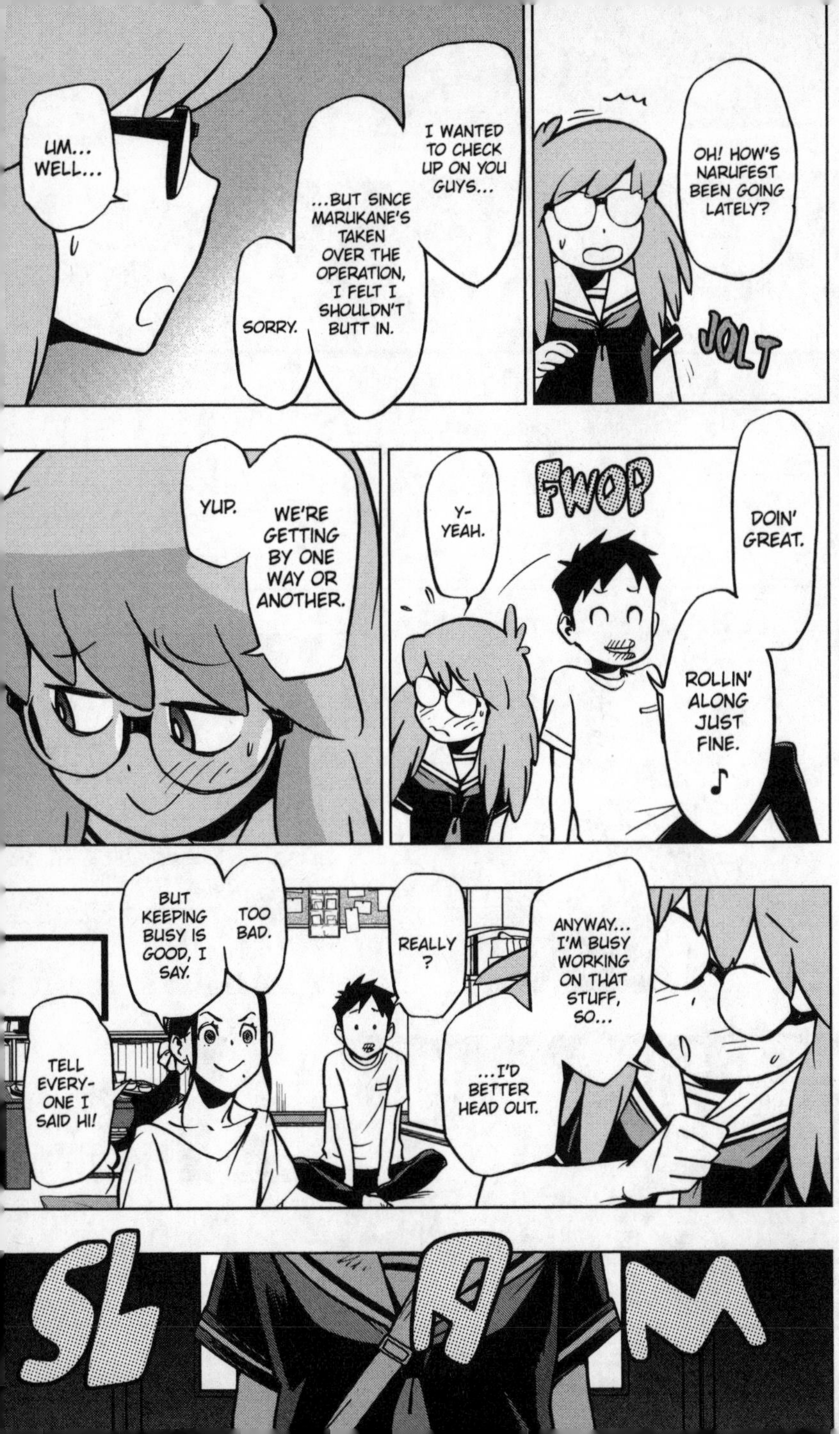
OH! HOW'S NARUFEST BEEN GOING LATELY?
JOLT
I WANTED TO CHECK UP ON YOU GUYS...
...BUT SINCE MARUKANE'S TAKEN OVER THE OPERATION, I FELT I SHOULDN'T BUTT IN.
SORRY.
UM... WELL...
DOIN' GREAT.
FWOP
Y- YEAH.
ROLLIN' ALONG JUST FINE. ♪
WE'RE GETTING BY ONE WAY OR ANOTHER.
YUP.
ANYWAY... I'M BUSY WORKING ON THAT STUFF, SO...
...I'D BETTER HEAD OUT.
REALLY ?
TOO BAD.
BUT KEEPING BUSY IS GOOD, I SAY.
TELL EVERY- ONE I SAID HI!
SLAM

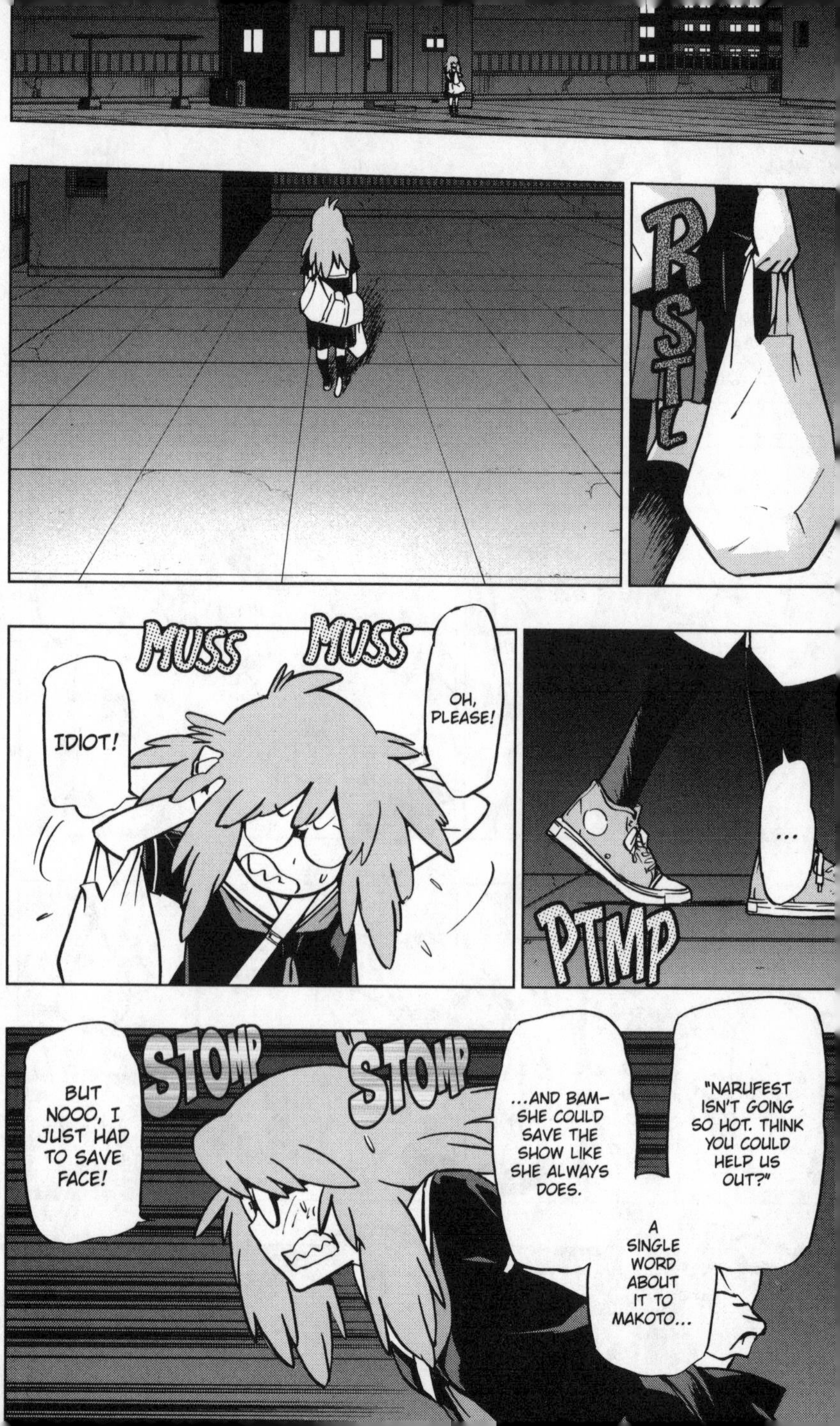
RSTL
...
PTMP
MUSS MUSS
OH, PLEASE!
IDIOT!
"NARUFEST ISN'T GOING SO HOT. THINK YOU COULD HELP US OUT?"
A SINGLE WORD ABOUT IT TO MAKOTO...
...AND BAM—SHE COULD SAVE THE SHOW LIKE SHE ALWAYS DOES.
STOMP STOMP
BUT NOOO, I JUST HAD TO SAVE FACE!

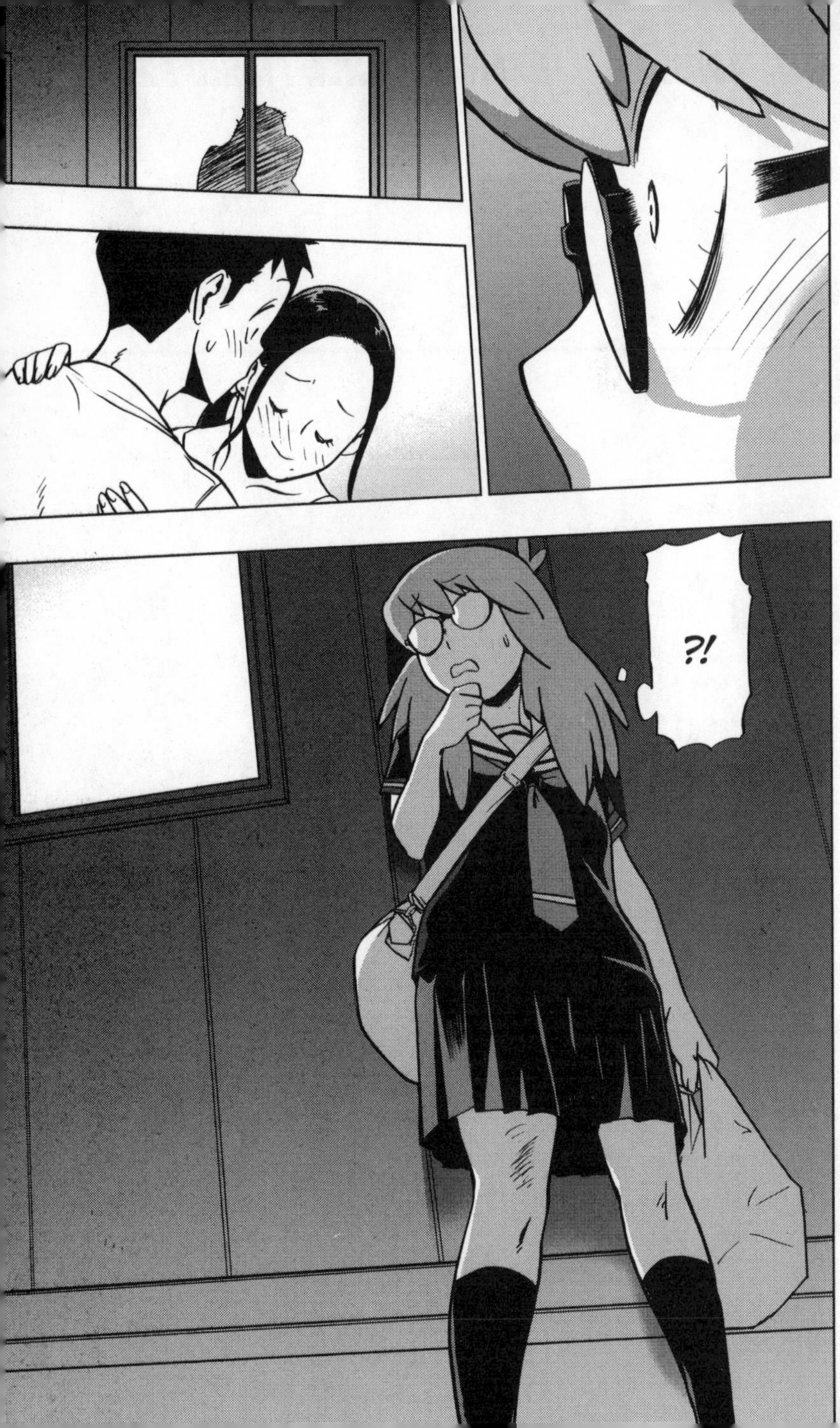
?!

THE TWINS & THE TRIO, THREE YEARS LATER

THE ROUGH DESIGN

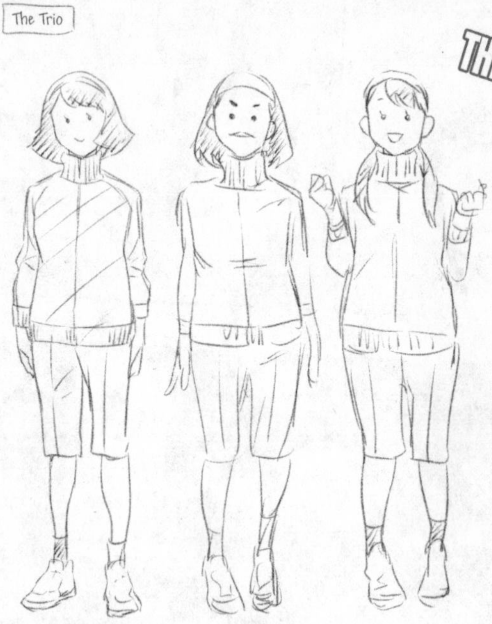
The Trio

BEHIND THE SCENES

To show the growth and changes over three years, I wanted the twins' designs to reflect the different paths they're taking—and of course, the Saint Lila's girls had to grow up, literally.

However, the trio is clearly too much to handle in terms of panel space, now that they're so big!

—Furuhashi

The trio's windbreakers and headbands represent the soul they inherited from the dance club president.

—Betten

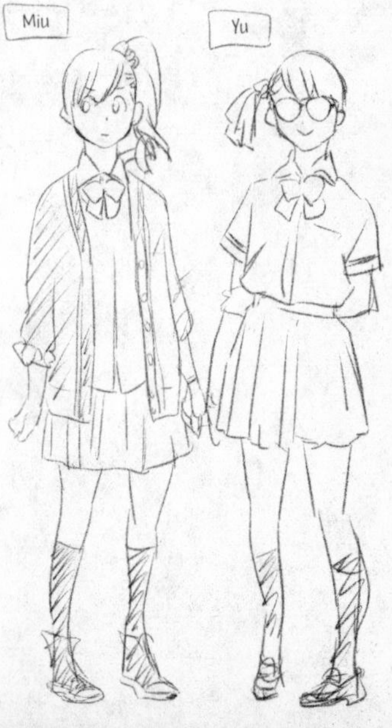
Miu
Yu

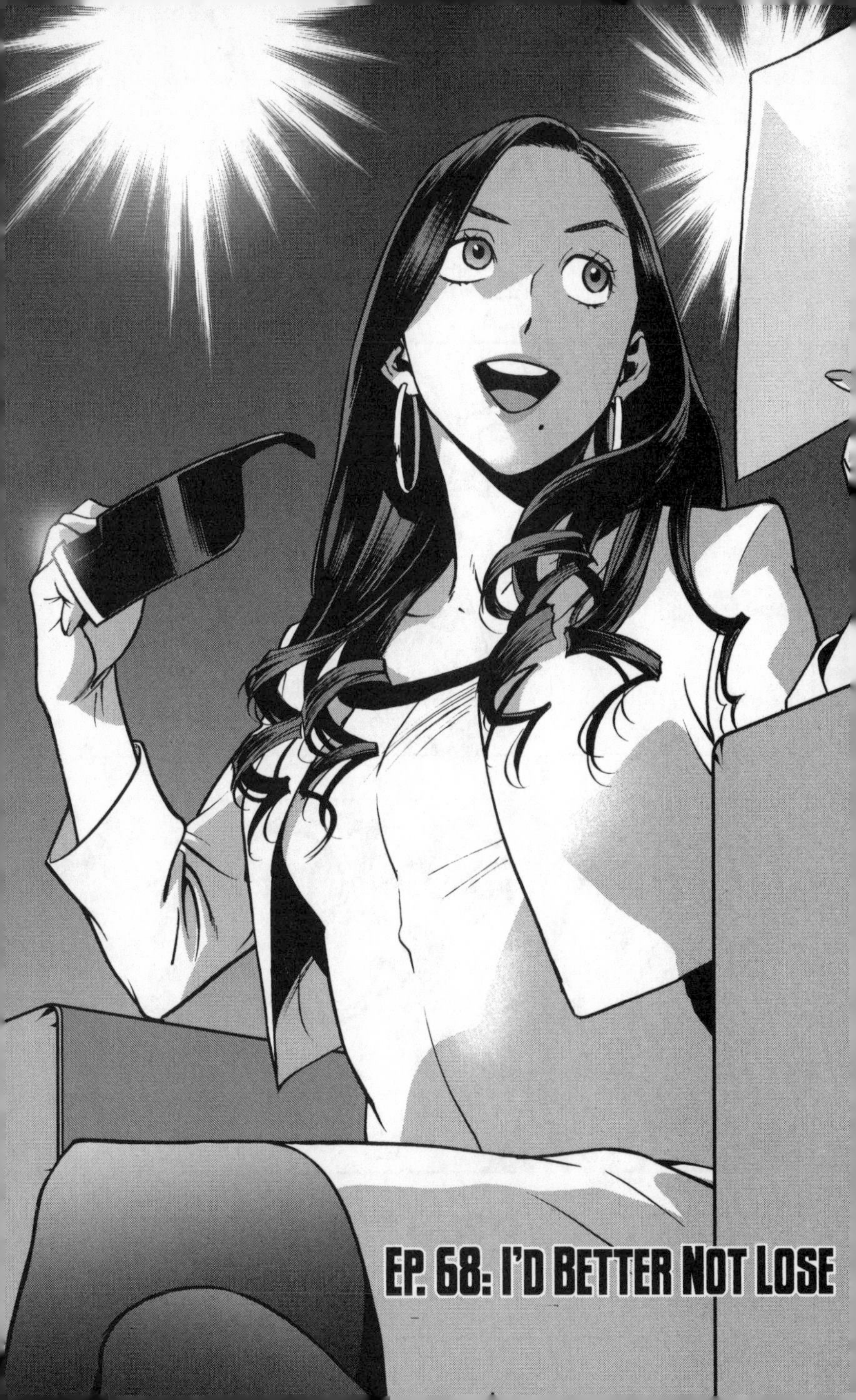
EP. 68: I'D BETTER NOT LOSE

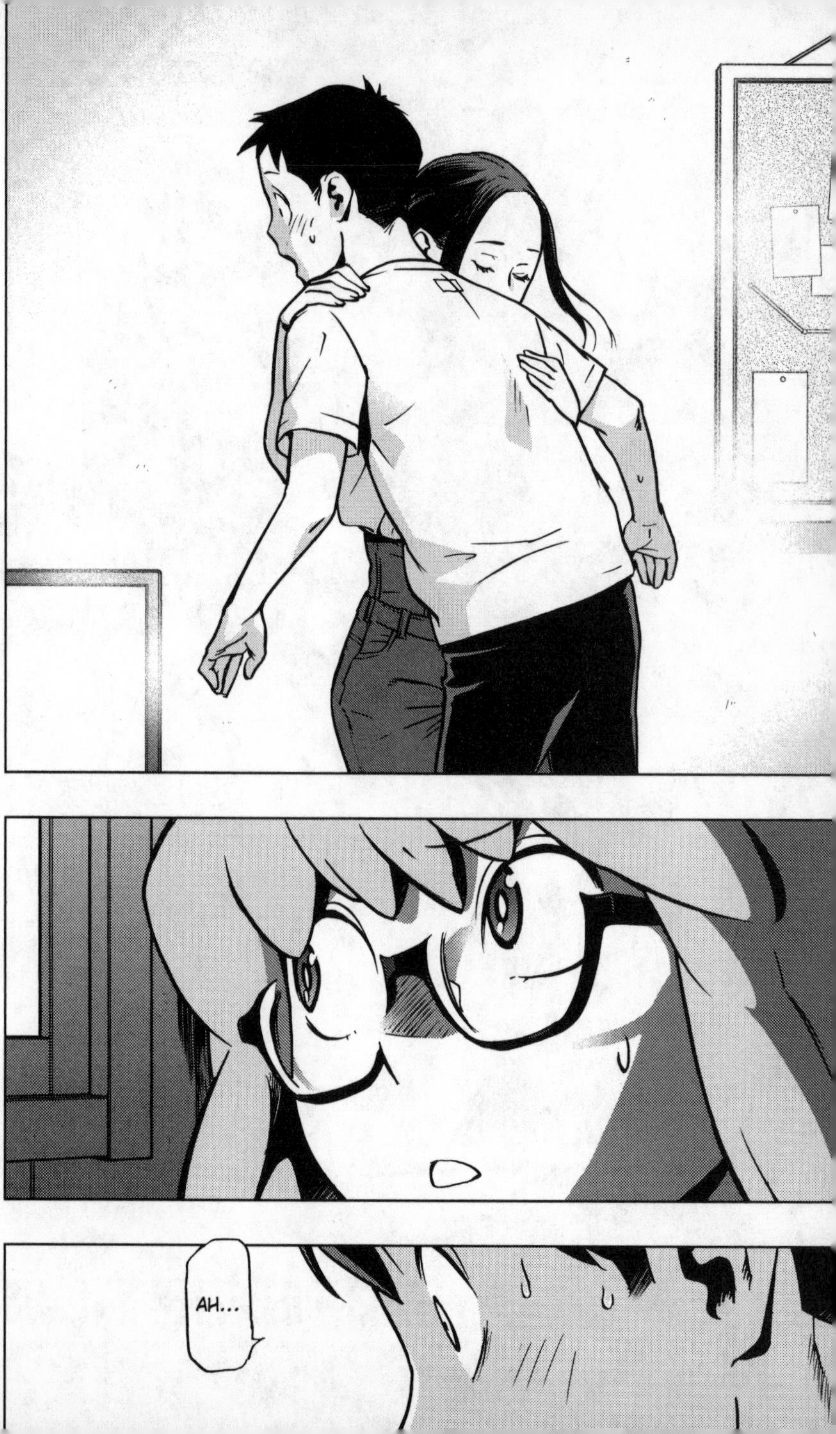
AH...

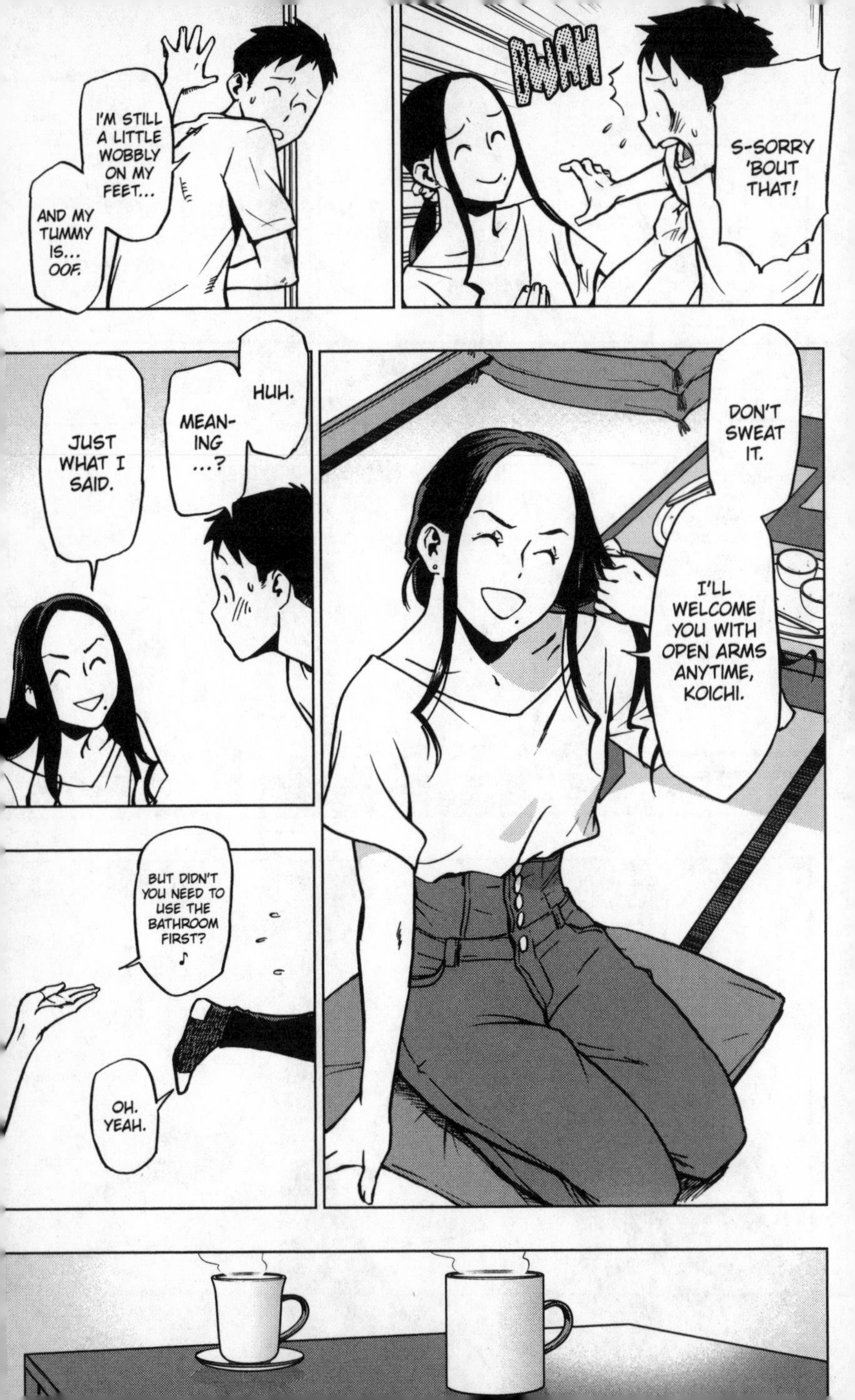
BWAH
S-SORRY 'BOUT THAT!
I'M STILL A LITTLE WOBBLY ON MY FEET...
AND MY TUMMY IS... OOF.
DON'T SWEAT IT.
I'LL WELCOME YOU WITH OPEN ARMS ANYTIME, KOICHI.
HUH.
MEAN-ING ...?
JUST WHAT I SAID.
BUT DIDN'T YOU NEED TO USE THE BATHROOM FIRST? ♪
OH. YEAH.

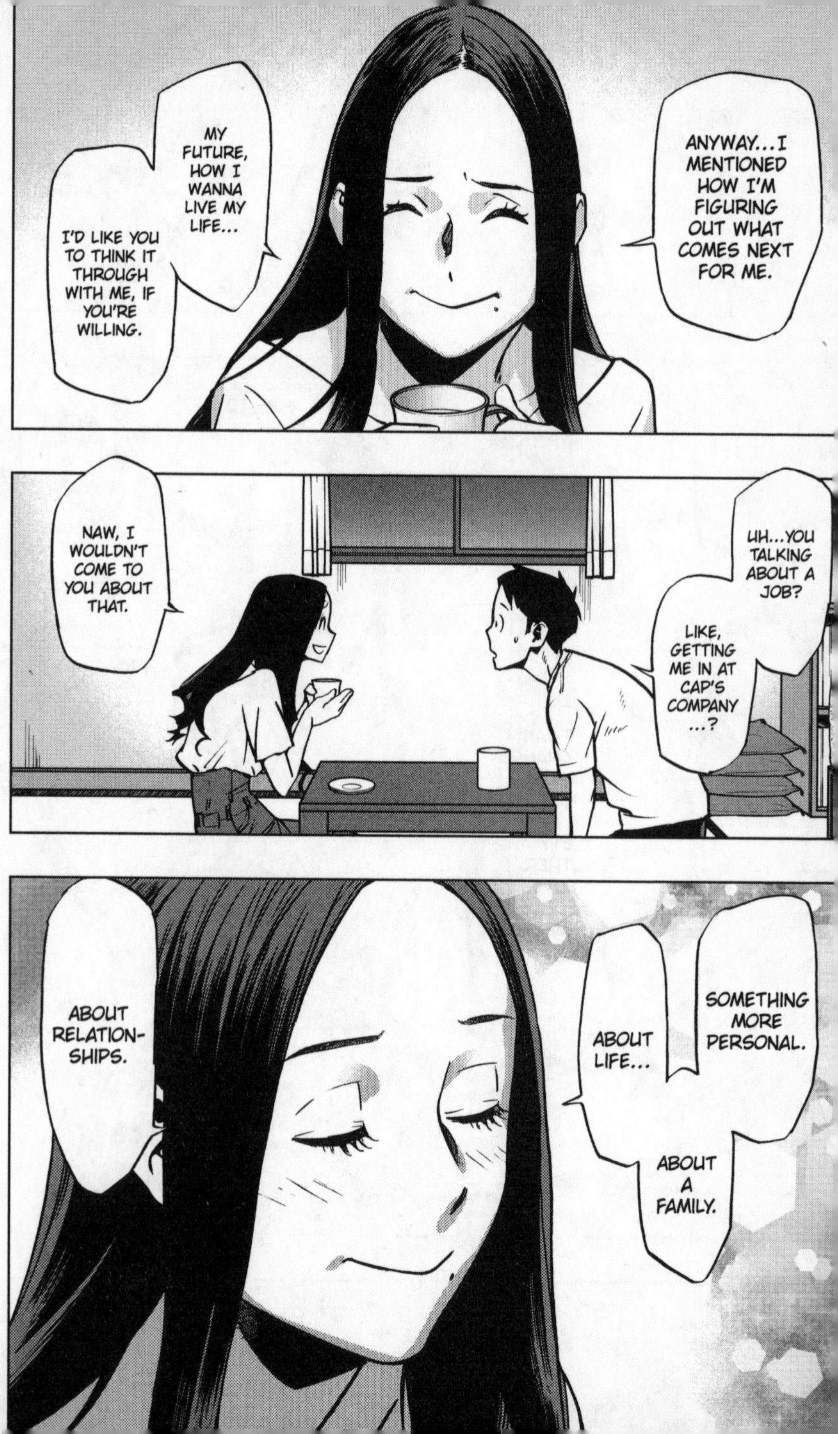
ANYWAY...I MENTIONED HOW I'M FIGURING OUT WHAT COMES NEXT FOR ME.
MY FUTURE, HOW I WANNA LIVE MY LIFE...
I'D LIKE YOU TO THINK IT THROUGH WITH ME, IF YOU'RE WILLING.
UH...YOU TALKING ABOUT A JOB?
LIKE, GETTING ME IN AT CAP'S COMPANY ...?
NAW, I WOULDN'T COME TO YOU ABOUT THAT.
SOMETHING MORE PERSONAL.
ABOUT LIFE...
ABOUT A FAMILY.
ABOUT RELATION-SHIPS.

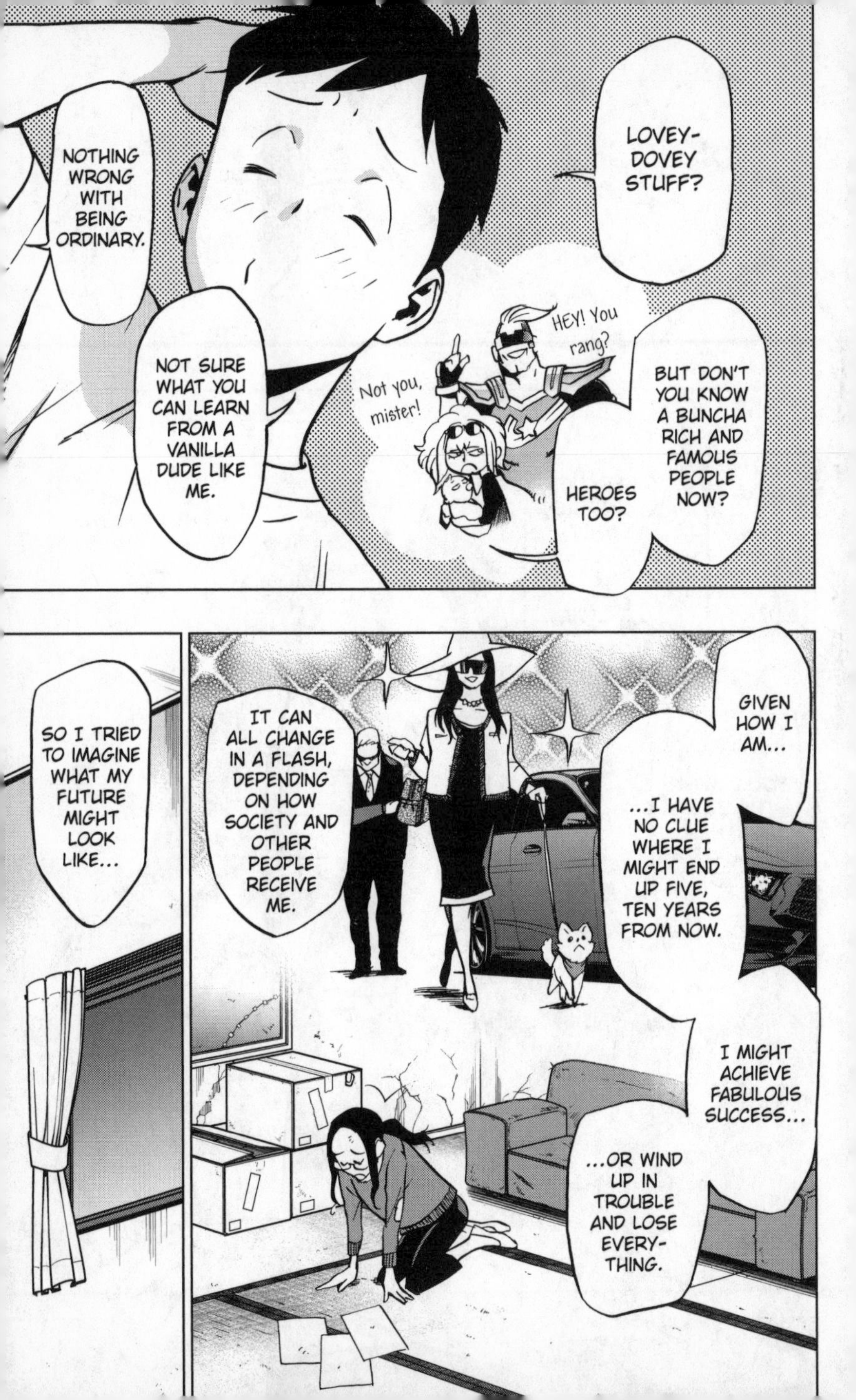
LOVEY-DOVEY STUFF?
BUT DON'T YOU KNOW A BUNCHA RICH AND FAMOUS PEOPLE NOW?
HEROES TOO?
HEY! You rang?
Not you, mister!
NOTHING WRONG WITH BEING ORDINARY.
NOT SURE WHAT YOU CAN LEARN FROM A VANILLA DUDE LIKE ME.
GIVEN HOW I AM...
...I HAVE NO CLUE WHERE I MIGHT END UP FIVE, TEN YEARS FROM NOW.
IT CAN ALL CHANGE IN A FLASH, DEPENDING ON HOW SOCIETY AND OTHER PEOPLE RECEIVE ME.
I MIGHT ACHIEVE FABULOUS SUCCESS...
...OR WIND UP IN TROUBLE AND LOSE EVERY-THING.
SO I TRIED TO IMAGINE WHAT MY FUTURE MIGHT LOOK LIKE...

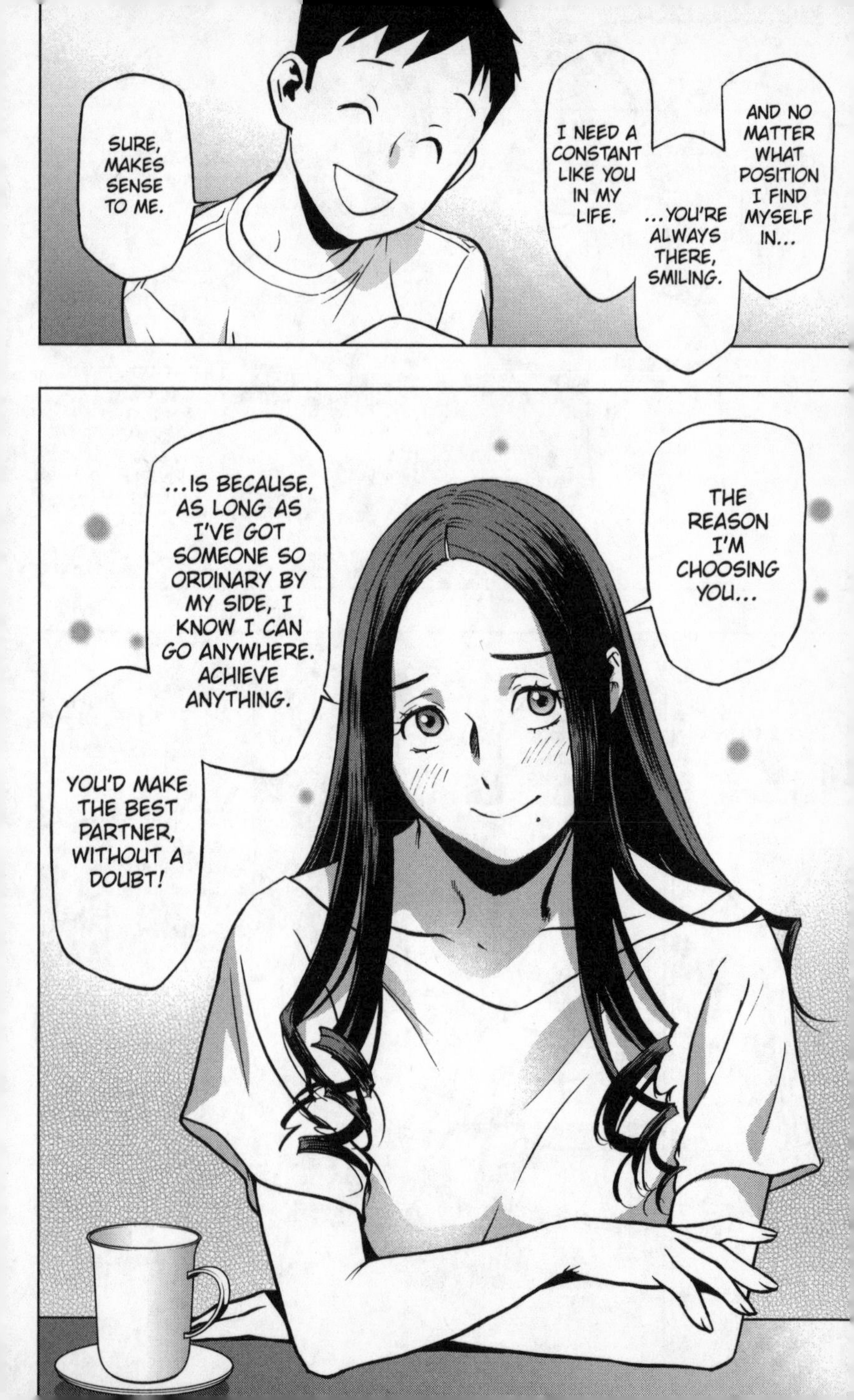
AND NO MATTER WHAT POSITION I FIND MYSELF IN...
...YOU'RE ALWAYS THERE, SMILING.
I NEED A CONSTANT LIKE YOU IN MY LIFE.
SURE, MAKES SENSE TO ME.
THE REASON I'M CHOOSING YOU...
...IS BECAUSE, AS LONG AS I'VE GOT SOMEONE SO ORDINARY BY MY SIDE, I KNOW I CAN GO ANYWHERE. ACHIEVE ANYTHING.
YOU'D MAKE THE BEST PARTNER, WITHOUT A DOUBT!

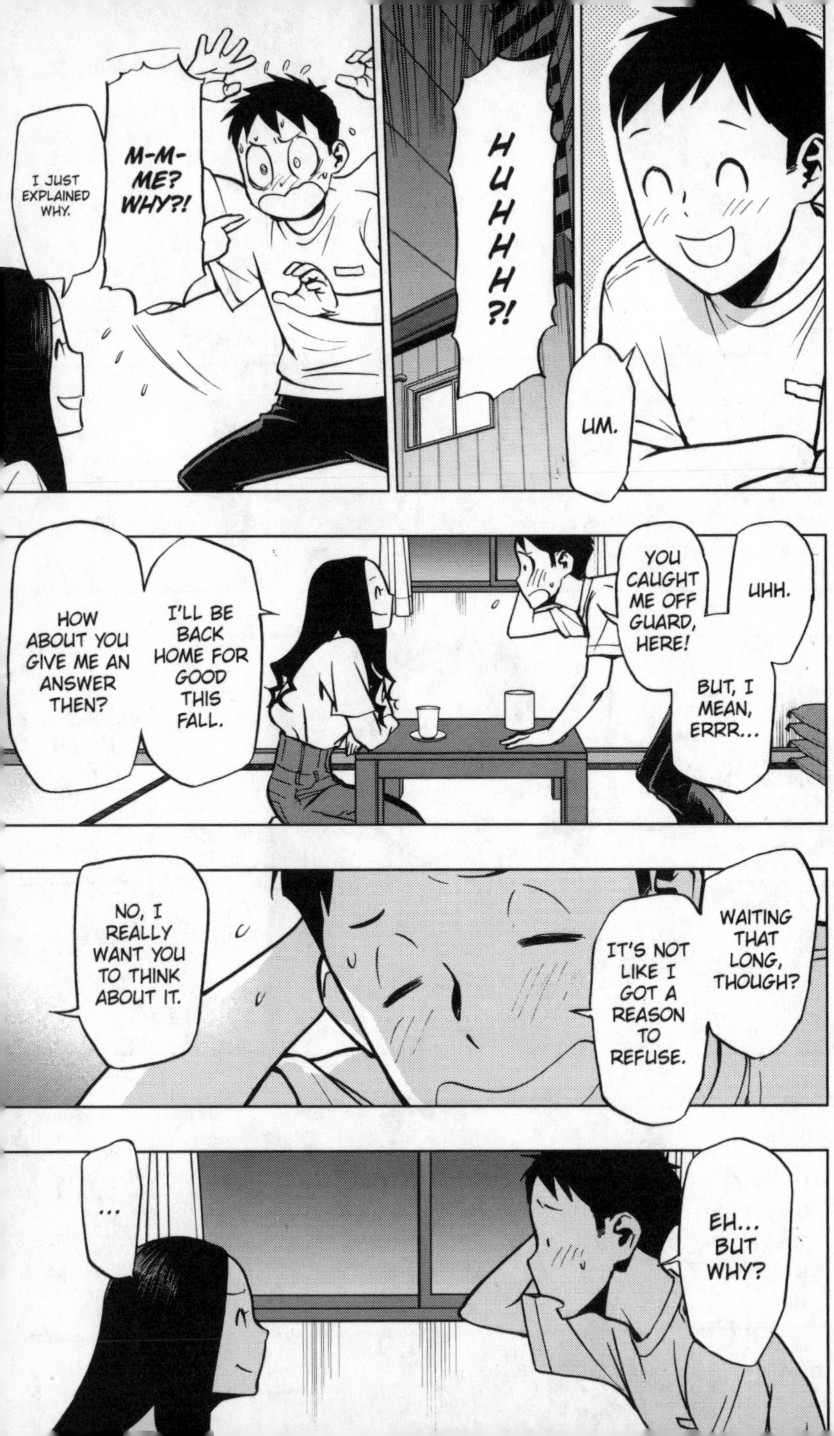
UM.
HUHHHH?!
M-M-ME? WHY?!
I JUST EXPLAINED WHY.
UHH.
YOU CAUGHT ME OFF GUARD, HERE!
BUT, I MEAN, ERRR...
I'LL BE BACK HOME FOR GOOD THIS FALL.
HOW ABOUT YOU GIVE ME AN ANSWER THEN?
WAITING THAT LONG, THOUGH?
IT'S NOT LIKE I GOT A REASON TO REFUSE.
NO, I REALLY WANT YOU TO THINK ABOUT IT.
EH... BUT WHY?
...

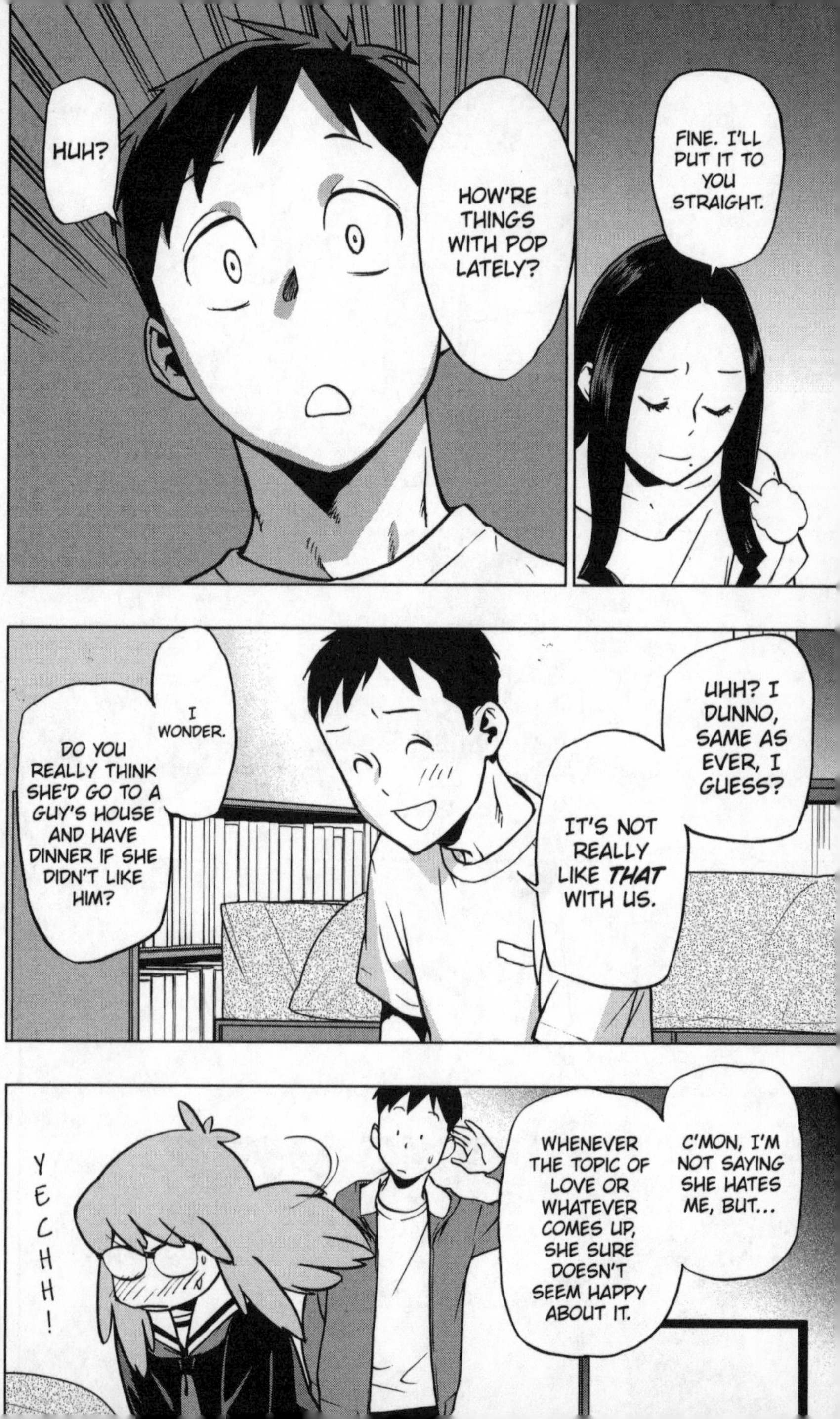
FINE. I'LL PUT IT TO YOU STRAIGHT.
HOW'RE THINGS WITH POP LATELY?
HUH?
UHH? I DUNNO, SAME AS EVER, I GUESS?
IT'S NOT REALLY LIKE *THAT* WITH US.
I WONDER.
DO YOU REALLY THINK SHE'D GO TO A GUY'S HOUSE AND HAVE DINNER IF SHE DIDN'T LIKE HIM?
C'MON, I'M NOT SAYING SHE HATES ME, BUT...
WHENEVER THE TOPIC OF LOVE OR WHATEVER COMES UP, SHE SURE DOESN'T SEEM HAPPY ABOUT IT.
YECHH!

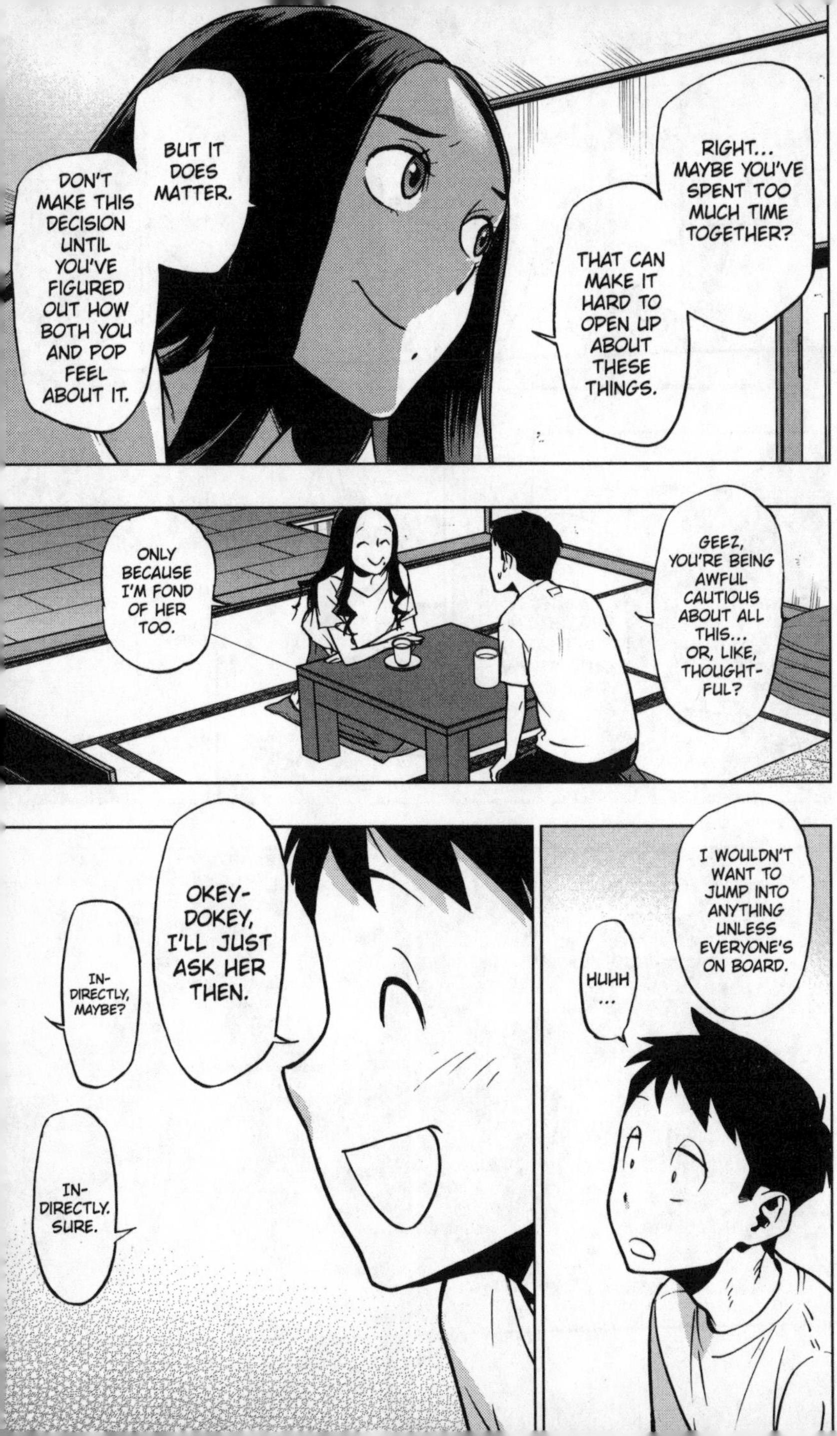
RIGHT... MAYBE YOU'VE SPENT TOO MUCH TIME TOGETHER?
THAT CAN MAKE IT HARD TO OPEN UP ABOUT THESE THINGS.
BUT IT DOES MATTER.
DON'T MAKE THIS DECISION UNTIL YOU'VE FIGURED OUT HOW BOTH YOU AND POP FEEL ABOUT IT.
GEEZ, YOU'RE BEING AWFUL CAUTIOUS ABOUT ALL THIS... OR, LIKE, THOUGHT-FUL?
ONLY BECAUSE I'M FOND OF HER TOO.
I WOULDN'T WANT TO JUMP INTO ANYTHING UNLESS EVERYONE'S ON BOARD.
HUHH ...
OKEY-DOKEY, I'LL JUST ASK HER THEN.
IN-DIRECTLY, MAYBE?
IN-DIRECTLY. SURE.

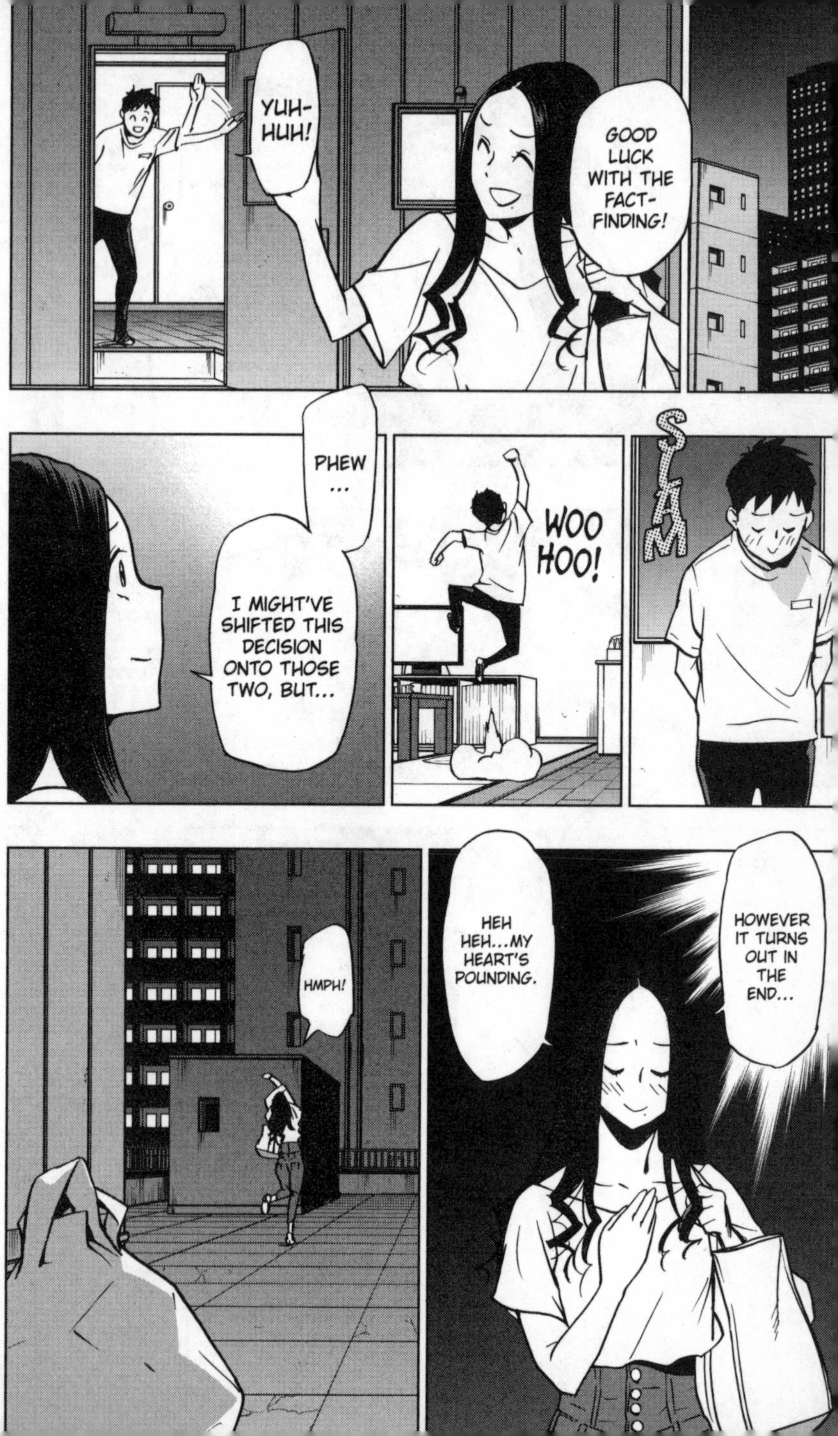
GOOD LUCK WITH THE FACT-FINDING!
YUH-HUH!
SLAM
WOO HOO!
PHEW...
I MIGHT'VE SHIFTED THIS DECISION ONTO THOSE TWO, BUT...
HOWEVER IT TURNS OUT IN THE END...
HEH HEH...MY HEART'S POUNDING.
HMPH!

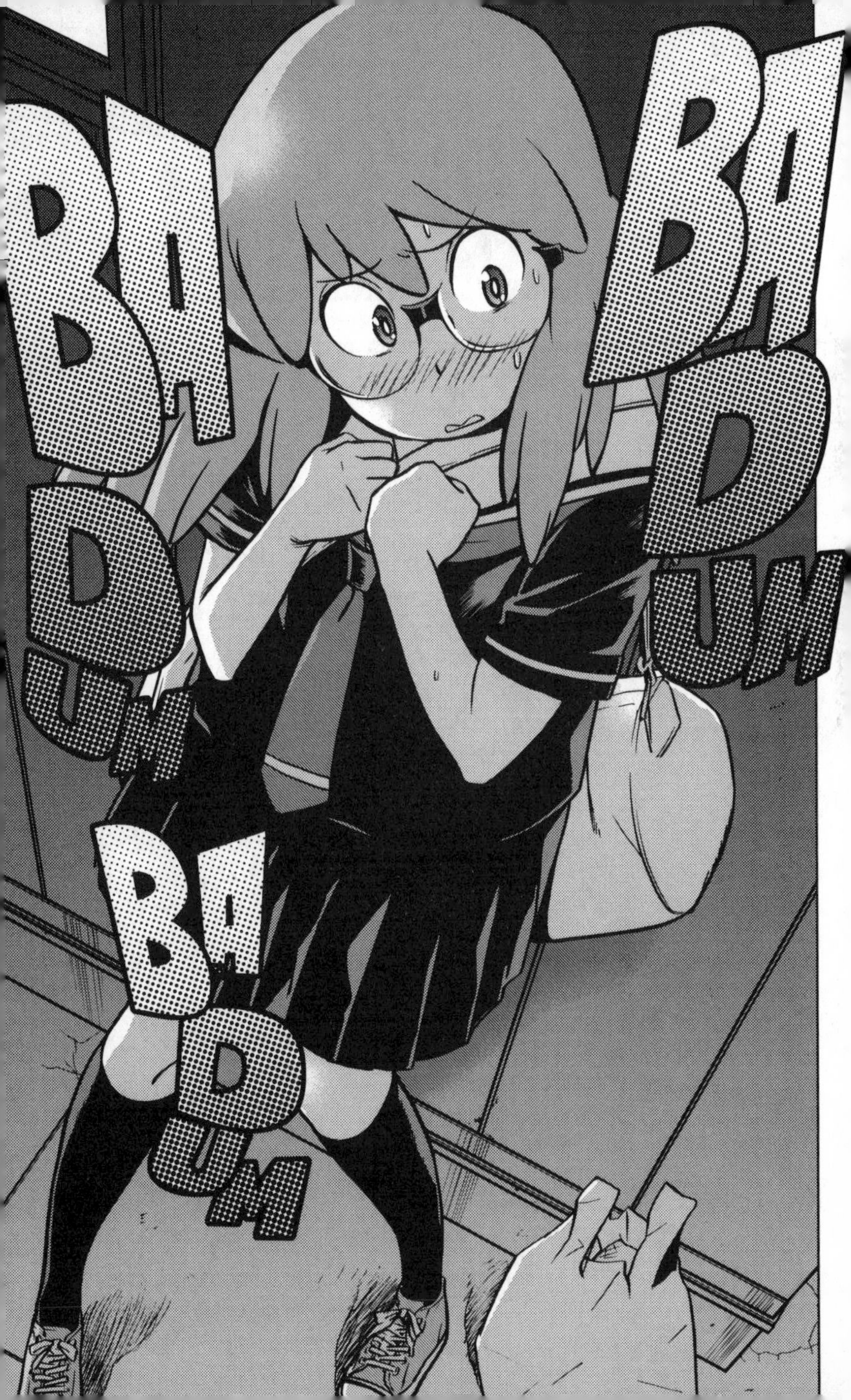
BA DUM
BA DUM
BA DUM

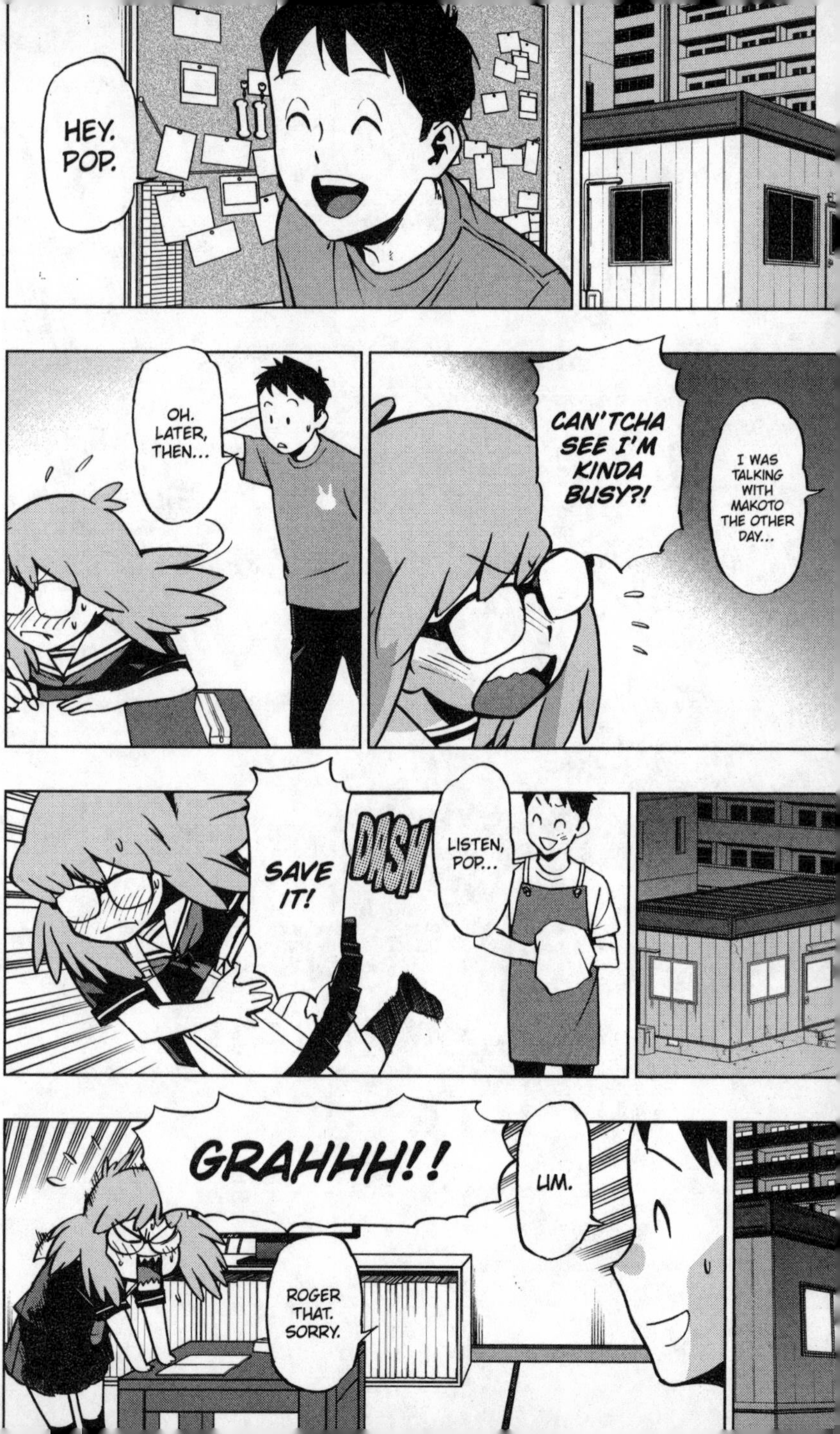
HEY. POP.
I WAS TALKING WITH MAKOTO THE OTHER DAY...
CAN'TCHA SEE I'M KINDA BUSY?!
OH. LATER, THEN...
LISTEN, POP...
DASH
SAVE IT!
GRAHHH!!
UM.
ROGER THAT. SORRY.

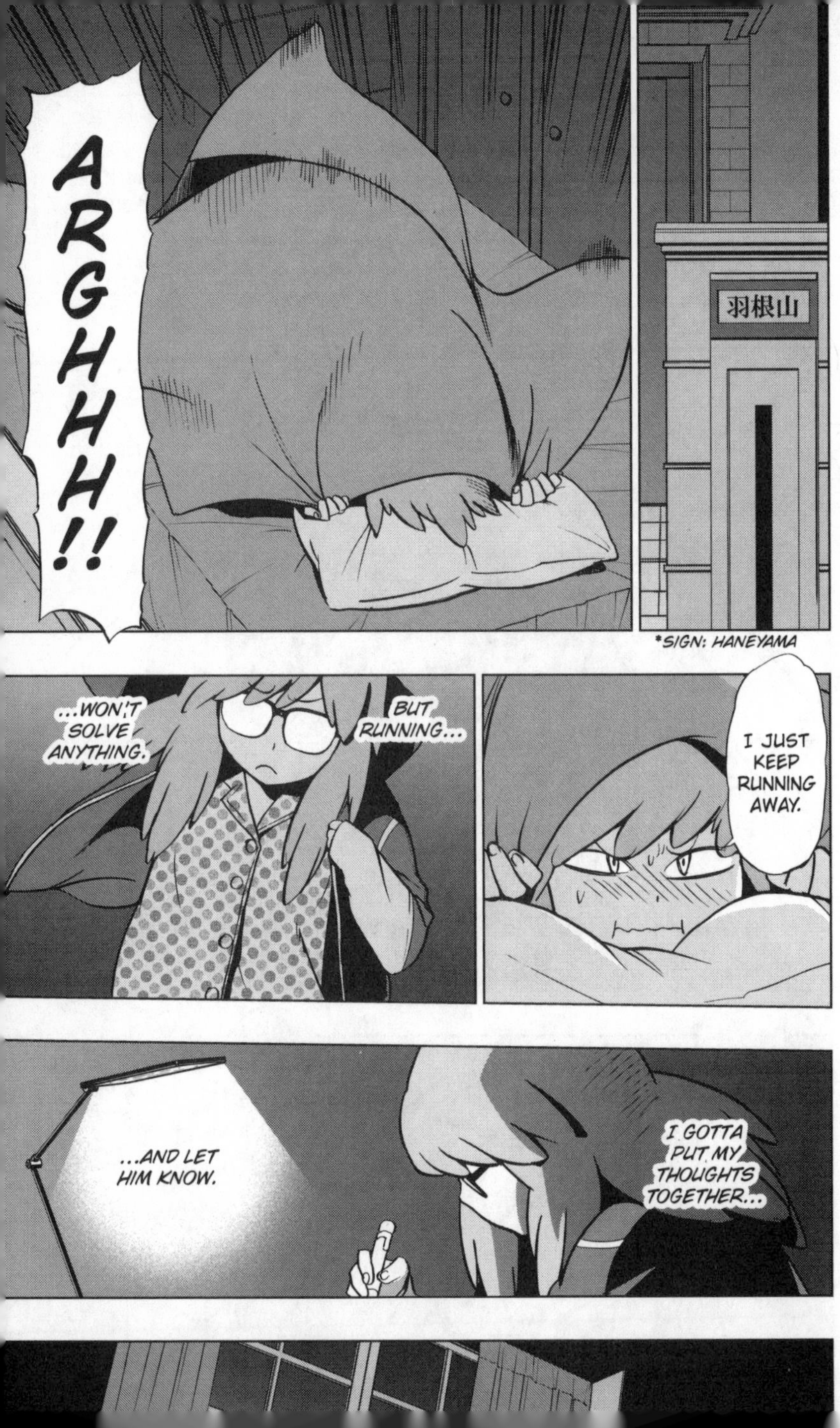
羽根山
ARGHHH!!
*SIGN: HANEYAMA
I JUST KEEP RUNNING AWAY.
BUT RUNNING...
...WON'T SOLVE ANYTHING.
I GOTTA PUT MY THOUGHTS TOGETHER...
...AND LET HIM KNOW.

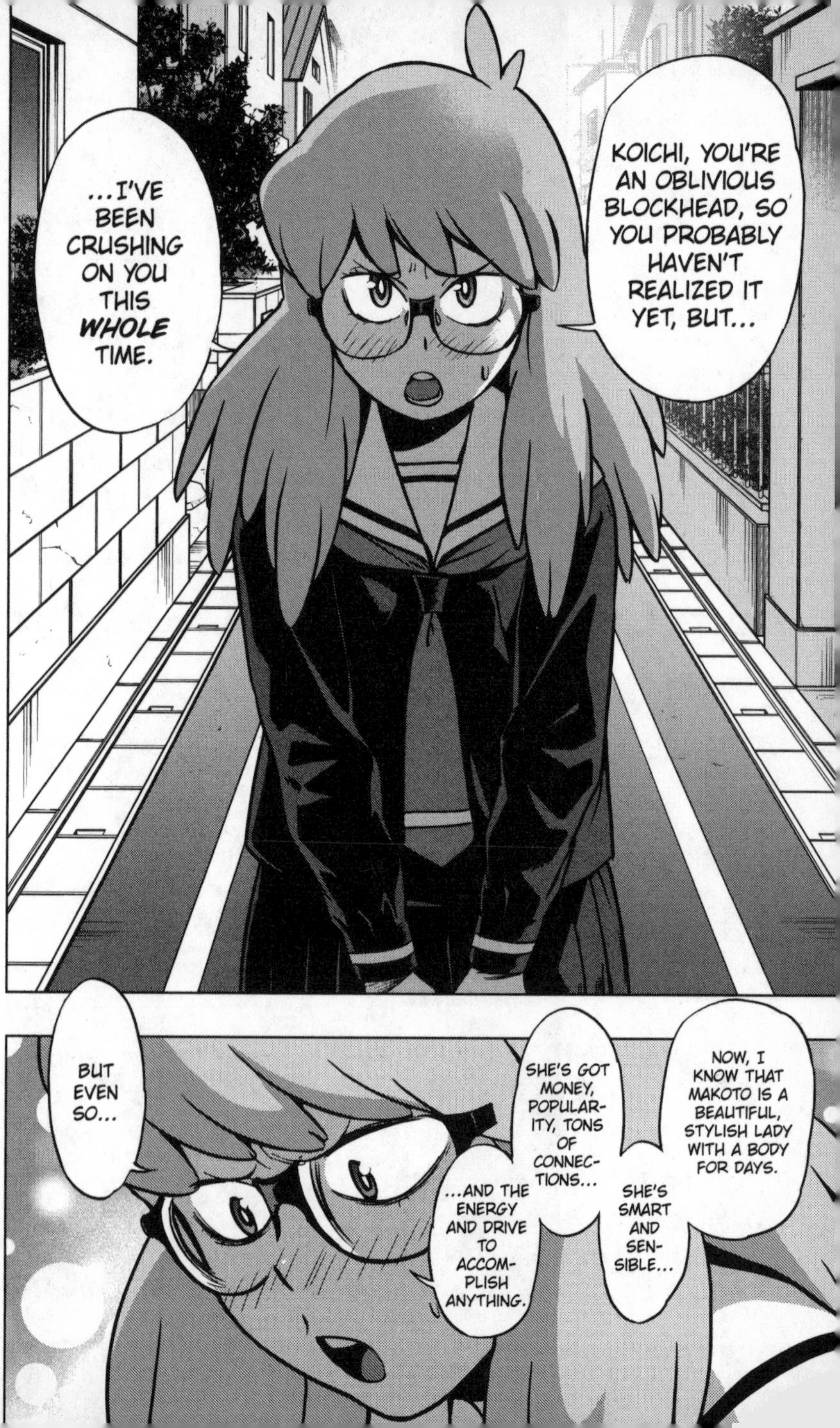
KOICHI, YOU'RE AN OBLIVIOUS BLOCKHEAD, SO YOU PROBABLY HAVEN'T REALIZED IT YET, BUT...
...I'VE BEEN CRUSHING ON YOU THIS ***WHOLE*** TIME.
NOW, I KNOW THAT MAKOTO IS A BEAUTIFUL, STYLISH LADY WITH A BODY FOR DAYS.
SHE'S SMART AND SEN-SIBLE...
SHE'S GOT MONEY, POPULAR-ITY, TONS OF CONNEC-TIONS...
...AND THE ENERGY AND DRIVE TO ACCOM-PLISH ANYTHING.
BUT EVEN SO...

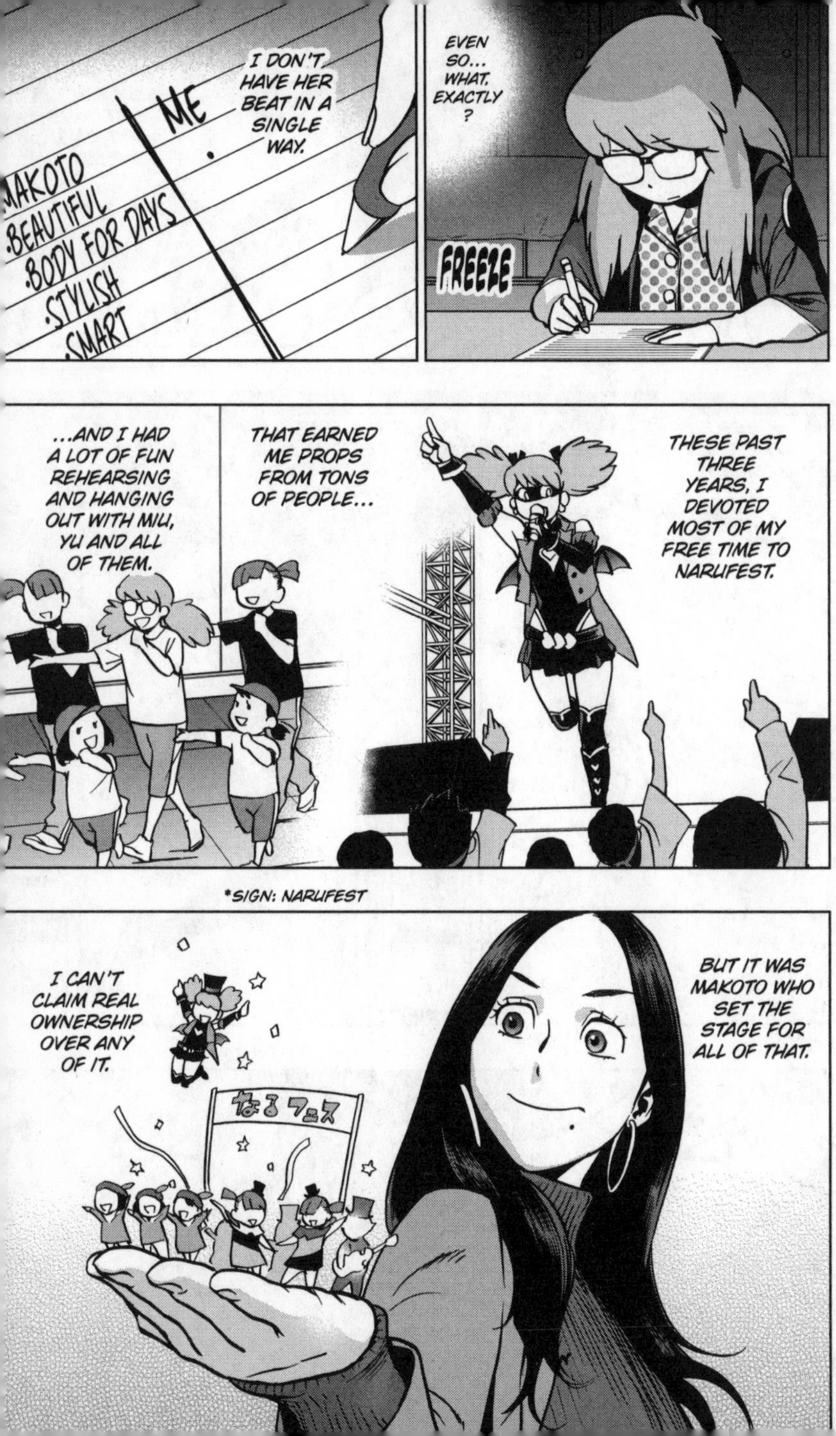
EVEN SO... WHAT, EXACTLY?
FREEZE
I DON'T HAVE HER BEAT IN A SINGLE WAY.
ME
MAKOTO
·BEAUTIFUL
·BODY FOR DAYS
·STYLISH
·SMART
THESE PAST THREE YEARS, I DEVOTED MOST OF MY FREE TIME TO NARUFEST.
THAT EARNED ME PROPS FROM TONS OF PEOPLE...
...AND I HAD A LOT OF FUN REHEARSING AND HANGING OUT WITH MIU, YU AND ALL OF THEM.
*SIGN: NARUFEST
BUT IT WAS MAKOTO WHO SET THE STAGE FOR ALL OF THAT.
I CAN'T CLAIM REAL OWNERSHIP OVER ANY OF IT.
なるフェス

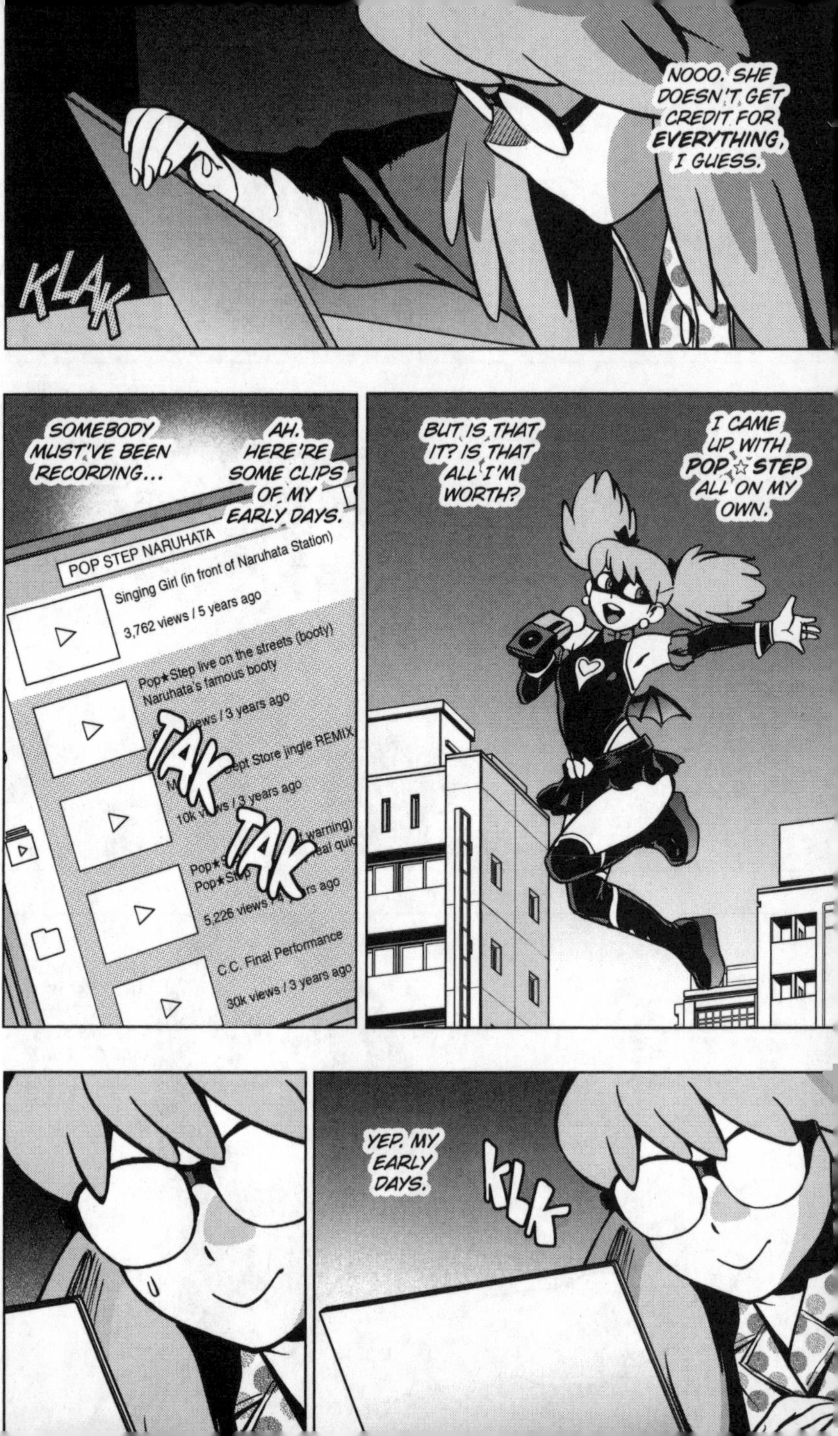
NOOO. SHE DOESN'T GET CREDIT FOR EVERYTHING, I GUESS.
KLAK
I CAME UP WITH POP☆STEP ALL ON MY OWN.
BUT IS THAT IT? IS THAT ALL I'M WORTH?
AH. HERE'RE SOME CLIPS OF MY EARLY DAYS.
SOMEBODY MUST'VE BEEN RECORDING...
POP STEP NARUHATA
POP STEP NARUHATA
Singing Girl (in front of Naruhata Station)
3,762 views / 5 years ago
Pop★Step live on the streets (booty)
Naruhata's famous booty
10k views / 3 years ago
5,226 views
C.C. Final Performance
30k views / 3 years ago
TAK
TAK
YEP. MY EARLY DAYS.
KLK

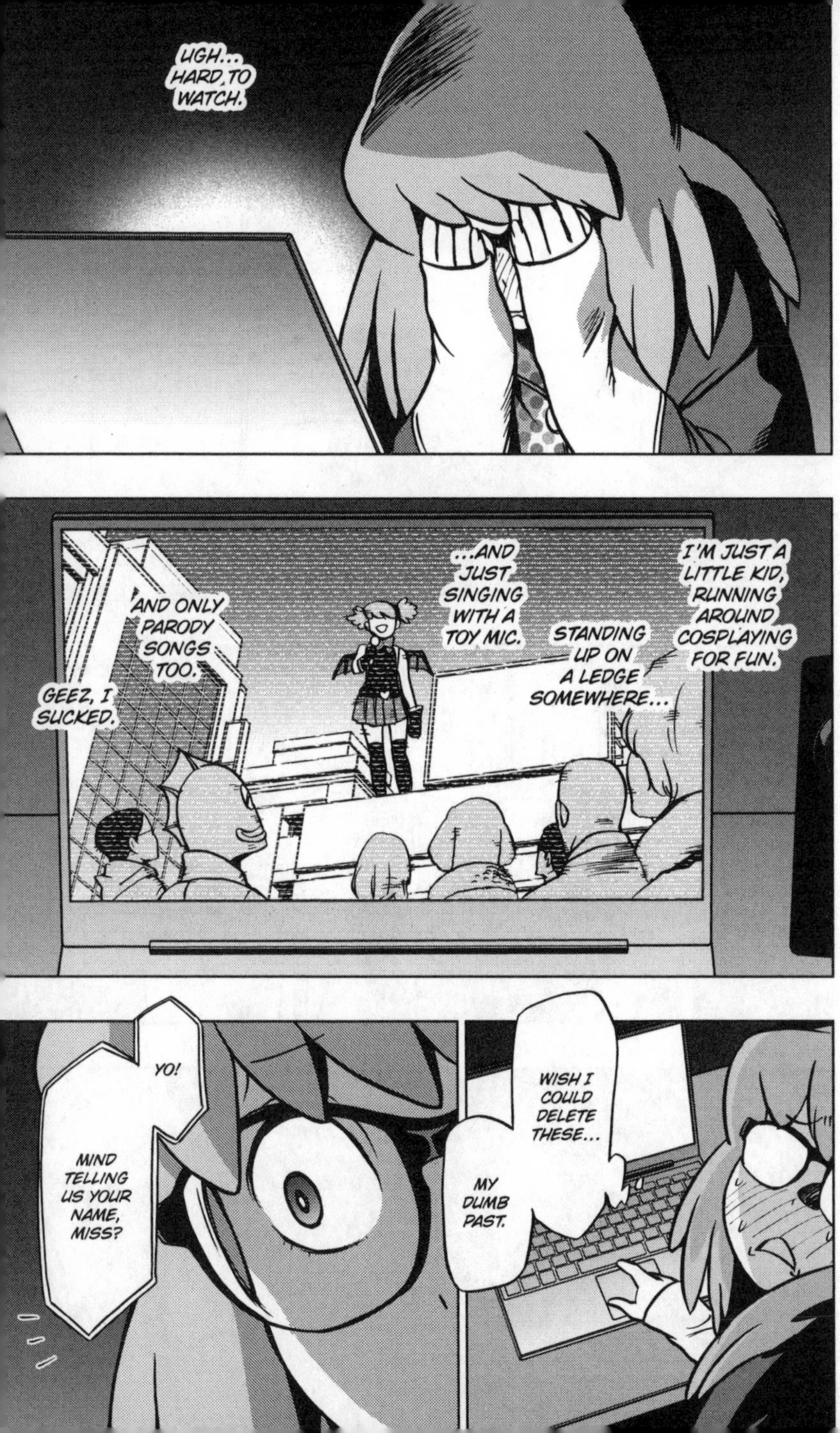
UGH... HARD TO WATCH.
I'M JUST A LITTLE KID, RUNNING AROUND COSPLAYING FOR FUN.
STANDING UP ON A LEDGE SOMEWHERE...
...AND JUST SINGING WITH A TOY MIC.
AND ONLY PARODY SONGS TOO.
GEEZ, I SUCKED.
WISH I COULD DELETE THESE...
MY DUMB PAST.
YO!
MIND TELLING US YOUR NAME, MISS?

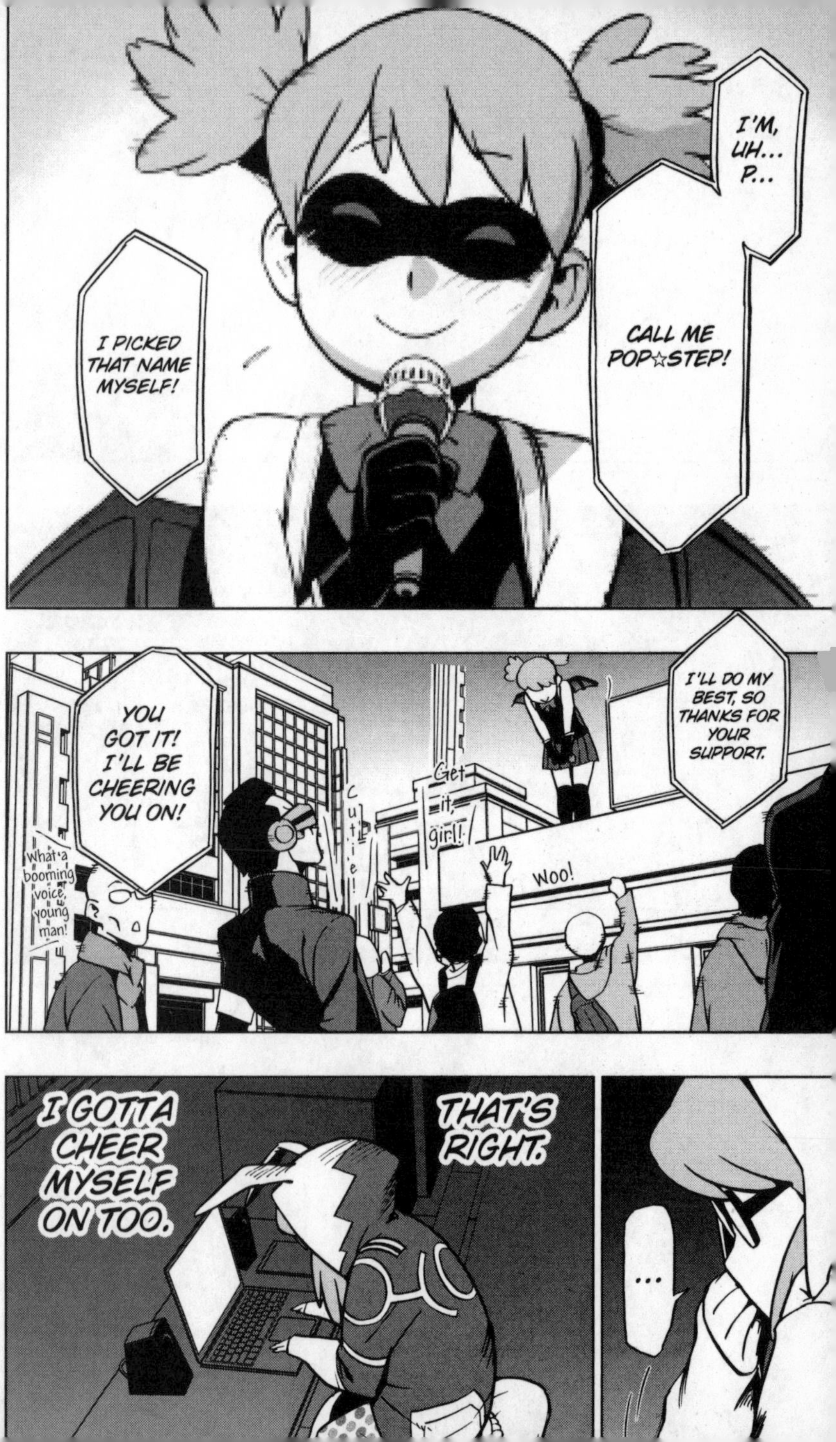

I'M, UH... P...
CALL ME POP☆STEP!
I PICKED THAT NAME MYSELF!
I'LL DO MY BEST, SO THANKS FOR YOUR SUPPORT.
YOU GOT IT! I'LL BE CHEERING YOU ON!
Get it, girl!
Cutie!
Woo!
What a booming voice, young man!
...
THAT'S RIGHT.
I GOTTA CHEER MYSELF ON TOO.

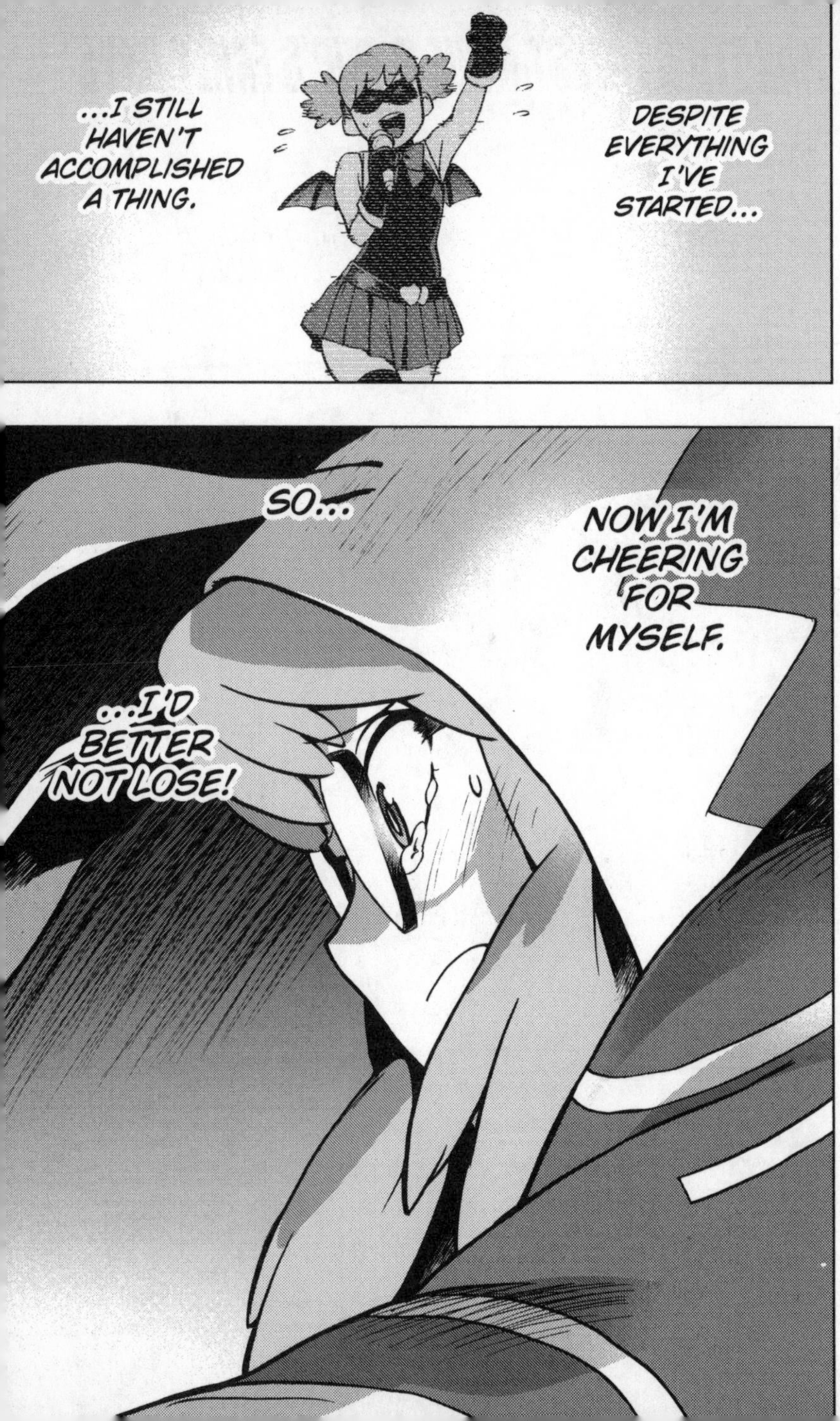
DESPITE EVERYTHING I'VE STARTED...
...I STILL HAVEN'T ACCOMPLISHED A THING.
NOW I'M CHEERING FOR MYSELF.
SO...
...I'D BETTER NOT LOSE!

MAKOTO'S LATEST MODE & POP'S EARLY DAYS

THE ROUGH DESIGN

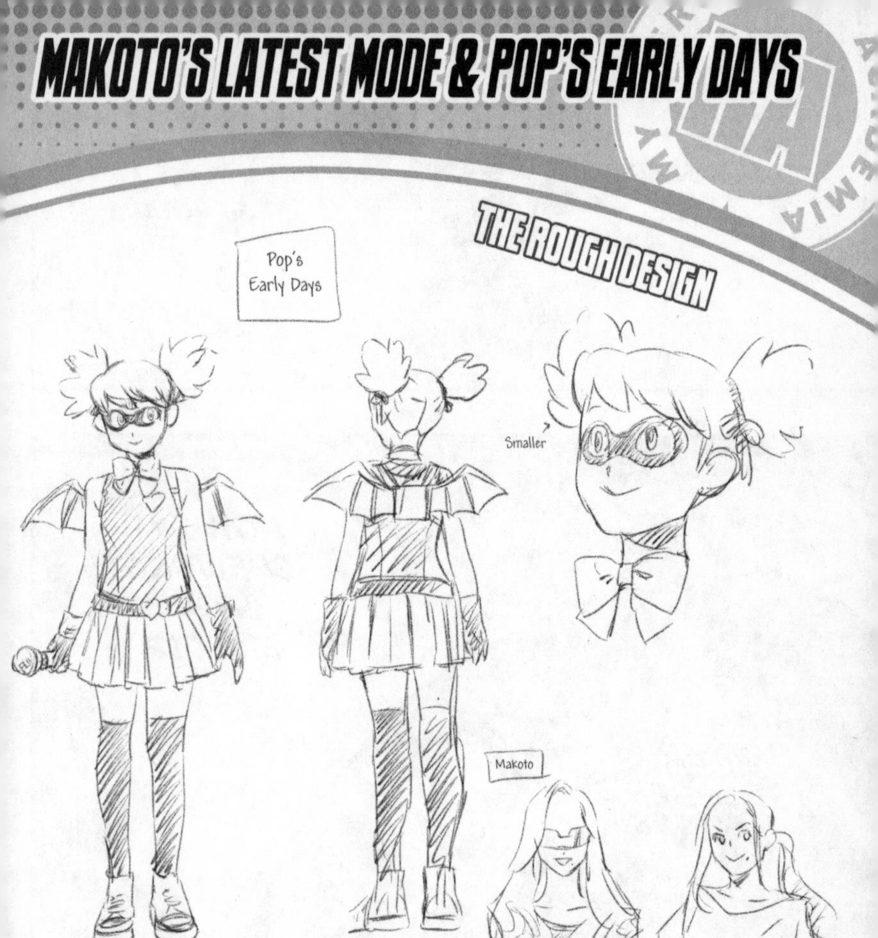
Pop's Early Days
Smaller

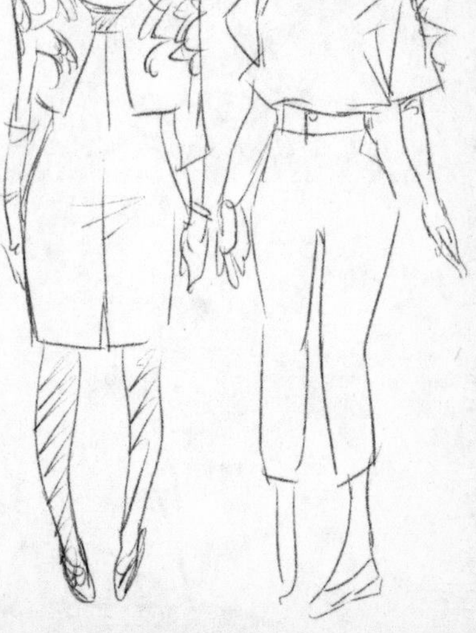
Makoto

BEHIND THE SCENES

Makoto is facing towards the future, while Pop is looking back at her own origins. Though it wasn't entirely intentional, I think that one scene creates some natural contrast between them.

The concept for Pop's first costume is "school-issued swimsuit" plus "party goods from the 100-yen shop." You're doing great, sweetie!

—Furuhashi

I like to try imagining what happened to transform Pop's first costume into her current one. (LOL)

—Betten

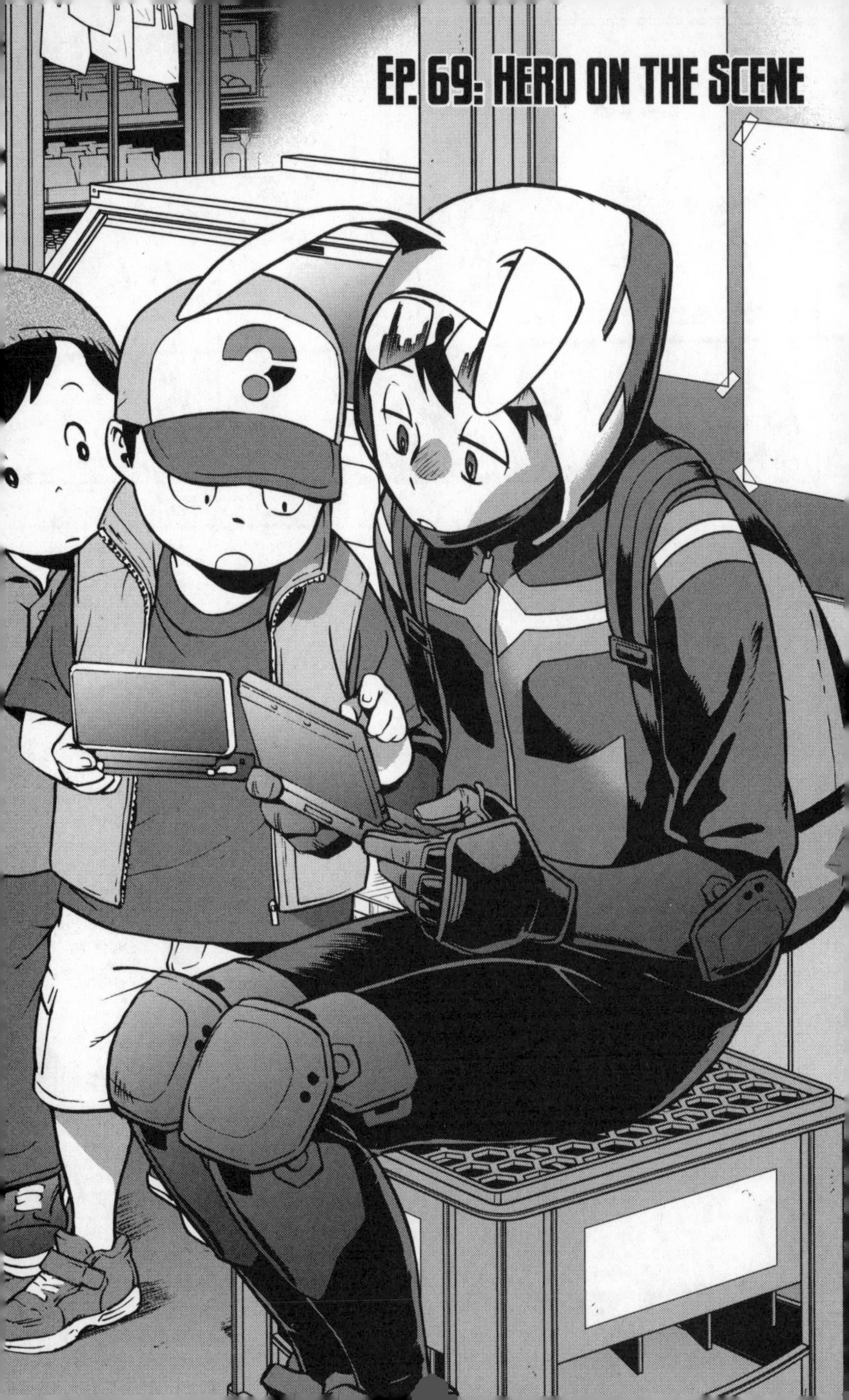
EP. 69: HERO ON THE SCENE

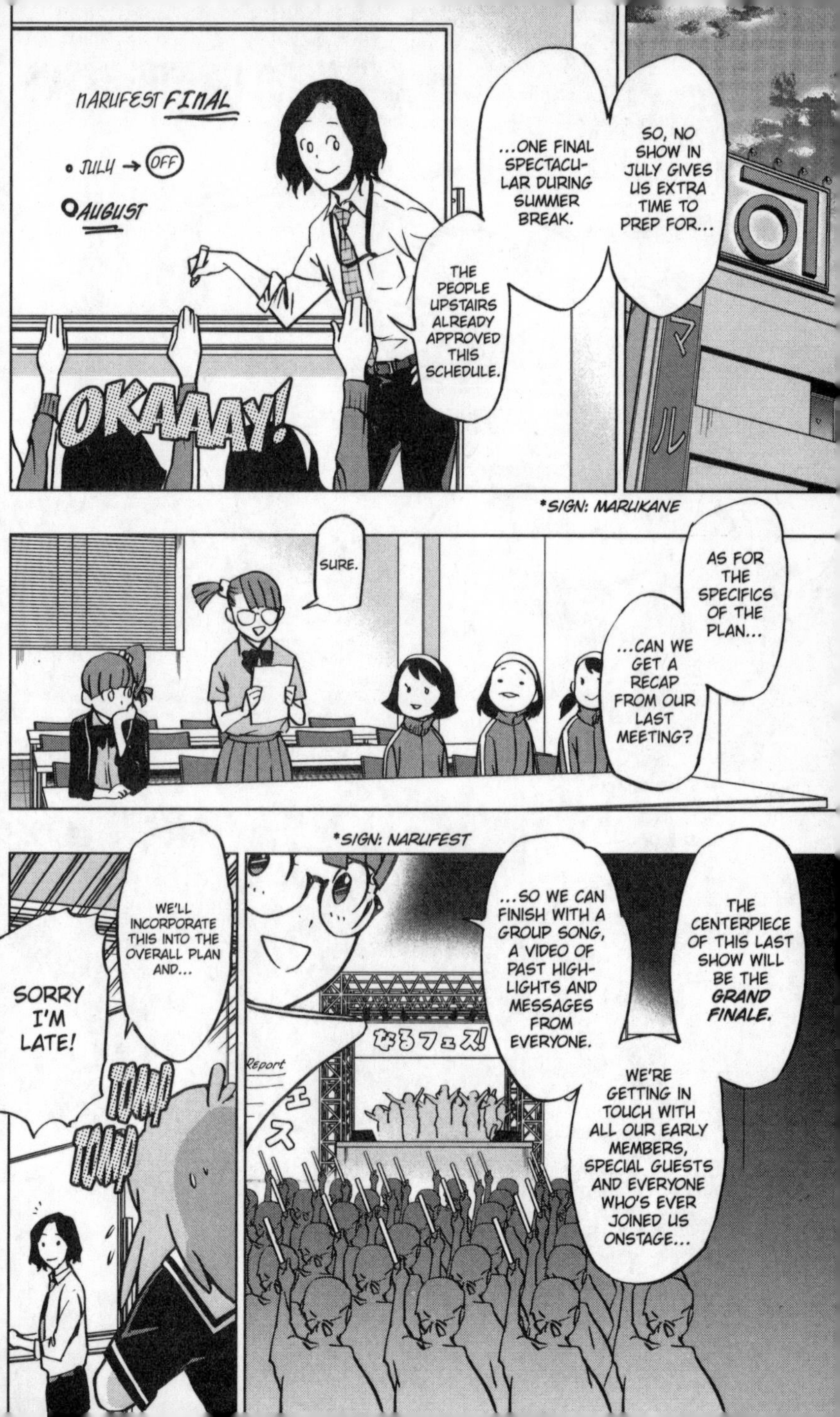
マル
NARUFEST FINAL
JULY → OFF
AUGUST
SO, NO SHOW IN JULY GIVES US EXTRA TIME TO PREP FOR...
...ONE FINAL SPECTACULAR DURING SUMMER BREAK.
THE PEOPLE UPSTAIRS ALREADY APPROVED THIS SCHEDULE.
OKAAAY!
*SIGN: MARUKANE
AS FOR THE SPECIFICS OF THE PLAN...
...CAN WE GET A RECAP FROM OUR LAST MEETING?
SURE.
*SIGN: NARUFEST
THE CENTERPIECE OF THIS LAST SHOW WILL BE THE ***GRAND FINALE.***
...SO WE CAN FINISH WITH A GROUP SONG, A VIDEO OF PAST HIGHLIGHTS AND MESSAGES FROM EVERYONE.
WE'RE GETTING IN TOUCH WITH ALL OUR EARLY MEMBERS, SPECIAL GUESTS AND EVERYONE WHO'S EVER JOINED US ONSTAGE...
なるフェス!
Report
WE'LL INCORPORATE THIS INTO THE OVERALL PLAN AND...
SORRY I'M LATE!
TOMP TOMP

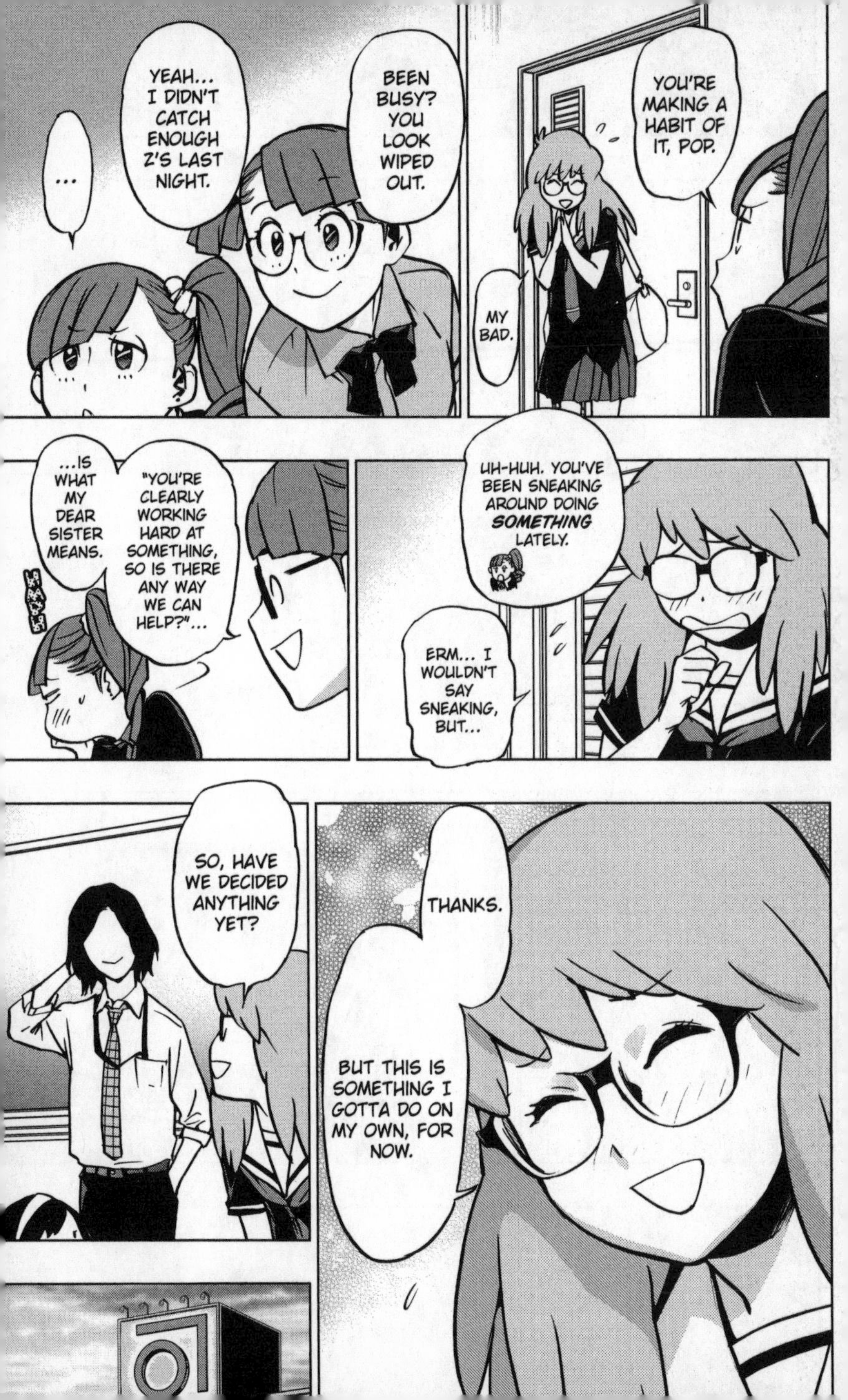
YOU'RE MAKING A HABIT OF IT, POP.
MY BAD.
BEEN BUSY? YOU LOOK WIPED OUT.
YEAH... I DIDN'T CATCH ENOUGH Z'S LAST NIGHT.
...
UH-HUH. YOU'VE BEEN SNEAKING AROUND DOING **SOMETHING** LATELY.
ERM... I WOULDN'T SAY SNEAKING, BUT...
"YOU'RE CLEARLY WORKING HARD AT SOMETHING, SO IS THERE ANY WAY WE CAN HELP?"...
...IS WHAT MY DEAR SISTER MEANS.
THANKS.
BUT THIS IS SOMETHING I GOTTA DO ON MY OWN, FOR NOW.
SO, HAVE WE DECIDED ANYTHING YET?

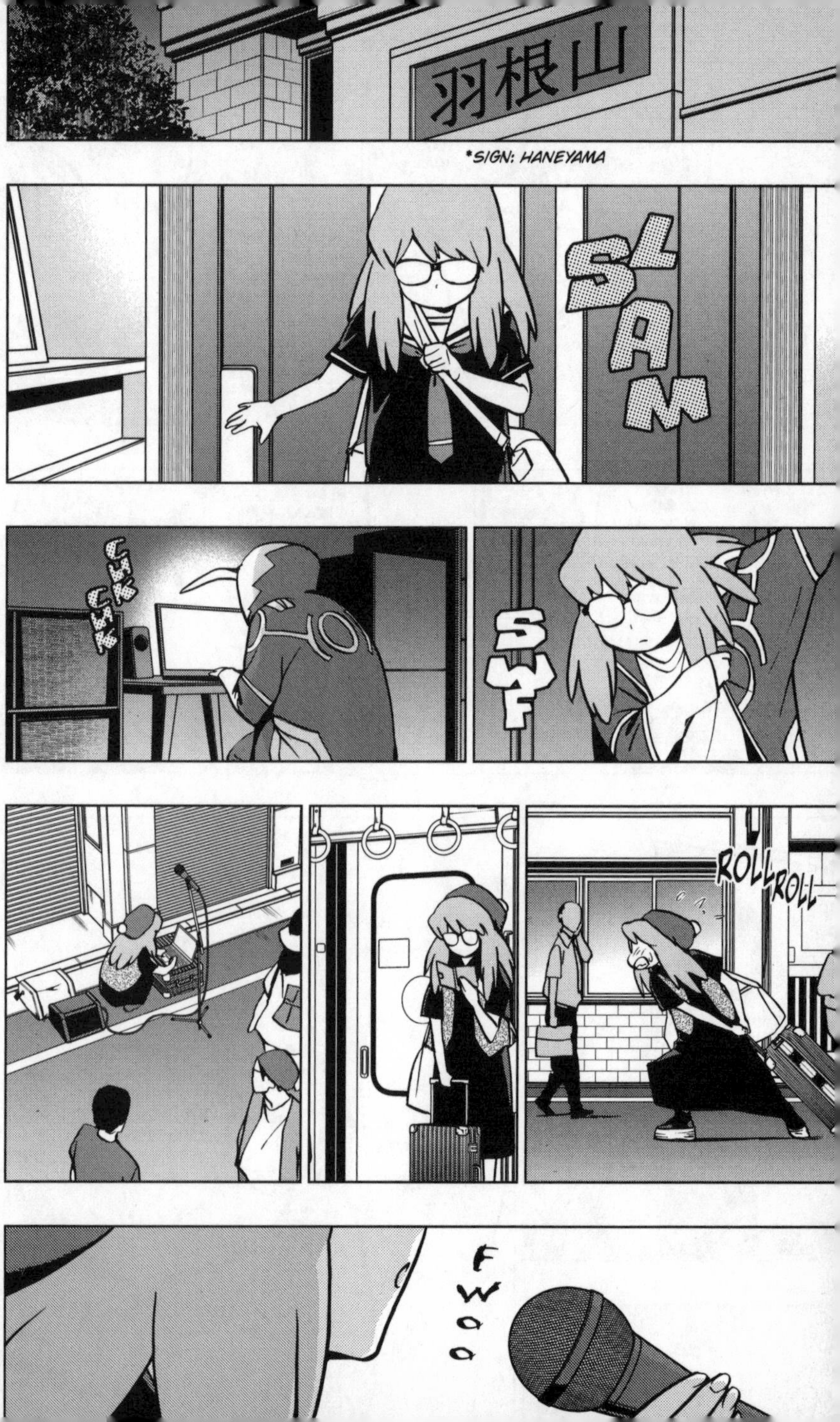
羽根山
*SIGN: HANEYAMA
SLAM
SWF
CHK CHK
ROLL ROLL
FWOO

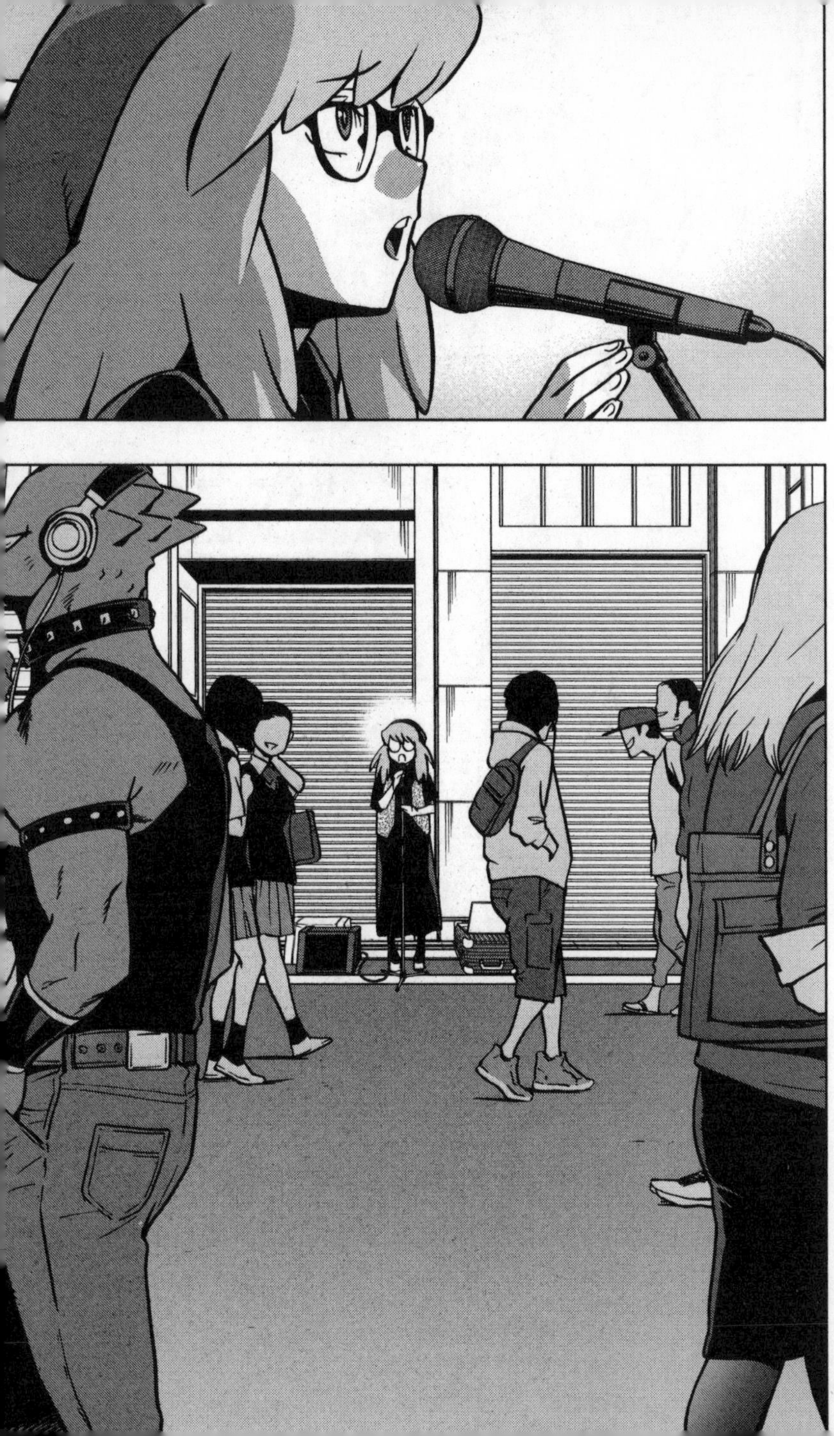

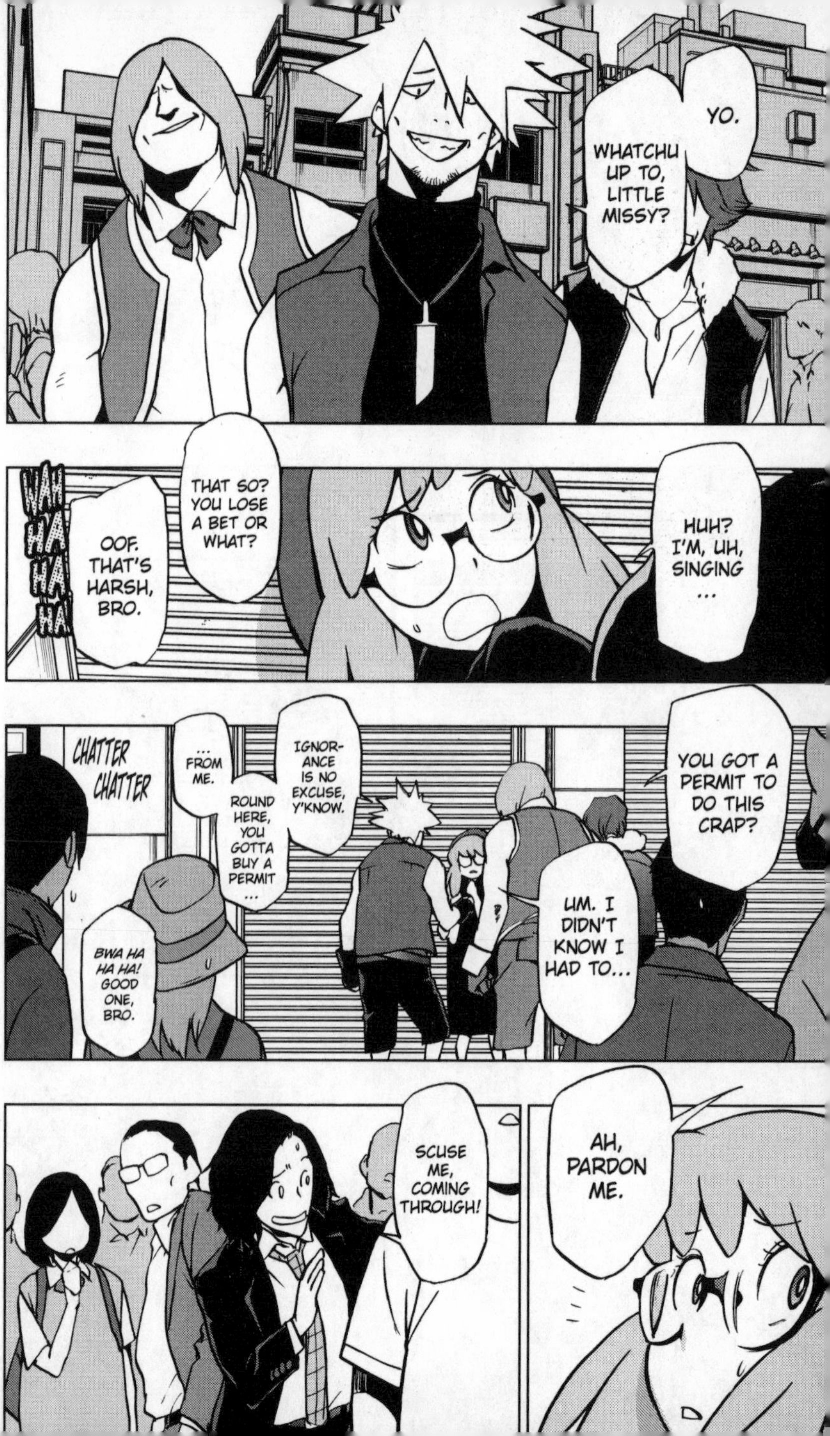
YO.
WHATCHU UP TO, LITTLE MISSY?
HUH? I'M, UH, SINGING ...
THAT SO? YOU LOSE A BET OR WHAT?
OOF. THAT'S HARSH, BRO.
WAH HA HA HA HA
YOU GOT A PERMIT TO DO THIS CRAP?
UM. I DIDN'T KNOW I HAD TO...
IGNOR-ANCE IS NO EXCUSE, Y'KNOW.
ROUND HERE, YOU GOTTA BUY A PERMIT ...
... FROM ME.
BWA HA HA HA! GOOD ONE, BRO.
CHATTER CHATTER
AH, PARDON ME.
SCUSE ME, COMING THROUGH!

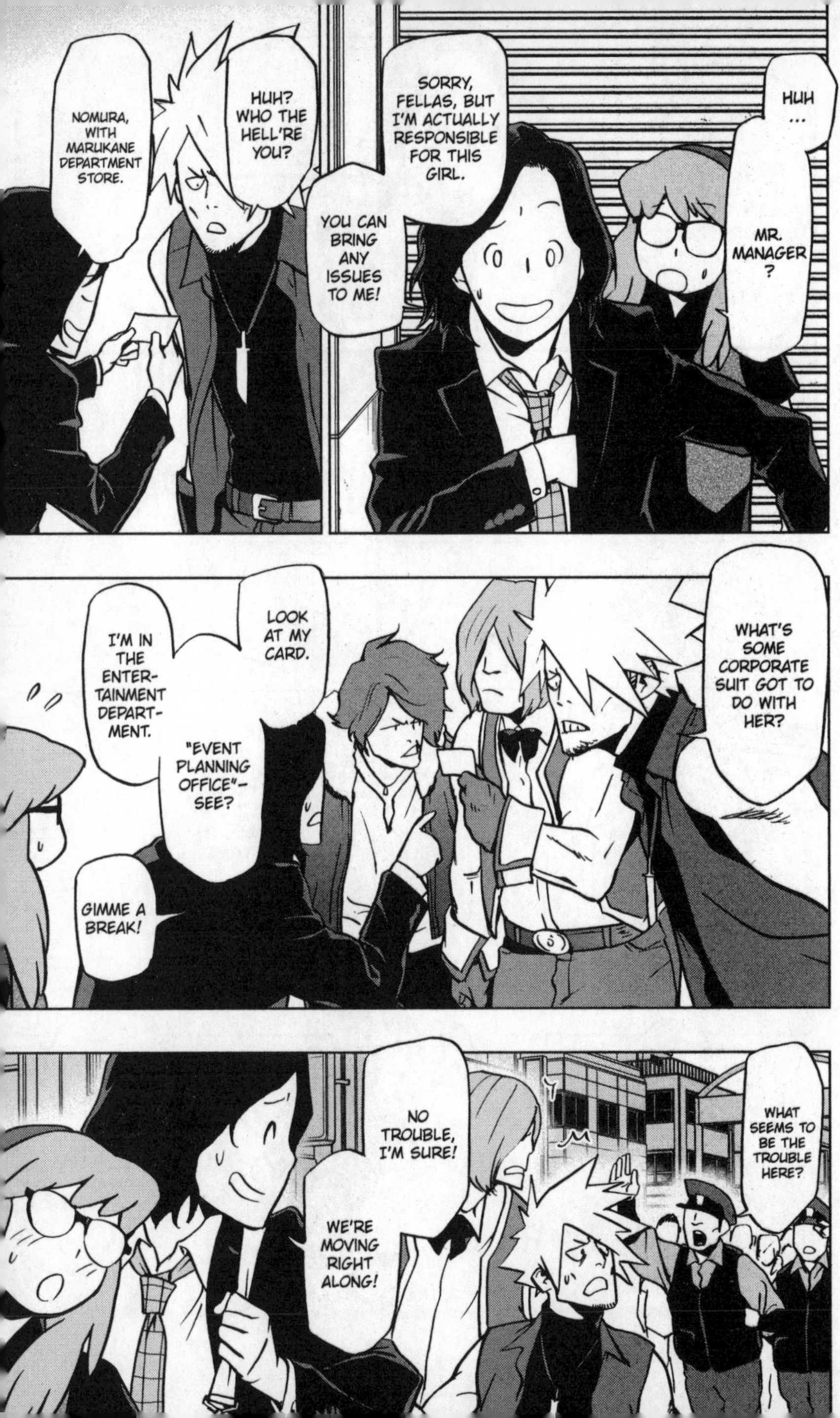
HUH ...
MR. MANAGER?
SORRY, FELLAS, BUT I'M ACTUALLY RESPONSIBLE FOR THIS GIRL.
YOU CAN BRING ANY ISSUES TO ME!
HUH? WHO THE HELL'RE YOU?
NOMURA, WITH MARUKANE DEPARTMENT STORE.
WHAT'S SOME CORPORATE SUIT GOT TO DO WITH HER?
LOOK AT MY CARD.
I'M IN THE ENTERTAINMENT DEPARTMENT.
"EVENT PLANNING OFFICE"—SEE?
GIMME A BREAK!
WHAT SEEMS TO BE THE TROUBLE HERE?
NO TROUBLE, I'M SURE!
WE'RE MOVING RIGHT ALONG!

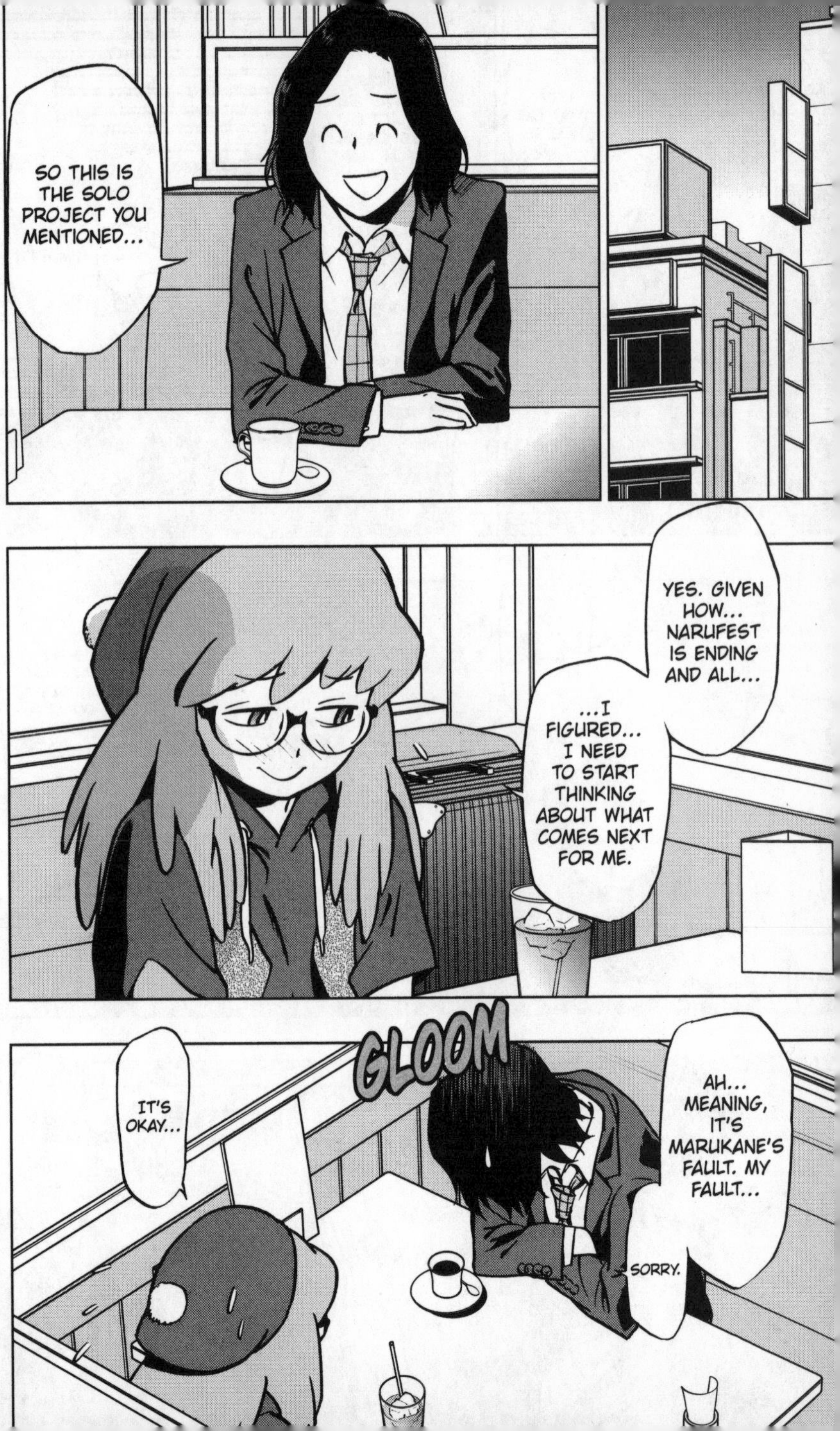
SO THIS IS THE SOLO PROJECT YOU MENTIONED...
YES. GIVEN HOW... NARUFEST IS ENDING AND ALL...
...I FIGURED... I NEED TO START THINKING ABOUT WHAT COMES NEXT FOR ME.
GLOOM
AH... MEANING, IT'S MARUKANE'S FAULT. MY FAULT...
SORRY.
IT'S OKAY...

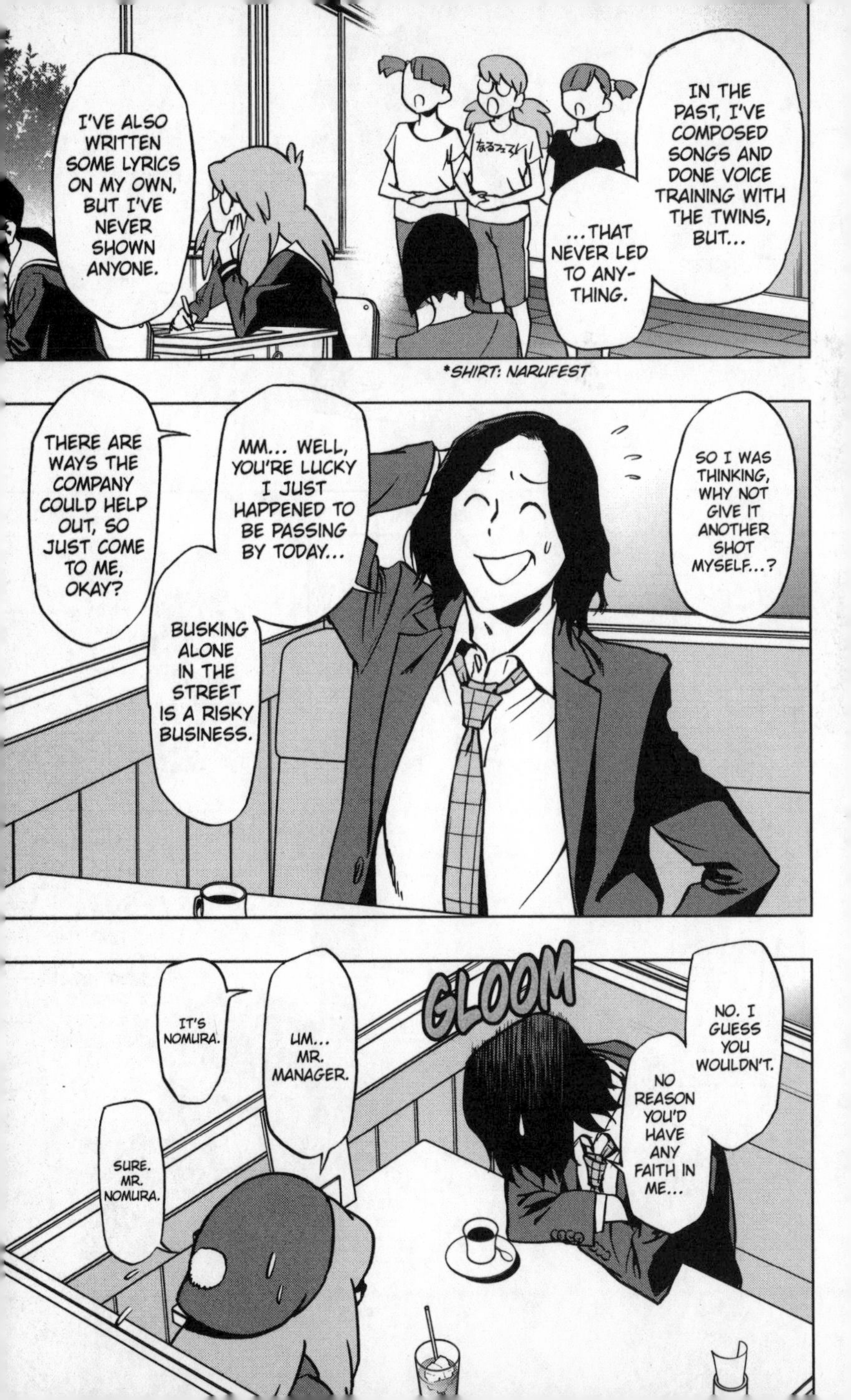
IN THE PAST, I'VE COMPOSED SONGS AND DONE VOICE TRAINING WITH THE TWINS, BUT...
...THAT NEVER LED TO ANY-THING.
I'VE ALSO WRITTEN SOME LYRICS ON MY OWN, BUT I'VE NEVER SHOWN ANYONE.
SO I WAS THINKING, WHY NOT GIVE IT ANOTHER SHOT MYSELF...?
MM... WELL, YOU'RE LUCKY I JUST HAPPENED TO BE PASSING BY TODAY...
BUSKING ALONE IN THE STREET IS A RISKY BUSINESS.
THERE ARE WAYS THE COMPANY COULD HELP OUT, SO JUST COME TO ME, OKAY?
GLOOM
NO. I GUESS YOU WOULDN'T.
NO REASON YOU'D HAVE ANY FAITH IN ME...
UM... MR. MANAGER.
IT'S NOMURA.
SURE. MR. NOMURA.

*SHIRT: NARUFEST

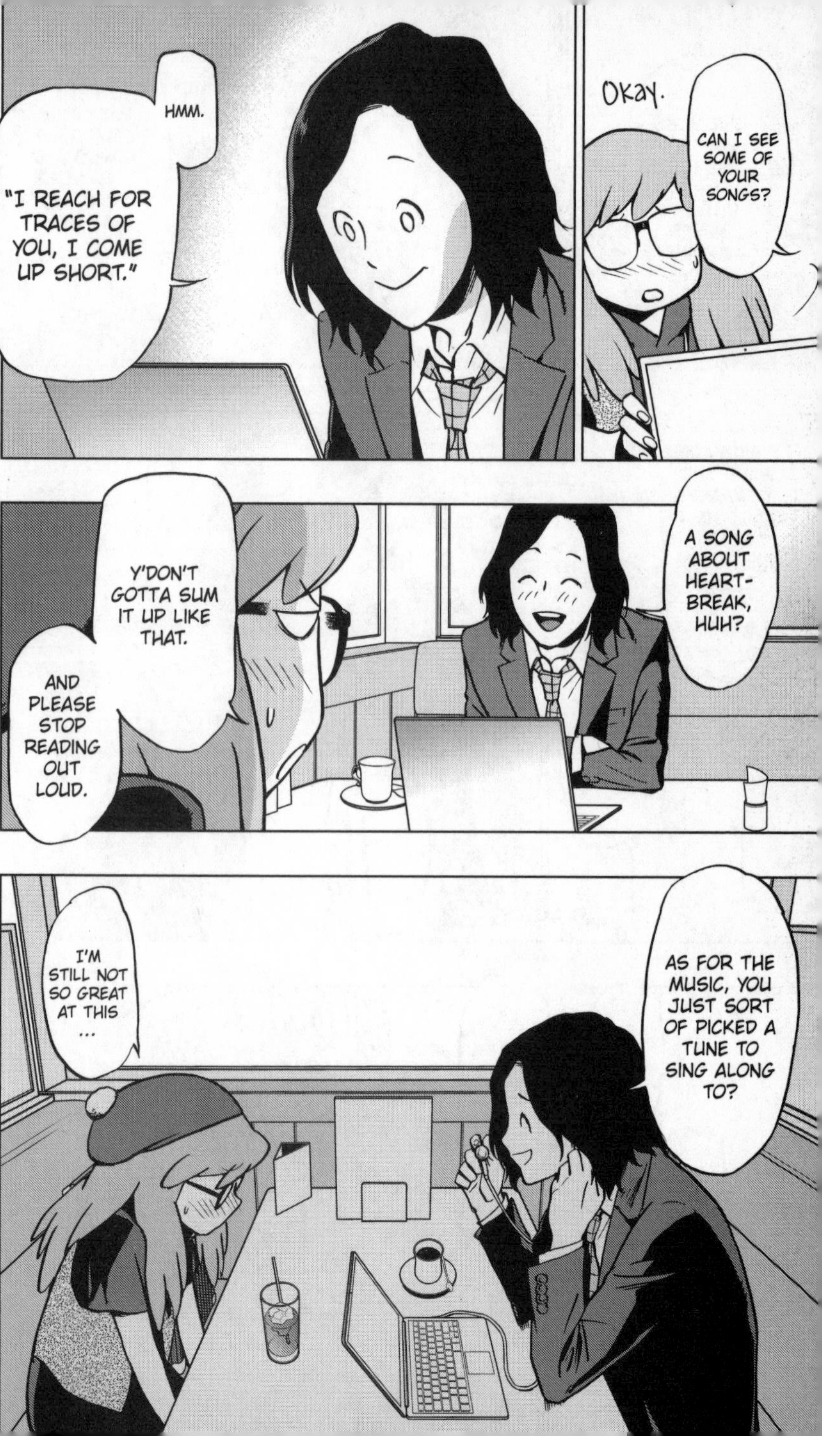
CAN I SEE SOME OF YOUR SONGS?
Okay.
HMM.
"I REACH FOR TRACES OF YOU, I COME UP SHORT."
A SONG ABOUT HEART-BREAK, HUH?
Y'DON'T GOTTA SUM IT UP LIKE THAT.
AND PLEASE STOP READING OUT LOUD.
AS FOR THE MUSIC, YOU JUST SORT OF PICKED A TUNE TO SING ALONG TO?
I'M STILL NOT SO GREAT AT THIS ...

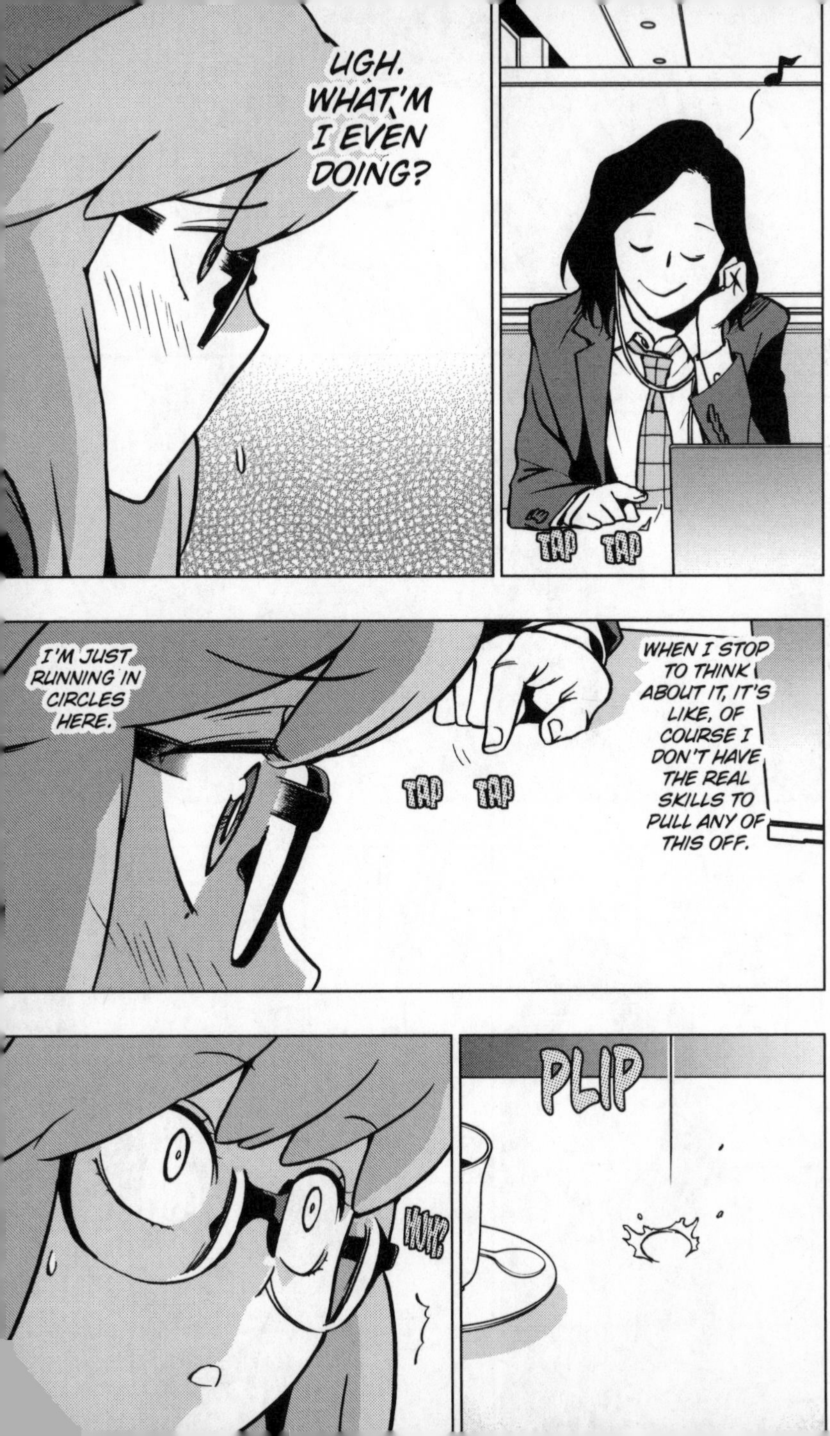
TAP TAP
UGH. WHAT'M I EVEN DOING?
WHEN I STOP TO THINK ABOUT IT, IT'S LIKE, OF COURSE I DON'T HAVE THE REAL SKILLS TO PULL ANY OF THIS OFF.
TAP TAP
I'M JUST RUNNING IN CIRCLES HERE.
PLIP
HUH?

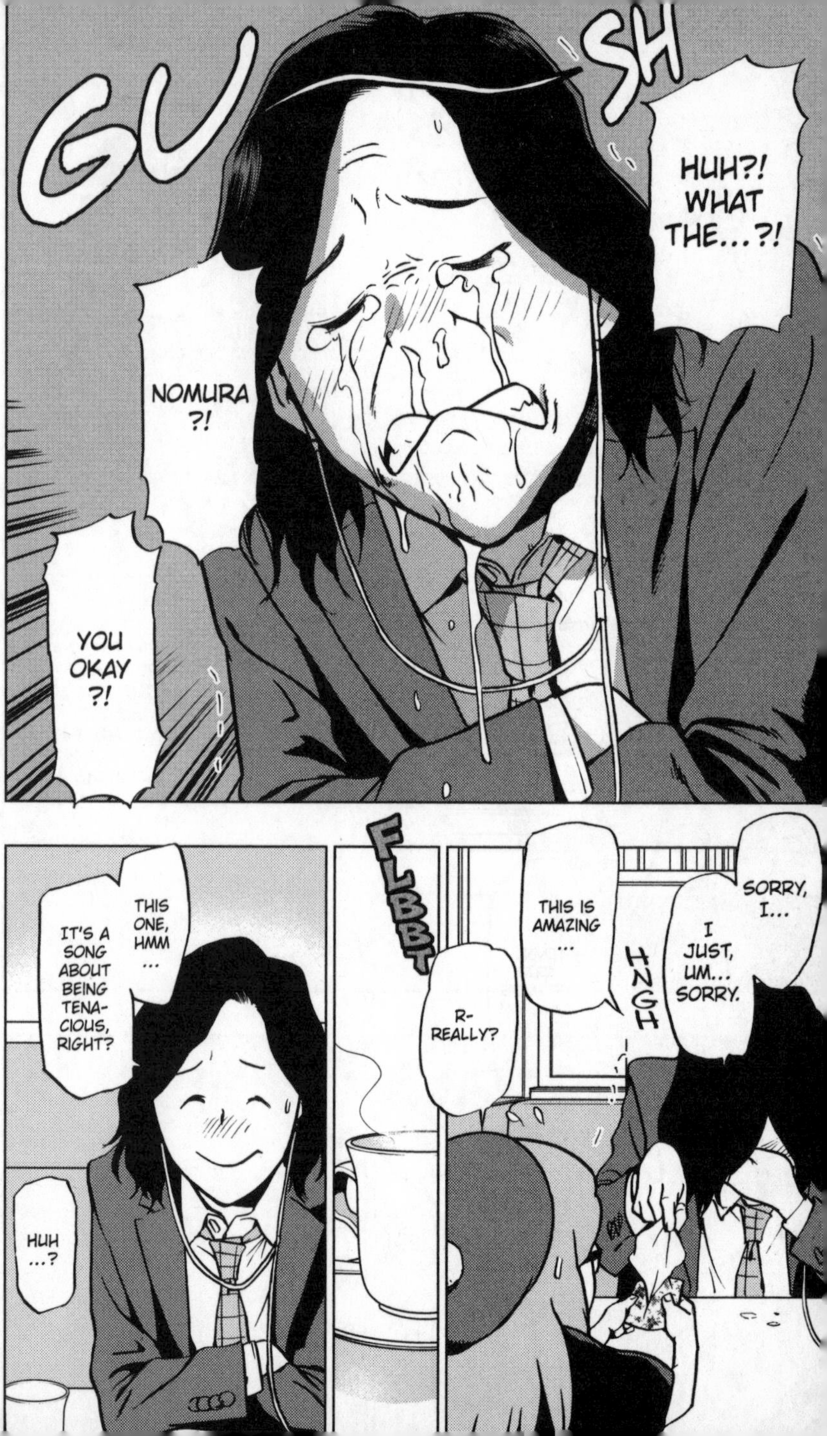
GUSH
HUH?! WHAT THE...?!
NOMURA ?!
YOU OKAY ?!
SORRY, I...
I JUST, UM... SORRY.
HNGH
THIS IS AMAZING ...
R-REALLY?
FLBBT
THIS ONE, HMM ...
IT'S A SONG ABOUT BEING TENA-CIOUS, RIGHT?
HUH ...?

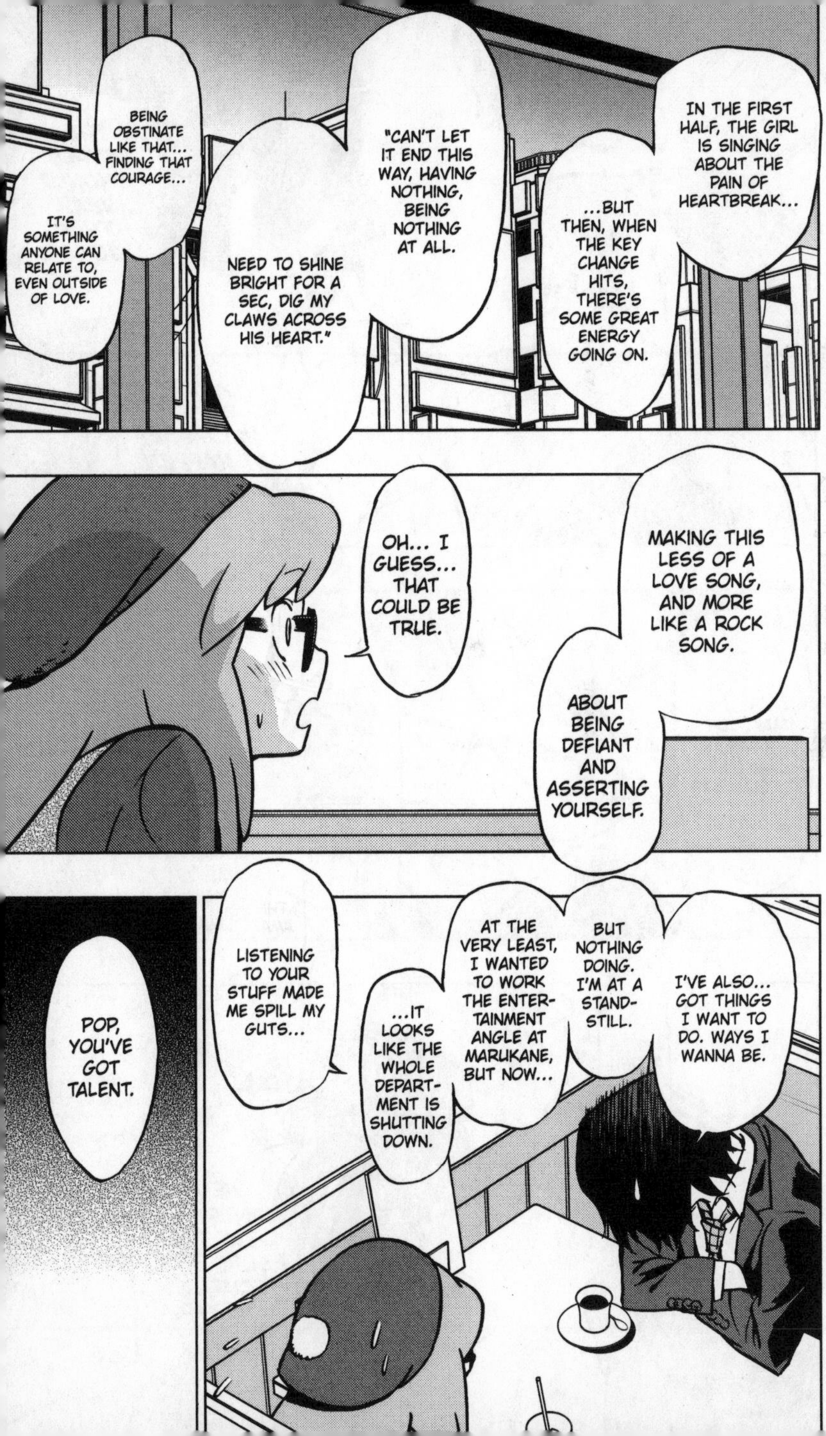
IN THE FIRST HALF, THE GIRL IS SINGING ABOUT THE PAIN OF HEARTBREAK...
...BUT THEN, WHEN THE KEY CHANGE HITS, THERE'S SOME GREAT ENERGY GOING ON.
"CAN'T LET IT END THIS WAY, HAVING NOTHING, BEING NOTHING AT ALL.
NEED TO SHINE BRIGHT FOR A SEC, DIG MY CLAWS ACROSS HIS HEART."
BEING OBSTINATE LIKE THAT... FINDING THAT COURAGE...
IT'S SOMETHING ANYONE CAN RELATE TO, EVEN OUTSIDE OF LOVE.
MAKING THIS LESS OF A LOVE SONG, AND MORE LIKE A ROCK SONG.
ABOUT BEING DEFIANT AND ASSERTING YOURSELF.
OH... I GUESS... THAT COULD BE TRUE.
I'VE ALSO... GOT THINGS I WANT TO DO. WAYS I WANNA BE.
BUT NOTHING DOING. I'M AT A STAND-STILL.
AT THE VERY LEAST, I WANTED TO WORK THE ENTER-TAINMENT ANGLE AT MARUKANE, BUT NOW...
...IT LOOKS LIKE THE WHOLE DEPART-MENT IS SHUTTING DOWN.
LISTENING TO YOUR STUFF MADE ME SPILL MY GUTS...
POP, YOU'VE GOT TALENT.

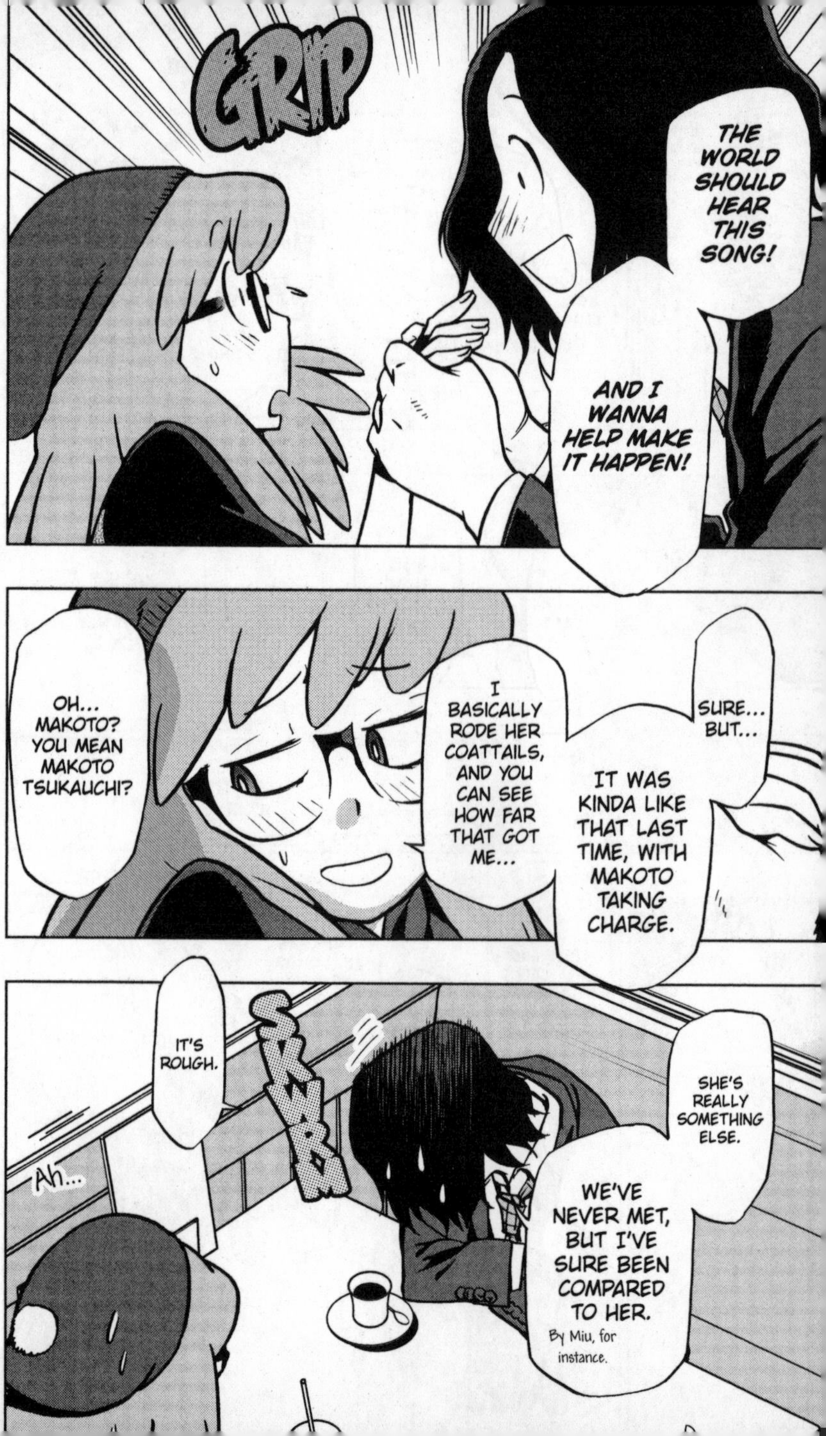
GRIP
THE WORLD SHOULD HEAR THIS SONG!
AND I WANNA HELP MAKE IT HAPPEN!
SURE... BUT...
IT WAS KINDA LIKE THAT LAST TIME, WITH MAKOTO TAKING CHARGE.
I BASICALLY RODE HER COATTAILS, AND YOU CAN SEE HOW FAR THAT GOT ME...
OH... MAKOTO? YOU MEAN MAKOTO TSUKAUCHI?
SHE'S REALLY SOMETHING ELSE.
WE'VE NEVER MET, BUT I'VE SURE BEEN COMPARED TO HER.
By Miu, for instance.
IT'S ROUGH.
Ah...

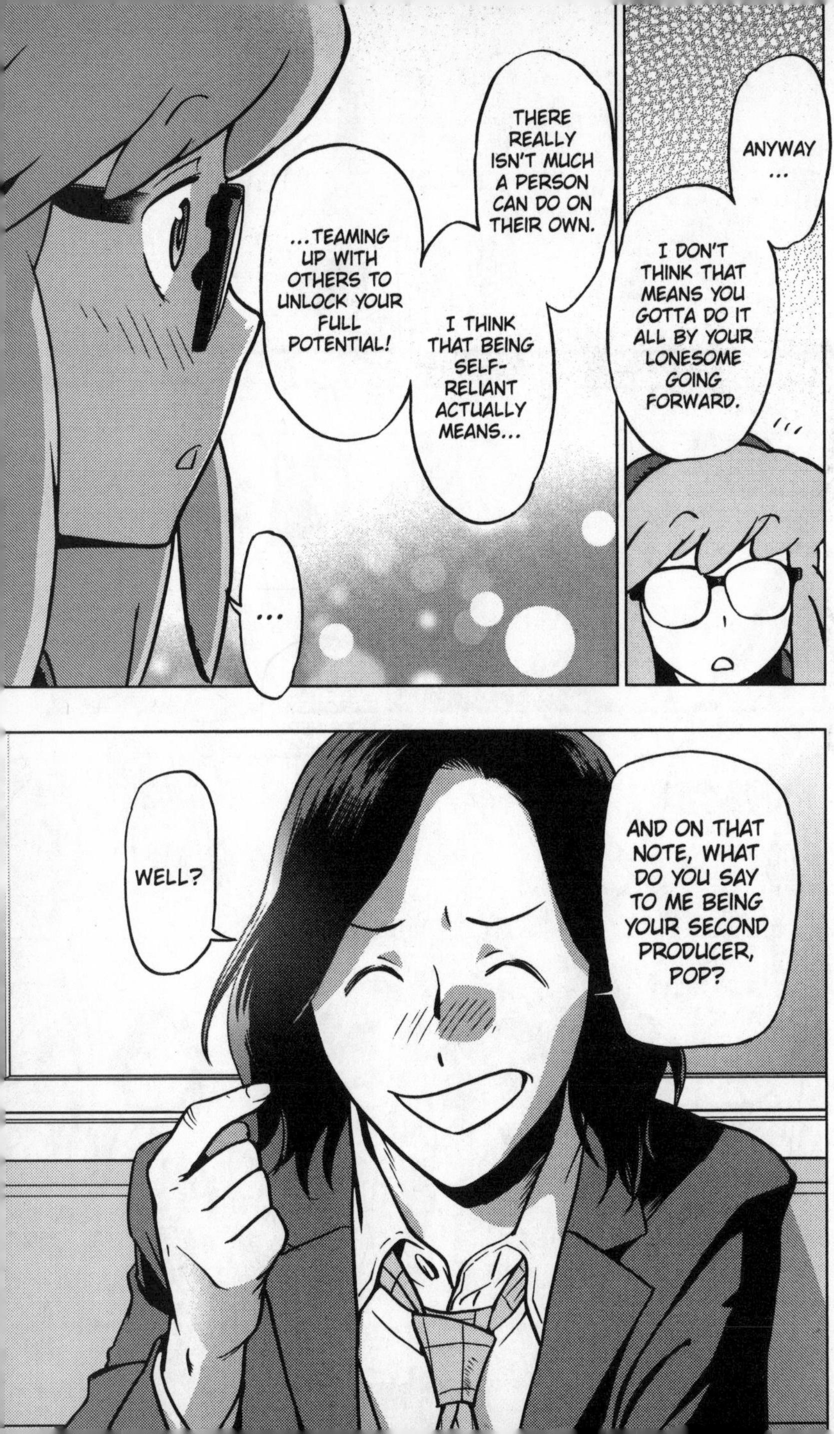
ANYWAY ...
I DON'T THINK THAT MEANS YOU GOTTA DO IT ALL BY YOUR LONESOME GOING FORWARD.
...
THERE REALLY ISN'T MUCH A PERSON CAN DO ON THEIR OWN.
I THINK THAT BEING SELF-RELIANT ACTUALLY MEANS...
...TEAMING UP WITH OTHERS TO UNLOCK YOUR FULL POTENTIAL!
...
AND ON THAT NOTE, WHAT DO YOU SAY TO ME BEING YOUR SECOND PRODUCER, POP?
WELL?

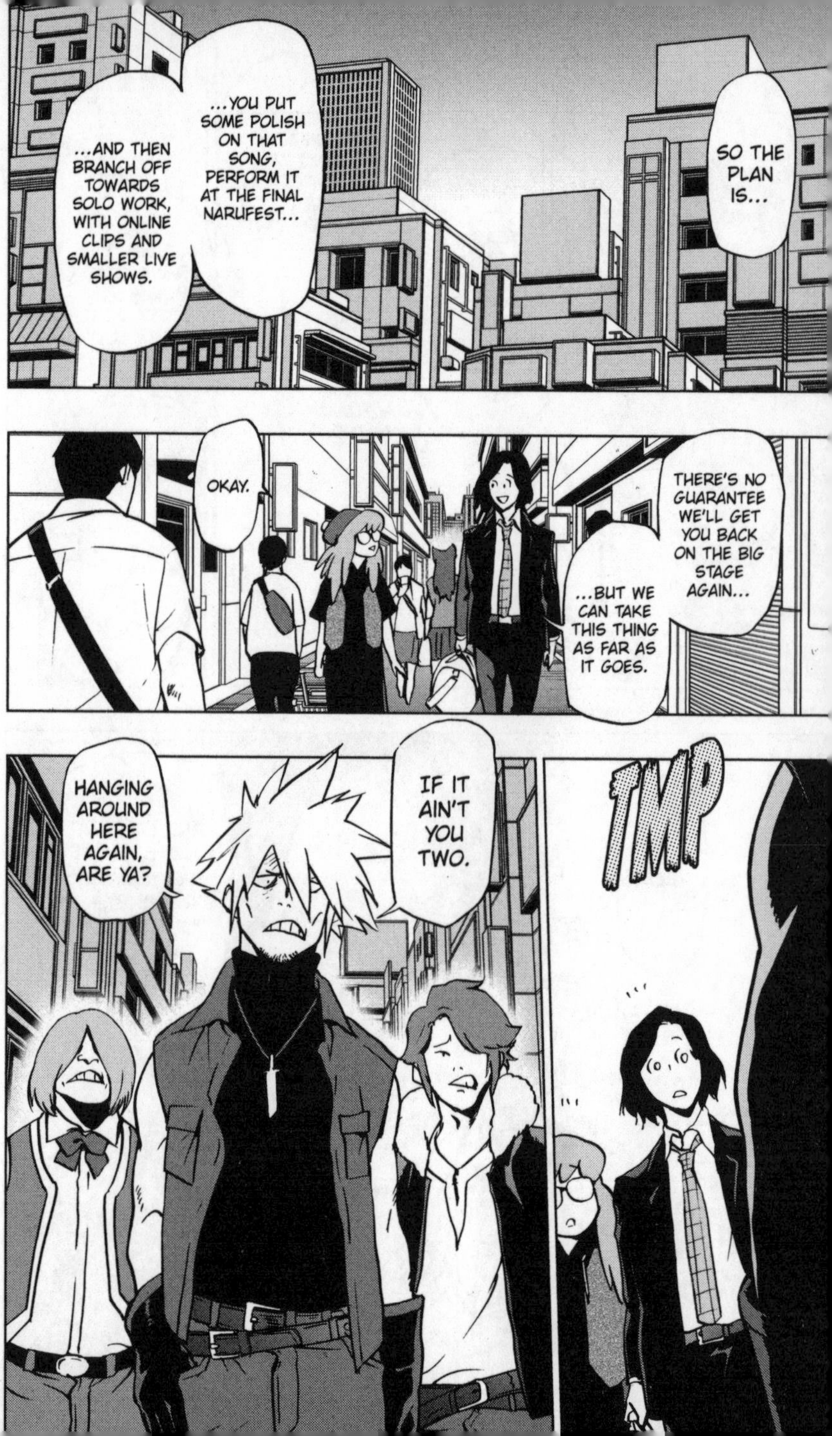
SO THE PLAN IS...
...YOU PUT SOME POLISH ON THAT SONG, PERFORM IT AT THE FINAL NARUFEST...
...AND THEN BRANCH OFF TOWARDS SOLO WORK, WITH ONLINE CLIPS AND SMALLER LIVE SHOWS.
THERE'S NO GUARANTEE WE'LL GET YOU BACK ON THE BIG STAGE AGAIN...
...BUT WE CAN TAKE THIS THING AS FAR AS IT GOES.
OKAY.
TMP
IF IT AIN'T YOU TWO.
HANGING AROUND HERE AGAIN, ARE YA?

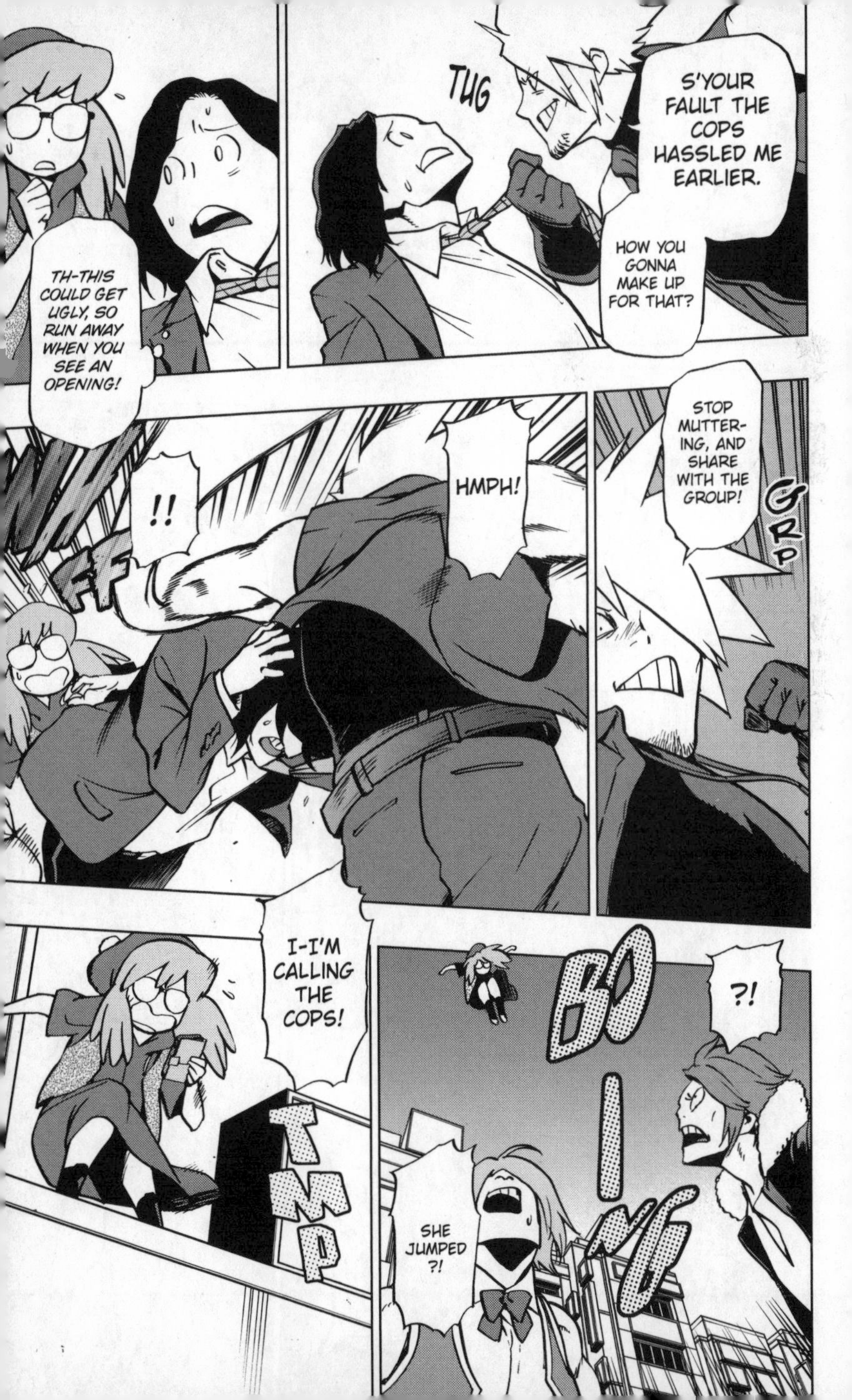
TUG
S'YOUR FAULT THE COPS HASSLED ME EARLIER.
HOW YOU GONNA MAKE UP FOR THAT?
TH-THIS COULD GET UGLY, SO RUN AWAY WHEN YOU SEE AN OPENING!
STOP MUTTER-ING, AND SHARE WITH THE GROUP!
GRP
HMPH!
!!
FF
BOING
?!
SHE JUMPED ?!
I-I'M CALLING THE COPS!
TMP

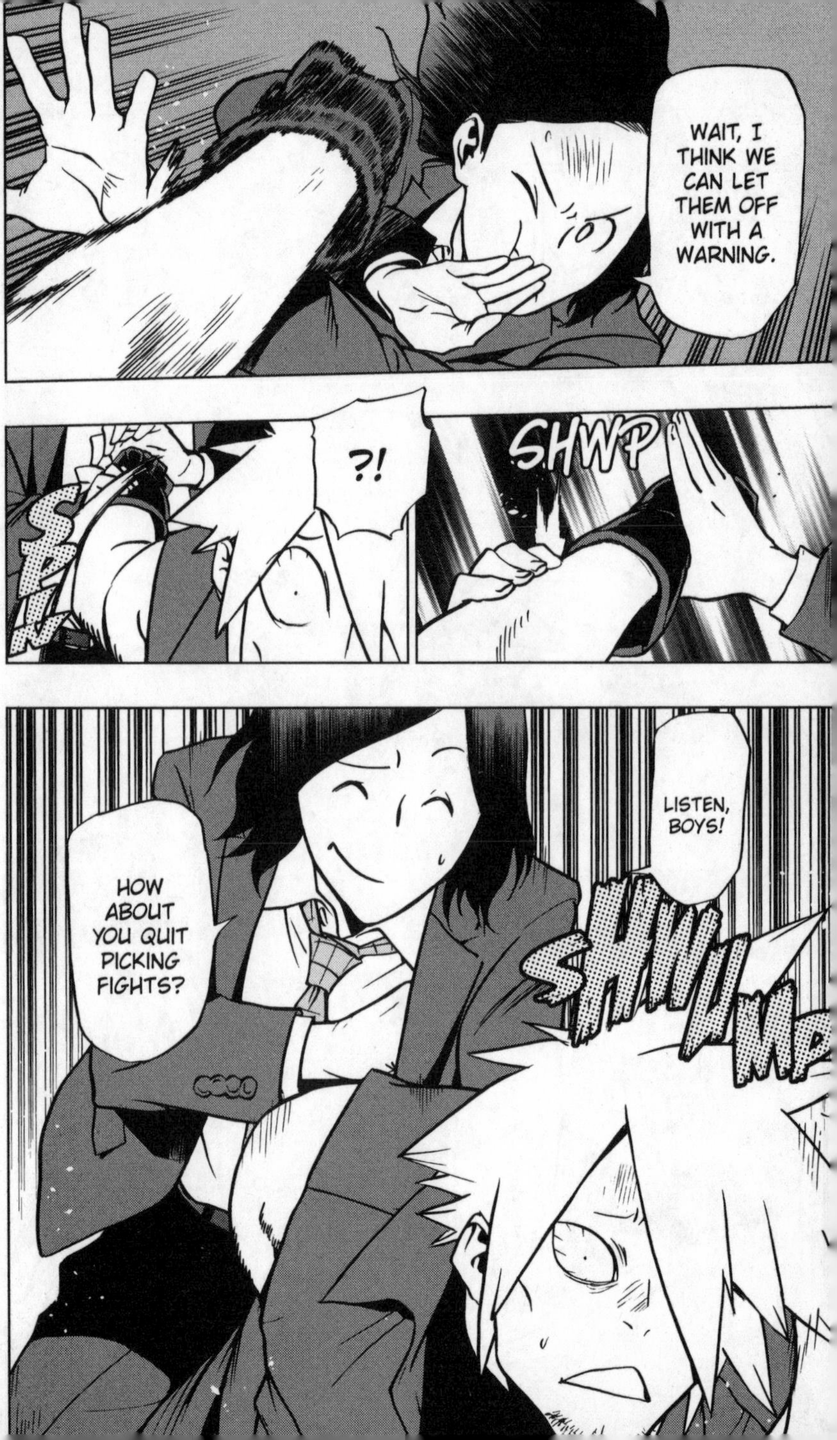
WAIT, I THINK WE CAN LET THEM OFF WITH A WARNING.
SHWP
?!
LISTEN, BOYS!
HOW ABOUT YOU QUIT PICKING FIGHTS?
SHWUMP

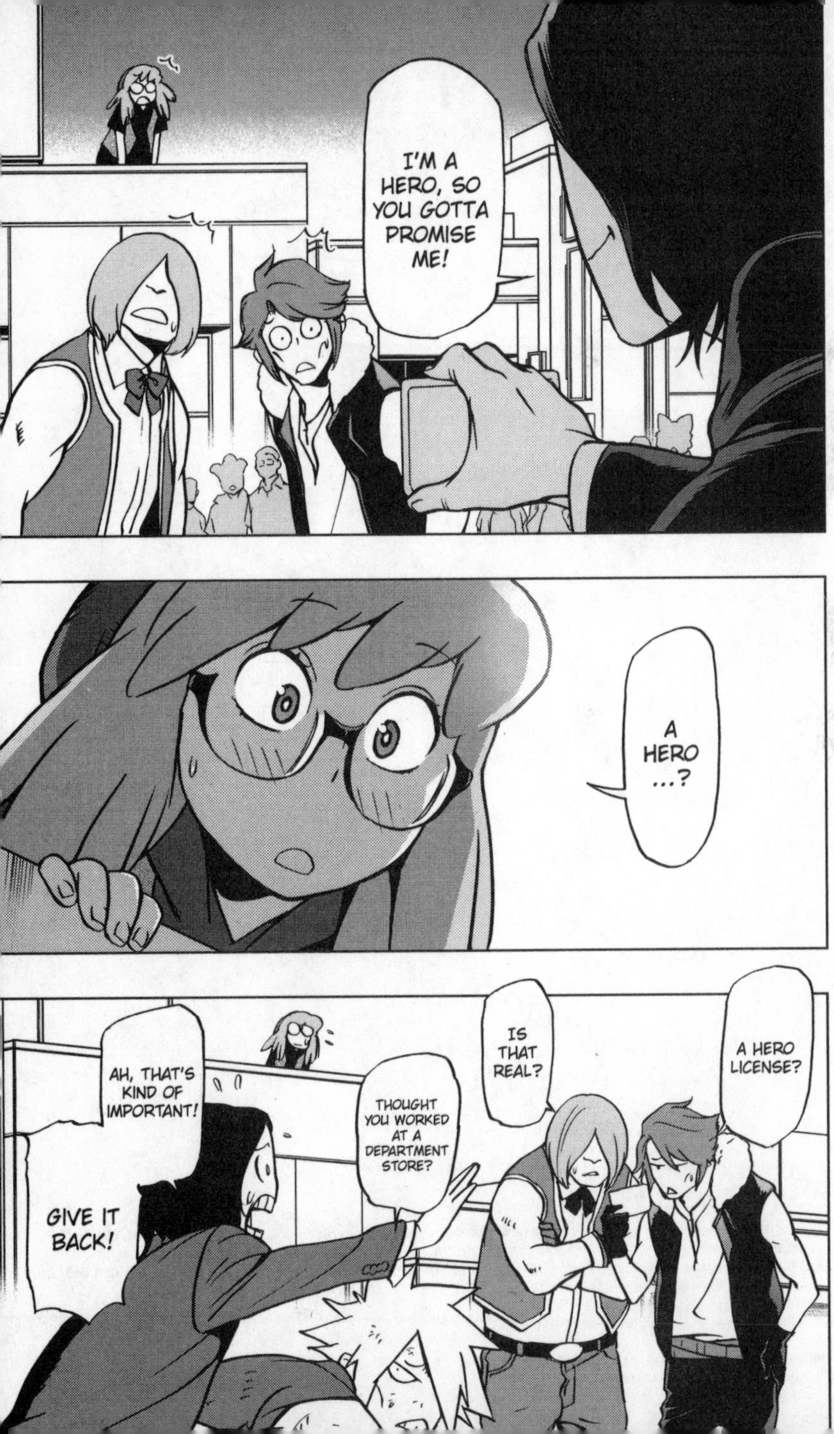

I'M A HERO, SO YOU GOTTA PROMISE ME!
A HERO ...?
A HERO LICENSE?
IS THAT REAL?
THOUGHT YOU WORKED AT A DEPARTMENT STORE?
AH, THAT'S KIND OF IMPORTANT!
GIVE IT BACK!

NOMURA

THE ROUGH DESIGN

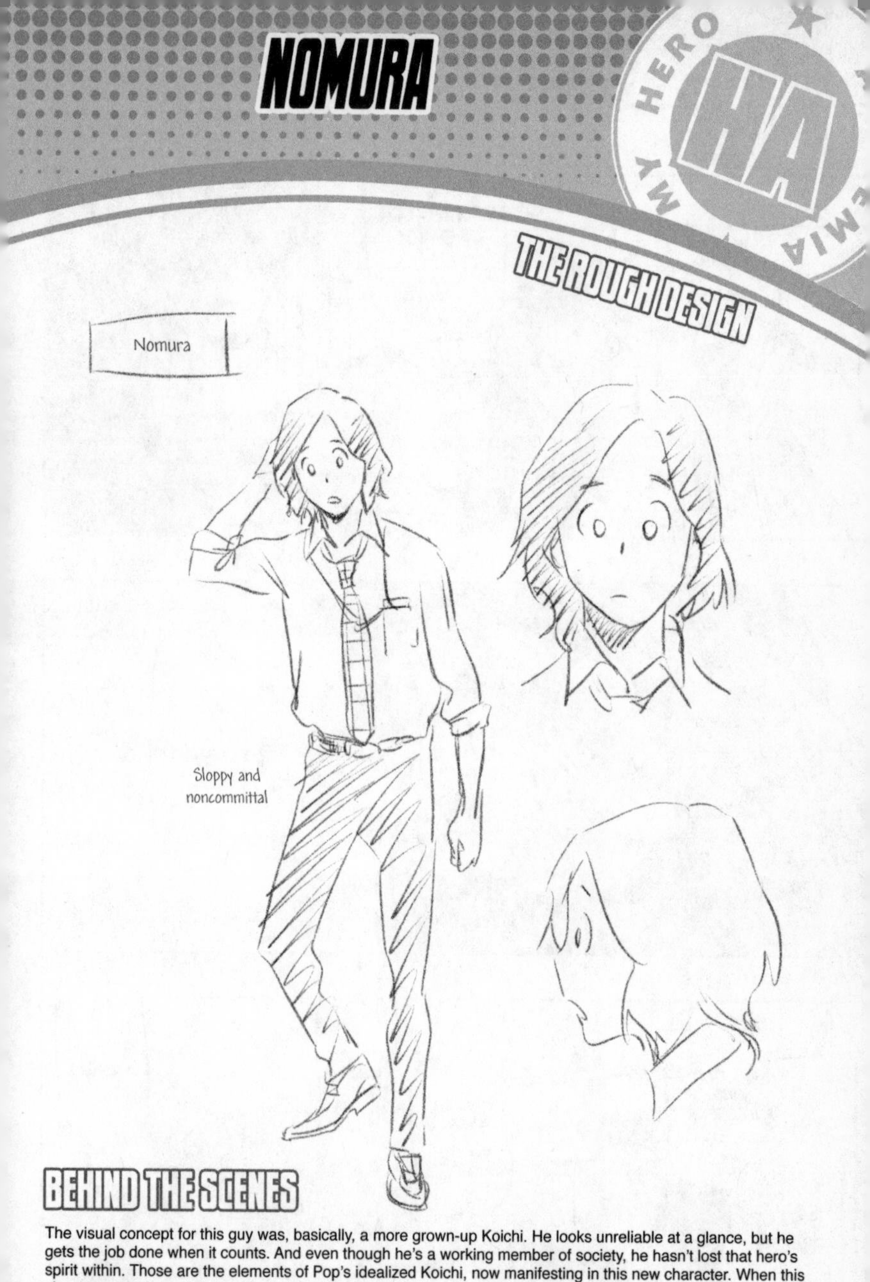
Nomura
Sloppy and noncommittal

BEHIND THE SCENES

The visual concept for this guy was, basically, a more grown-up Koichi. He looks unreliable at a glance, but he gets the job done when it counts. And even though he's a working member of society, he hasn't lost that hero's spirit within. Those are the elements of Pop's idealized Koichi, now manifesting in this new character. When this chapter was released, I was glad to hear feedback like "Pop should just end up with this dude!"

—Furuhashi

He just had to be utterly dull and ordinary. ^^

—Betten

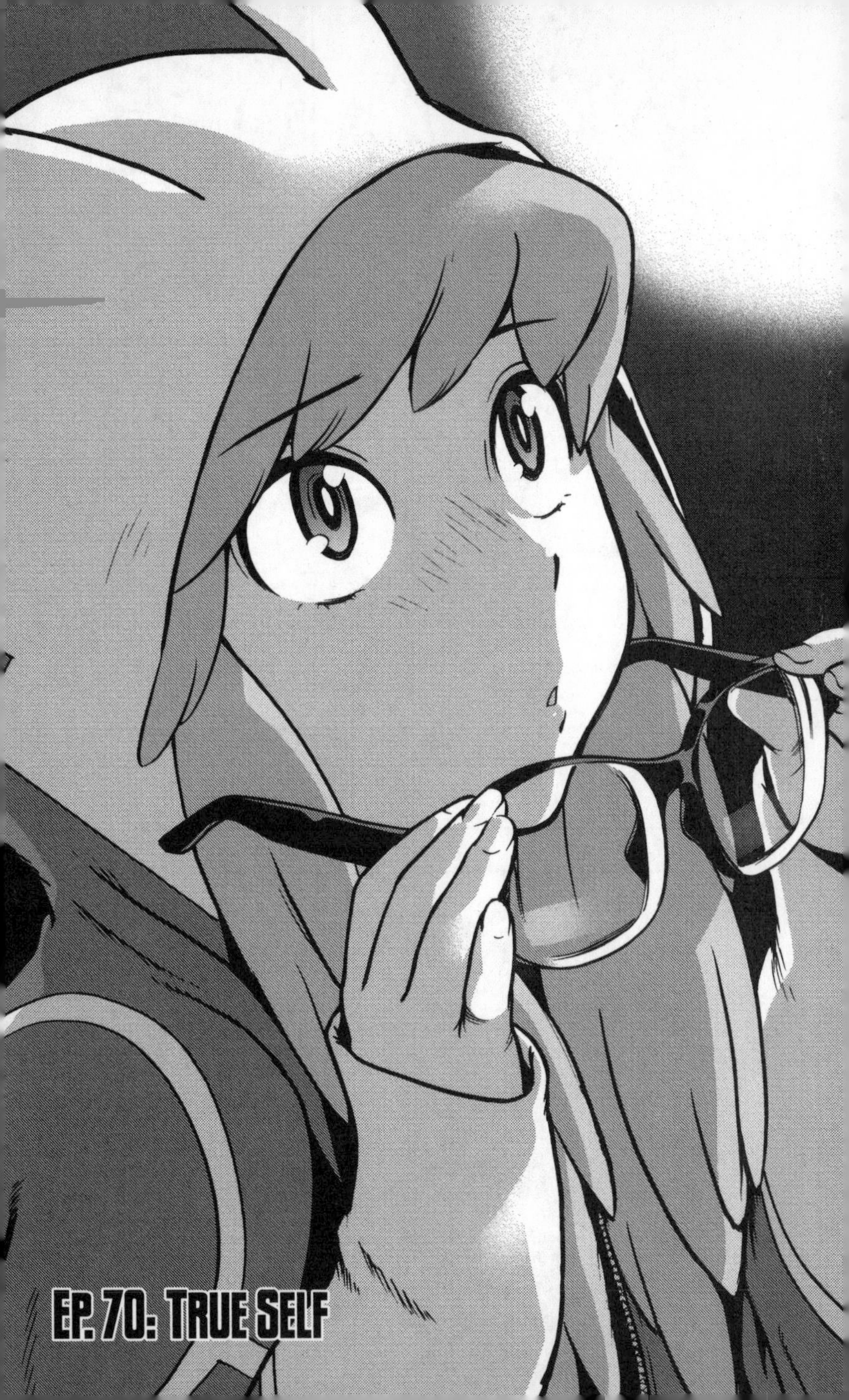
EP. 70: TRUE SELF

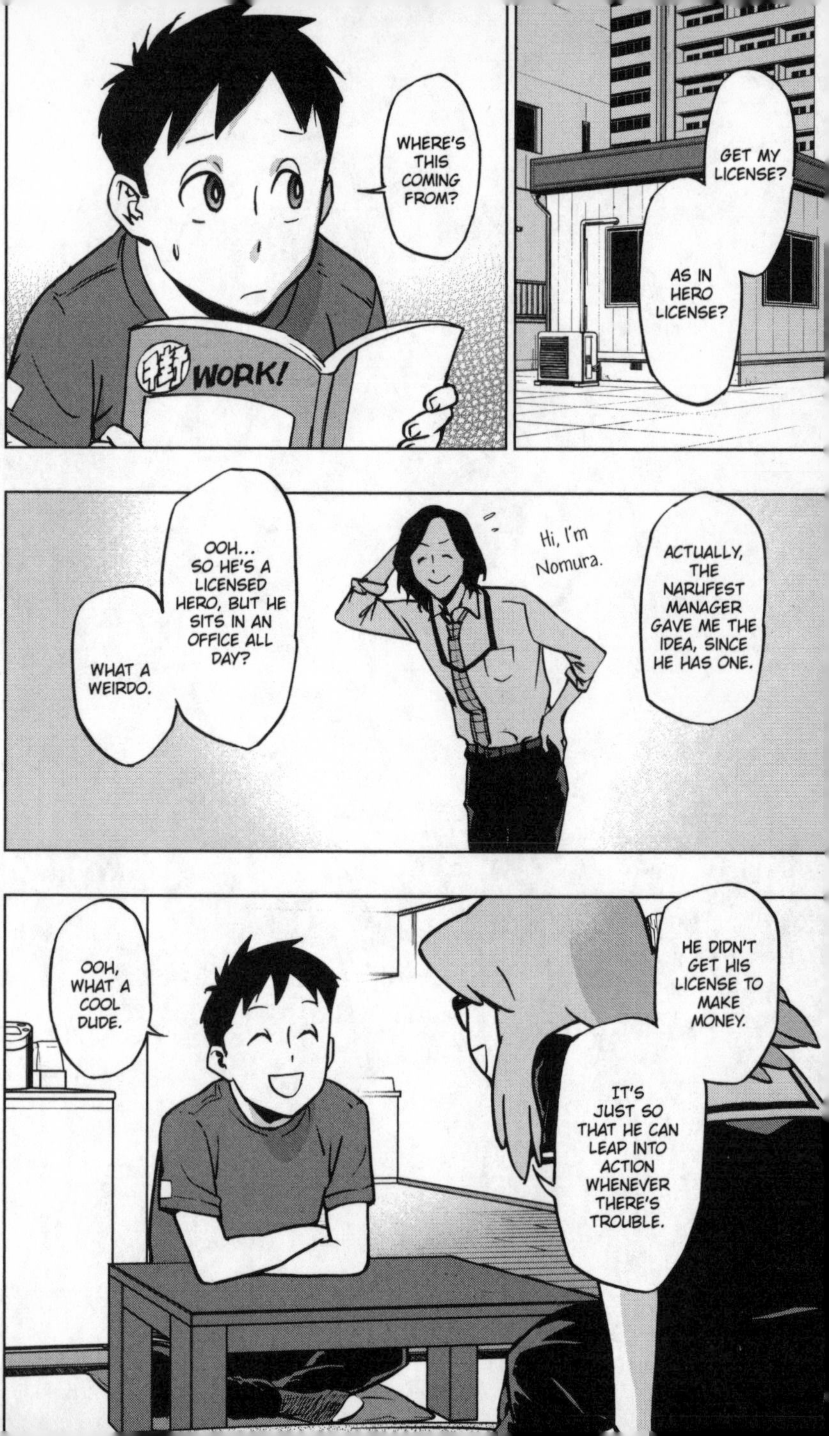
GET MY LICENSE?
AS IN HERO LICENSE?
WHERE'S THIS COMING FROM?
WORK!
ACTUALLY, THE NARUFEST MANAGER GAVE ME THE IDEA, SINCE HE HAS ONE.
Hi, I'm Nomura.
OOH... SO HE'S A LICENSED HERO, BUT HE SITS IN AN OFFICE ALL DAY?
WHAT A WEIRDO.
HE DIDN'T GET HIS LICENSE TO MAKE MONEY.
IT'S JUST SO THAT HE CAN LEAP INTO ACTION WHENEVER THERE'S TROUBLE.
OOH, WHAT A COOL DUDE.

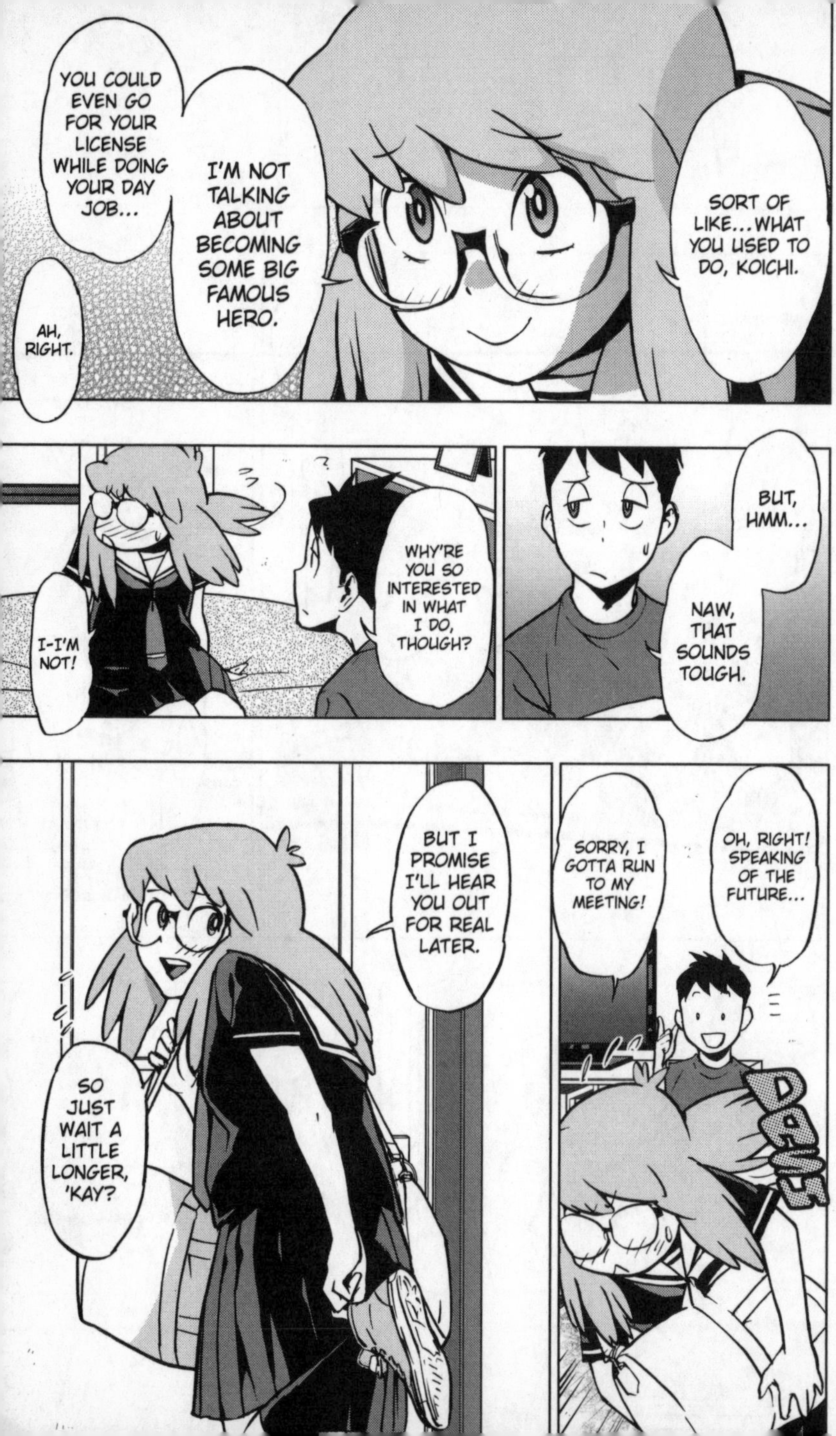
SORT OF LIKE...WHAT YOU USED TO DO, KOICHI.
I'M NOT TALKING ABOUT BECOMING SOME BIG FAMOUS HERO.
YOU COULD EVEN GO FOR YOUR LICENSE WHILE DOING YOUR DAY JOB...
AH, RIGHT.
BUT, HMM...
NAW, THAT SOUNDS TOUGH.
WHY'RE YOU SO INTERESTED IN WHAT I DO, THOUGH?
I-I'M NOT!
OH, RIGHT! SPEAKING OF THE FUTURE...
SORRY, I GOTTA RUN TO MY MEETING!
DASH
BUT I PROMISE I'LL HEAR YOU OUT FOR REAL LATER.
SO JUST WAIT A LITTLE LONGER, 'KAY?

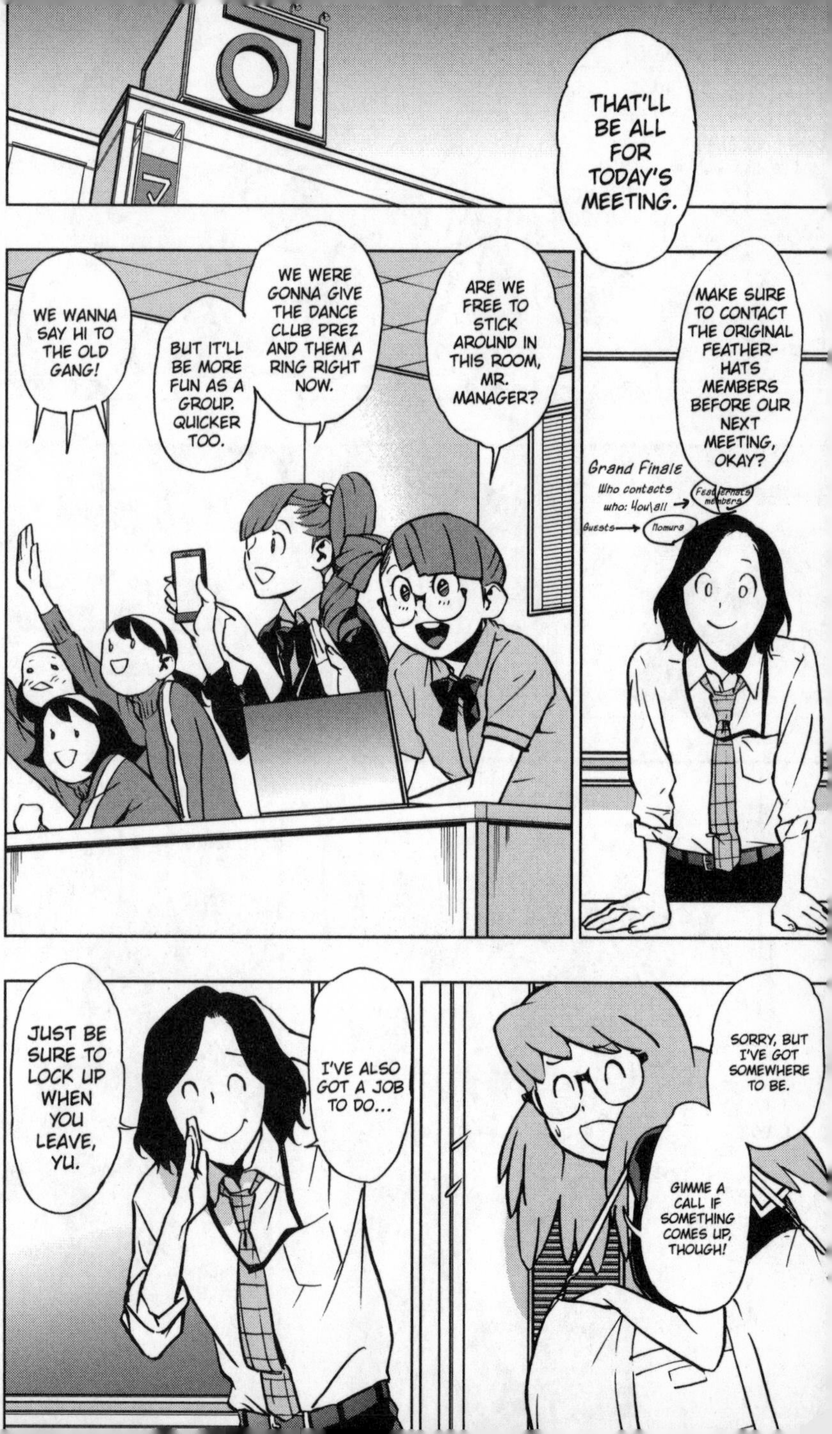
THAT'LL BE ALL FOR TODAY'S MEETING.
MAKE SURE TO CONTACT THE ORIGINAL FEATHER-HATS MEMBERS BEFORE OUR NEXT MEETING, OKAY?
Grand Finale
Who contacts who: You\all
members
Guests
Nomura
ARE WE FREE TO STICK AROUND IN THIS ROOM, MR. MANAGER?
WE WERE GONNA GIVE THE DANCE CLUB PREZ AND THEM A RING RIGHT NOW.
BUT IT'LL BE MORE FUN AS A GROUP. QUICKER TOO.
WE WANNA SAY HI TO THE OLD GANG!
SORRY, BUT I'VE GOT SOMEWHERE TO BE.
GIMME A CALL IF SOMETHING COMES UP, THOUGH!
I'VE ALSO GOT A JOB TO DO...
JUST BE SURE TO LOCK UP WHEN YOU LEAVE, YU.

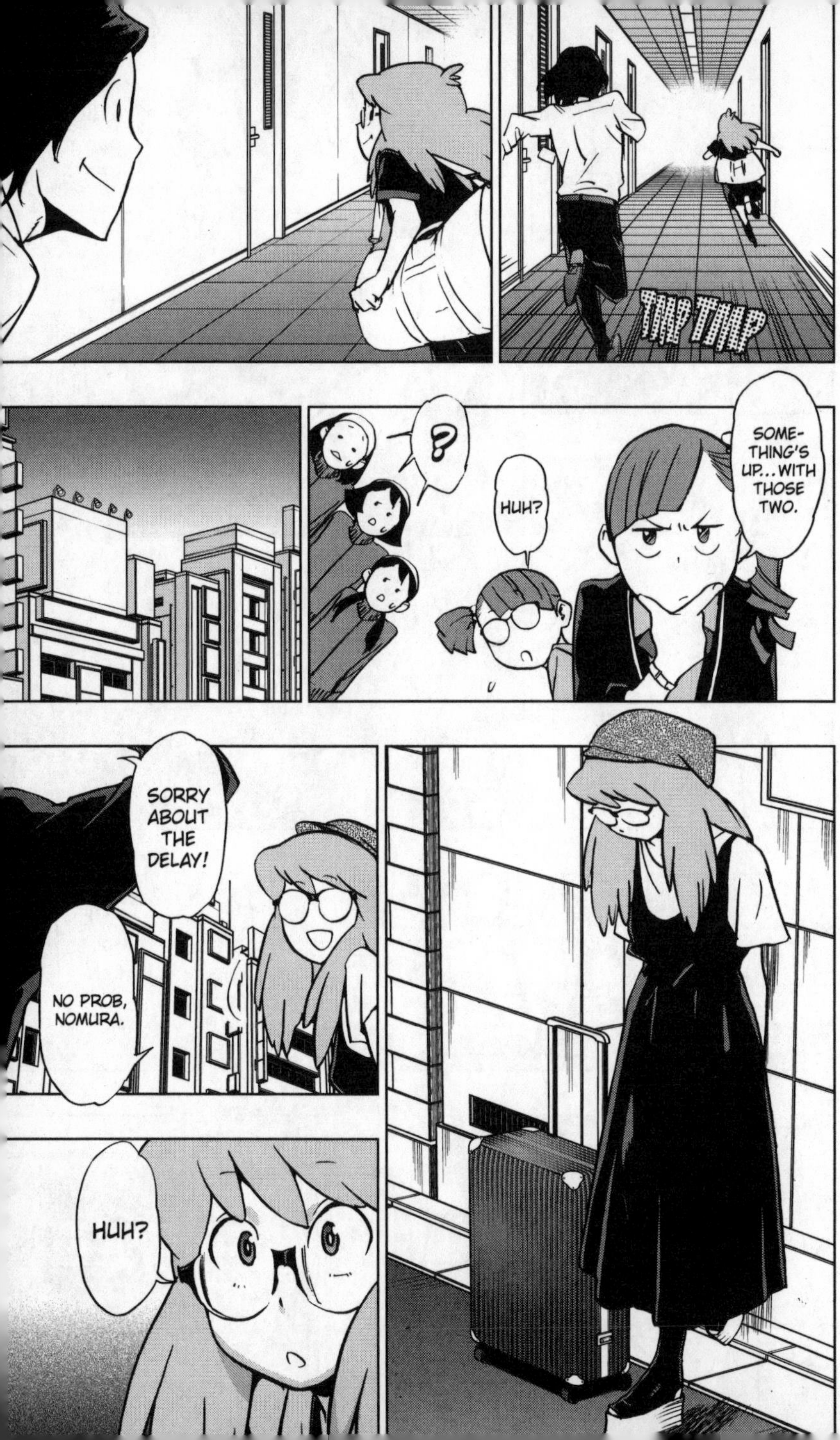
TMP TMP
SOME-THING'S UP...WITH THOSE TWO.
HUH?
?
SORRY ABOUT THE DELAY!
NO PROB, NOMURA.
HUH?

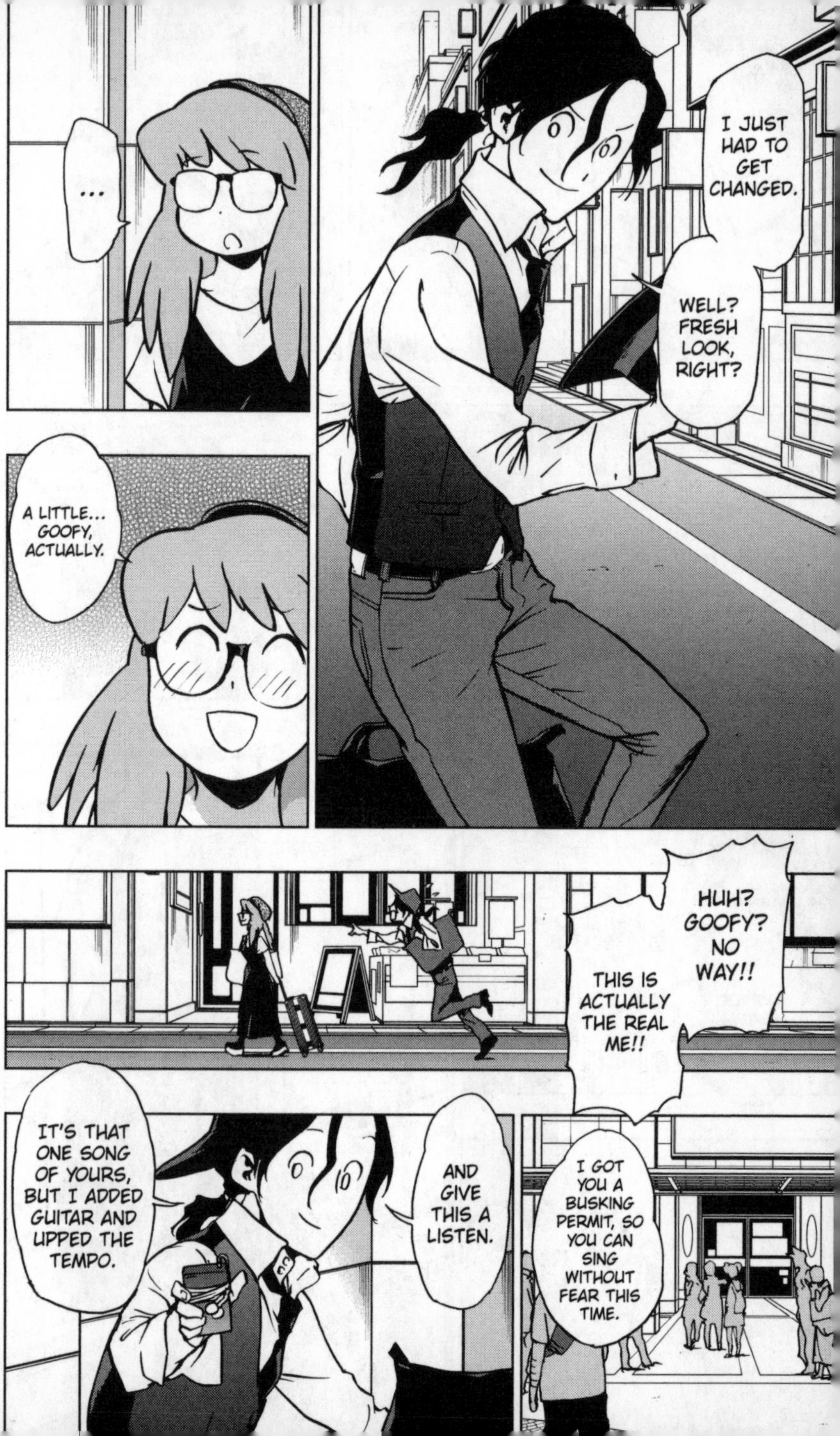
I JUST HAD TO GET CHANGED.
WELL? FRESH LOOK, RIGHT?
...
A LITTLE... GOOFY, ACTUALLY.
HUH? GOOFY? NO WAY!!
THIS IS ACTUALLY THE REAL ME!!
I GOT YOU A BUSKING PERMIT, SO YOU CAN SING WITHOUT FEAR THIS TIME.
AND GIVE THIS A LISTEN.
IT'S THAT ONE SONG OF YOURS, BUT I ADDED GUITAR AND UPPED THE TEMPO.

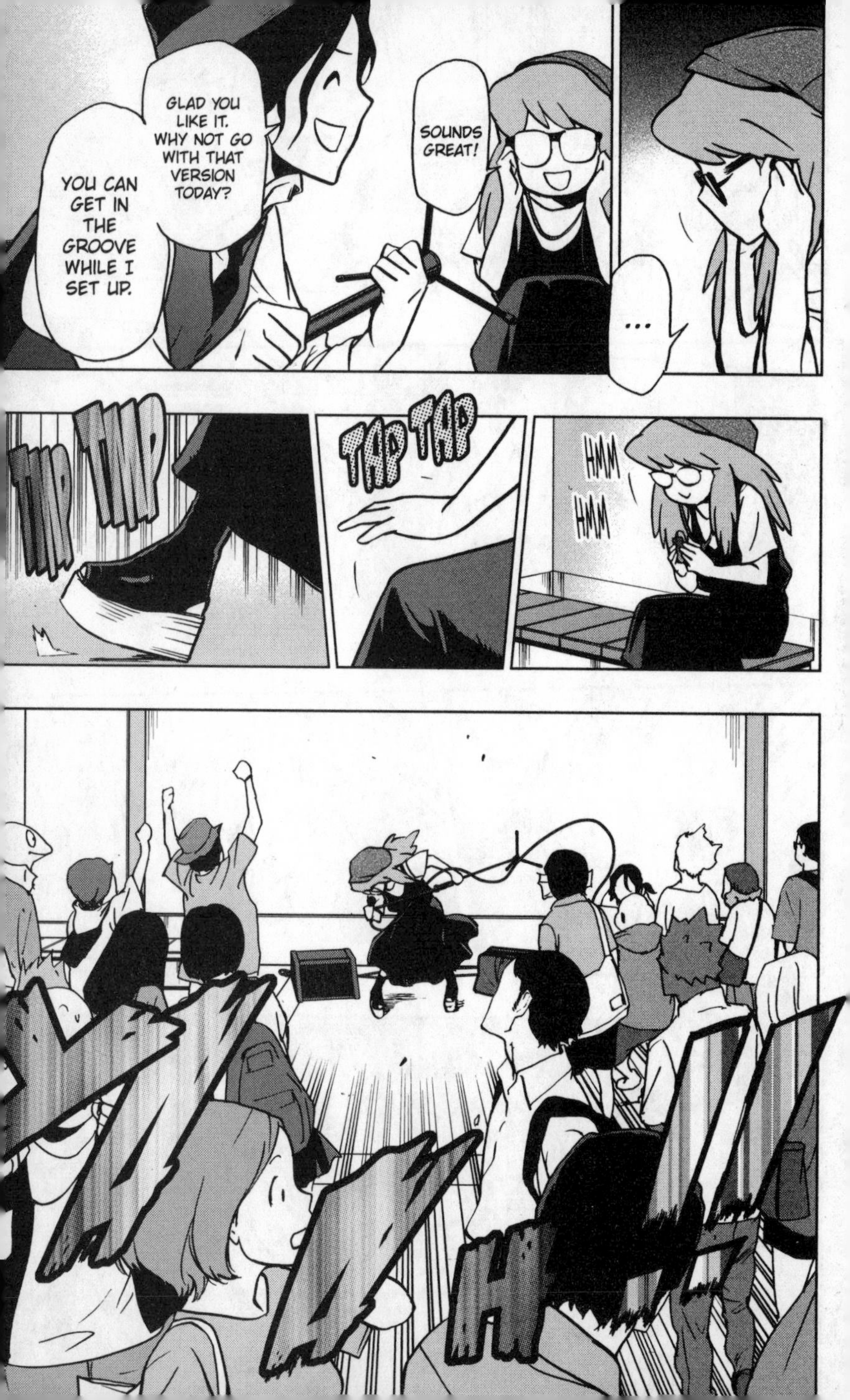
...
SOUNDS GREAT!
GLAD YOU LIKE IT. WHY NOT GO WITH THAT VERSION TODAY?
YOU CAN GET IN THE GROOVE WHILE I SET UP.
HMM HMM
THP THP
THP THP

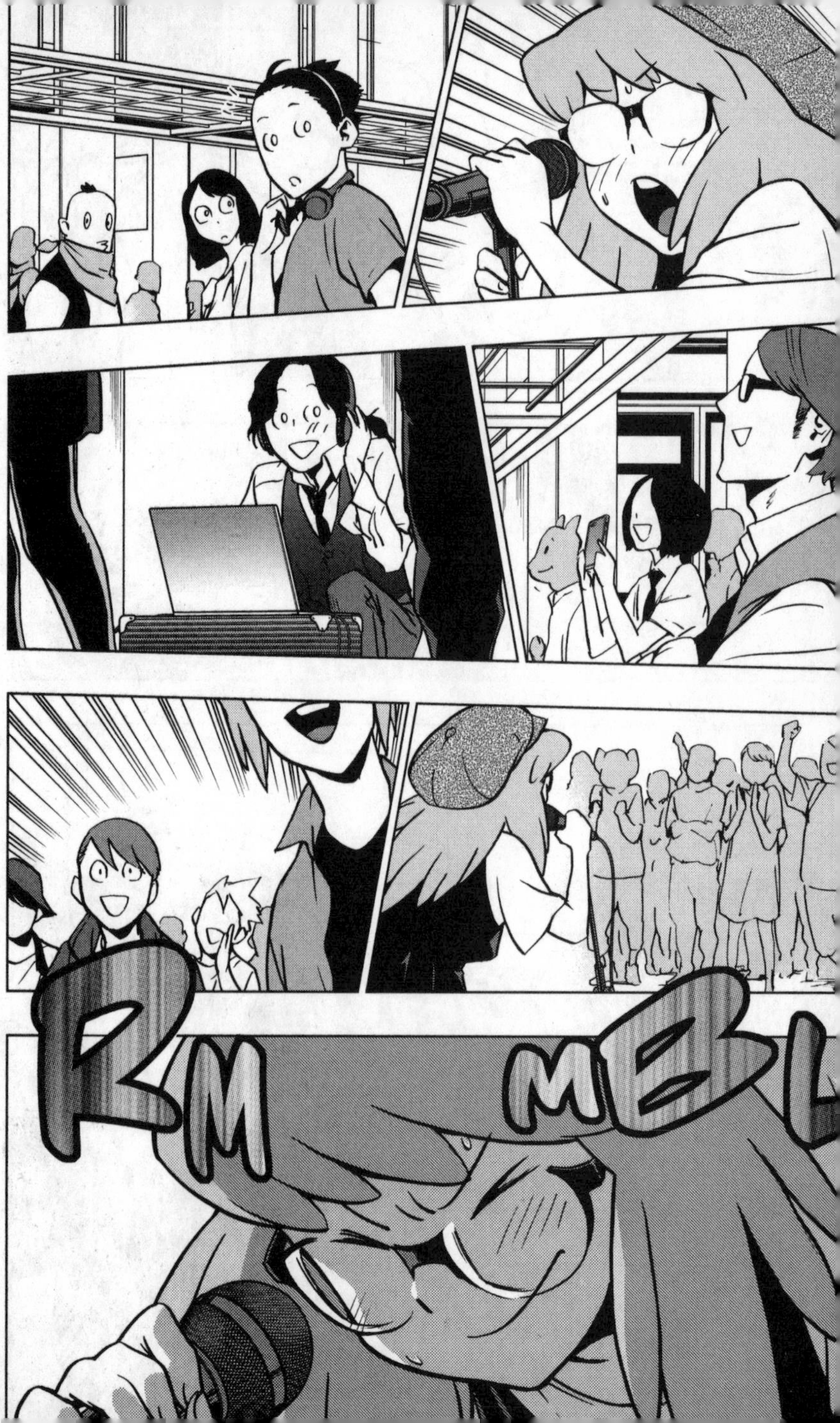
RM MBL

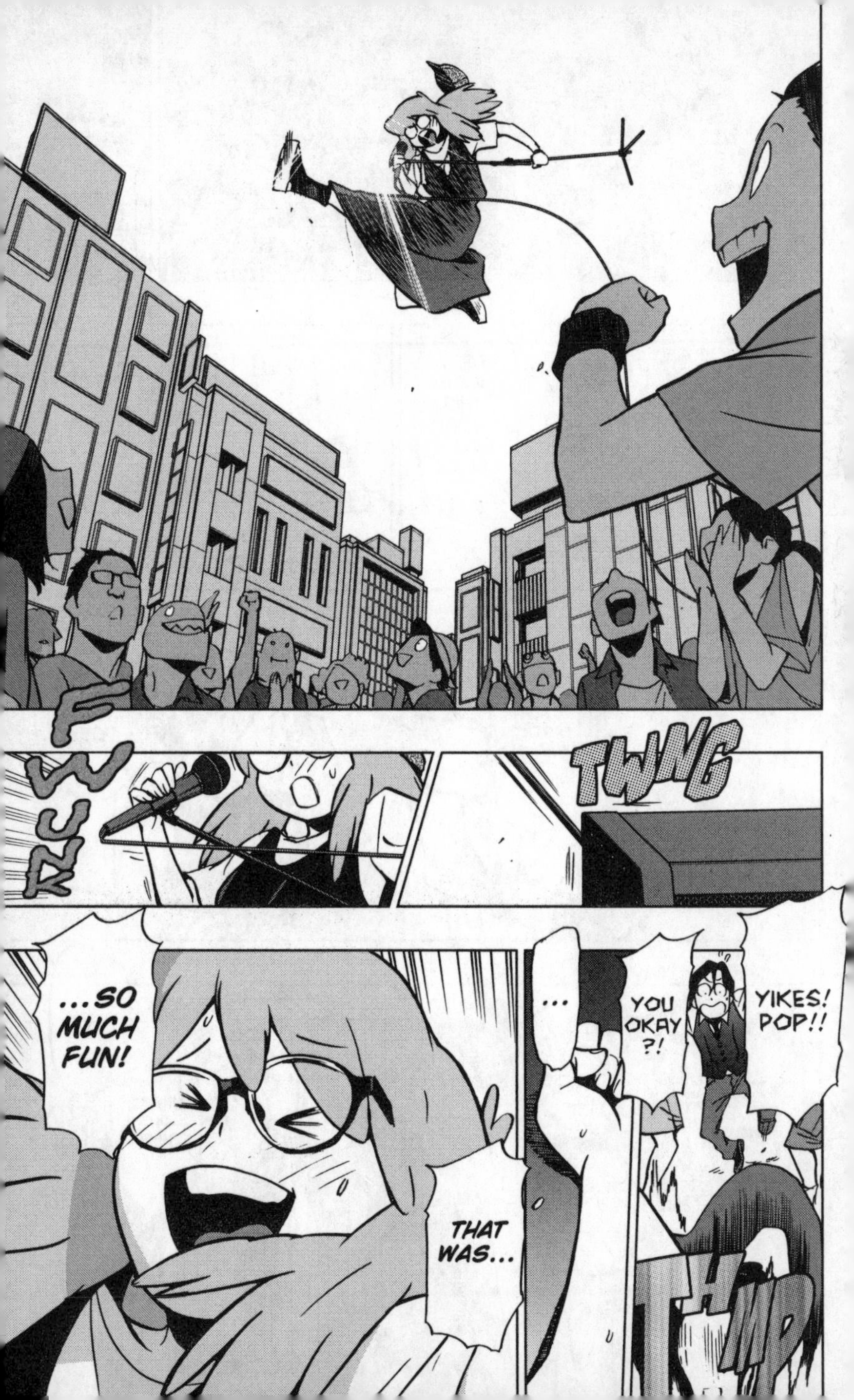
TWNG
YIKES! POP!!
YOU OKAY ?!
...
THAT WAS...
...SO MUCH FUN!

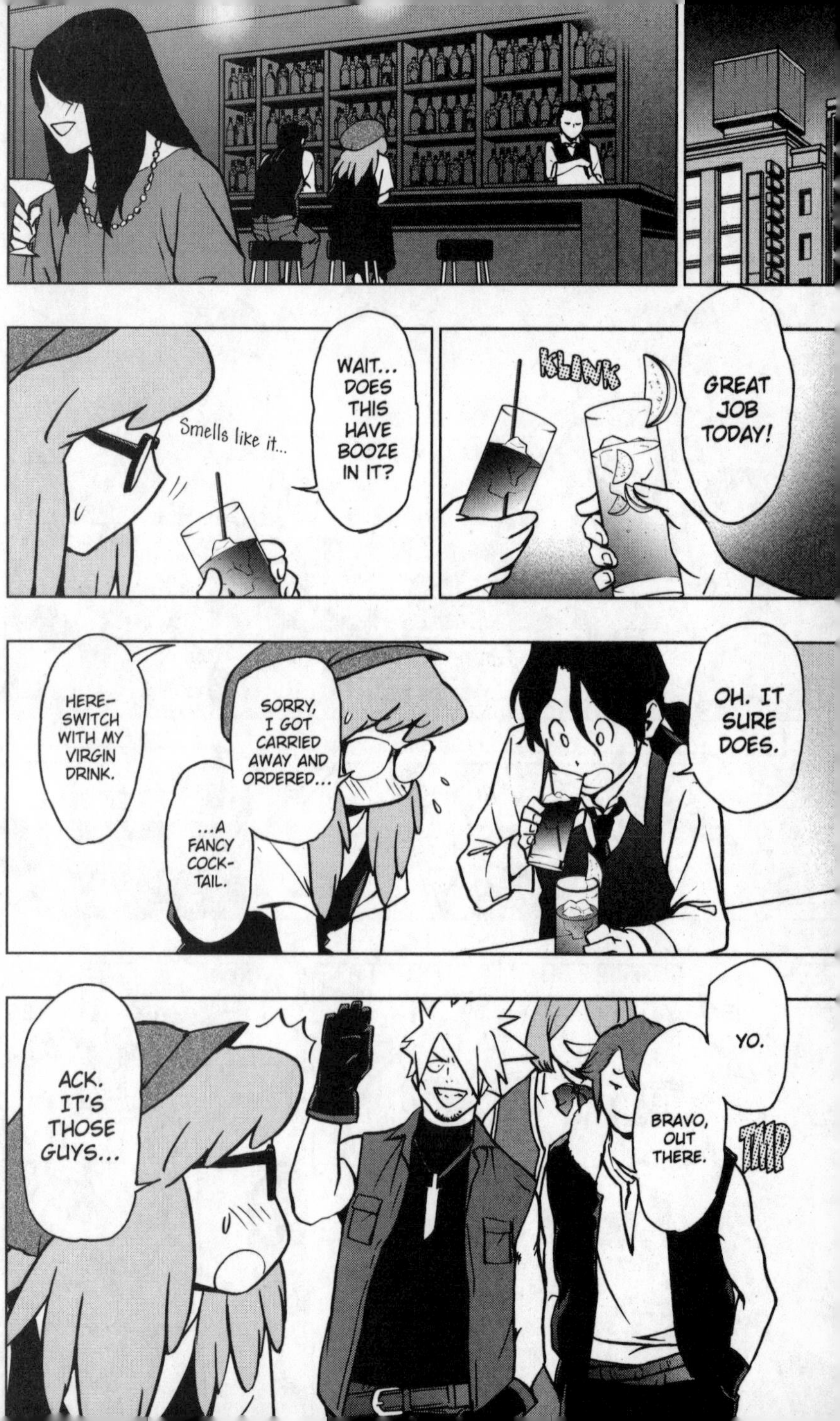
GREAT JOB TODAY!
KLINK
WAIT... DOES THIS HAVE BOOZE IN IT?
Smells like it...
OH. IT SURE DOES.
SORRY, I GOT CARRIED AWAY AND ORDERED...
...A FANCY COCK-TAIL.
HERE-SWITCH WITH MY VIRGIN DRINK.
YO.
BRAVO, OUT THERE.
TMP
ACK. IT'S THOSE GUYS...

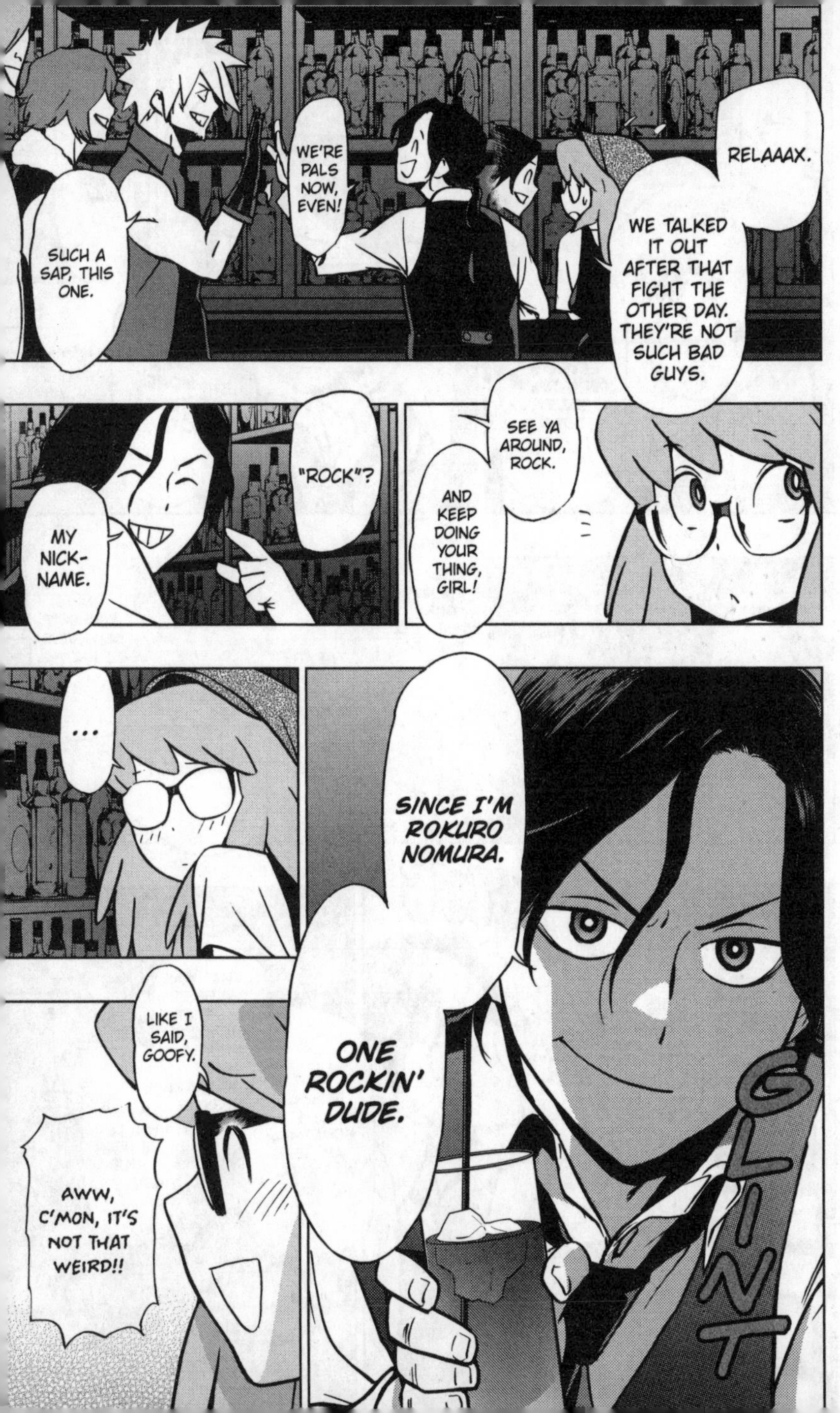
RELAAAX.
WE TALKED IT OUT AFTER THAT FIGHT THE OTHER DAY. THEY'RE NOT SUCH BAD GUYS.
WE'RE PALS NOW, EVEN!
SUCH A SAP, THIS ONE.
SEE YA AROUND, ROCK.
AND KEEP DOING YOUR THING, GIRL!
"ROCK"?
MY NICK-NAME.
SINCE I'M ROKURO NOMURA.
ONE ROCKIN' DUDE.
GLINT
...
LIKE I SAID, GOOFY.
AWW, C'MON, IT'S NOT THAT WEIRD!!

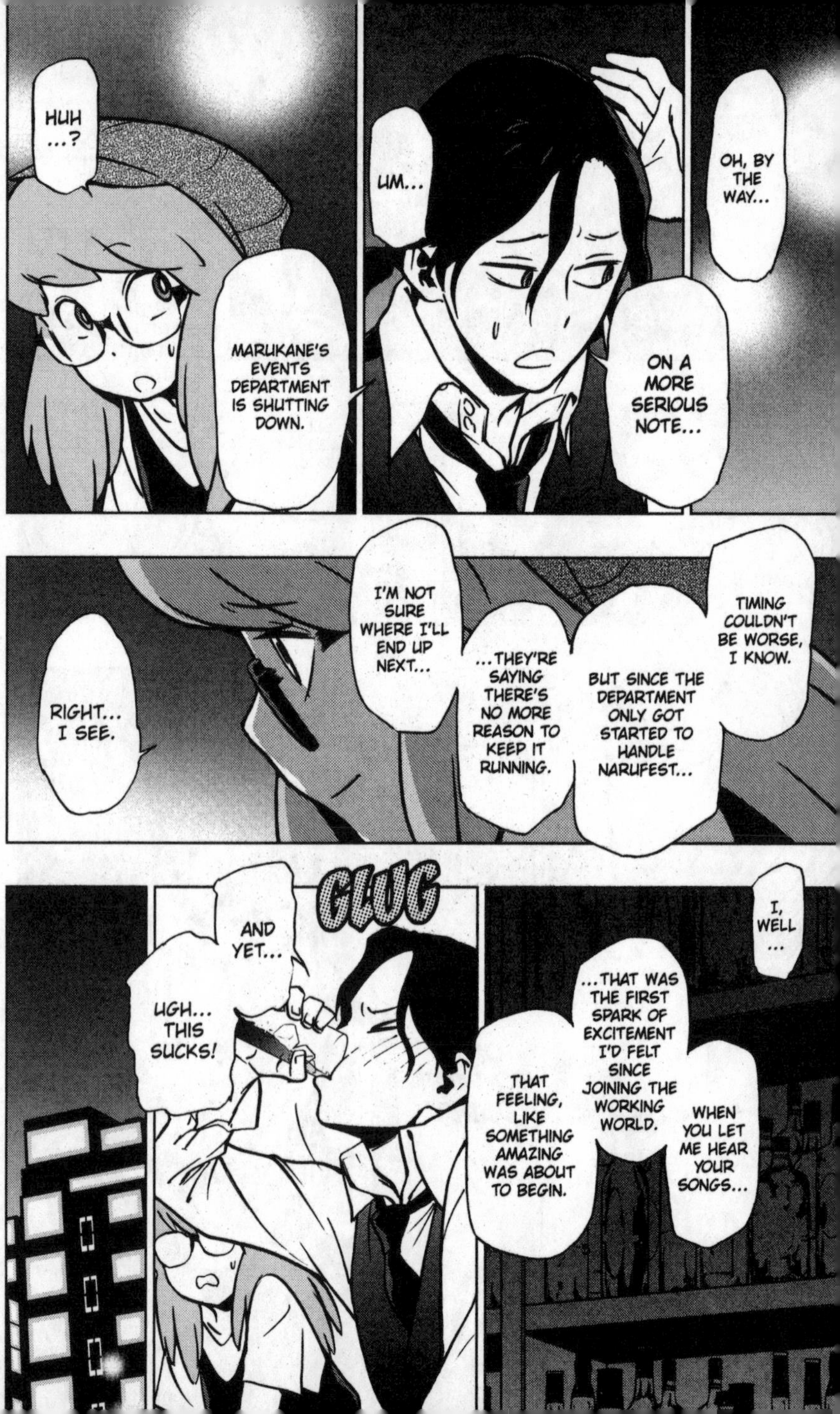
OH, BY THE WAY...
ON A MORE SERIOUS NOTE...
UM...
MARUKANE'S EVENTS DEPARTMENT IS SHUTTING DOWN.
HUH ...?
TIMING COULDN'T BE WORSE, I KNOW.
BUT SINCE THE DEPARTMENT ONLY GOT STARTED TO HANDLE NARUFEST...
...THEY'RE SAYING THERE'S NO MORE REASON TO KEEP IT RUNNING.
I'M NOT SURE WHERE I'LL END UP NEXT...
RIGHT... I SEE.
I, WELL ...
WHEN YOU LET ME HEAR YOUR SONGS...
...THAT WAS THE FIRST SPARK OF EXCITEMENT I'D FELT SINCE JOINING THE WORKING WORLD.
THAT FEELING, LIKE SOMETHING AMAZING WAS ABOUT TO BEGIN.
GLUG
AND YET...
UGH... THIS SUCKS!

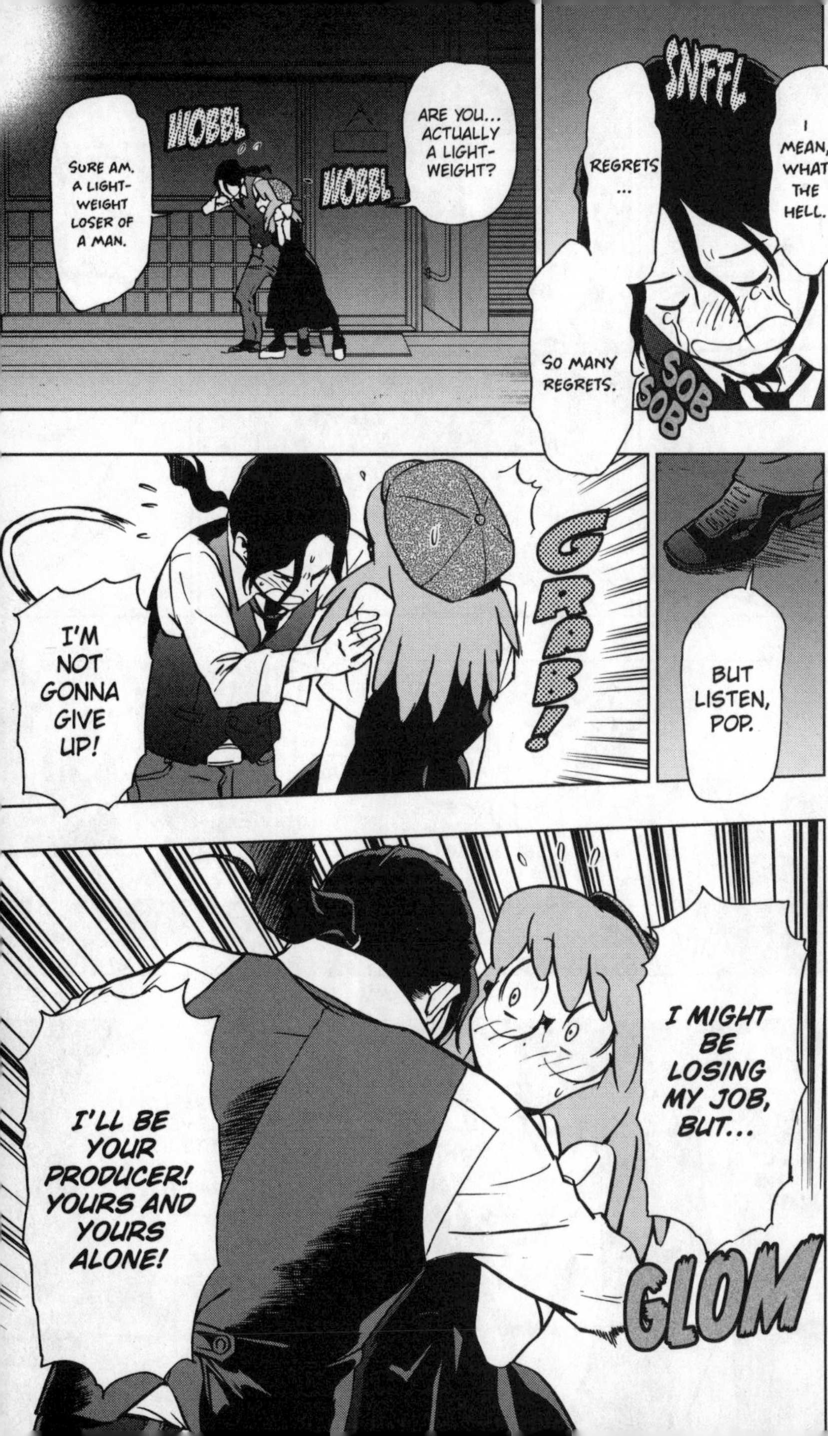
SNFFL
I MEAN, WHAT THE HELL.
REGRETS...
SO MANY REGRETS.
SOB SOB
ARE YOU... ACTUALLY A LIGHT-WEIGHT?
WOBBL
WOBBL
SURE AM. A LIGHT-WEIGHT LOSER OF A MAN.
BUT LISTEN, POP.
GRAB!
I'M NOT GONNA GIVE UP!
I MIGHT BE LOSING MY JOB, BUT...
I'LL BE YOUR PRODUCER! YOURS AND YOURS ALONE!
GLOM

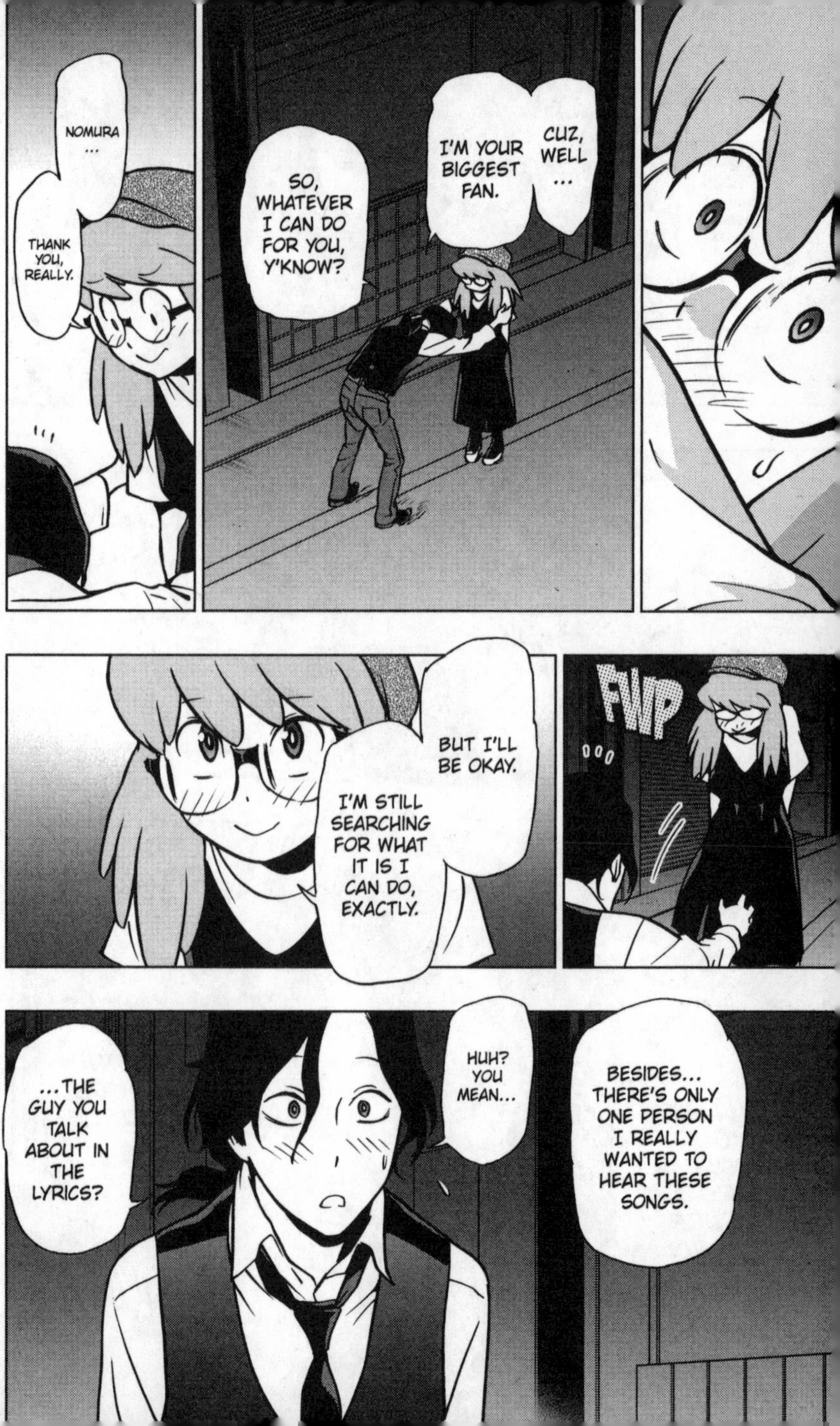
CUZ, WELL ...
I'M YOUR BIGGEST FAN.
SO, WHATEVER I CAN DO FOR YOU, Y'KNOW?
NOMURA ...
THANK YOU, REALLY.
FWP
BUT I'LL BE OKAY.
I'M STILL SEARCHING FOR WHAT IT IS I CAN DO, EXACTLY.
BESIDES... THERE'S ONLY ONE PERSON I REALLY WANTED TO HEAR THESE SONGS.
HUH? YOU MEAN...
...THE GUY YOU TALK ABOUT IN THE LYRICS?

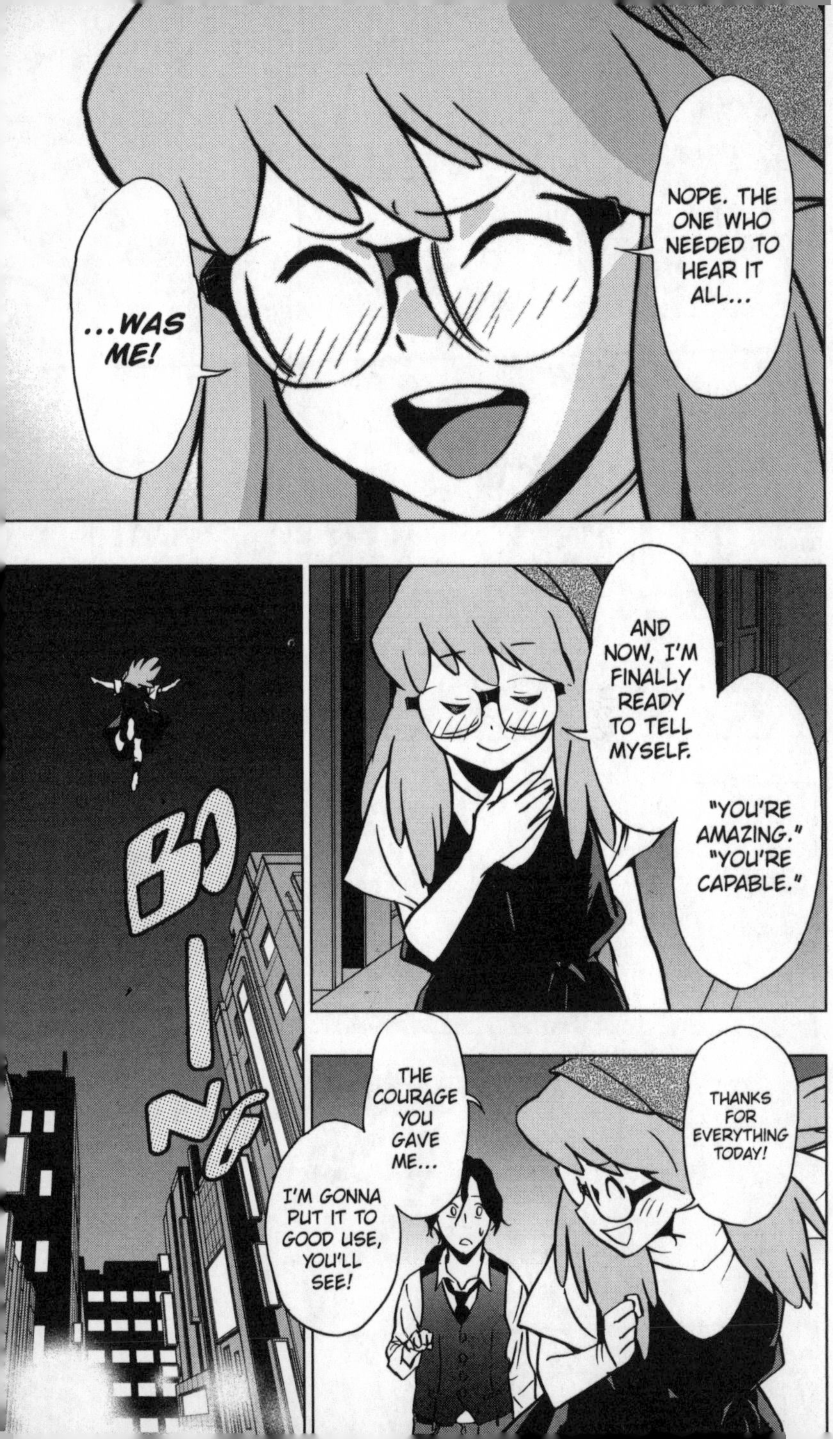
NOPE. THE ONE WHO NEEDED TO HEAR IT ALL...
...WAS ME!
AND NOW, I'M FINALLY READY TO TELL MYSELF.
"YOU'RE AMAZING." "YOU'RE CAPABLE."
THANKS FOR EVERYTHING TODAY!
THE COURAGE YOU GAVE ME...
I'M GONNA PUT IT TO GOOD USE, YOU'LL SEE!
BO-I-NG

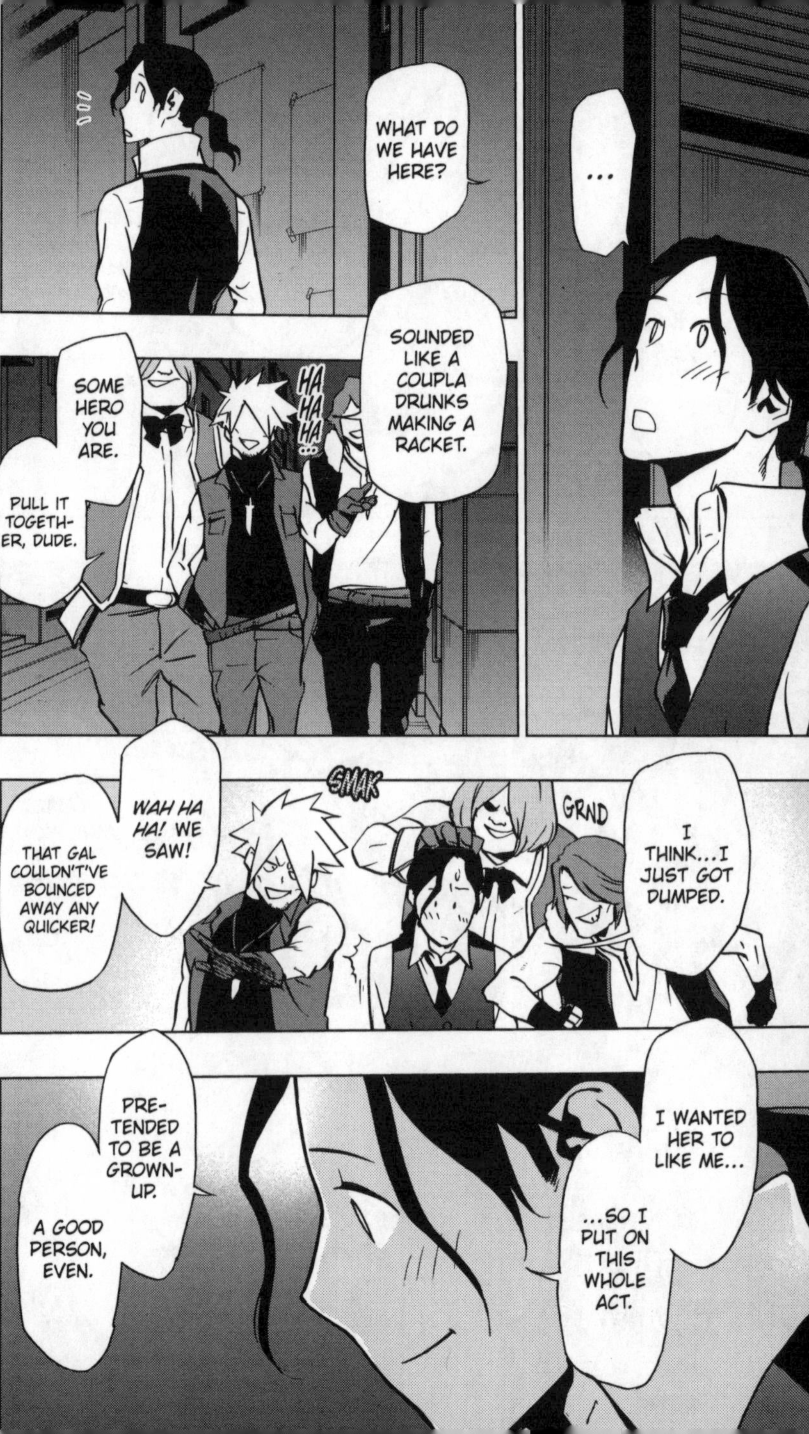
...
WHAT DO WE HAVE HERE?
SOUNDED LIKE A COUPLA DRUNKS MAKING A RACKET.
HA HA HA...
SOME HERO YOU ARE.
PULL IT TOGETH-ER, DUDE.
I THINK...I JUST GOT DUMPED.
GRND
SMAK
WAH HA HA! WE SAW!
THAT GAL COULDN'T'VE BOUNCED AWAY ANY QUICKER!
I WANTED HER TO LIKE ME...
...SO I PUT ON THIS WHOLE ACT.
PRE-TENDED TO BE A GROWN-UP.
A GOOD PERSON, EVEN.

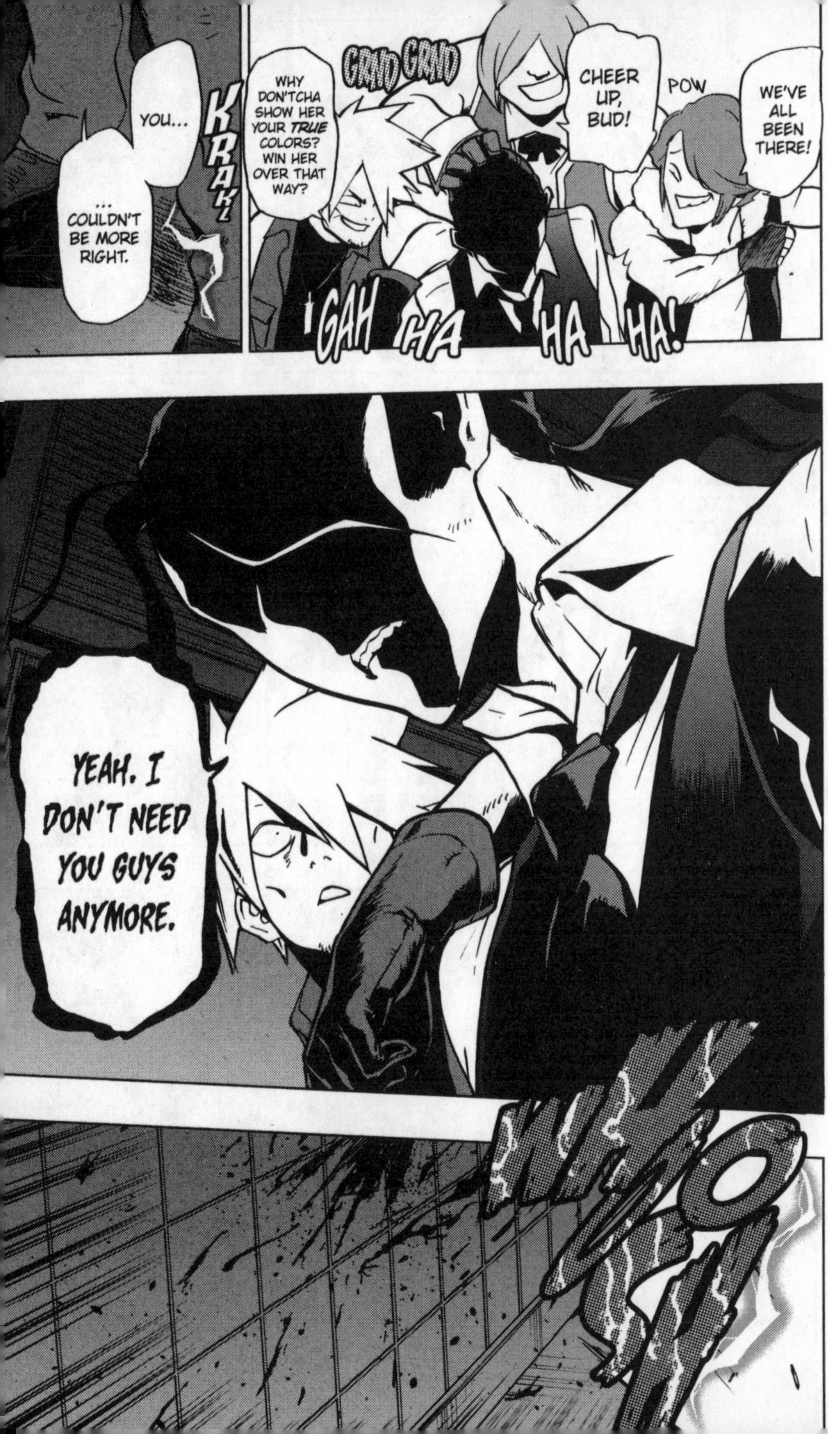
WE'VE ALL BEEN THERE!
POW
CHEER UP, BUD!
GRND GRND
WHY DON'TCHA SHOW HER YOUR *TRUE* COLORS? WIN HER OVER THAT WAY?
GAH HA HA HA!
KRAK
YOU...
...COULDN'T BE MORE RIGHT.
YEAH. I DON'T NEED YOU GUYS ANYMORE.

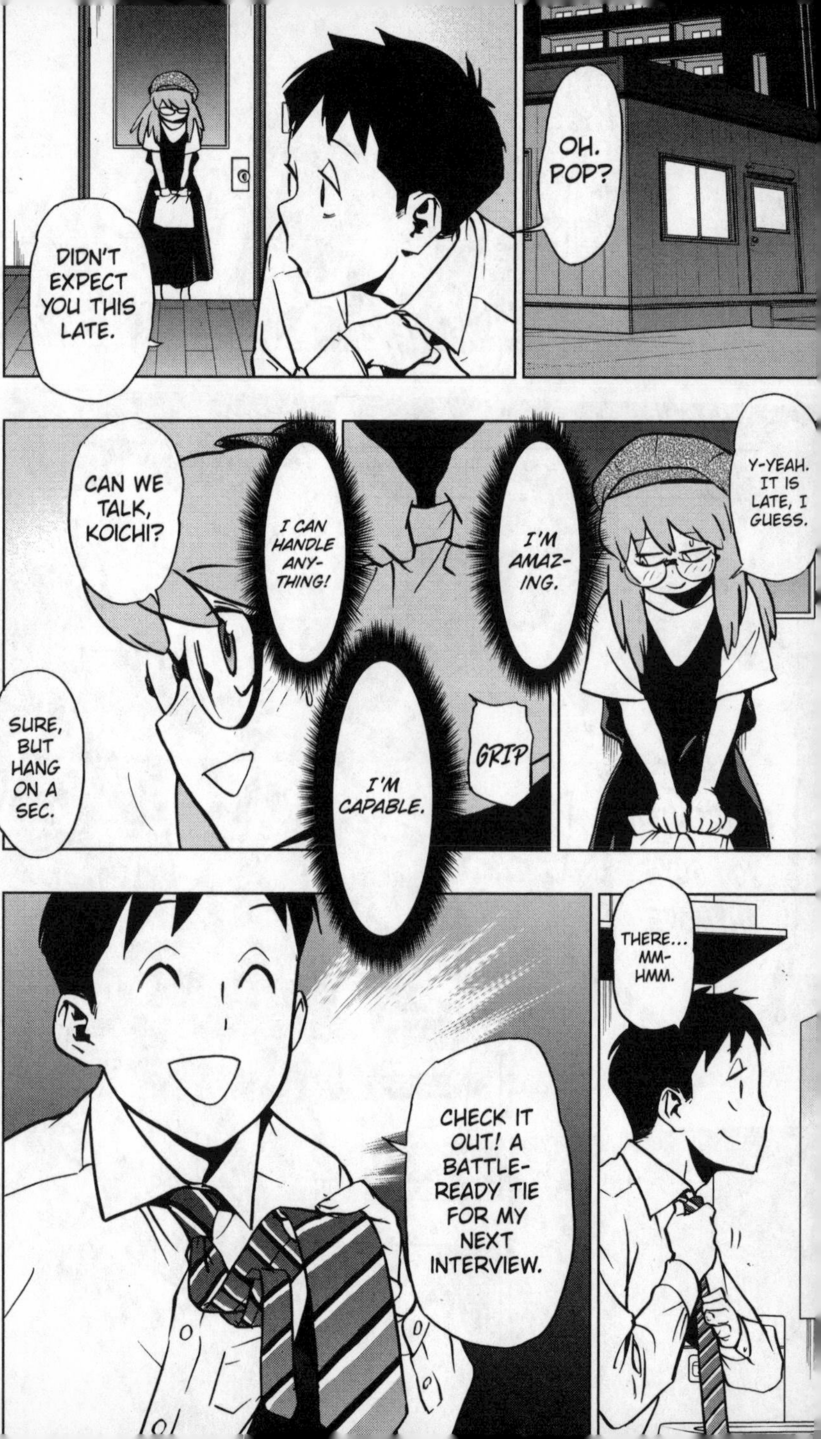

OH. POP?
DIDN'T EXPECT YOU THIS LATE.
Y-YEAH. IT IS LATE, I GUESS.
GRIP
I'M AMAZING.
I CAN HANDLE ANYTHING!
I'M CAPABLE.
CAN WE TALK, KOICHI?
SURE, BUT HANG ON A SEC.
THERE... MM-HMM.
CHECK IT OUT! A BATTLE-READY TIE FOR MY NEXT INTERVIEW.

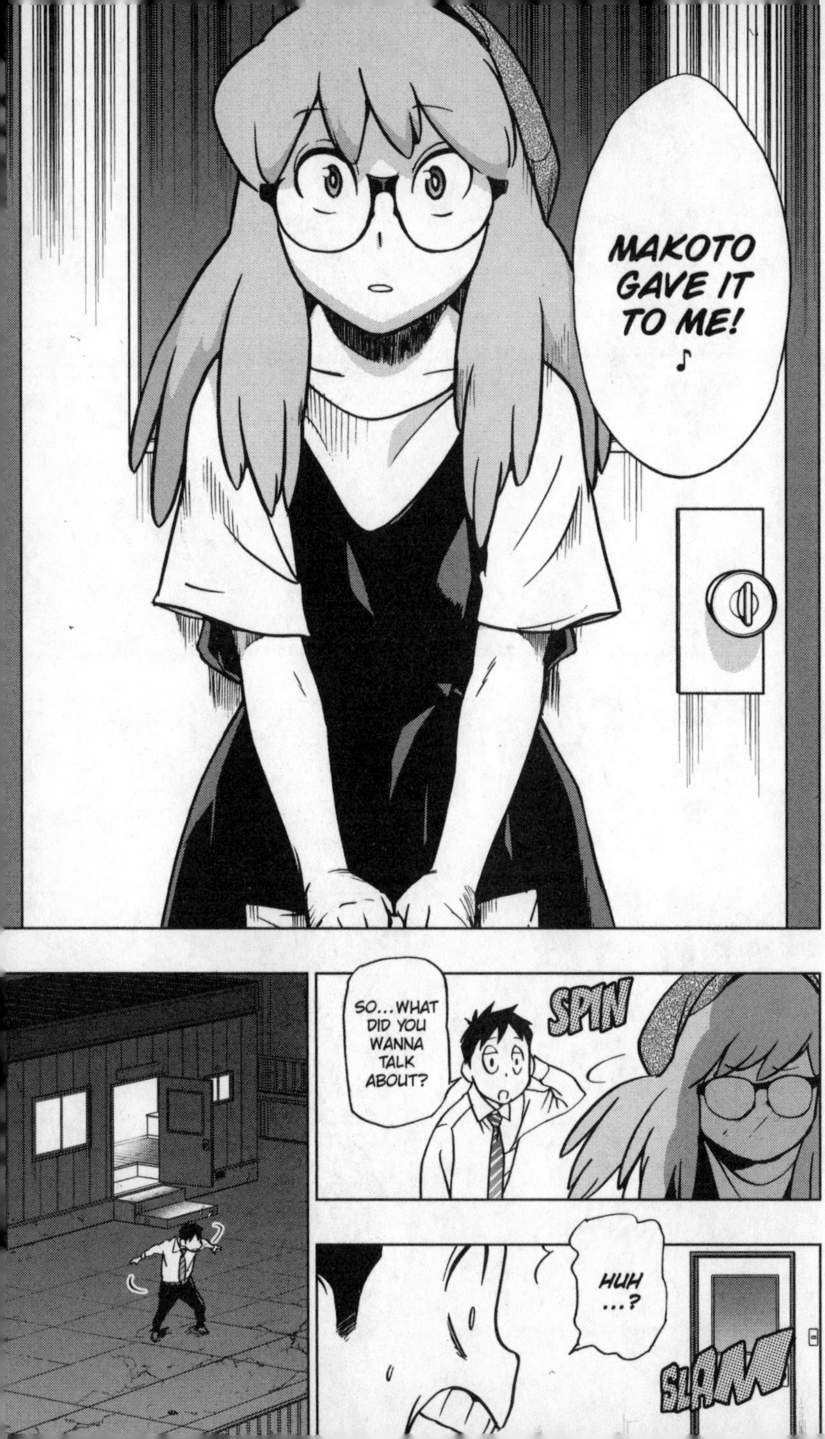
MAKOTO GAVE IT TO ME! ♪
SO...WHAT DID YOU WANNA TALK ABOUT?
SPIN
HUH ...?
SLAM

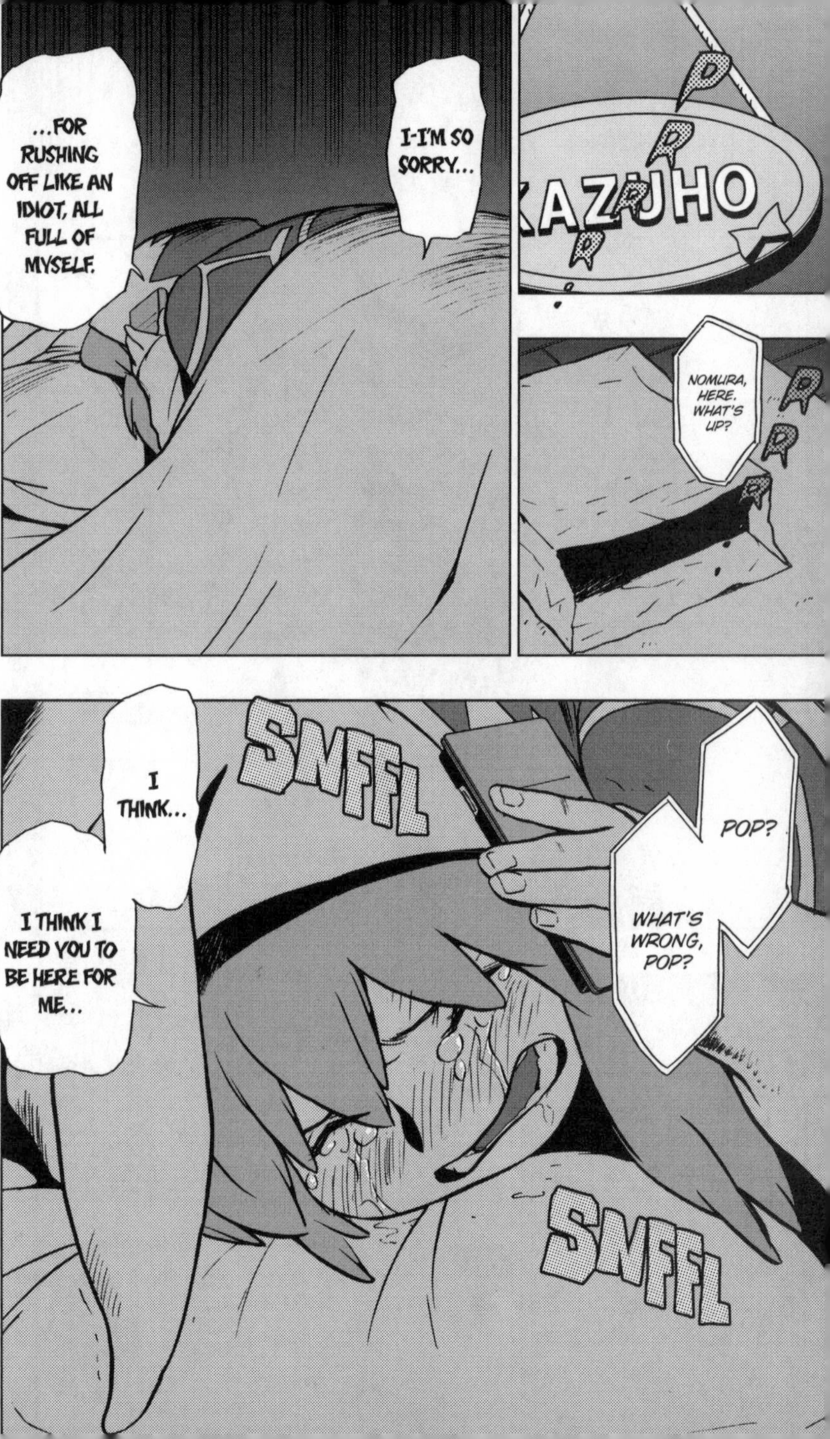
NOMURA, HERE. WHAT'S UP?
I-I'M SO SORRY...
...FOR RUSHING OFF LIKE AN IDIOT, ALL FULL OF MYSELF.
POP?
WHAT'S WRONG, POP?
SNFFL
I THINK...
I THINK I NEED YOU TO BE HERE FOR ME...
SNFFL

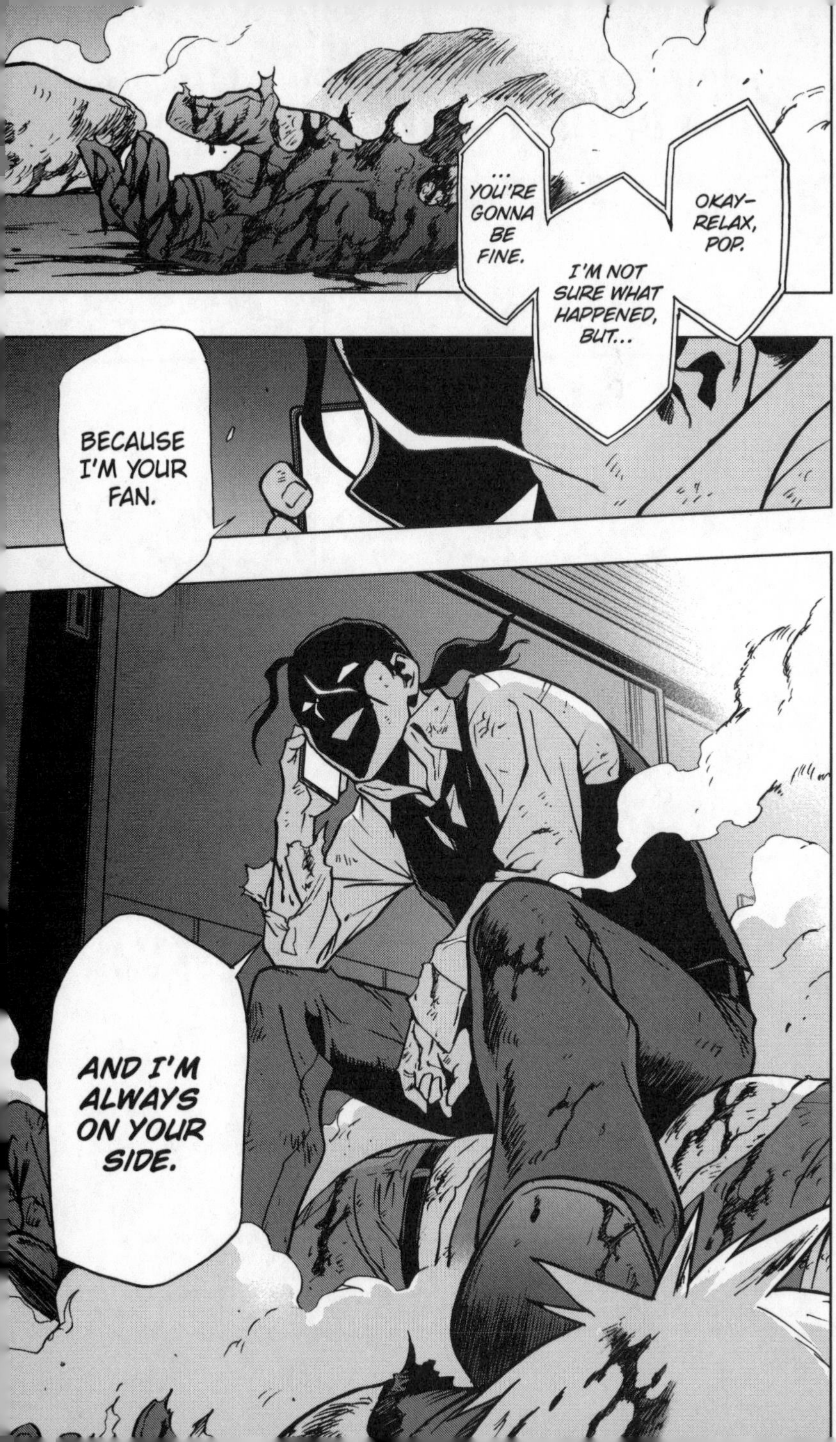
OKAY—RELAX, POP.
I'M NOT SURE WHAT HAPPENED, BUT...
...YOU'RE GONNA BE FINE.
BECAUSE I'M YOUR FAN.
AND I'M ALWAYS ON YOUR SIDE.

ROCK (STREET CLOTHES)

MY HERO ACADEMIA / HA

THE ROUGH DESIGN

New Villain (Concept)

Messy bangs

Thick and sturdy belt

Like Shotaro from *Kamen Rider W*, or the guys from *Tiger & Bunny*

BEHIND THE SCENES

Betten-san gave me this design for Number 6's "Rock" persona a while back, but since the character needed to disguise himself and operate in the shadows for so long, we couldn't make use of this version until now. So the feeling now is "Here he is, finally!"

—Furuhashi

Since Furuhashi-san wanted this guy's exterior to suggest that he could be a heroic protagonist, some elements of his street clothes are taken from those of a certain *Kamen Rider* duo and the main characters in *Tiger & Bunny*. Having his facial features almost transform when his true identity is revealed is a trick you see a lot in *JoJo's Bizarre Adventure*. Incidentally, "This is something you see a lot in *JoJo*," is an oft-used phrase in our planning meetings. (LOL)

—Betten

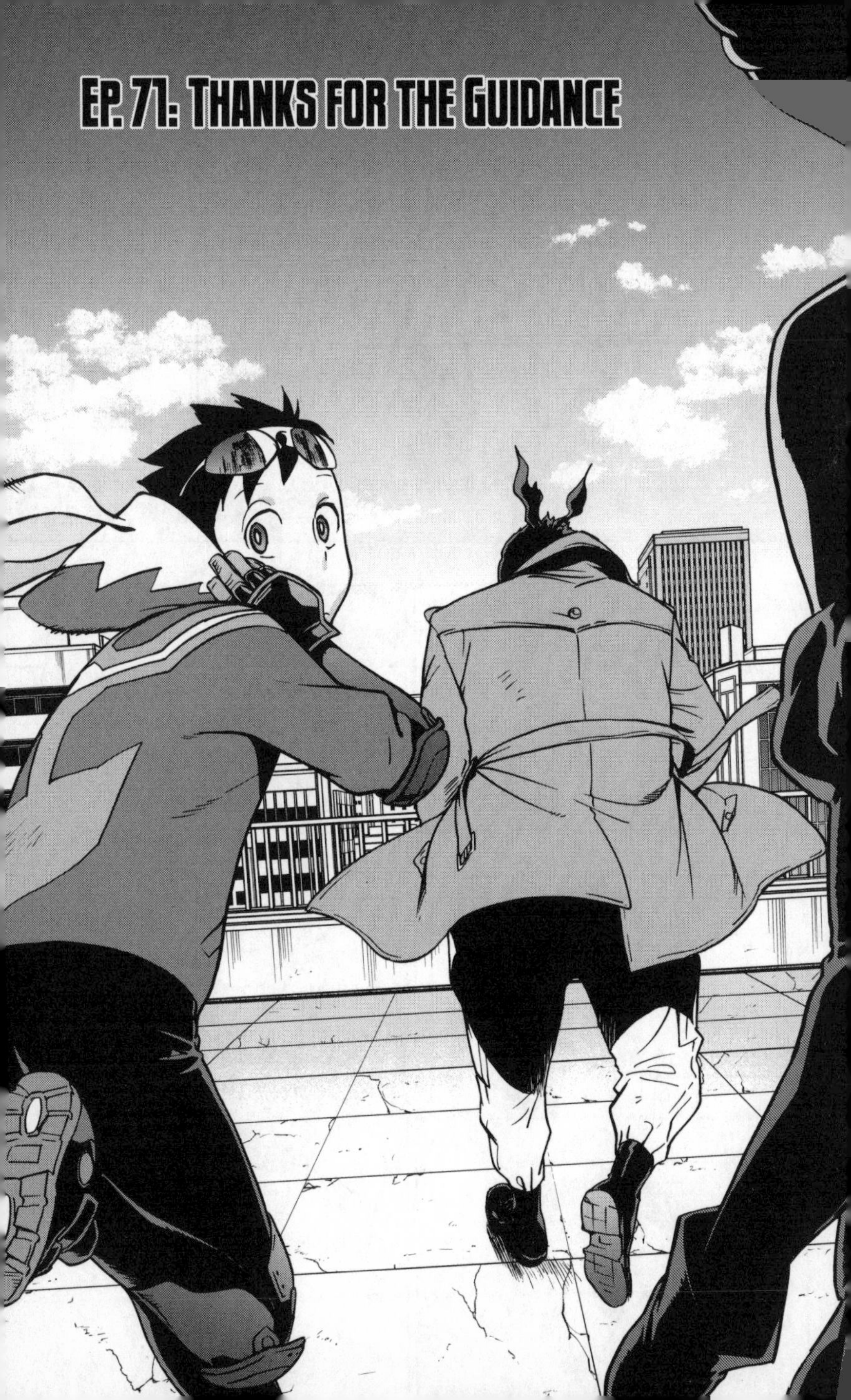
Ep. 71: Thanks for the Guidance

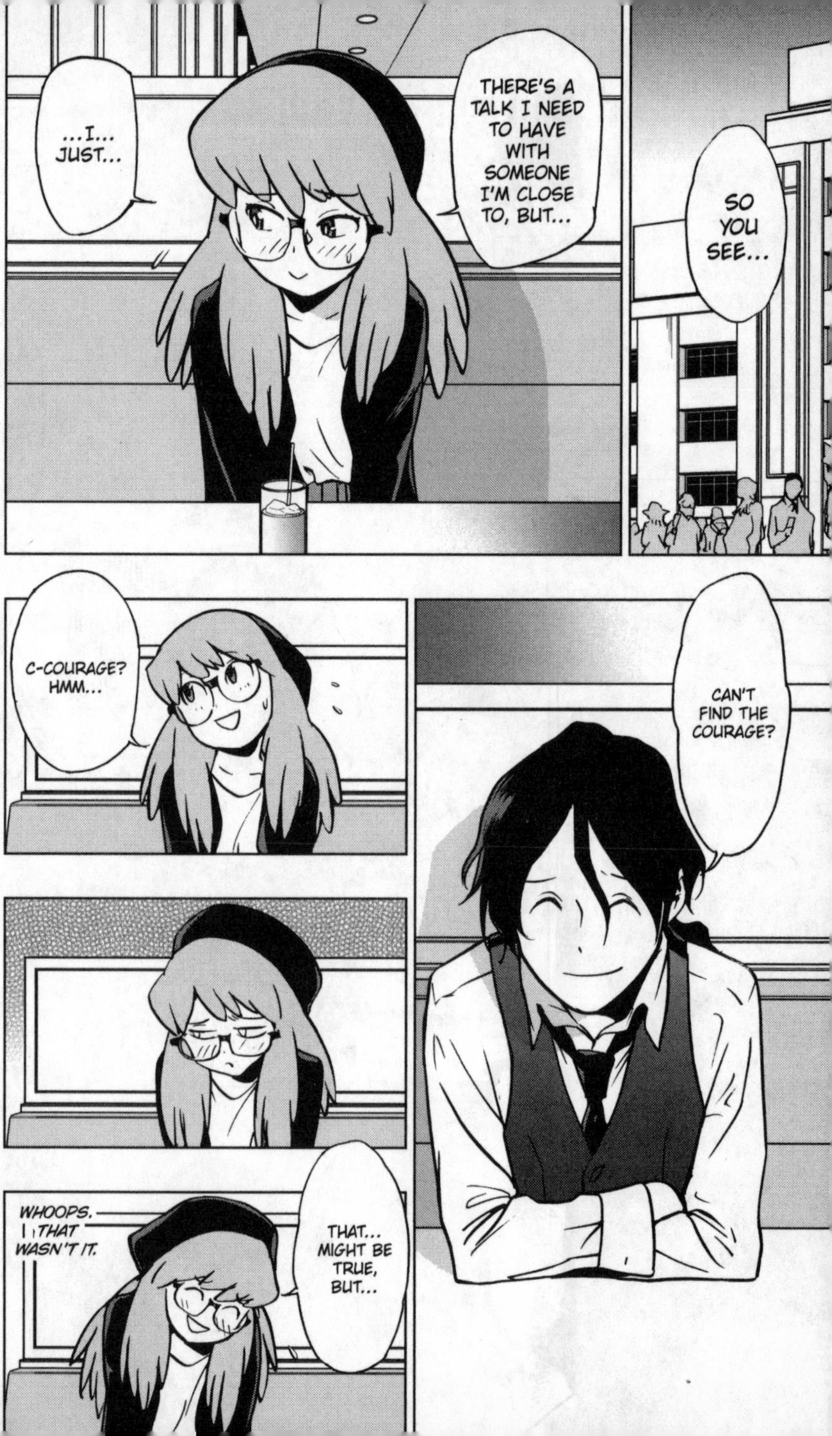
SO YOU SEE...
THERE'S A TALK I NEED TO HAVE WITH SOMEONE I'M CLOSE TO, BUT...
...I... JUST...
CAN'T FIND THE COURAGE?
C-COURAGE? HMM...
THAT... MIGHT BE TRUE, BUT...
WHOOPS. THAT WASN'T IT.

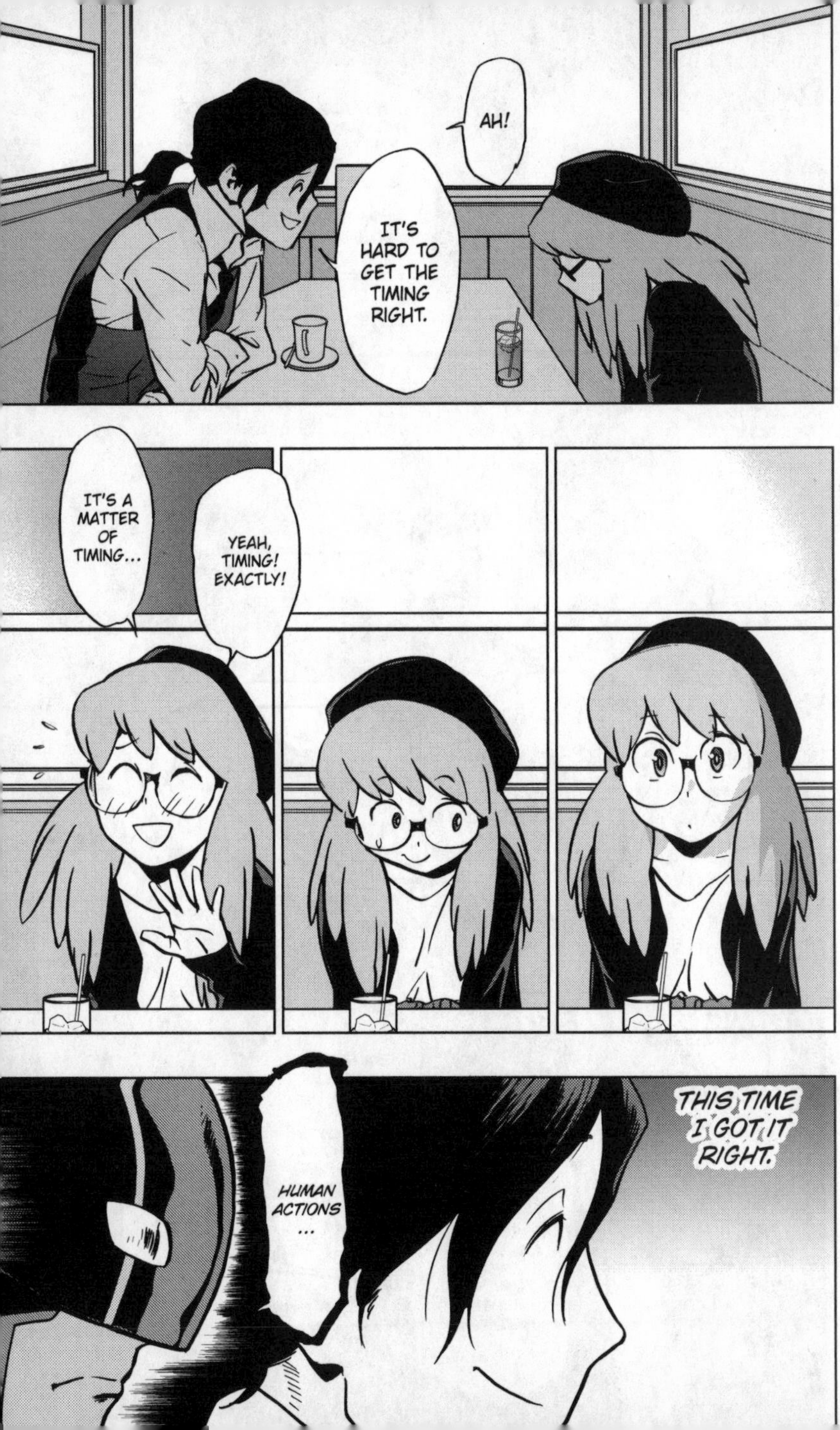
AH!
IT'S HARD TO GET THE TIMING RIGHT.
IT'S A MATTER OF TIMING...
YEAH, TIMING! EXACTLY!
THIS TIME I GOT IT RIGHT.
HUMAN ACTIONS ...

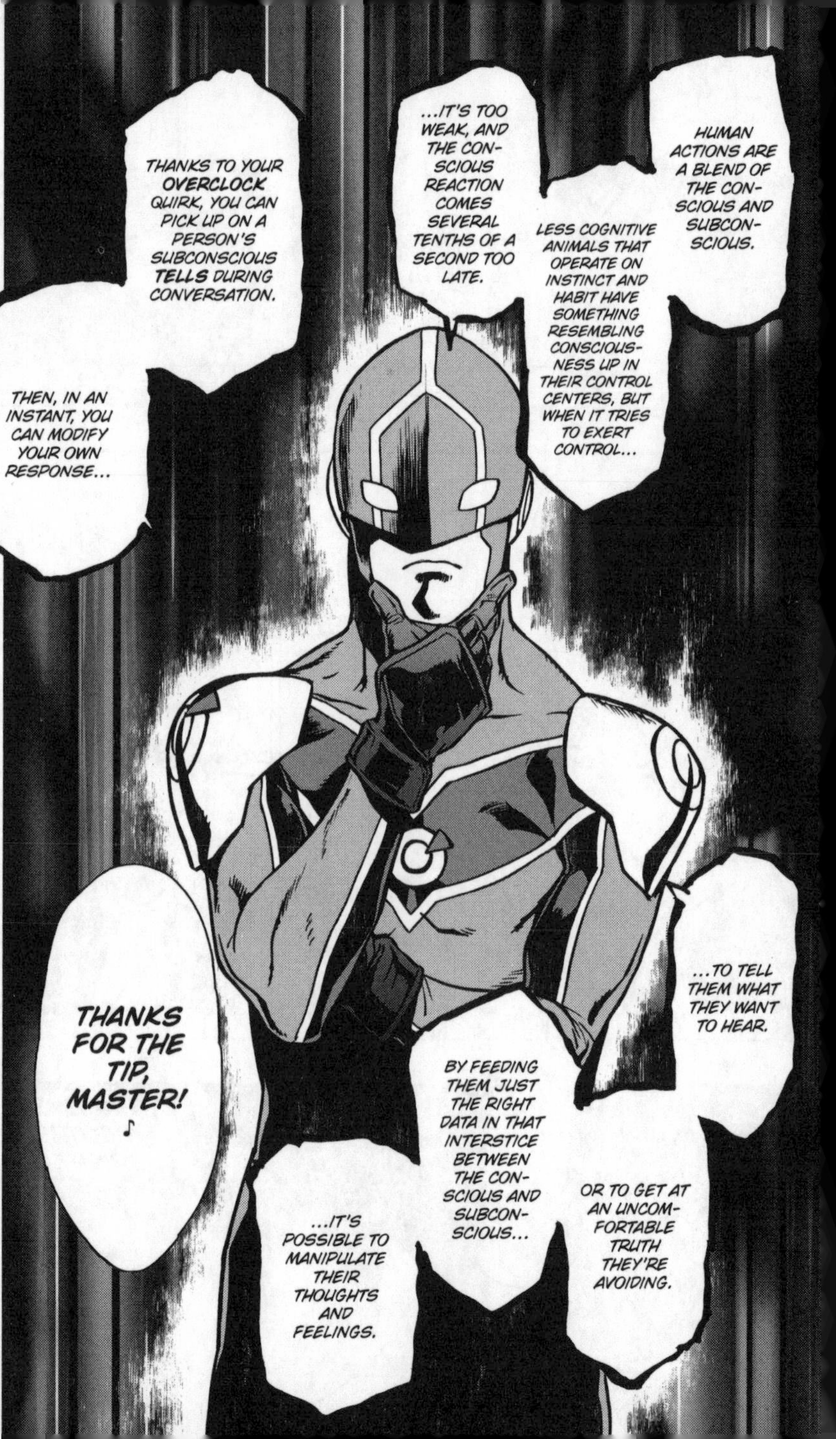
HUMAN ACTIONS ARE A BLEND OF THE CONSCIOUS AND SUBCONSCIOUS.
LESS COGNITIVE ANIMALS THAT OPERATE ON INSTINCT AND HABIT HAVE SOMETHING RESEMBLING CONSCIOUSNESS UP IN THEIR CONTROL CENTERS, BUT WHEN IT TRIES TO EXERT CONTROL...
...IT'S TOO WEAK, AND THE CONSCIOUS REACTION COMES SEVERAL TENTHS OF A SECOND TOO LATE.
THANKS TO YOUR **OVERCLOCK** QUIRK, YOU CAN PICK UP ON A PERSON'S SUBCONSCIOUS **TELLS** DURING CONVERSATION.
THEN, IN AN INSTANT, YOU CAN MODIFY YOUR OWN RESPONSE...
...TO TELL THEM WHAT THEY WANT TO HEAR.
OR TO GET AT AN UNCOMFORTABLE TRUTH THEY'RE AVOIDING.
BY FEEDING THEM JUST THE RIGHT DATA IN THAT INTERSTICE BETWEEN THE CONSCIOUS AND SUBCONSCIOUS...
...IT'S POSSIBLE TO MANIPULATE THEIR THOUGHTS AND FEELINGS.
THANKS FOR THE TIP, MASTER! ♪

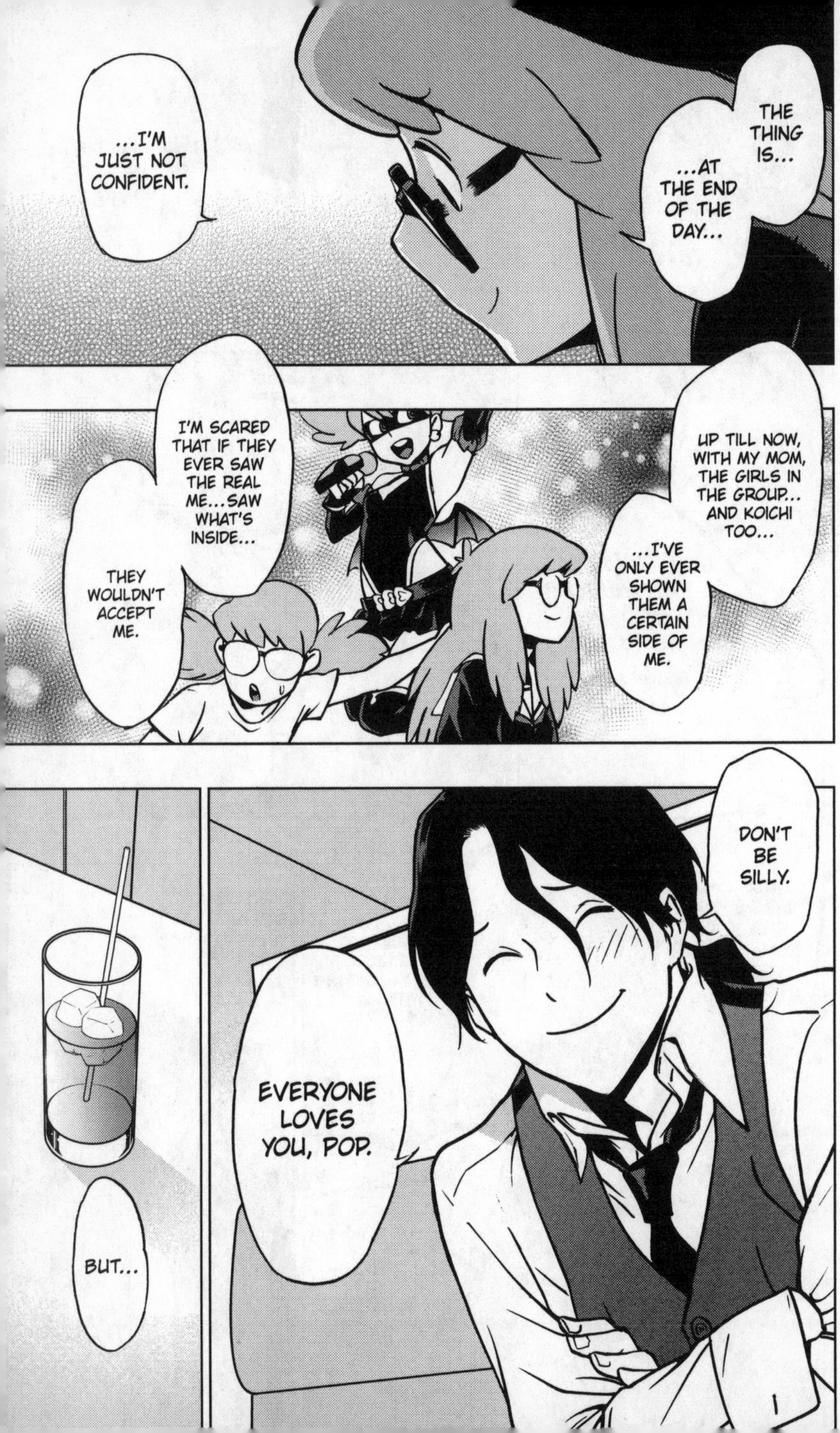
THE THING IS...
...AT THE END OF THE DAY...
...I'M JUST NOT CONFIDENT.
UP TILL NOW, WITH MY MOM, THE GIRLS IN THE GROUP... AND KOICHI TOO...
...I'VE ONLY EVER SHOWN THEM A CERTAIN SIDE OF ME.
I'M SCARED THAT IF THEY EVER SAW THE REAL ME...SAW WHAT'S INSIDE...
THEY WOULDN'T ACCEPT ME.
DON'T BE SILLY.
EVERYONE LOVES YOU, POP.
BUT...

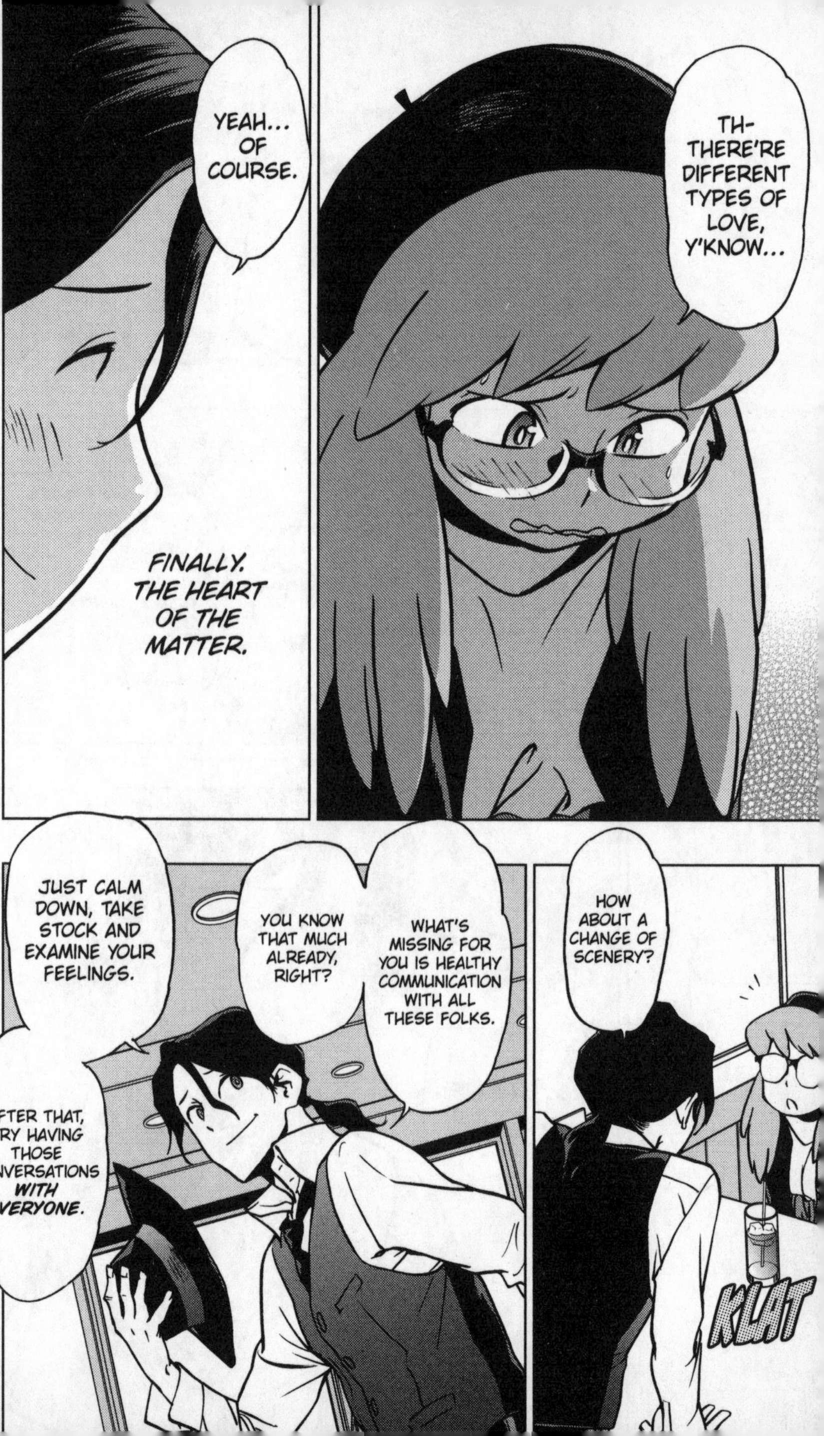
TH- THERE'RE DIFFERENT TYPES OF LOVE, Y'KNOW...
YEAH... OF COURSE.
FINALLY. THE HEART OF THE MATTER.
HOW ABOUT A CHANGE OF SCENERY?
KLAT
WHAT'S MISSING FOR YOU IS HEALTHY COMMUNICATION WITH ALL THESE FOLKS.
YOU KNOW THAT MUCH ALREADY, RIGHT?
JUST CALM DOWN, TAKE STOCK AND EXAMINE YOUR FEELINGS.
AFTER THAT, TRY HAVING THOSE CONVERSATIONS *WITH EVERYONE*.

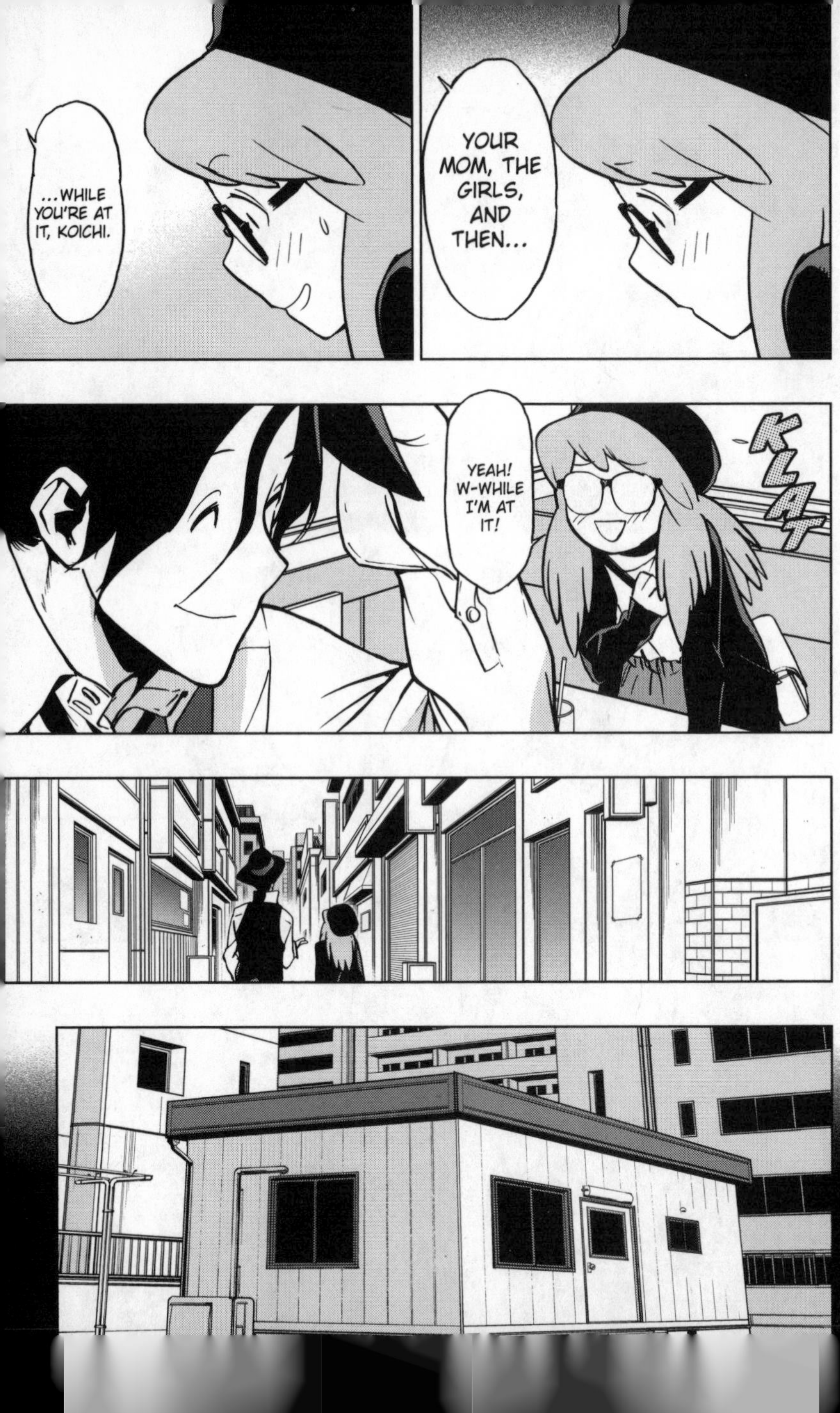
YOUR MOM, THE GIRLS, AND THEN...
...WHILE YOU'RE AT IT, KOICHI.
KLAT
YEAH! W-WHILE I'M AT IT!

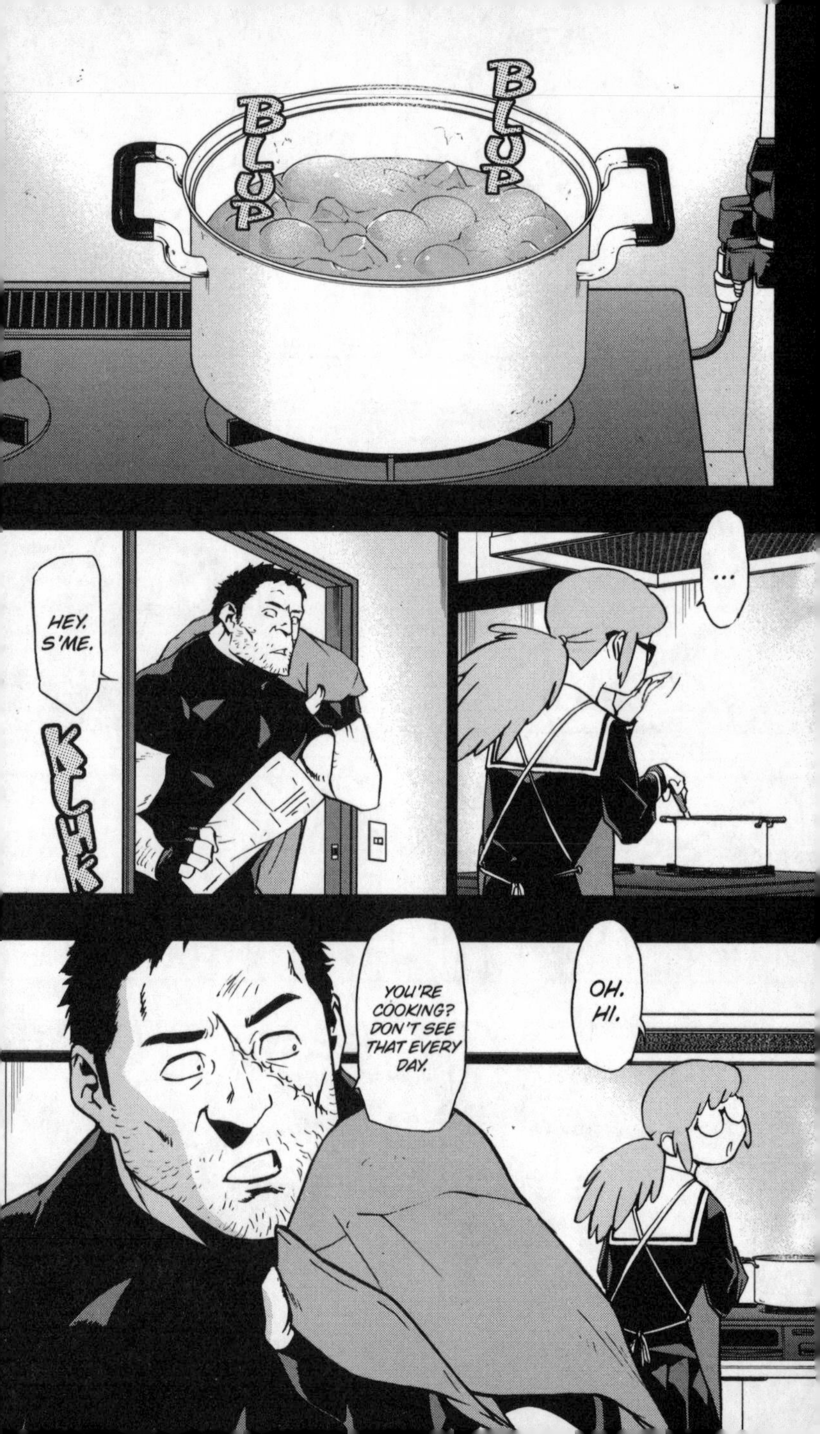
BLUP
BLUP
...
HEY. S'ME.
KLUNK
OH. HI.
YOU'RE COOKING? DON'T SEE THAT EVERY DAY.

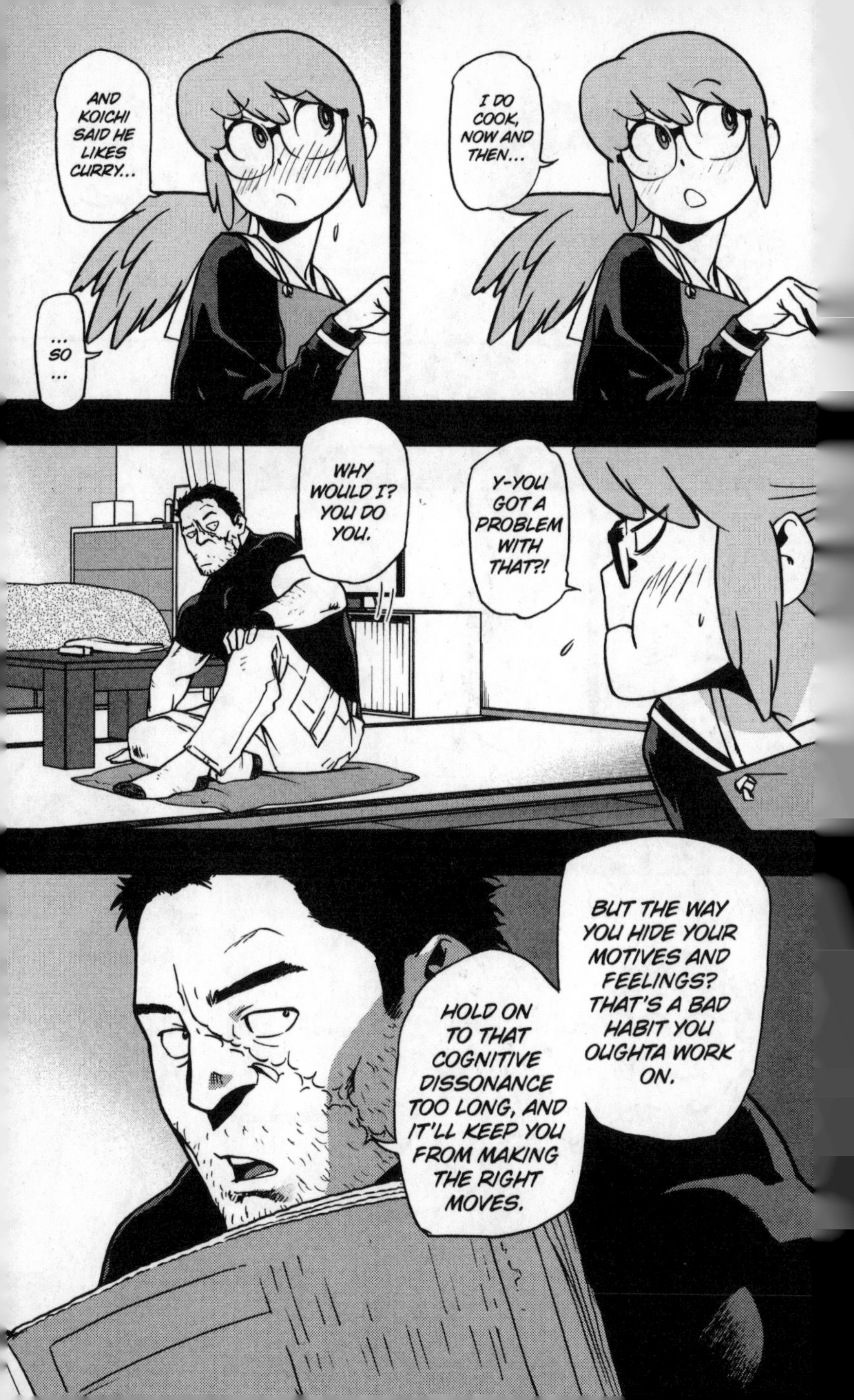
I DO COOK, NOW AND THEN...
AND KOICHI SAID HE LIKES CURRY...
... SO ...
Y-YOU GOT A PROBLEM WITH THAT?!
WHY WOULD I? YOU DO YOU.
BUT THE WAY YOU HIDE YOUR MOTIVES AND FEELINGS? THAT'S A BAD HABIT YOU OUGHTA WORK ON.
HOLD ON TO THAT COGNITIVE DISSONANCE TOO LONG, AND IT'LL KEEP YOU FROM MAKING THE RIGHT MOVES.

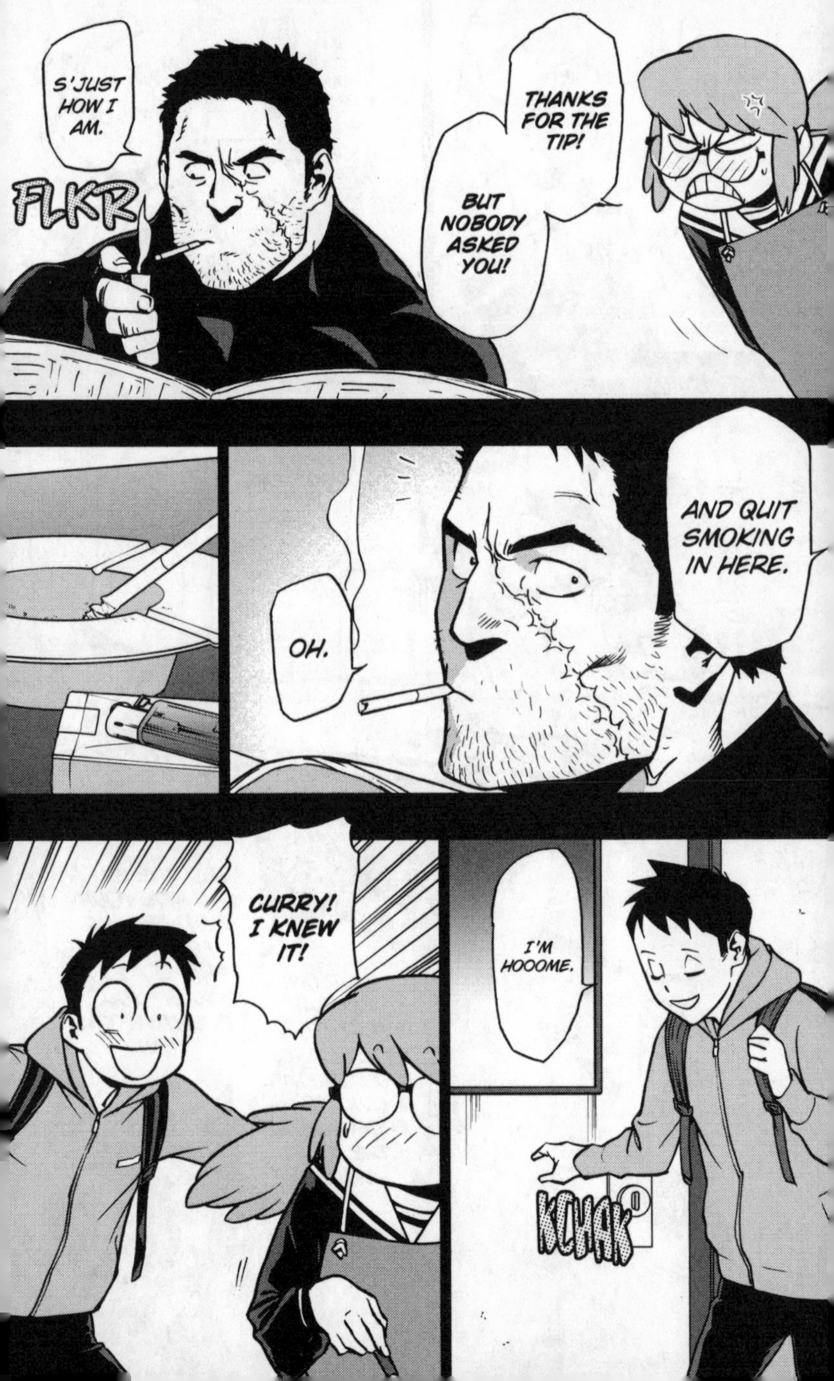
THANKS FOR THE TIP!
BUT NOBODY ASKED YOU!
S'JUST HOW I AM.
FLKR
AND QUIT SMOKING IN HERE.
OH.
I'M HOOOME.
KCHAK
CURRY! I KNEW IT!

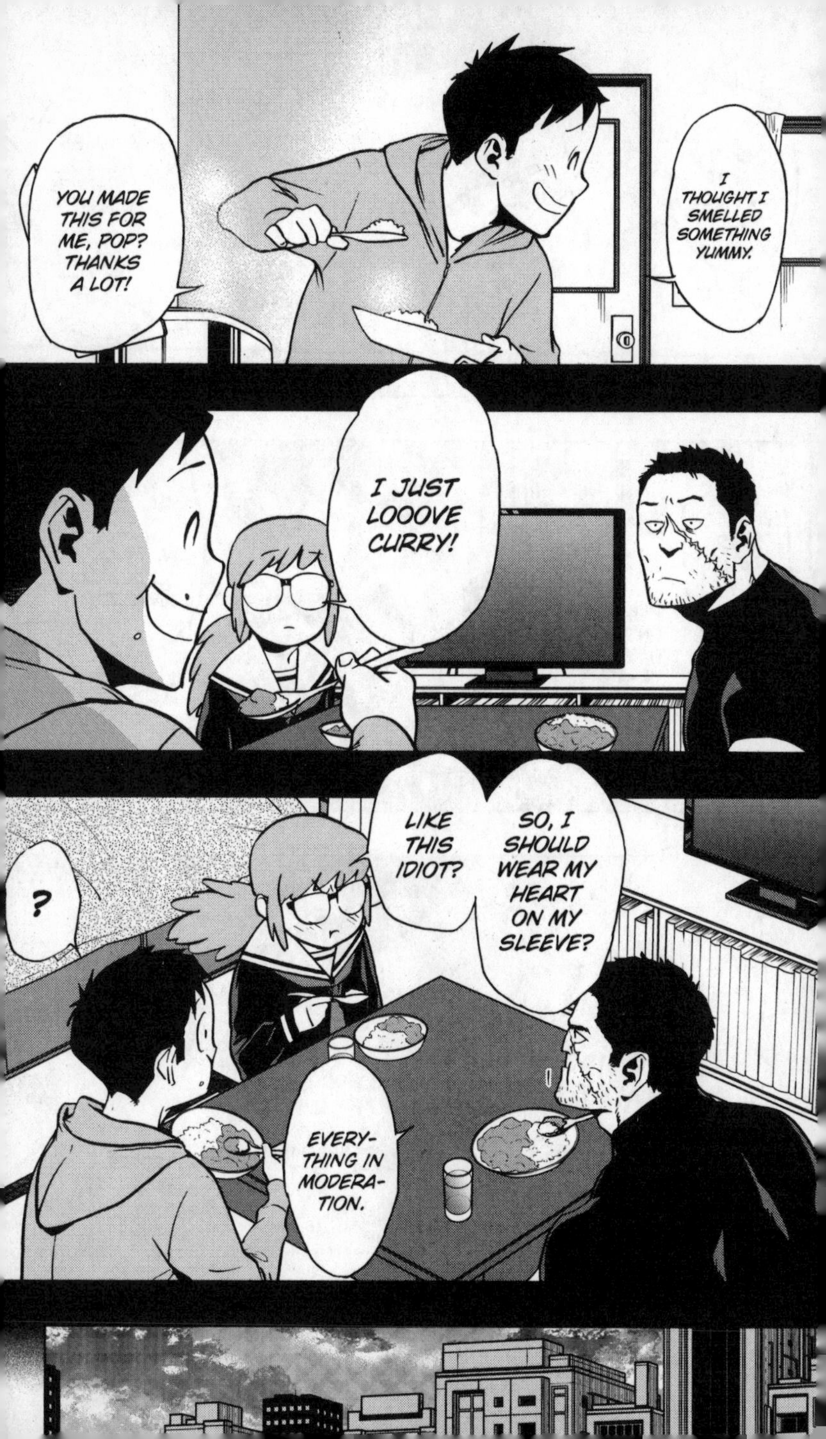
I THOUGHT I SMELLED SOMETHING YUMMY.
YOU MADE THIS FOR ME, POP? THANKS A LOT!
I JUST LOOOVE CURRY!
SO, I SHOULD WEAR MY HEART ON MY SLEEVE?
LIKE THIS IDIOT?
?
EVERY-THING IN MODERA-TION.

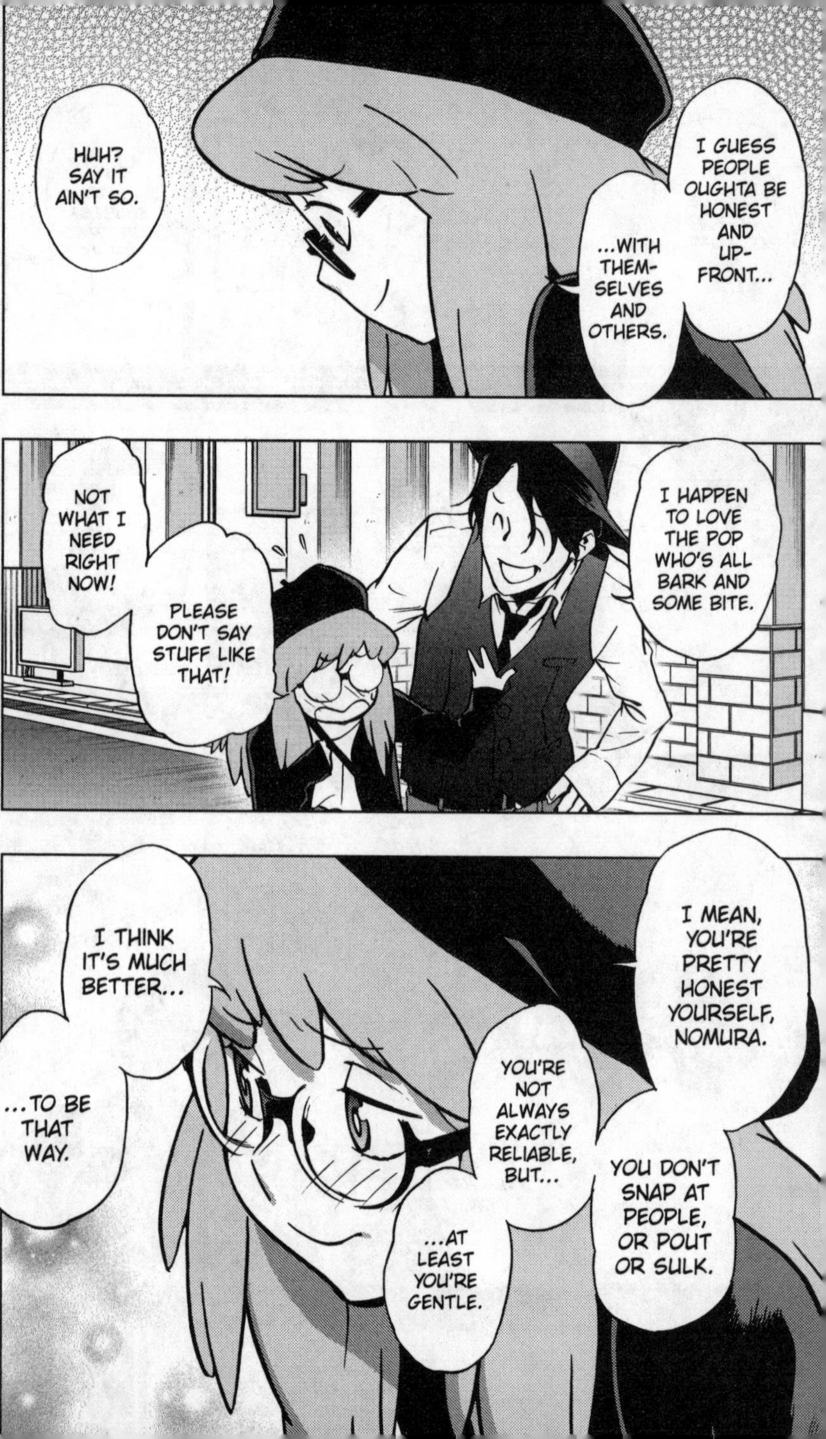
I GUESS PEOPLE OUGHTA BE HONEST AND UP-FRONT...
...WITH THEMSELVES AND OTHERS.
HUH? SAY IT AIN'T SO.
I HAPPEN TO LOVE THE POP WHO'S ALL BARK AND SOME BITE.
PLEASE DON'T SAY STUFF LIKE THAT!
NOT WHAT I NEED RIGHT NOW!
I MEAN, YOU'RE PRETTY HONEST YOURSELF, NOMURA.
YOU DON'T SNAP AT PEOPLE, OR POUT OR SULK.
YOU'RE NOT ALWAYS EXACTLY RELIABLE, BUT...
...AT LEAST YOU'RE GENTLE.
I THINK IT'S MUCH BETTER...
...TO BE THAT WAY.

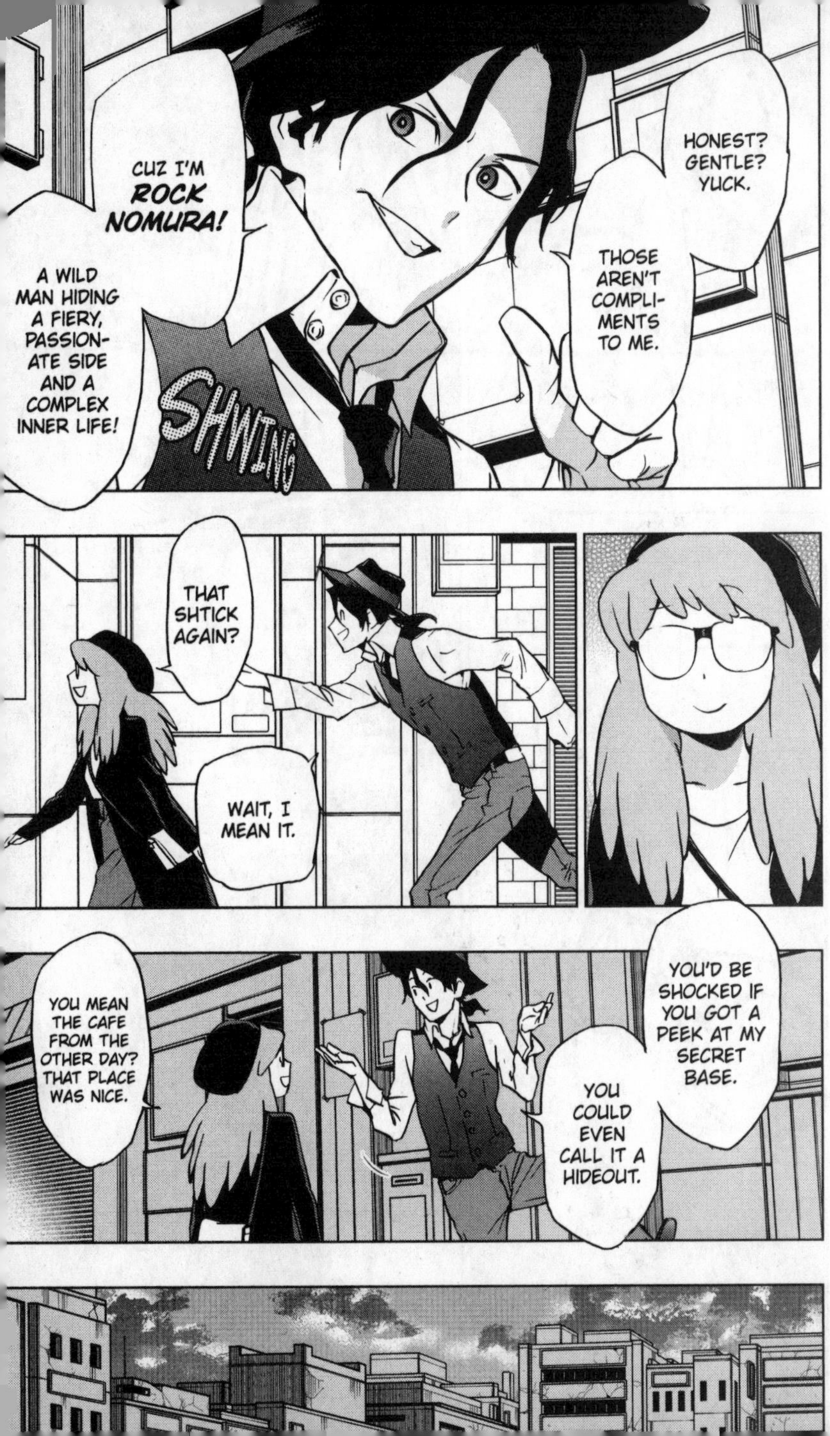
HONEST? GENTLE? YUCK.
THOSE AREN'T COMPLI-MENTS TO ME.
CUZ I'M **ROCK NOMURA!**
A WILD MAN HIDING A FIERY, PASSION-ATE SIDE AND A COMPLEX INNER LIFE!
SHWING
THAT SHTICK AGAIN?
WAIT, I MEAN IT.
YOU'D BE SHOCKED IF YOU GOT A PEEK AT MY SECRET BASE.
YOU COULD EVEN CALL IT A HIDEOUT.
YOU MEAN THE CAFE FROM THE OTHER DAY? THAT PLACE WAS NICE.

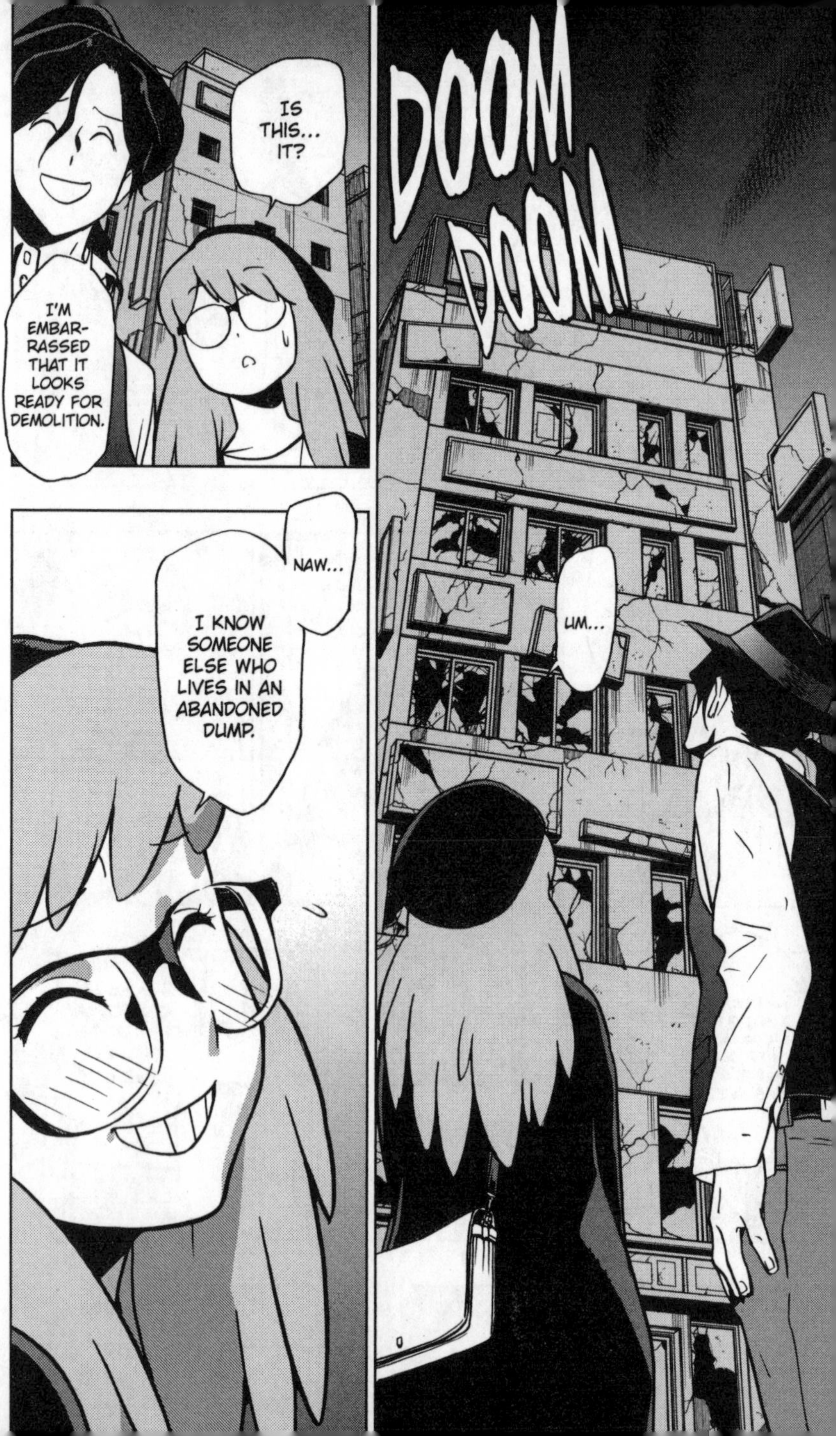
DOOM
DOOM
UM...
IS THIS... IT?
I'M EMBARRASSED THAT IT LOOKS READY FOR DEMOLITION.
NAW...
I KNOW SOMEONE ELSE WHO LIVES IN AN ABANDONED DUMP.

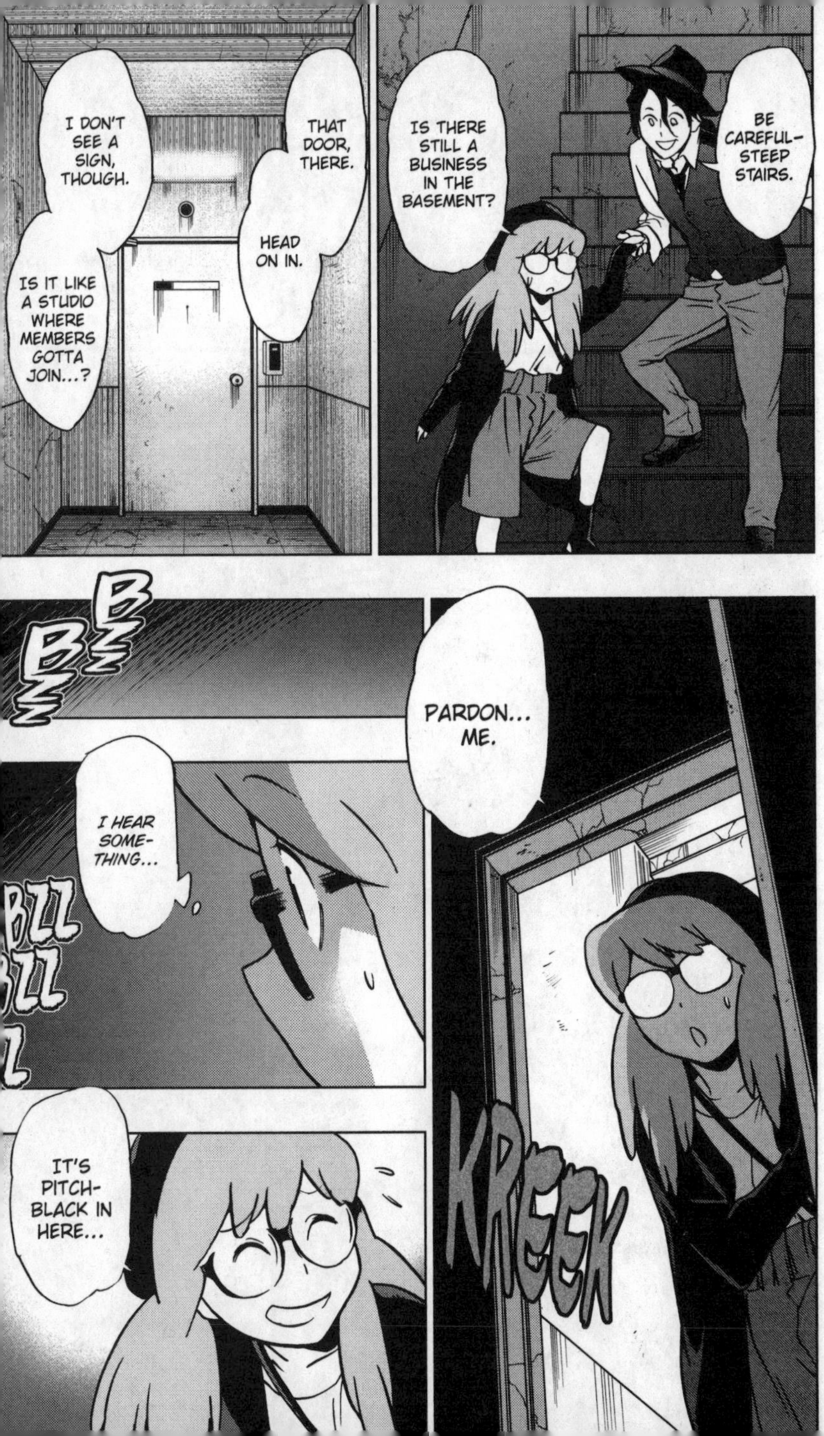
BE CAREFUL-STEEP STAIRS.
IS THERE STILL A BUSINESS IN THE BASEMENT?
THAT DOOR, THERE.
HEAD ON IN.
I DON'T SEE A SIGN, THOUGH.
IS IT LIKE A STUDIO WHERE MEMBERS GOTTA JOIN...?
PARDON... ME.
KREEK
BZZ
BZZ
I HEAR SOMETHING...
IT'S PITCH-BLACK IN HERE...

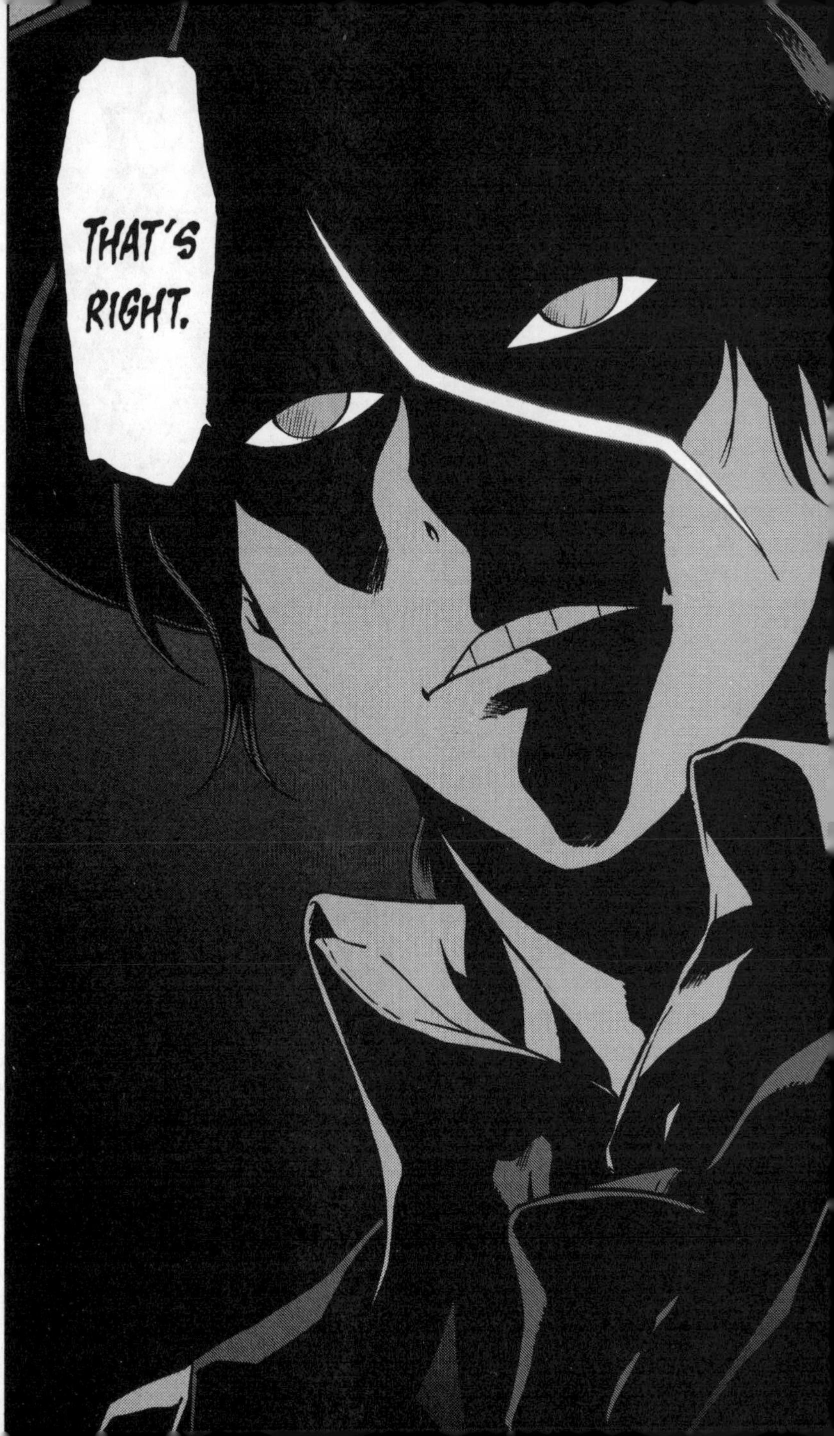
THAT'S RIGHT.

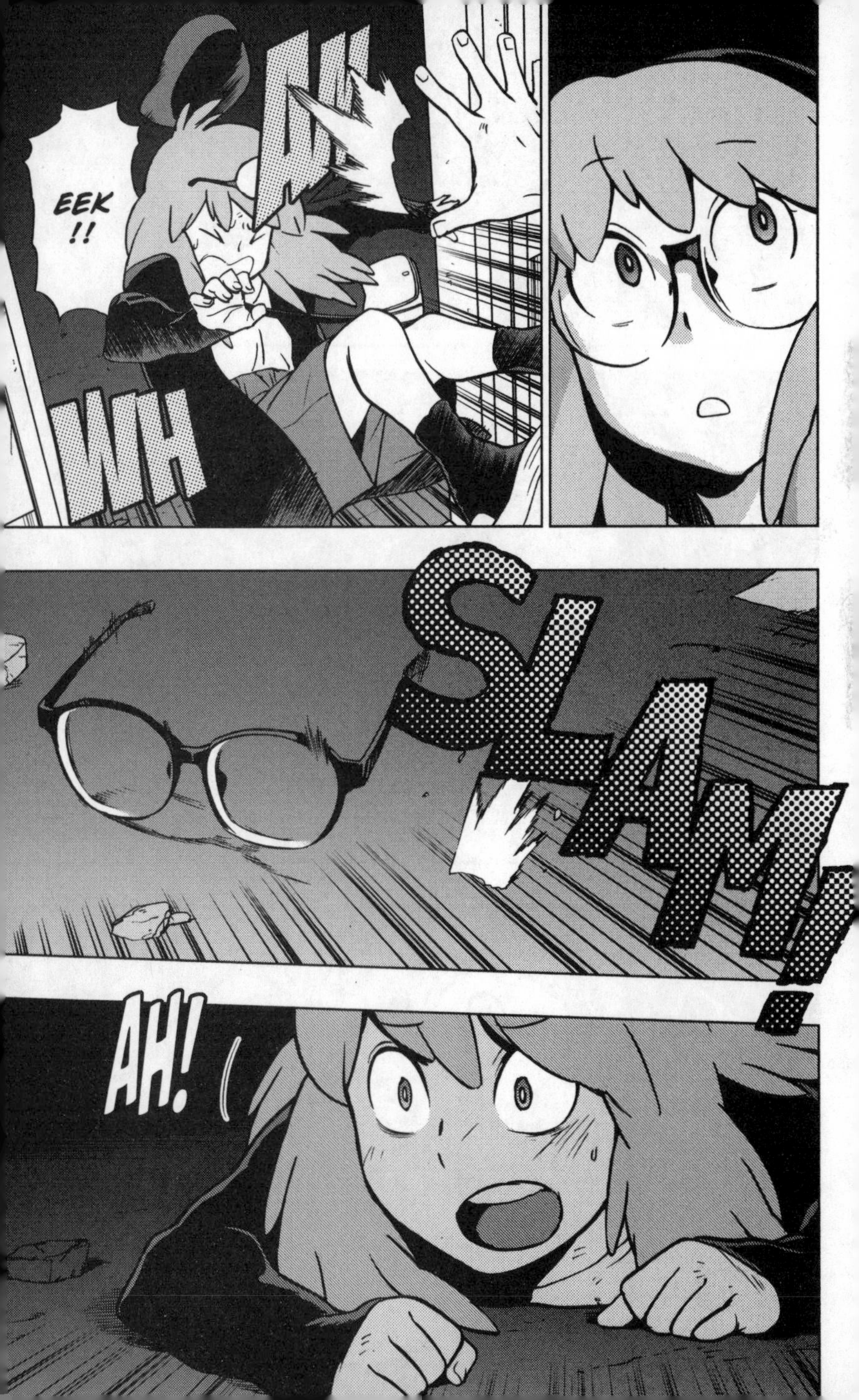
AH
EEK !!
WH
SLAM!!
AH!

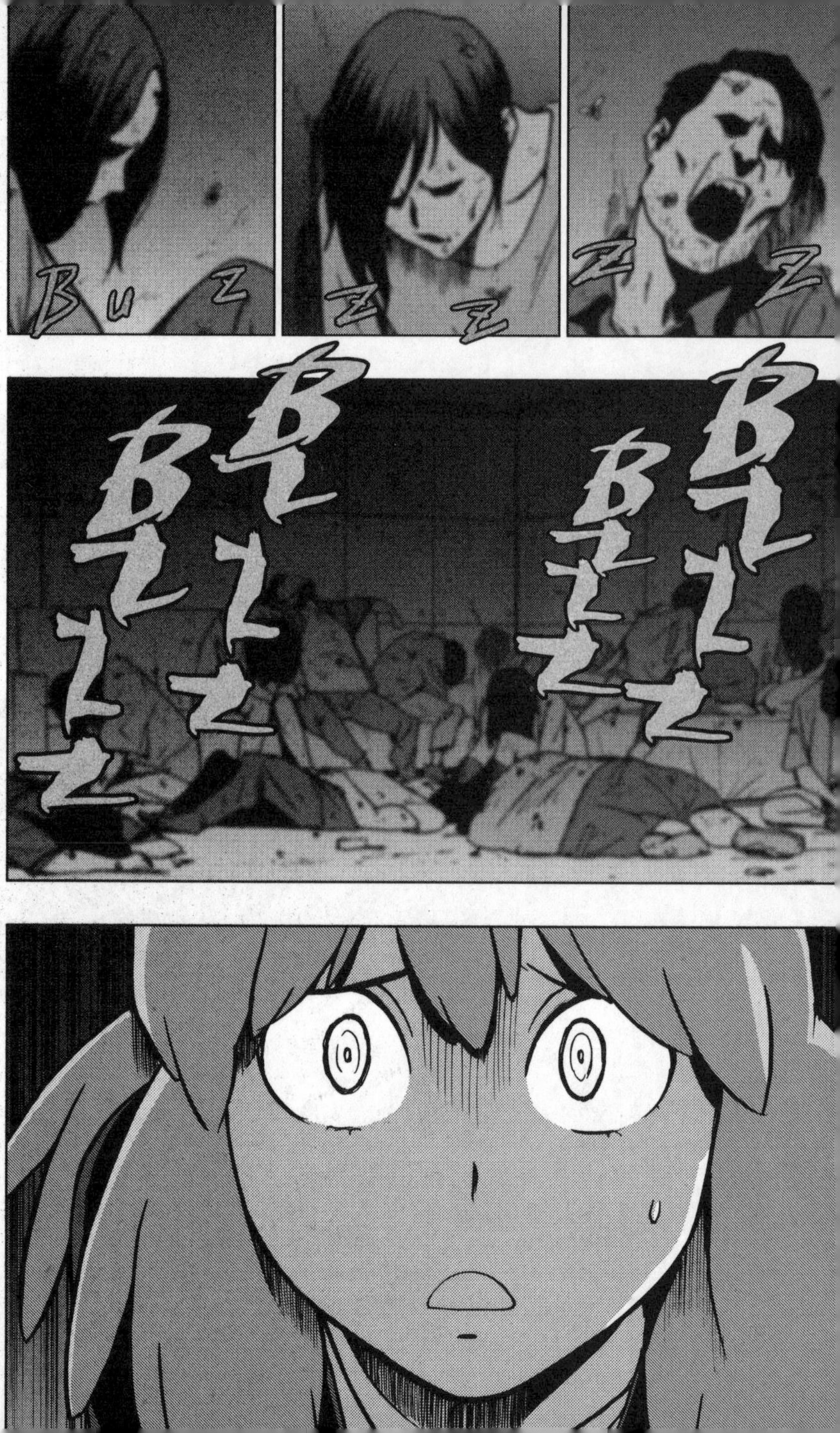
Buzzzzz
Bzzz
Bzzz
Bzzz
Bzzzz

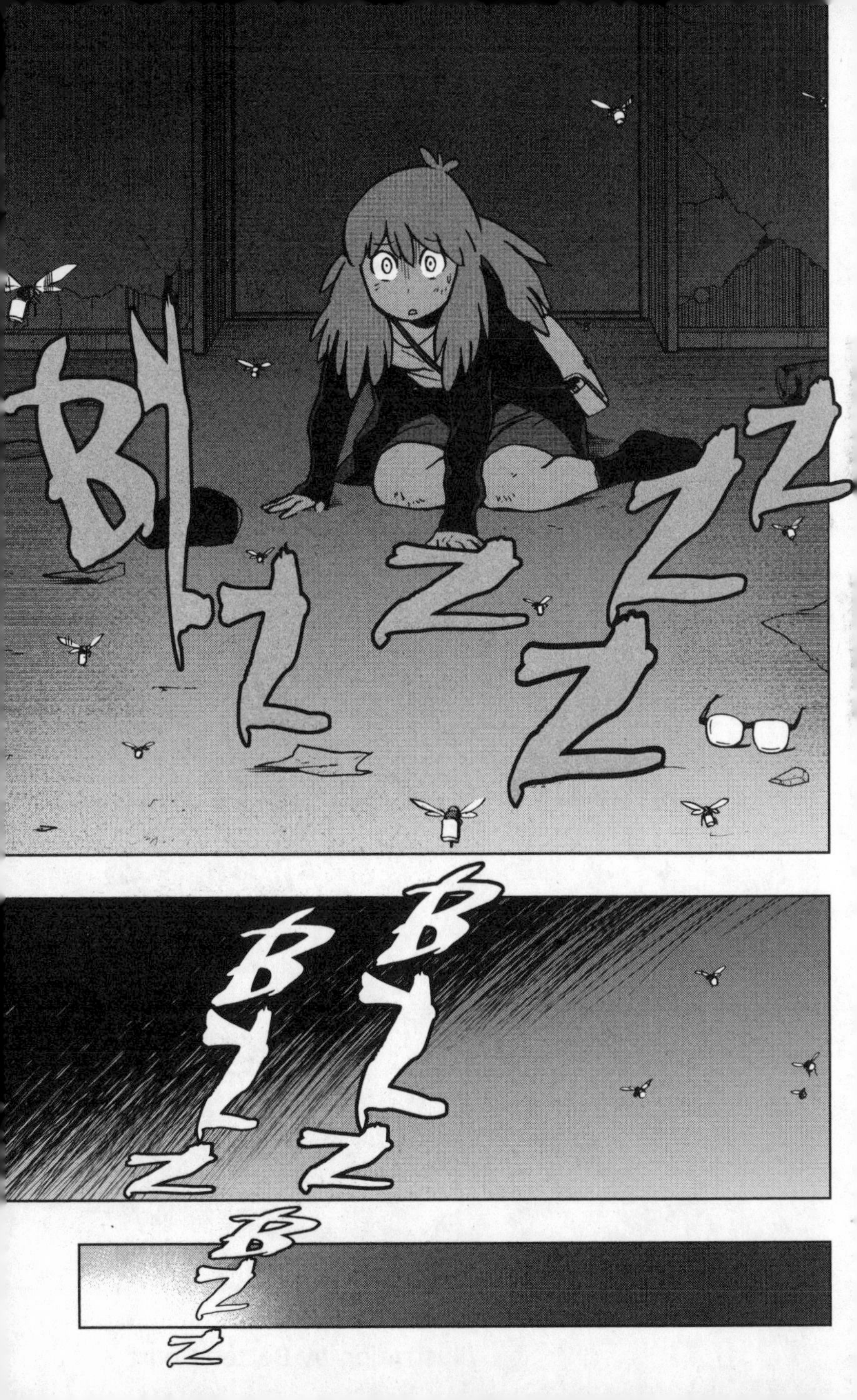
BZZZZZ
BZZ
BZZ
BZZ

"WHAT-IF"

ERASER HEAD Ver.

If Shota Aizawa hadn't become an educator

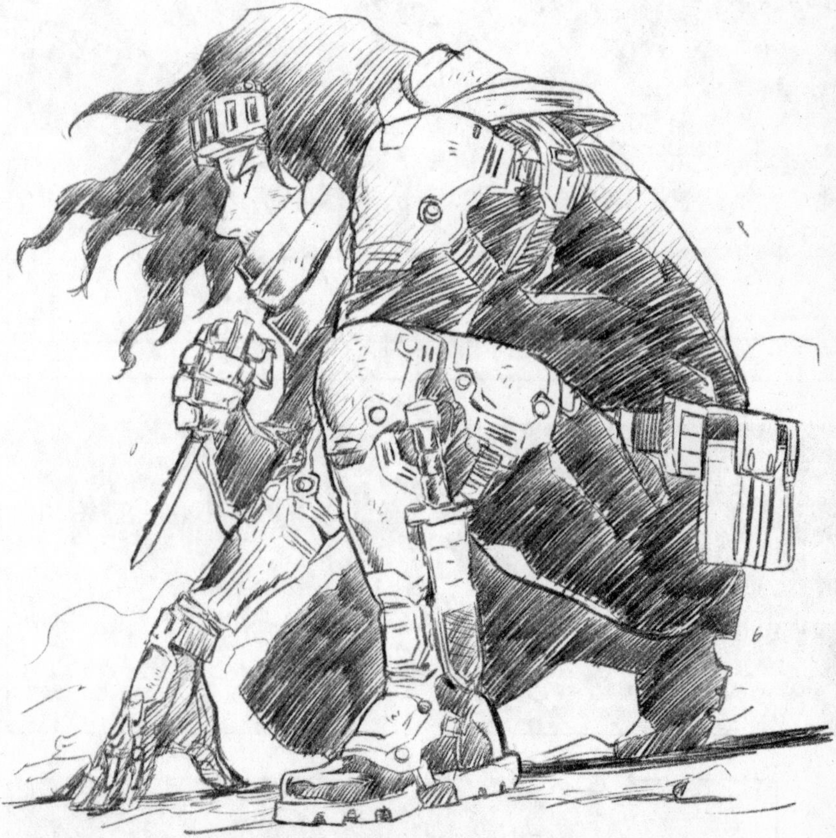

Illustration by Betten Court

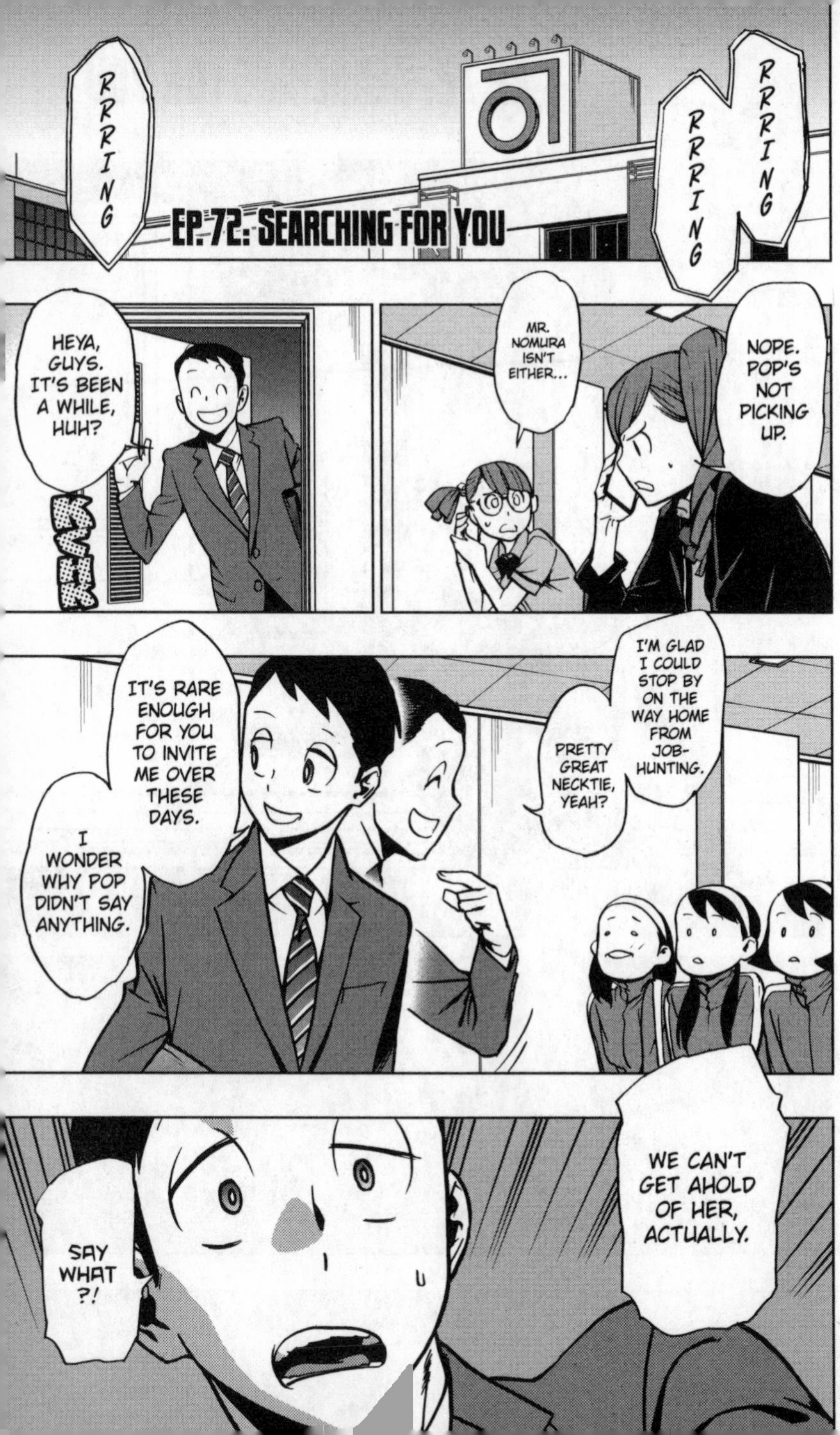
RRRING
RRRING
RRRING
EP. 72: SEARCHING FOR YOU
NOPE. POP'S NOT PICKING UP.
MR. NOMURA ISN'T EITHER...
HEYA, GUYS. IT'S BEEN A WHILE, HUH?
I'M GLAD I COULD STOP BY ON THE WAY HOME FROM JOB-HUNTING.
PRETTY GREAT NECKTIE, YEAH?
IT'S RARE ENOUGH FOR YOU TO INVITE ME OVER THESE DAYS.
I WONDER WHY POP DIDN'T SAY ANYTHING.
WE CAN'T GET AHOLD OF HER, ACTUALLY.
SAY WHAT?!

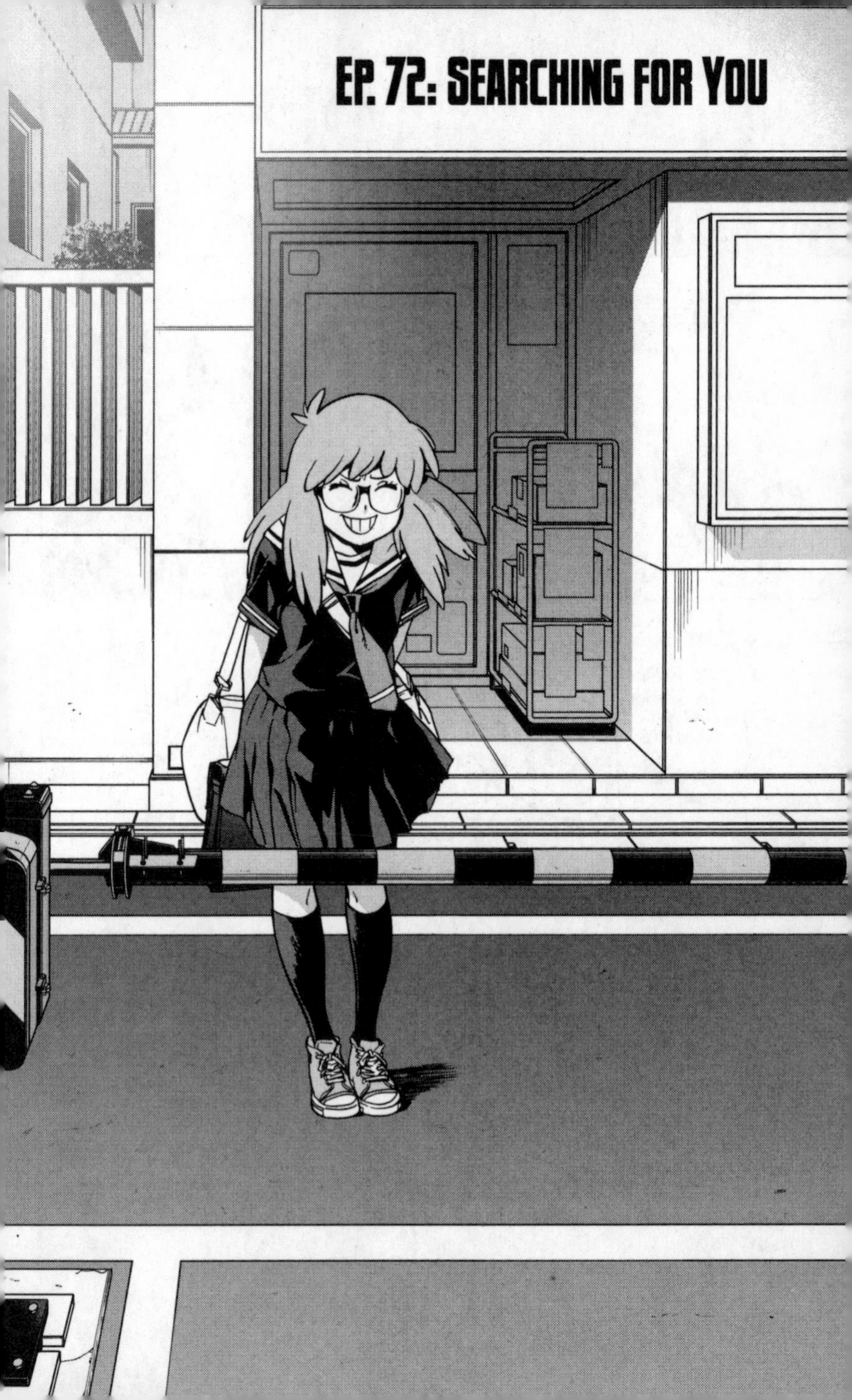
Ep. 72: Searching for You

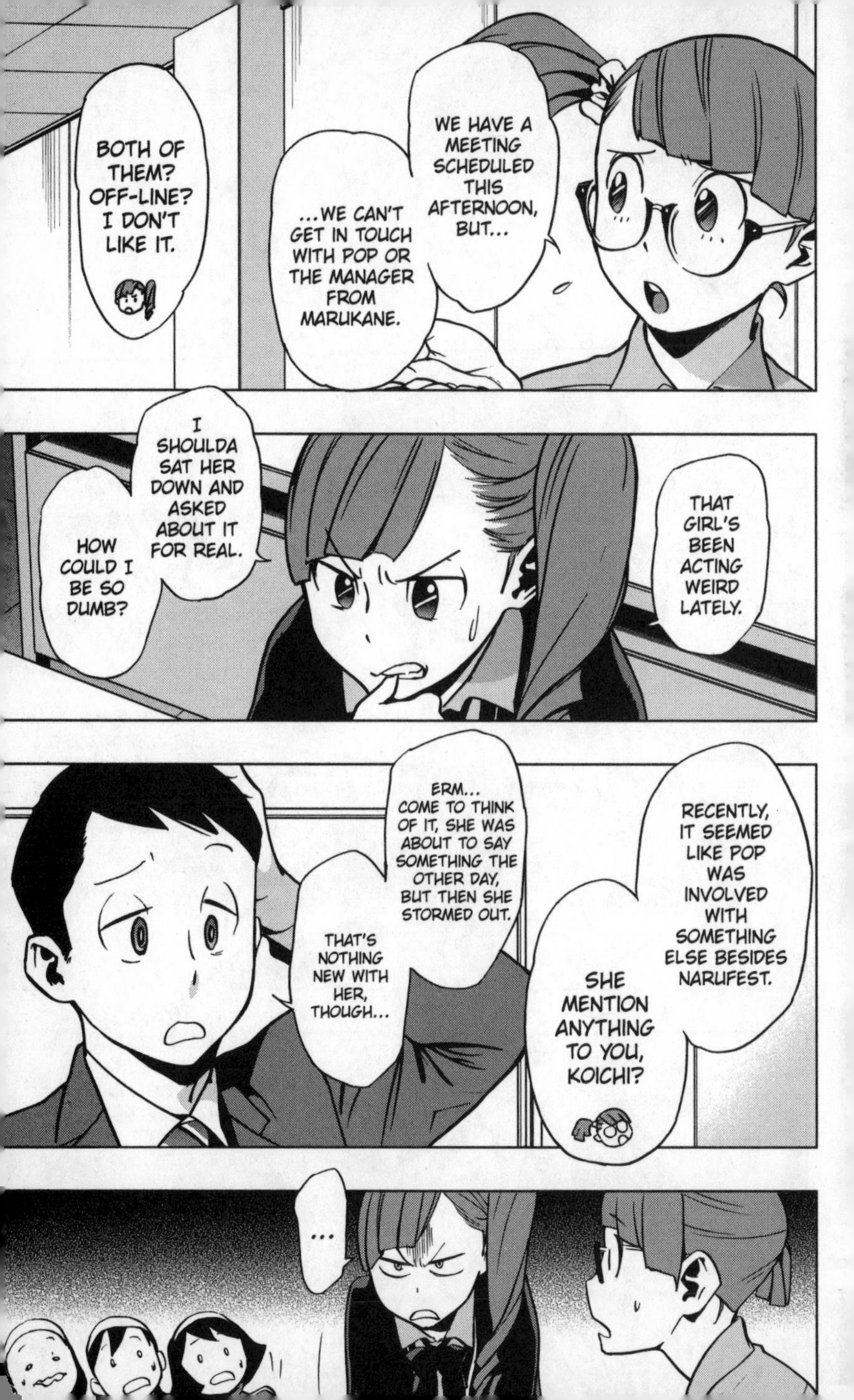
WE HAVE A MEETING SCHEDULED THIS AFTERNOON, BUT...
...WE CAN'T GET IN TOUCH WITH POP OR THE MANAGER FROM MARUKANE.
BOTH OF THEM? OFF-LINE? I DON'T LIKE IT.
THAT GIRL'S BEEN ACTING WEIRD LATELY.
I SHOULDA SAT HER DOWN AND ASKED ABOUT IT FOR REAL.
HOW COULD I BE SO DUMB?
RECENTLY, IT SEEMED LIKE POP WAS INVOLVED WITH SOMETHING ELSE BESIDES NARUFEST.
SHE MENTION ANYTHING TO YOU, KOICHI?
ERM... COME TO THINK OF IT, SHE WAS ABOUT TO SAY SOMETHING THE OTHER DAY, BUT THEN SHE STORMED OUT.
THAT'S NOTHING NEW WITH HER, THOUGH...
...

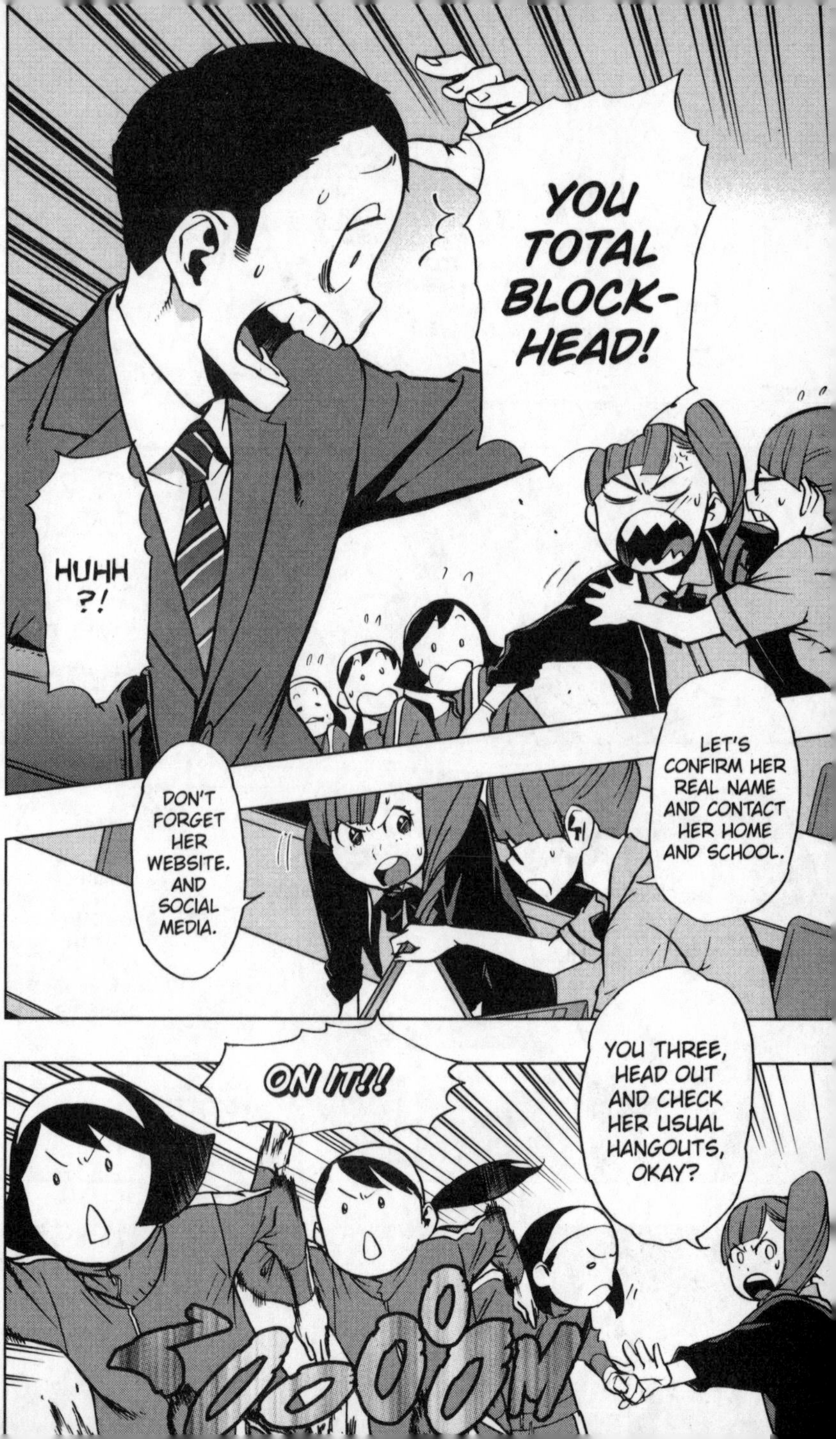
YOU TOTAL BLOCK-HEAD!
HUHH ?!
LET'S CONFIRM HER REAL NAME AND CONTACT HER HOME AND SCHOOL.
DON'T FORGET HER WEBSITE. AND SOCIAL MEDIA.
YOU THREE, HEAD OUT AND CHECK HER USUAL HANGOUTS, OKAY?
ON IT!!

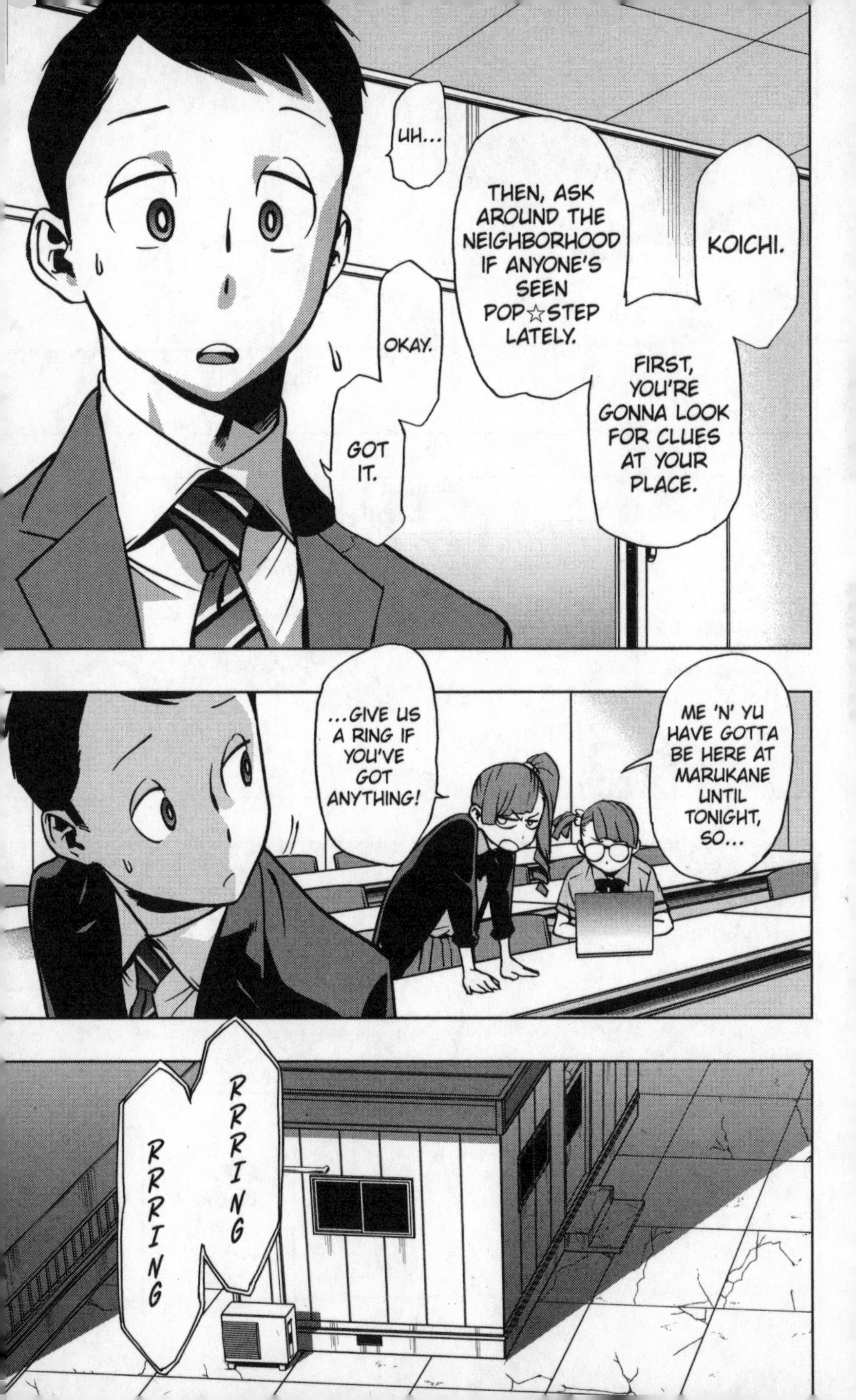
KOICHI.
FIRST, YOU'RE GONNA LOOK FOR CLUES AT YOUR PLACE.
THEN, ASK AROUND THE NEIGHBORHOOD IF ANYONE'S SEEN POP☆STEP LATELY.
UH...
OKAY.
GOT IT.
ME 'N' YU HAVE GOTTA BE HERE AT MARUKANE UNTIL TONIGHT, SO...
...GIVE US A RING IF YOU'VE GOT ANYTHING!
RRRING
RRRING

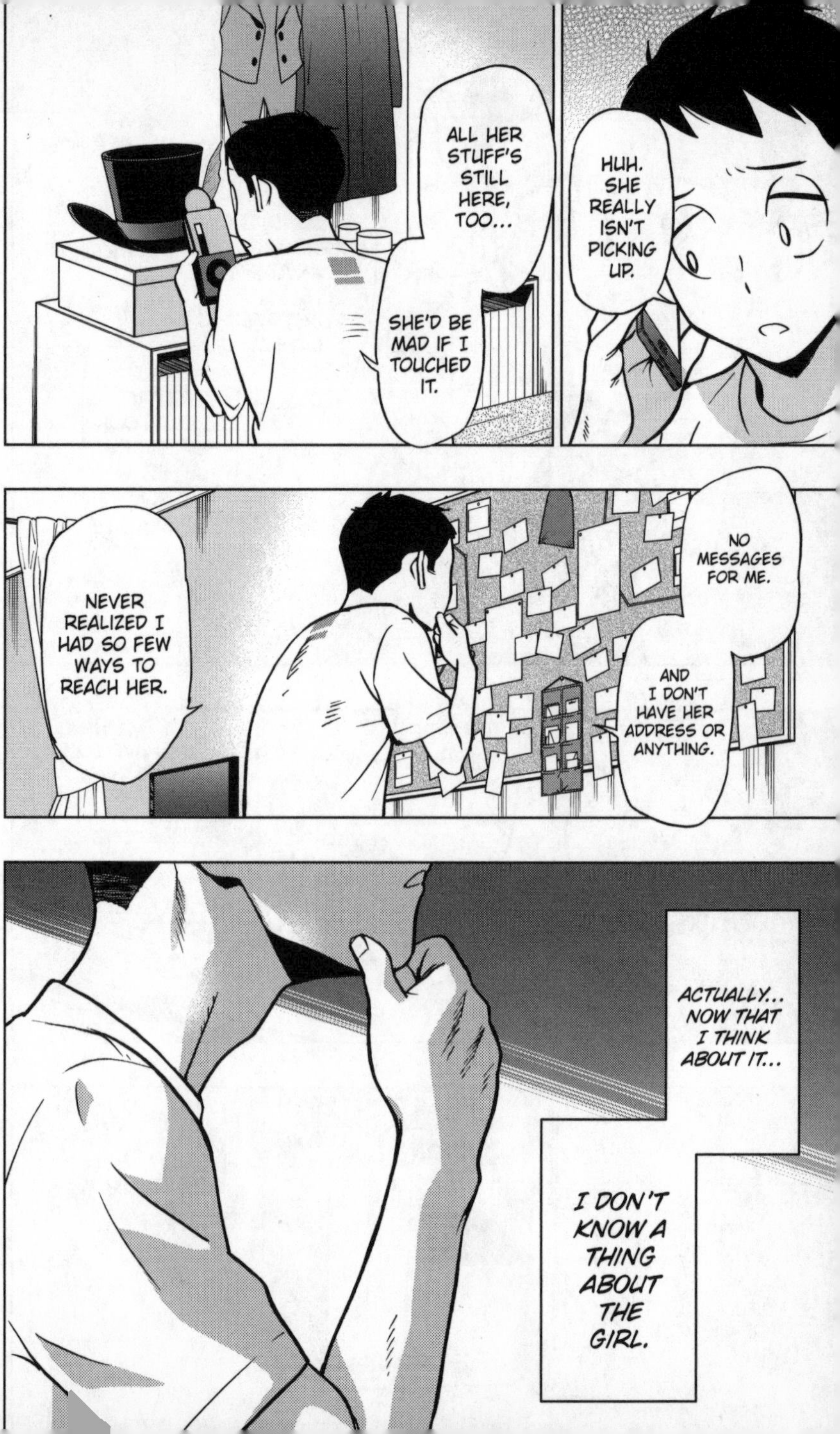
HUH. SHE REALLY ISN'T PICKING UP.
ALL HER STUFF'S STILL HERE, TOO...
SHE'D BE MAD IF I TOUCHED IT.
NO MESSAGES FOR ME.
AND I DON'T HAVE HER ADDRESS OR ANYTHING.
NEVER REALIZED I HAD SO FEW WAYS TO REACH HER.
ACTUALLY... NOW THAT I THINK ABOUT IT...
I DON'T KNOW A THING ABOUT THE GIRL.

SHE JUST POPPED INTO MY LIFE ONE DAY...

...AND THEN WE WERE ALWAYS TOGETHER.

I KINDA ASSUMED IT'D ALWAYS BE THAT WAY.

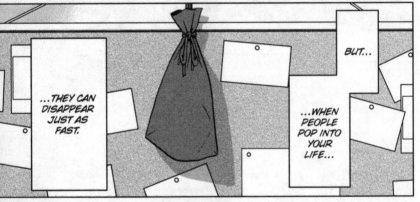

BUT...

...WHEN PEOPLE POP INTO YOUR LIFE...

...THEY CAN DISAPPEAR JUST AS FAST.

THERE WAS NO GUARANTEE THAT THERE'D ALWAYS BE A TOMORROW FOR US.

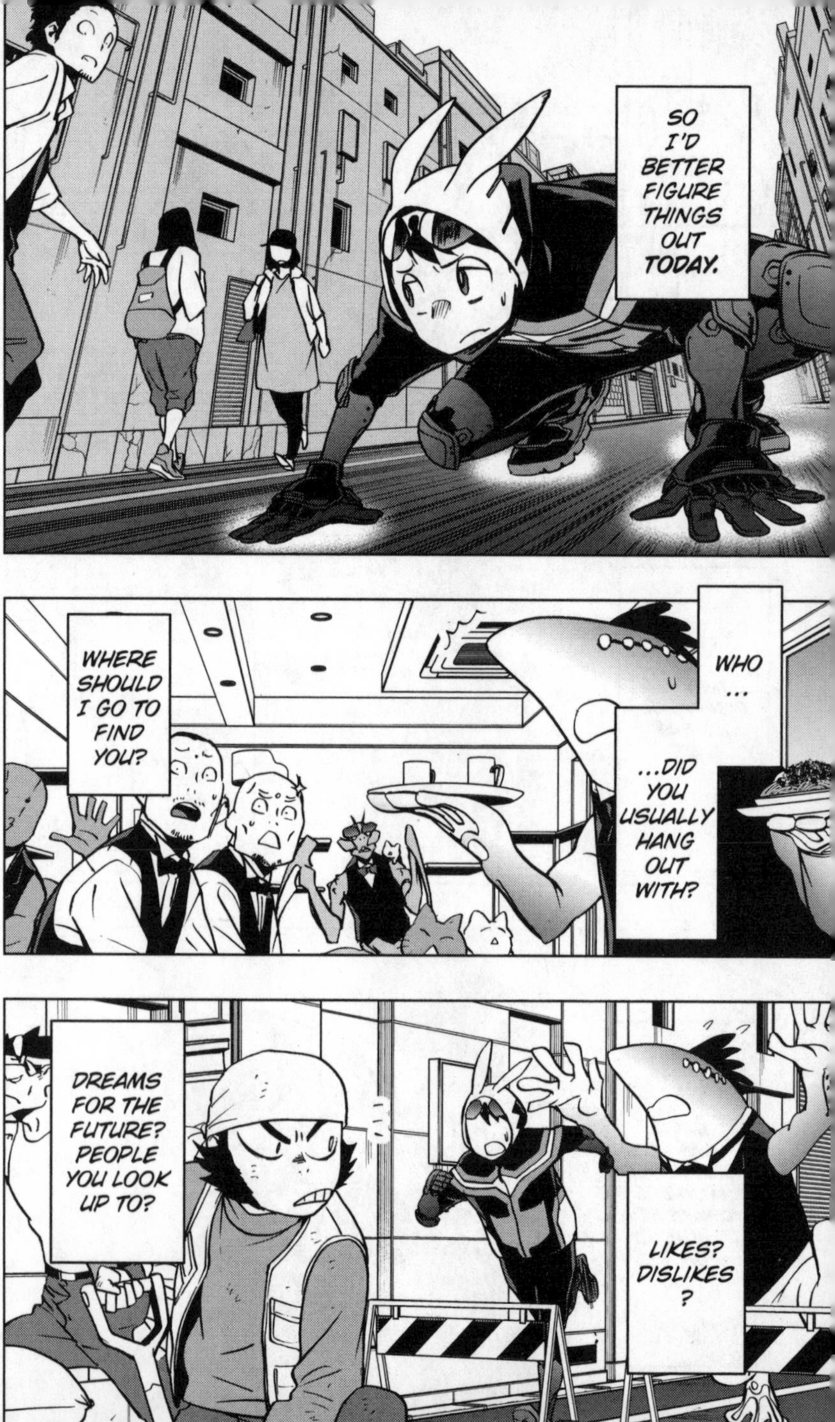
SO I'D BETTER FIGURE THINGS OUT TODAY.
WHO ...
...DID YOU USUALLY HANG OUT WITH?
WHERE SHOULD I GO TO FIND YOU?
LIKES? DISLIKES ?
DREAMS FOR THE FUTURE? PEOPLE YOU LOOK UP TO?

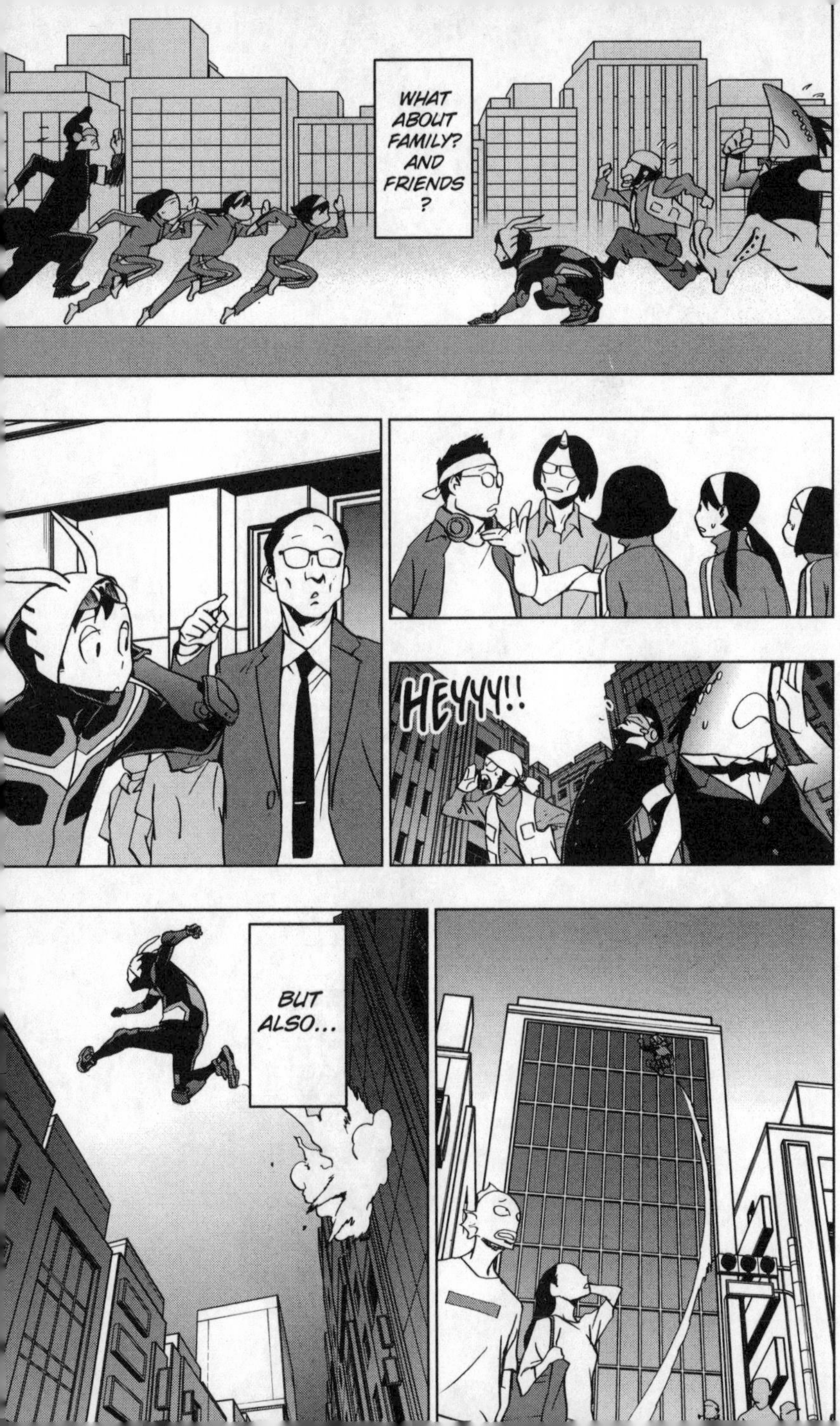
WHAT ABOUT FAMILY? AND FRIENDS ?
HEYYY!!
BUT ALSO...

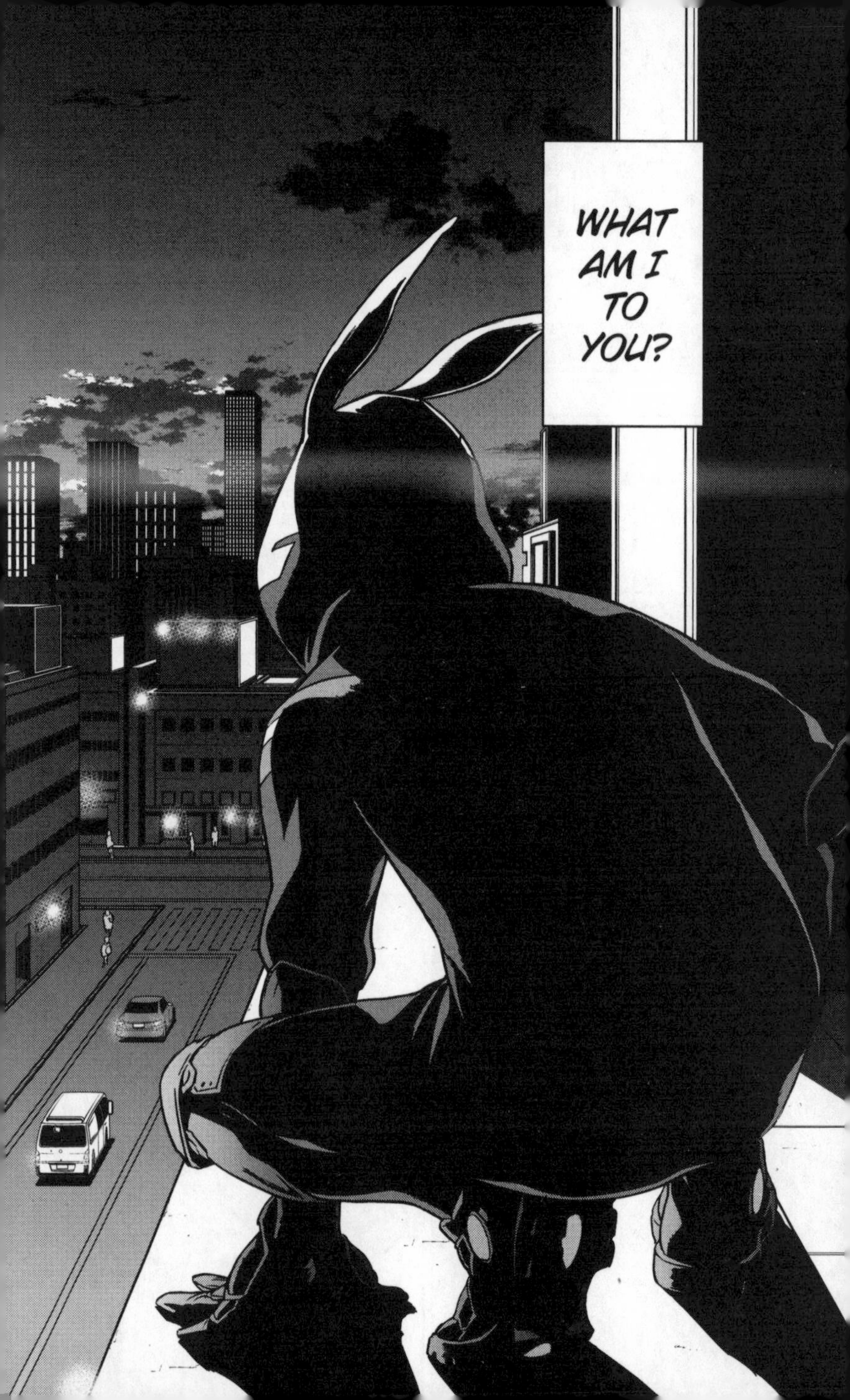
WHAT AM I TO YOU?

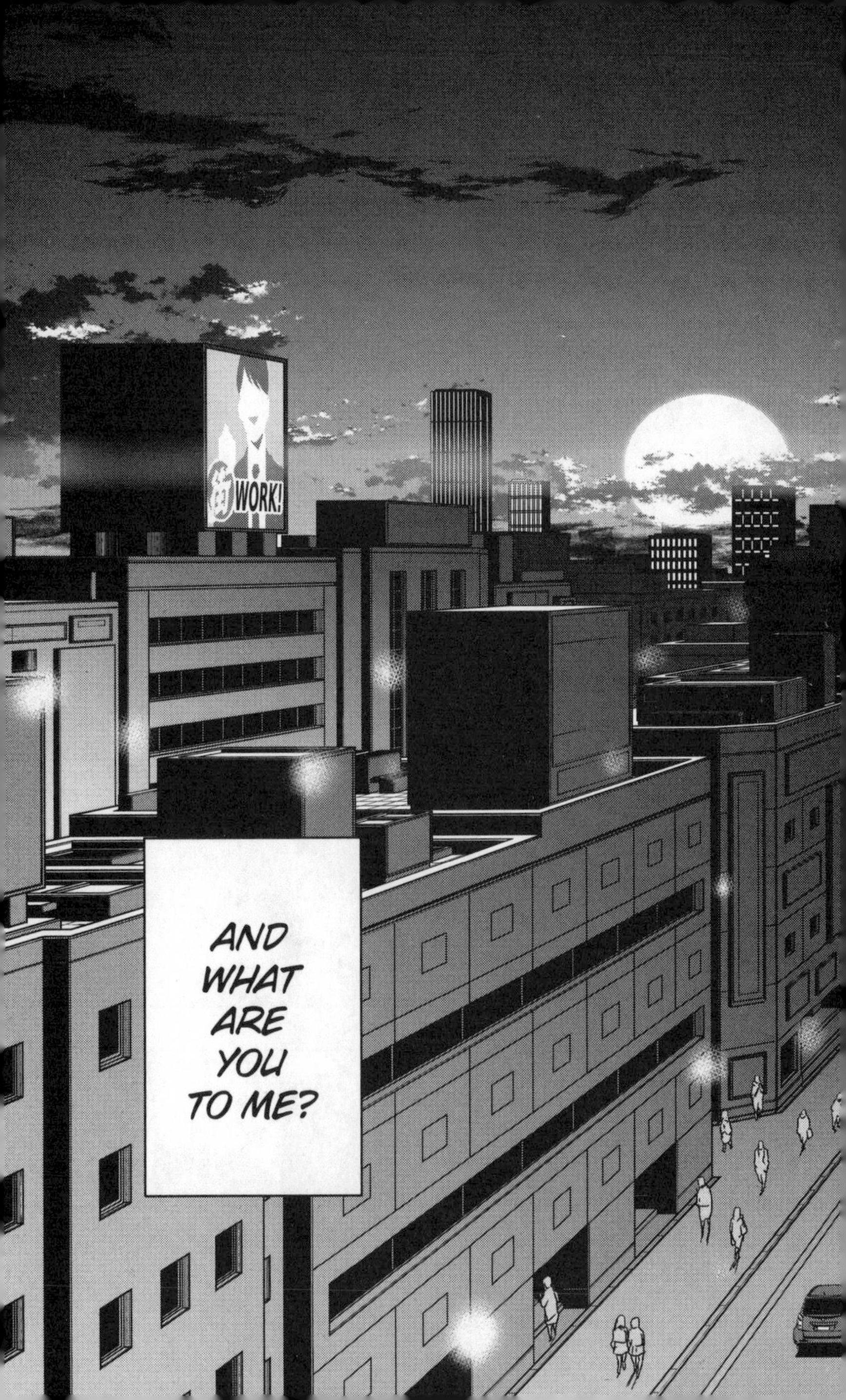
WORK!
AND WHAT ARE YOU TO ME?

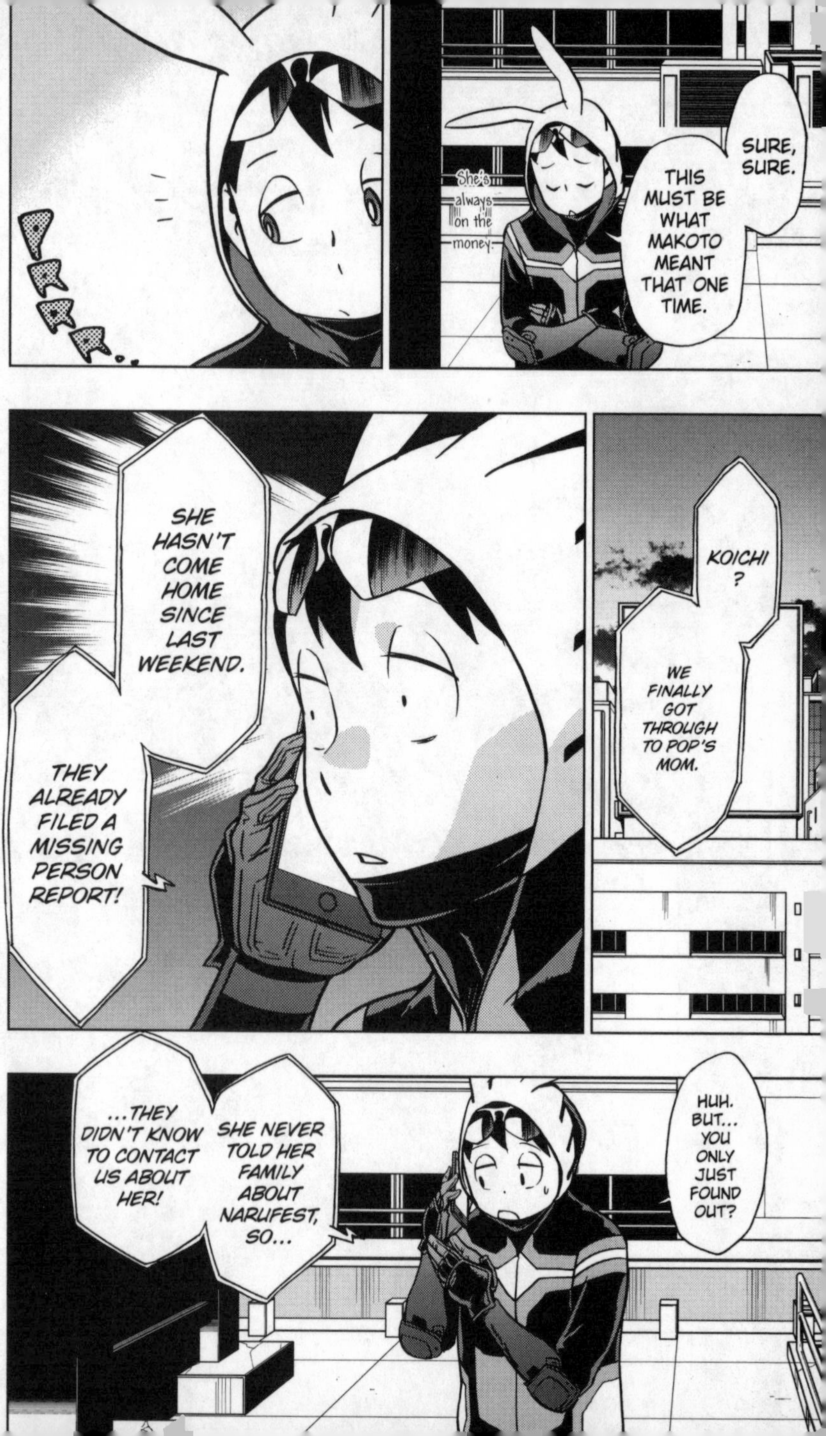
SURE, SURE.
THIS MUST BE WHAT MAKOTO MEANT THAT ONE TIME.
She's always on the money.
PRRR...
KOICHI?
WE FINALLY GOT THROUGH TO POP'S MOM.
SHE HASN'T COME HOME SINCE LAST WEEKEND.
THEY ALREADY FILED A MISSING PERSON REPORT!
HUH. BUT... YOU ONLY JUST FOUND OUT?
SHE NEVER TOLD HER FAMILY ABOUT NARUFEST, SO...
...THEY DIDN'T KNOW TO CONTACT US ABOUT HER!

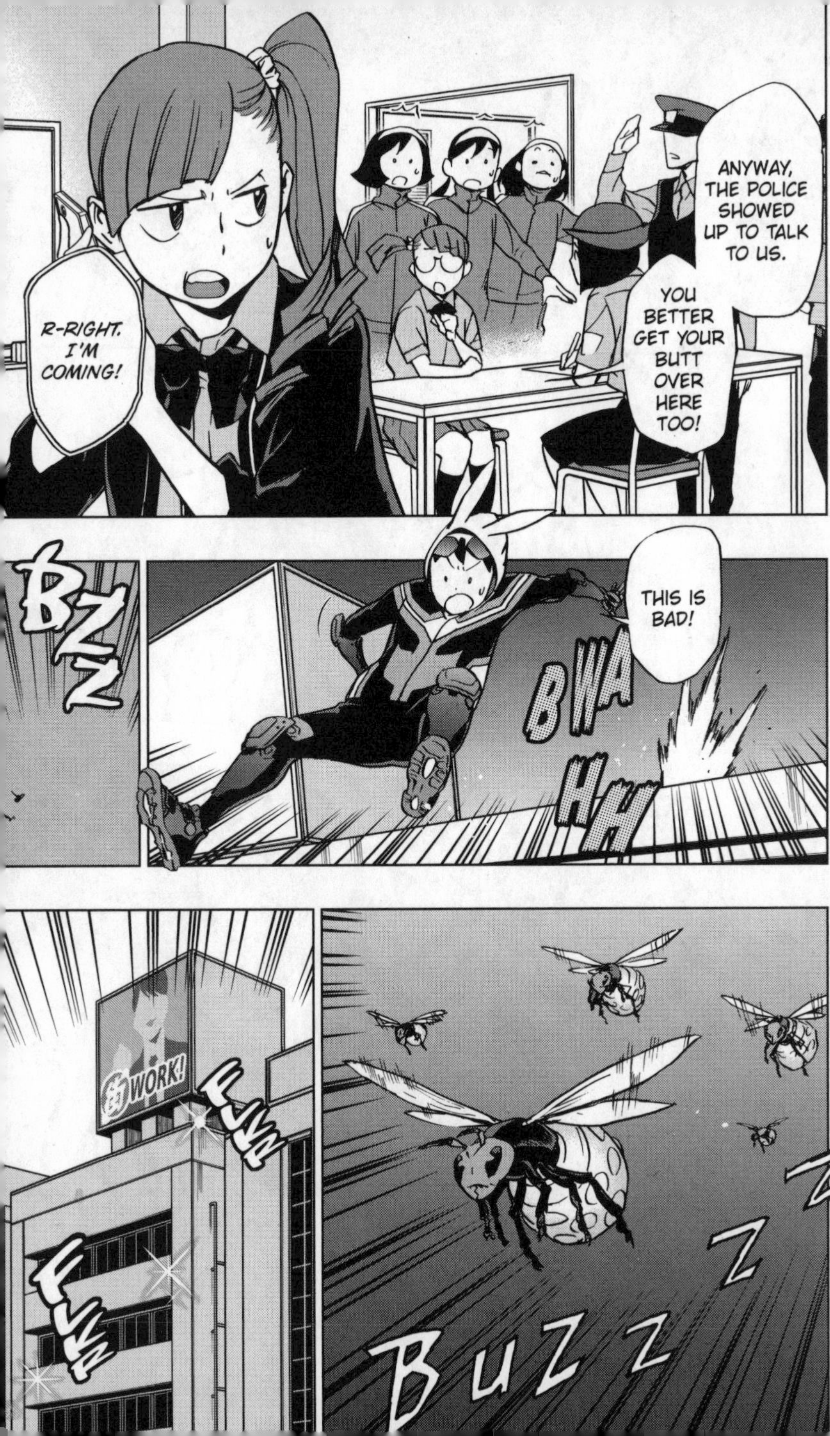
ANYWAY, THE POLICE SHOWED UP TO TALK TO US.
YOU BETTER GET YOUR BUTT OVER HERE TOO!
R-RIGHT. I'M COMING!
THIS IS BAD!
BWAHH
BZZZ
BUZZZ
WORK!

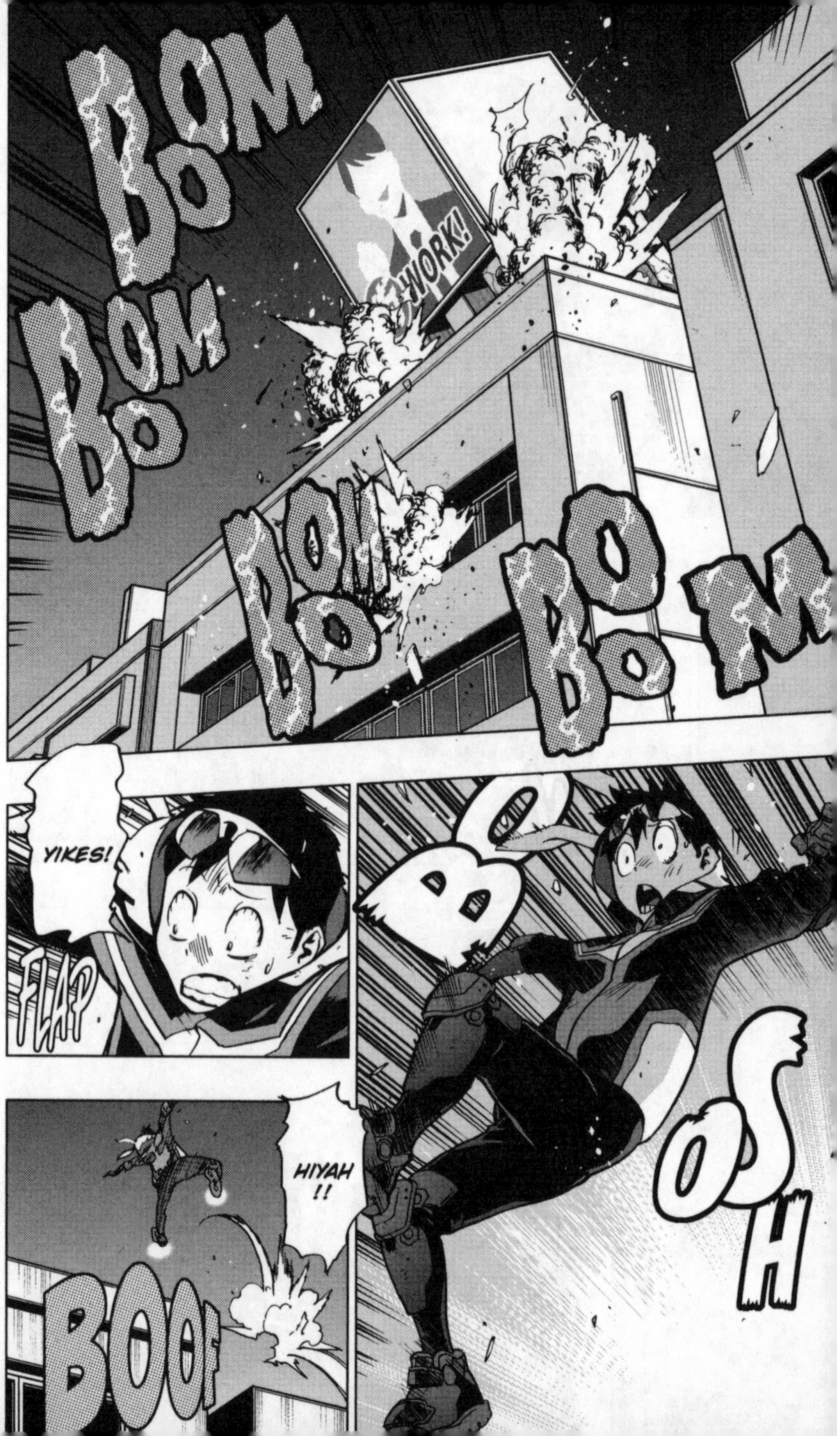

WORK!
BOOM
BOOM
BOOM
BOOM
BOOSH
YIKES!
FLAP
HIYAH!!
BOOF

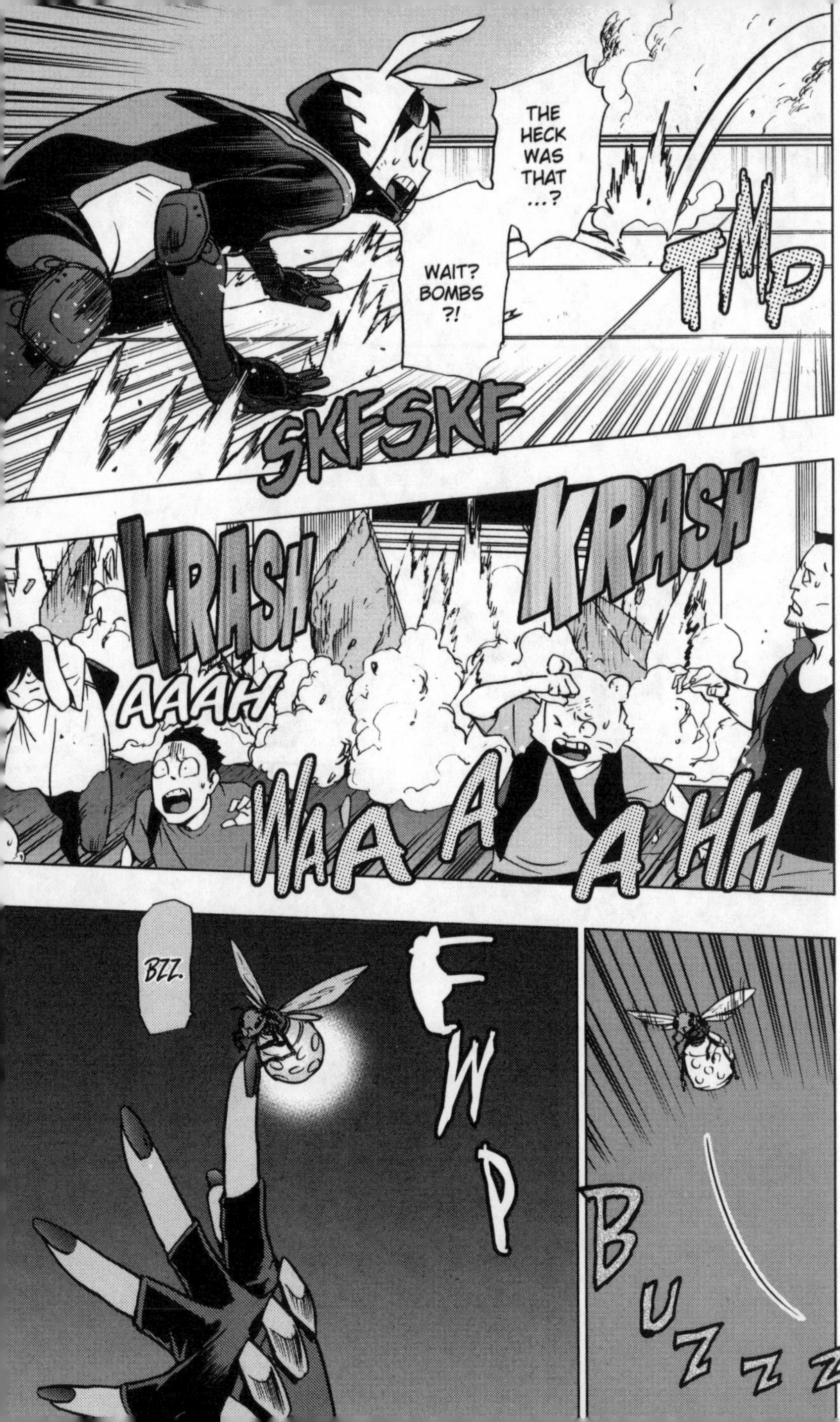

TMP
THE HECK WAS THAT ...?
WAIT? BOMBS ?!
SKFSKF
KRASH
KRASH
AAAH
WAAAAHH
BUZZZZ
BZZ.
FWP

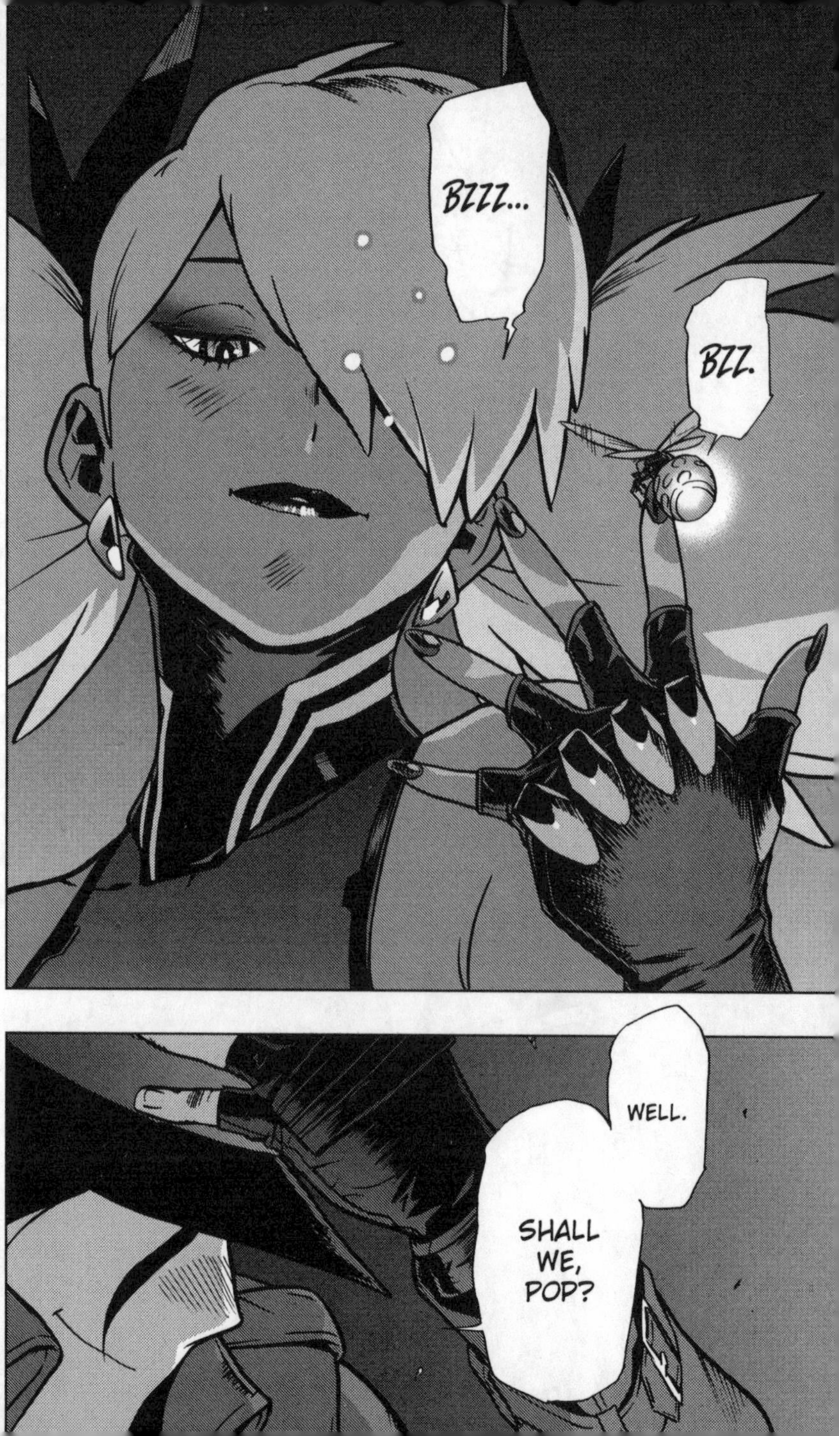
BZZZ...
BZZ.
WELL.
SHALL WE, POP?

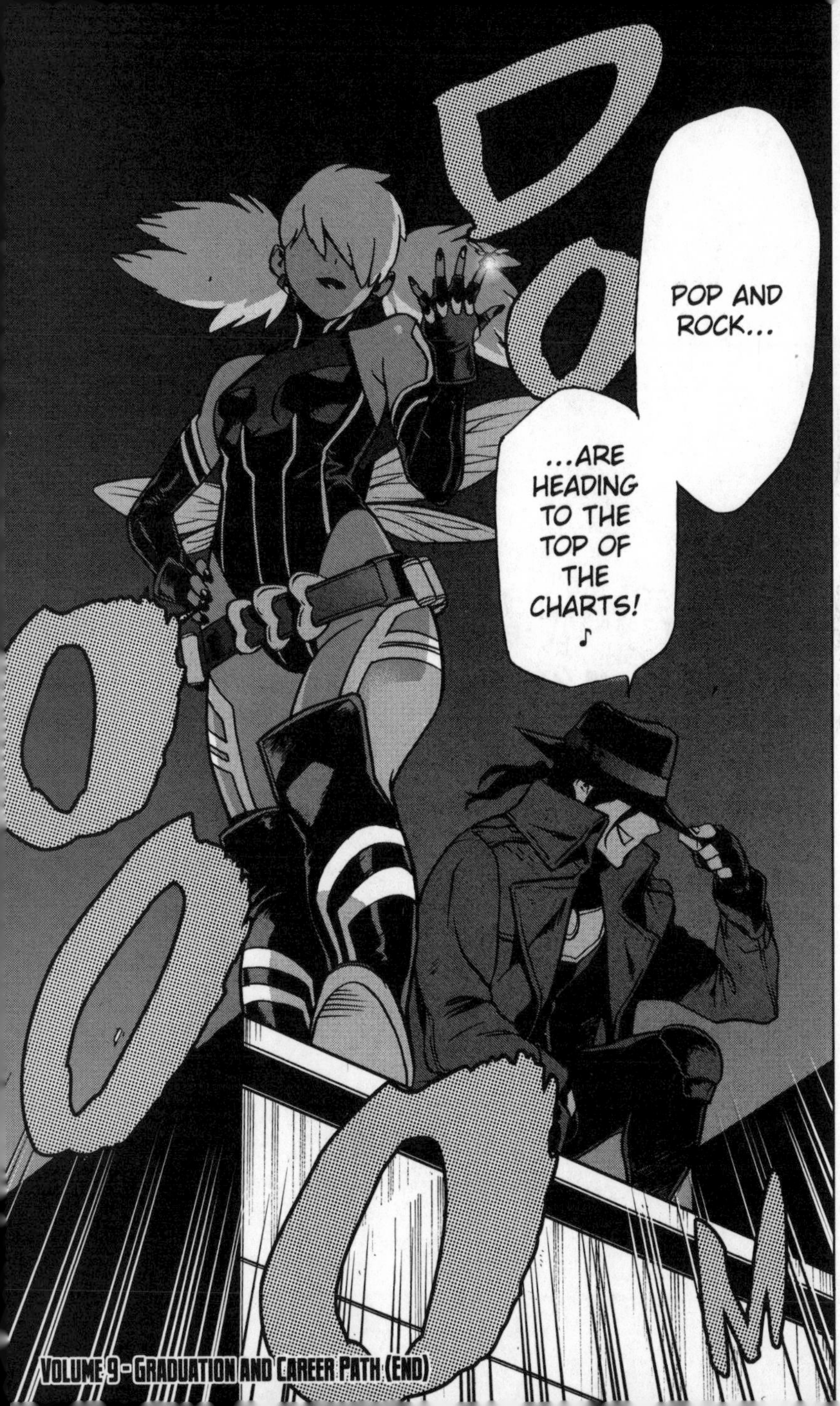
DOOOOM
POP AND ROCK...
...ARE HEADING TO THE TOP OF THE CHARTS! ♪
VOLUME 9 - GRADUATION AND CAREER PATH (END)

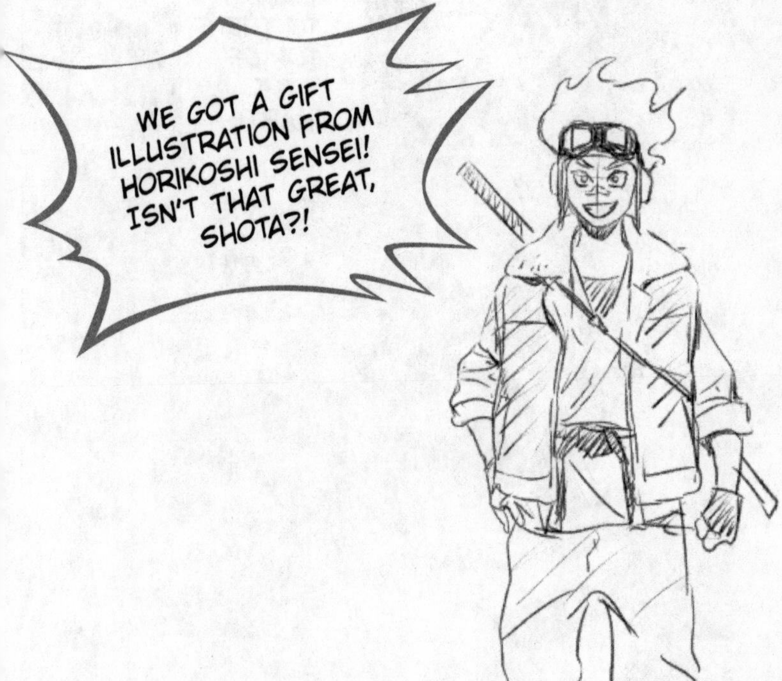
WE GOT A GIFT ILLUSTRATION FROM HORIKOSHI SENSEI! ISN'T THAT GREAT, SHOTA?!

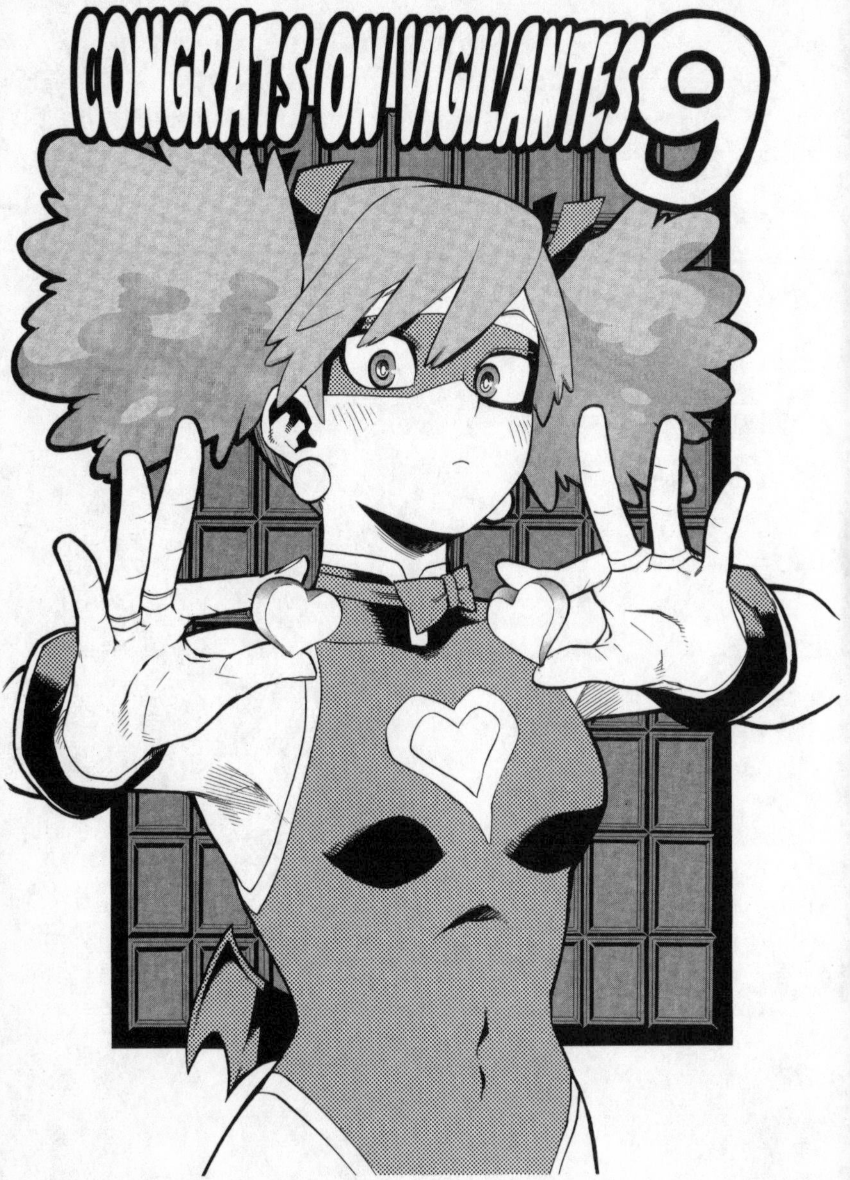
CONGRATS ON VIGILANTES 9

Message from Kohei Horikoshi

HIDEYUKI FURUHASHI

Vigilantes is a story about not wanting to grow up and postponing social responsibility, so one necessary element concerns the death of one's dreams. That's something that's hard to talk about in the main series, so it's the perfect theme for the spin-off.

BETTEN COURT

The really explosive developments begin in this volume, and while you readers may be shocked by what happens, keep in mind that I'm the very first person to go "Huhh!?" and "Oh god!!" (not out loud, but inside) while drawing these scenes.

MY HERO ACADEMIA VIGILANTES

VOLUME 9
SHONEN JUMP Manga Edition

STORY: HIDEYUKI FURUHASHI
ART: BETTEN COURT
ORIGINAL CONCEPT: KOHEI HORIKOSHI

Translation & English Adaptation/Caleb Cook
Touch-Up Art & Lettering/John Hunt
Designer/Julian [JR] Robinson
Editor/Mike Montesa

Printed in the U.S.A.

Published by VIZ Media, LLC
P.O. Box 77010
San Francisco, CA 94107

10 9 8 7 6 5 4 3 2 1
First printing, March 2021

VIZ MEDIA
viz.com

SHONEN JUMP

ratings.viz.com
RATED T TEEN

PARENTAL ADVISORY
MY HERO ACADEMIA: VIGILANTES is rated T for Teen and is recommended for ages 13 and up. This volume contains fantasy violence.

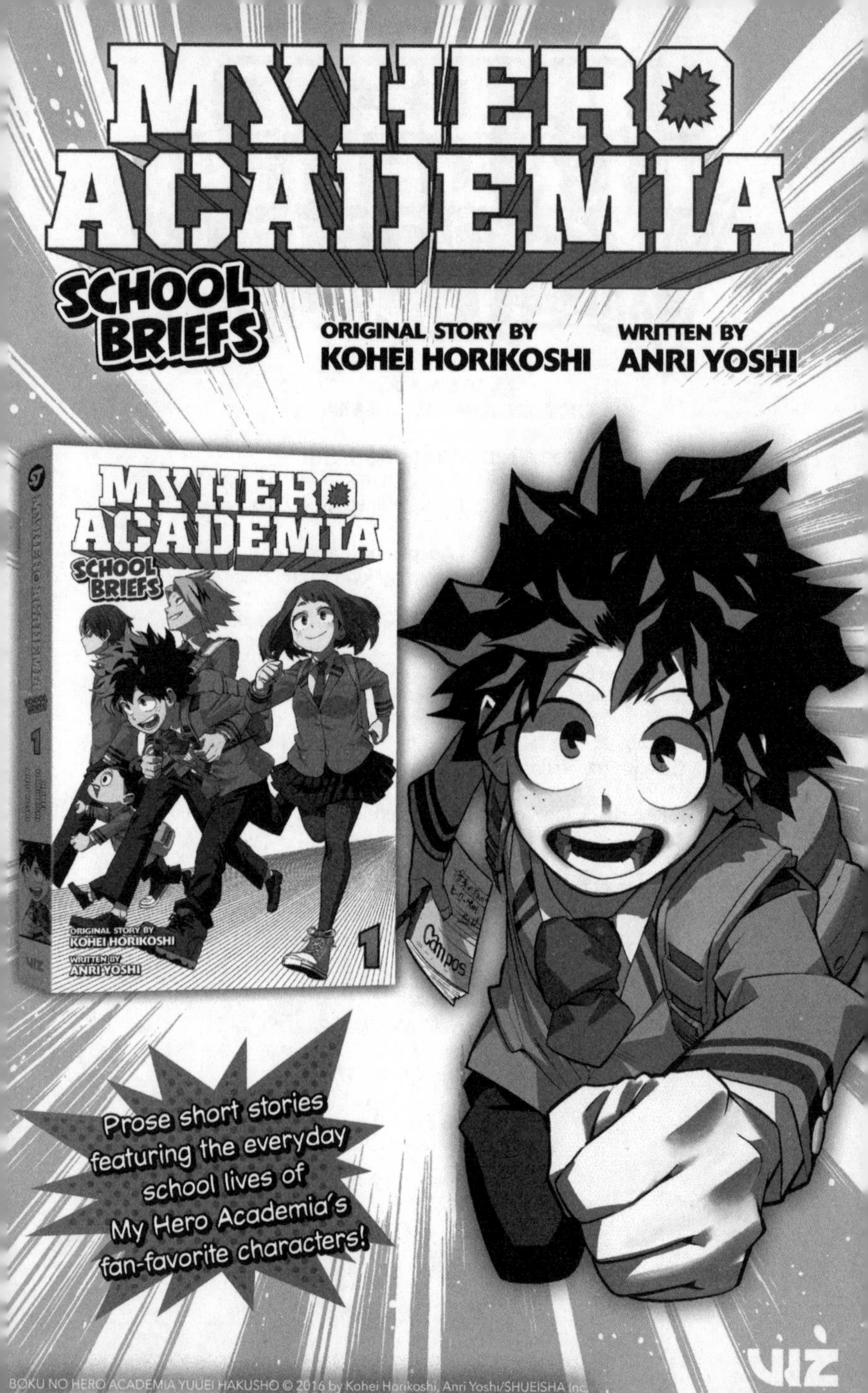

MY HERO ACADEMIA
SCHOOL BRIEFS

ORIGINAL STORY BY
KOHEI HORIKOSHI

WRITTEN BY
ANRI YOSHI

Prose short stories featuring the everyday school lives of My Hero Academia's fan-favorite characters!

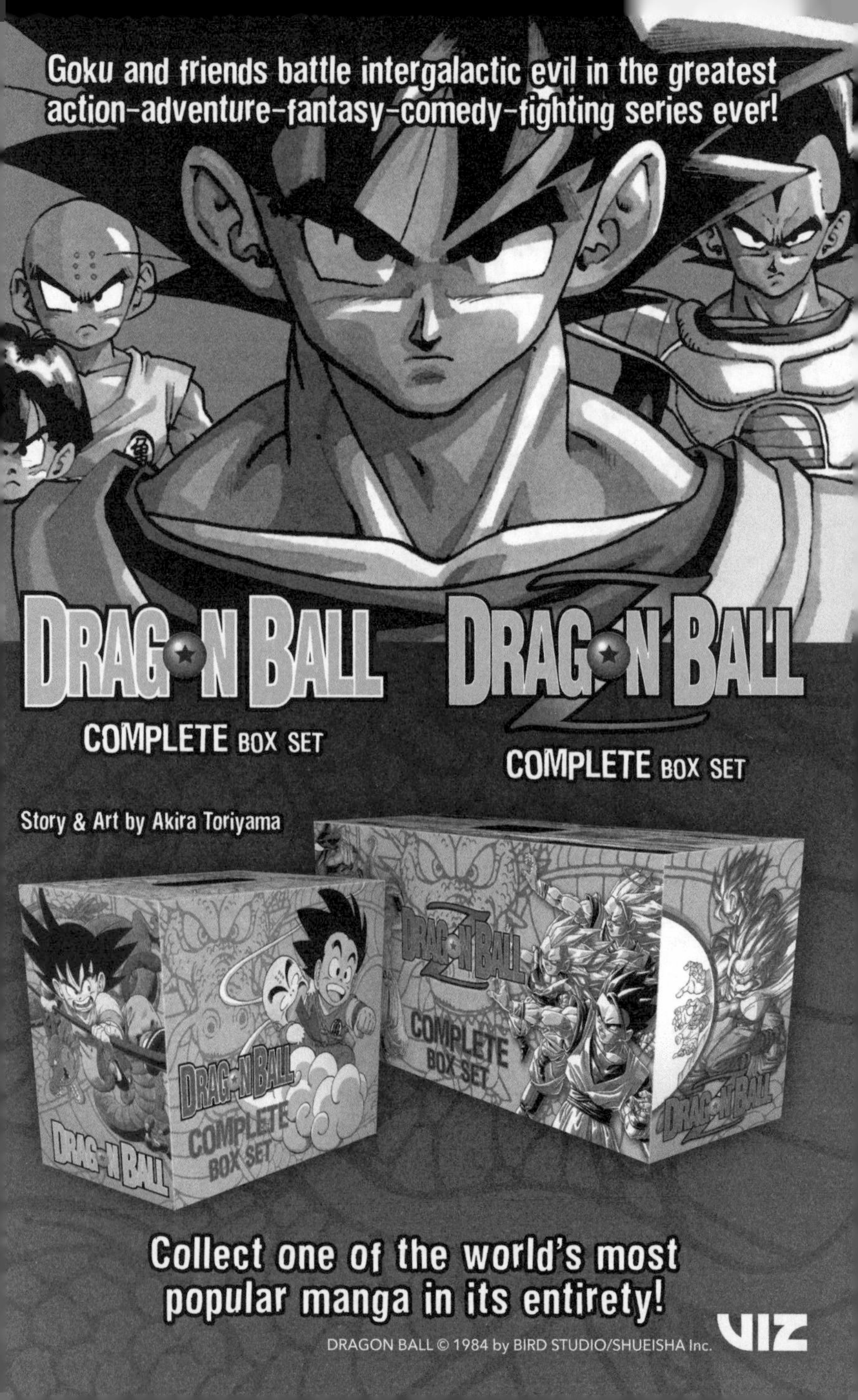

Goku and friends battle intergalactic evil in the greatest action-adventure-fantasy-comedy-fighting series ever!

DRAG☆N BALL
COMPLETE BOX SET

DRAG☆N BALL Z
COMPLETE BOX SET

Story & Art by Akira Toriyama

Collect one of the world's most popular manga in its entirety!

VIZ

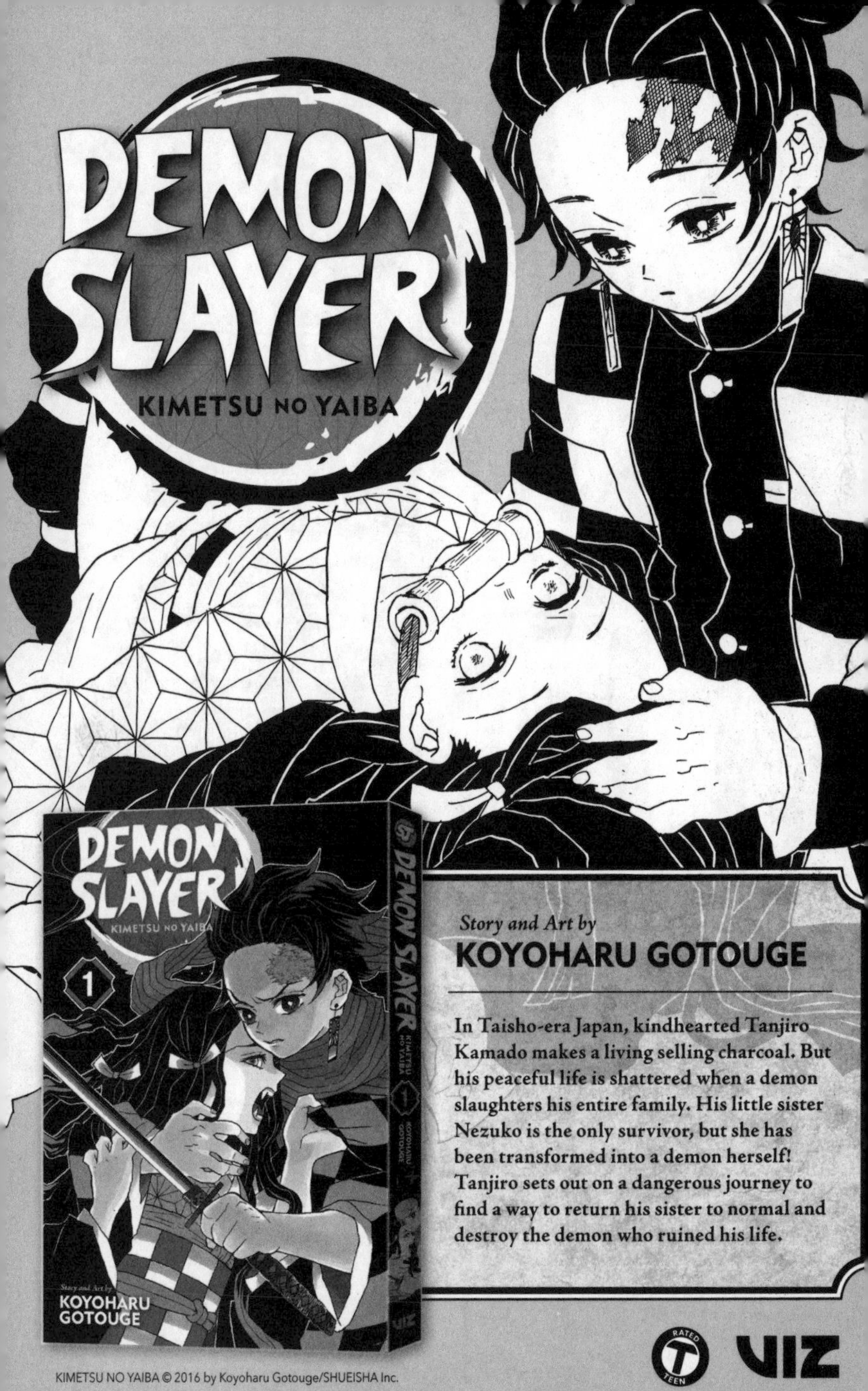
DEMON SLAYER
KIMETSU NO YAIBA
DEMON SLAYER
KIMETSU NO YAIBA
1
Story and Art by
KOYOHARU GOTOUGE
DEMON SLAYER
KIMETSU NO YAIBA
1
KOYOHARU GOTOUGE
VIZ
Story and Art by
KOYOHARU GOTOUGE
In Taisho-era Japan, kindhearted Tanjiro Kamado makes a living selling charcoal. But his peaceful life is shattered when a demon slaughters his entire family. His little sister Nezuko is the only survivor, but she has been transformed into a demon herself! Tanjiro sets out on a dangerous journey to find a way to return his sister to normal and destroy the demon who ruined his life.
RATED T TEEN
VIZ

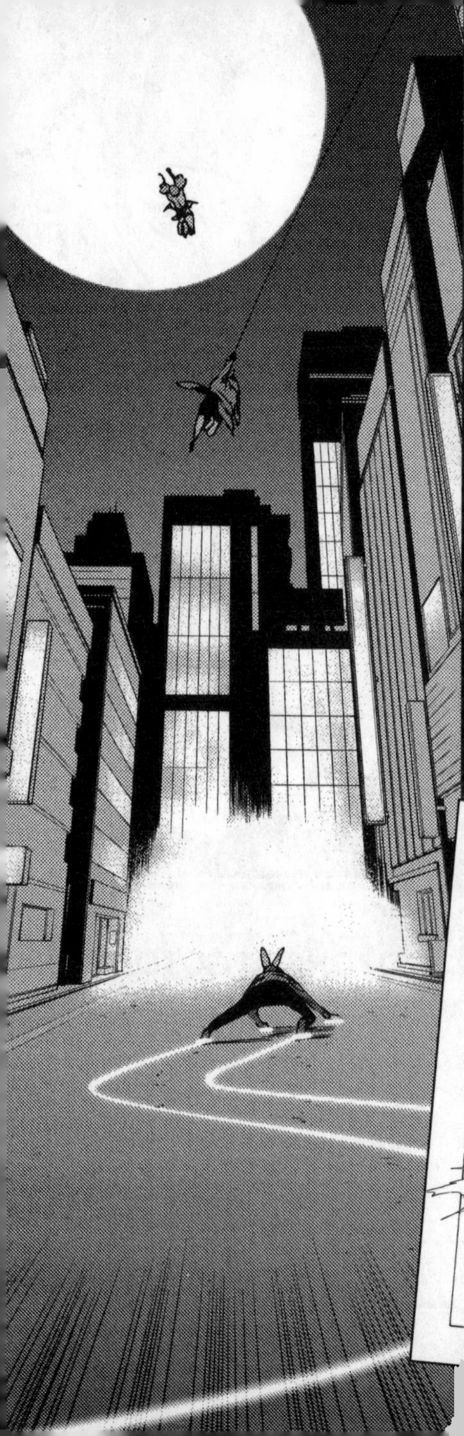

YOU'RE READING THE WRONG WAY!!

MY HERO ACADEMIA VIGILANTES reads from right to left, starting in the upper-right corner. Japanese is read from right to left, meaning that action, sound effects and word-balloon order are completely reversed from English order.

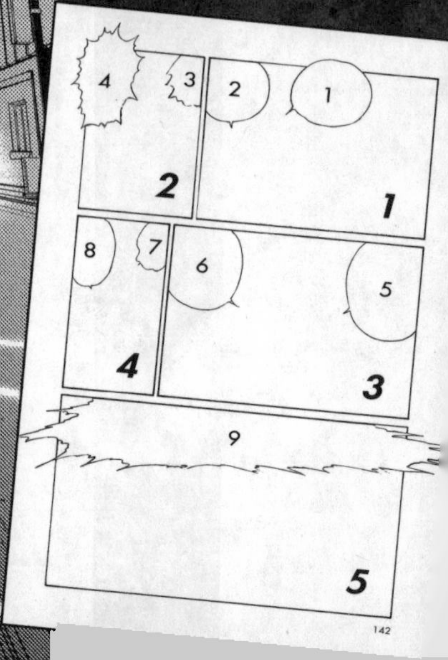